THE SOUTH

*A TREASURY OF
ART AND LITERATURE*

THE SOUTH

A TREASURY OF
ART AND LITERATURE

*For Debbi and OZ Crosby, from
Lynn D Stewart—Merry Christmas!
regards and best wishes,
Lisa Howorth
oxford, mississippi
12·15·93*

Edited by Lisa Howorth

*Center for the Study of Southern Culture
at The University of Mississippi*

Hugh Lauter Levin Associates, Inc.

Distributed by Macmillan Publishing Company, New York

Copyright © 1993, Hugh Lauter Levin Associates, Inc.
Design by Ken Scaglia
Editorial production by Deborah Zindell

Printed in Hong Kong. Bound in China
ISBN 0–88363–593–3

Garcilaso de la Vega. From *The Florida of the Inca* Translated and edited by John Grier Varner and Jeannette Johnson Varner. Copyright © 1951, The University of Texas Press. Courtesy of the publisher.

Captain John Smith. From *The Complete Works of Captain John Smith, 1580–1631.* Edited by Philip L. Barbour. Published for the Institute of Early American History and Culture, Williamsburg, Virginia. Copyright © 1986 by The University of North Carolina Press. Reprinted by permission of the publisher.

John Lawson. From *A New Voyage to Carolina.* London. 1709.

Mark Catesby. From *The Natural History of Carolina, Florida, and the Bahama Islands.* London: B. White, 1771.

William Bartram. From *The Travels of William Bartram,* by Francis Harper. Copyright © 1958 by Yale University Press, Inc. Reprinted by permission of the publisher.

William Byrd. From *The Secret Diary of William Byrd of Westover, 1709–1712.* Edited by Louis B. Wright and Marion Tinling. The Dietz Press, 1941.

Eliza Lucas Pinckney. From *The Letterbook of Eliza Lucas Pinckney, 1739–1762.* Edited by Eliza Pinckney and Marvin R. Zahniser. Copyright © 1972 by The University of North Carolina Press. Reprinted by permission of the publisher.

Reverend Charles Woodmason. "On Correct Behavior in Church." From *The Carolina Backcountry on the Eve of the Revolution: The Journal and Other Writings of Charles Woodmason, Anglican Itinerant.* Edited by Richard J. Hooker. Published for the Institute of Early American History and Culture, Williamsburg, Virginia. Copyright © 1953, renewed 1981 by The University of North Carolina Press. Reprinted by permission of the publisher.

Patrick Henry. Excerpt from a speech delivered to the Virginia Assembly, March 23, 1775.

Eliza Wilkinson. "A Day of Terror." From *Letters of Eliza Wilkinson.* 1779.

Anonymous. "The Dance." From *Songs and Ballads of the American Revolution.* 1781.

St. George Tucker. From *St. George Tucker's Journal of the Siege of Yorktown, 1781.*

Thomas Jefferson. From *The Domestic Life of Thomas Jefferson Compiled from Family Letters and Reminiscences, by his Great-Granddaughter, Sarah N. Randolph.* Harper and Brothers, 1871.

Martha Laurens Ramsay. From *Memoirs of the Life of Martha Laurens Ramsay.* 1812.

Alex Haley. From *Roots.* Copyright © 1976 by Alex Haley. Used by permission of Doubleday, a division of Bantam Doubleday Dell Publishing Group, Inc.

John Newton. "Amazing Grace." 1789.

Will D. Campbell. From *Providence.* Copyright © 1992 by Will D. Campbell. Reprinted with permission of Longstreet Press.

T. Addison Richards. From "The Landscape of the South." Reprinted from *Harper's New Monthly Magazine,* May 1853.

J. P. Kennedy. From *Swallow Barn, or Sojourn in the Old Dominion.* George P. Putnam, 1851.

Frederick Douglass. From *Narrative of the Life of Frederick Douglass, an American Slave.* The Anti-Slavery Office, 1845.

From the *West Tennessee Democrat,* 1853.

Anonymous. "Go Down, Moses." 1872.

Daniel Decatur Emmet. "Dixie." 1859.

Alexis de Tocqueville. From *Journey to America.* Translated by George Lawrence. Edited by J.P. Mayer. Anchor Books, 1971.

Frances Anne Kemble. From *Journal of a Residence on a Georgia Plantation* in 1838–1839. Harper and Brothers, 1863.

Charles Dickens. From *American Notes and Pictures from Italy.* 1862–1868.

Frederick Law Olmsted. From *A Journey in the Seaboard Slave States.* 1856.

Henry Adams. From *The Education of Henry Adams.* Copyright 1918 by The Massachusetts Historical Society. Copyright 1931 by The Modern Library, Inc. Copyright 1946 by Charles Francis Adams.

Mary Chesnut. From *The Private Mary Chesnut. The Unpublished Civil War Diaries.* Copyright 1984 by C. Vann Woodward, Elisabeth Muhlenfeld, McCoy Metts Hill, Barbara G. Carpenter, Sally Bland Johnson, and Katherine W. Herbert. Reprinted by permission of Harold Ober Associates Incorporated.

John S. Jackman. From *Diary of a Confederate Soldier.* Copyright 1990 by The University of South Carolina Press. Reprinted with permission of the publisher.

Caroline Seabury. From *The Diary of Caroline Seabury, 1854–1863.* Edited and with an introduction by Suzanne Bunkers. Copyright 1991 by the Board of Regents of The University of Wisconsin System. Reprinted by permission of The University of Wisconsin Press.

Jeremiah Gage. "A Dying Soldier's Letter to His Mother." July 3, 1863.

Shelby Foote. From *The Civil War: A Narrative.* Volume II. Copyright © 1963 by Shelby Foote. Reprinted by permission of Random House, Inc.

Dolly Lunt Burge. From *The Diary of Dolly Lunt Burge.* Edited by James I. Robertson, Jr. Copyright 1962 by The University of Georgia Press. Reprinted by permission of The University of Georgia Press.

Margaret Mitchell. From *Gone with the Wind.* Copyright 1936 by Macmillan Publishing Co., Inc. Copyright renewed 1964 by Stephens Mitchell and Trust Company of Georgia as Executors of Margaret Mitchell Marsh. Copyright renewed 1964 by Stephens Mitchell. Reprinted by permission of William Morris Agency.

Robert E. Lee. The General's farewell address to his troops, April 10, 1865.

Father Ryan. "The Conquered Banner." from *Poems: Patriotic, Religious, Miscellaneous* by Abram J. Ryan. Baltimore: The Baltimore Publishing Company, 1889.

John James Audubon. From Delineations of American Scenery and Character. New York: G.A. Baker & Company, 1926.

Joel Chandler Harris. From *Uncle Remus.* Copyright 1881 by the Century Collection, and 1883 by Joel Chandler Harris.

Mark Twain. From *Life on the Mississippi.* Copyright 1944 by the Mark Twain Company.

Lyle Saxon. From *Fabulous New Orleans.* Copyright 1928 by The Century Company.

Vance Randolph. "Pissing in the Snow" from *Pissing in the Snow and Other Ozark Folktales.* Copyright 1976 by The University of Illinois Press.

Sidney Lanier. "Song of the Chattahoochee." Charles Scribner's Sons, 1884.

Kate Chopin. "The Storm." Reprinted by permission of Louisiana State University Press from *The Complete Works of Kate Chopin, Volume II,* edited by Per Seyersted. Copyright 1969 by Louisiana State University Press.

Jean Toomer. "Georgia Dusk." From *Cane.* Copyright 1923 by Boni and Liveright. Copyright renewed 1951 by Jean Toomer.

W.C. Handy. From *Father of the Blues.* Copyright 1941 by W.C. Handy. Reprinted by permission of Macmillan Publishing Company.

Ida Cox. "Southern Woman's Blues."

Florence Reece and James Farmer. "Which Side Are You On?" Copyright 1947, 1963 by Stormking Music Inc. All rights reserved. Used by Permission.

Jimmie Rodgers. "Train Whistle Blues." Copyright © 1930 by Peer International Corporation. Copyright renewed. International Copyright Secured. All Rights Reserved. Used by Permission.

Alfred E. Brumley. "I'll Fly Away." Integrated Copyright. Used by permission.

Thomas A. Dorsey. "Take My Hand, Precious Lord." © 1938 (renewed) UNICHAPPELL MUSIC INC. All Rights Reserved. Used by Permission.

A.P. Carter. "Can the Circle Be Unbroken?" Copyright © 1947, 1954 by Peer International Corporation. Copyright Renewed. International Copyright Secured. All Rights Reserved. Used by Permission.

Bill Monroe. "Blue Moon of Kentucky." Copyright © 1947, 1954 by Peer International Corporation. Copyright Renewed. International Copyright Secured. All Rights Reserved. Used by permission.

Hank Williams. "Jambalaya." Copyright 1952 Fred Rose Music, Inc. Acuff-Rose.

Theodore Rosengarten. From *All God's Dangers: The Life of Nate Shaw.* Copyright © 1974 by Theodore Rosengarten. Reprinted by permission of Alfred A. Knopf, Inc.

Zora Neale Hurston. From *Mules and Men.* J.B. Lippincott Company 1935. Copyright 1935 by Zora Neale Hurston. Reprinted by permission of HarperCollins Publishers, Inc.

James Agee and Walker Evans. From *Let Us Now Praise Famous Men.* Copyright 1939 and 1940 by James Agee. Copyright 1941 by James Agee and Walker Evans. Copyright © renewed 1969 by Mia Fritsch Agee and Walker Evans. Reprinted by permission of Houghton Mifflin Co. All rights reserved.

Henry Woodfin Grady. From *The New South and Other Addresses.* First published in 1904.

Andrew Nelson Lytle. From "The Hind Tit"; from *I'll Take My Stand: The South and the Agrarian Tradition by Twelve Southerners.* Copyright 1930 by Harper & Brothers. Renewed copyright 1958 by Donald Davison.

William Alexander Percy. From *Lanterns on the Levee.* Copyright 1941 Alfred A. Knopf, Inc. and renewed 1969 by LeRoy Pratt Percy. Reprinted by permission of the publisher.

Thomas Wolfe. From *Look Homeward, Angel.* Reprinted with permission of Charles Scribner's Sons, an imprint of Macmillan Publishing Company. Copyright 1929 by Charles Scribner's Sons, renewed © 1957 by Edward C. Ashwell, as Administrator C.T.A. of the Estate of Thomas Wolfe and/or Fred W. Wolfe.

Allen Tate. "The Trout Map." From *Collected Poems 1919–1976,* by Allen Tate. Copyright © 1977 by Allen Tate. Reprinted by permission of Farrar, Straus & Giroux.

William Faulkner. From *Absalom, Absalom!* Copyright 1936 by William Faulkner and renewed 1964 by Estelle Faulkner and Jill Faulkner Summers. Reprinted by permission of Random House, Inc.

Richard Wright. From *Black Boy: A Record of Childhood and Youth.* Copyright 1937, 1942, 1944, 1945 by Richard Wright. Reprinted by permission of HarperCollins Publishers, Inc.

W.J. Cash. From *The Mind of the South.* Copyright 1941 by Alfred A. Knopf, Inc. and renewed 1969 by Mary R. Maury. Reprinted by permission of Alfred A. Knopf, Inc.

Joseph Mitchell. "I Blame It All on Mamma." from *Up in the Old Hotel and Other Stories.* Copyright © 1938, 1939, 1940, 1941, 1942, 1943, 1944, 1945, 1947, 1948, 1949, 1951, 1952, 1955, 1956, 1959, 1964, 1965, 1966, 1968, 1969, 1970, 1971, 1972, 1973, 1975, 1976, 1977, 1979, 1980, 1983, 1984, 1987, 1992 by Joseph Mitchell. Reprinted by permission of Random House, Inc.

Tennessee Williams. From *A Streetcar Named Desire.* Copyright 1947 by Tennessee Williams.

Carson McCullers. From "The Heart is a Lonely Hunter." Copyright 1940 by Carson McCullers. Copyright © renewed 1967 by Carson McCullers. Reprinted by permission of Houghton Mifflin Co. All rights reserved.

Eudora Welty. "Why I Live at the P.O." From *A Curtain of Green and Other Stories.* Copyright 1941 and renewed 1969 by Eudora Welty. Reprinted by permission of Harcourt Brace & Company.

Robert Penn Warren. From *All the King's Men.* Copyright 1946 and renewed 1974 by Robert Penn Warren. Reprinted by permission of Harcourt Brace & Company.

Flannery O'Connor. "Enoch and the Gorilla," From *The Complete Stories.* Copyright © 1971 by the Estate of Mary Flannery O'Connor. Reprinted by permission of Farrar, Straus & Giroux.

Truman Capote. From "A Christmas Memory." Copyright 1956 by Truman Capote. Copyright renewed. Reprinted by permission of Random House, Inc.

Margaret Walker Alexander. "For My People." Copyright 1942 by Yale University Press.

Red Barber and Robert Creamer. From *Rhubarb in the Catbird Seat.* Copyright © 1968 by Walter L. Barber and Robert Creamer. Used by permission of Doubleday a division of Bantam, Doubleday Dell Publishing Group, Inc.

Rosa Parks. From *Rosa Parks: My Story,* by Rosa Parks with Jim Haskins. Copyright © 1992 by Rosa Parks. Used by permission of Dial Books for Young Readers, a division of Penguin Books USA Inc.

"We Shall Overcome" Copyright © 1960, 1963 by Ludlow Music, Inc.

Martin Luther King, Jr. Excerpt from a speech in Washington D.C.

Tom Wolfe. Excerpt from "The Last American Hero." From *The Kandy-Kolored Tangerine-Flake Streamline Baby.* Copyright © 1965 by Tom Wolfe.

Hunter S. Thompson. From *The Great Shark Hunt: Strange Tales from a Strange Time.* Copyright © 1979 by Hunter S. Thompson. From *Scanlon's Monthly,* June 1970.

Walker Percy. "Bourbon." From *Signposts in a Strange Land.* Copyright © 1991 by Mary Bernice Percy.

Florence King. "The Cult of Southern Womanhood." Copyright 1975 by Florence King.

Craig Claiborne. From "A Feast Made for Laughter." Used with permission of the author.

Roy Blount, Jr. "Song to Grits." From *One Fell Soup, or I'm Just a Bug on the Windshield of Life.* Copyright © 1975 by Roy Blount, Jr. First appeared in Eastern Airlines Magazine. By permission of Little, Brown and Company.

Reynolds Price. From *Clear Pictures: First Loves, First Guides.* Copyright 1968, 1989 by Reynolds Price. Reprinted by permission of Macmillan Publishing Company.

Harper Lee. From *To Kill a Mockingbird.* Copyright 1960 by Harper Lee. Use by permission of HarperCollins Publishers, Inc.

Wendell Berry. "The Contrariness of the Mad Farmer." Copyright © 1964, 1968, 1969, 1970, 1973, 1977, 1980, 1982, 1984 by Wendell Berry.

James Dickey. "The Sheep Child." Reprinted from *Falling, May Day, Sermon & Other Poems.* Copyright © 1982 by James Dickey, Wesleyan University Press. By permission of The University Press of New England.

Willie Morris. From *North Toward Home.* Copyright © 1967 by Willie Morris. Reprinted by permission of the Joan Daves Literary Agency.

John Kennedy Toole. From *A Confederacy of Dunces.* Copyright 1980 by Thelma Toole. Reprinted by permission of Louisiana State University Press.

Alice Walker. "Everyday Use." From *In Love & Trouble: Stories of Black Women.* Copyright © 1973 by Alice Walker, reprinted by permission of Harcourt Brace & Company.

Peter Taylor. From *In the Miro District and Other Stories.* Copyright © 1974, 1975, 1976, 1977 by Peter Taylor. Reprinted by permission of Alfred A. Knopf, Inc.

William Styron. From *Sophie's Choice.* Copyright © 1976, 1978, 1979 by William Styron. Reprinted by permission of Random House, Inc.

Harry Crews. From *A Childhood: The Biography of a Place.* Copyright © 1978 by Harry Crews. Used by permission of HarperCollins Publishers, Inc.

Barry Hannah. "Knowing He Was Not My Kind Yet I Followed." from *Airships.* Copyright.© 1970, 1974, 1975, 1976, 1977, 1978 by Barry Hannah. Reprinted by permission of Alfred A. Knopf, Inc.

Alfred Uhry. From *Driving Miss Daisy.* Copyright © 1986, 1987 by Alfred Uhry. Reprinted by permission of Theatre Communications Group.

ACKNOWLEDGMENTS

My immense gratitude is due the writers, artists, museums, archives, collectors, and publishers who have allowed us to reproduce their work. Kimberly J. Tuck and the Robert M. Hicklin, Jr. Collection in Spartanburg, South Carolina, the Morris Museum in Augusta, Georgia, the Historic New Orleans Collection, and Kenneth Barnes and the Roger Houston Ogden Collection in New Orleans were particularly helpful. I also wish to thank Hugh L. Levin, Bill Ferris and Ann Abadie, Debby Zindell and Ken Scaglia, the University of Mississippi Library, especially John Cloy, Thomas Verich, Sharonne Sarthou and Access Services, Larry Brown, Richard Howorth, Bob Haws, Jay Johnson, Jay Watson, Anthony Walton, the Kentucky Derby Museum, Charles Hudson, John Shelton Reed, Judy McWillie, Warren Steele, Dannal Perry, Kenneth Holditch, Greg Horne, Dave Nelson, William Griffith, and Amy Wood. Bill Martin provided speedy photographic services, and Charles Reagan Wilson, the Diderot of Dixie, allowed me to relentlessly rifle his brain and bookshelf.

Special thanks go to Kate Stofko Funk, with me in the beginning, and to Leslie Carola, with me to the end.

For Claire, Beckett, and Lee, and all the children of the South with the hope that they will come to know the great artistic and literary legacy of their region.

Lisa Howorth

CONTENTS

	ACKNOWLEDGMENTS	5
	INTRODUCTION	10
A NEW EDEN	GARCILASO DE LA VEGA: from *The Florida of the Inca*	27
	CAPTAIN JOHN SMITH: from "The Description of Virginia"	29
	JOHN LAWSON: from *A New Voyage to Carolina*	31
	MARK CATESBY: from *The Natural History of Carolina, Florida, and the Bahama Islands*	33
	WILLIAM BARTRAM: from *The Travels of William Bartram*	35
THE EMERGING SOUTH	WILLIAM BYRD: from *The Secret Diary of William Byrd of Westover*	37
	ELIZA LUCAS PINCKNEY: from *The Letterbook of Eliza Lucas Pinckney*	39
	REVEREND CHARLES WOODMASON: "On Correct Behavior in Church"	49
	PATRICK HENRY: Liberty or Death Speech	50
	ELIZA WILKINSON: from *Letters of Eliza Wilkinson*	52
	ANONYMOUS: "The Dance"	54
	ST. GEORGE TUCKER: from "St. George Tucker's Journal of the Siege of Yorktown, 1781"	56
	THOMAS JEFFERSON: from *The Domestic Life of Thomas Jefferson*	58
	MARTHA LAURENS RAMSAY: from *Memoirs of the Life of Martha Laurens Ramsay*	59
	ALEX HALEY: from *Roots*	60
	JOHN NEWTON: "Amazing Grace"	63
	WILL D. CAMPBELL: from *Providence*	64
THE OLD SOUTH	T. ADDISON RICHARDS: from "The Landscape of the South"	75
	J.P. KENNEDY: from *Swallow Barn, or Sojourn in the Old Dominion*	77
	FREDERICK DOUGLASS: from *Narrative of the Life of Frederick Douglass, An American Slave*	80
	From the *West Tennessee Democrat*: To Catch a Runaway Slave	83
	ANONYMOUS: "Go Down, Moses"	83
	DANIEL DECATUR EMMETT: "Dixie"	85
OUTSIDERS VIEW THE OLD SOUTH	ALEXIS DE TOCQUEVILLE: from *Journey to America*	86
	FRANCES ANNE KEMBLE: from *Journal of a Residence on a Georgia Plantation*	87
	CHARLES DICKENS: from *American Notes and Pictures from Italy*	97
	FREDERICK LAW OLMSTED: from *A Journey in the Seaboard Slave States*	99
	HENRY ADAMS: from *The Education of Henry Adams*	102

THE CIVIL WAR	MARY CHESNUT: from *The Private Mary Chesnut*	*104*
AND THE	JOHN S. JACKMAN: from *Diary of a Confederate Soldier*	*106*
LOST CAUSE	CAROLINE SEABURY: from *The Diary of Caroline Seabury*	*108*
	JEREMIAH GAGE: A Dying Soldier's Letter to His Mother	*110*
	SHELBY FOOTE: from *The Civil War: A Narrative*	*111*
	DOLLY LUNT BURGE: from *The Diary of Dolly Lunt Burge*	*122*
	MARGARET MITCHELL: from *Gone with the Wind*	*125*
	ROBERT E. LEE: The General's Farewell Address to His Troops	*128*
	FATHER RYAN: "The Conquered Banner"	*128*
LOCAL COLOR	JOHN JAMES AUDUBON: from *Delineations of American Scenery and Character*	*130*
	JOEL CHANDLER HARRIS: from *Uncle Remus*	*133*
	MARK TWAIN: from *Life on the Mississippi*	*134*
	LYLE SAXON: from "Have a Good Time While You Can"	*146*
	VANCE RANDOLPH: "Pissing in the Snow"	*149*
	SIDNEY LANIER: "Song of the Chattahoochee"	*150*
	KATE CHOPIN: "The Storm"	*152*
	JEAN TOOMER: "Georgia Dusk"	*156*
SOUTHERN FOLK	W.C. HANDY: from *Father of the Blues*	*157*
	IDA COX: "Southern Woman's Blues"	*158*
	FLORENCE REECE and JAMES FARMER: "Which Side Are You On?"	*159*
	JIMMIE RODGERS: "Train Whistle Blues"	*177*
	ALBERT E. BRUMLEY: "I'll Fly Away"	*178*
	THOMAS ANDREW DORSEY: "Take My Hand, Precious Lord"	*179*
	A.P. CARTER: "Can the Circle Be Unbroken?"	*179*
	BILL MONROE: "Blue Moon of Kentucky"	*180*
	HANK WILLIAMS: "Jambalaya"	*181*
	THEODORE ROSENGARTEN: from *All God's Dangers: The Life of Nate Shaw*	*182*
	ZORA NEALE HURSTON: from *Mules and Men*	*184*
	JAMES AGEE and WALKER EVANS: from *Let Us Now Praise Famous Men*	*187*
THE MODERN	HENRY WOODFIN GRADY: from "The New South"	*188*
SOUTH	ANDREW NELSON LYTLE: from "The Hind Tit"	*190*
	WILLIAM ALEXANDER PERCY: from *Lanterns on the Levee*	*201*
	THOMAS WOLFE: from *Look Homeward, Angel*	*203*
	ALLEN TATE: "The Trout Map"	*205*
	WILLIAM FAULKNER: from *Absalom, Absalom!*	*207*
	RICHARD WRIGHT: from *Black Boy*	*210*

W. J. CASH: from *The Mind of the South* ... *214*

JOSEPH MITCHELL: "I Blame It All on Mamma" ... *216*

TENNESSEE WILLIAMS: from *A Streetcar Named Desire* ... *229*

CARSON McCULLERS: from "The Heart Is a Lonely Hunter" ... *232*

EUDORA WELTY: "Why I Live at the P.O." ... *235*

ROBERT PENN WARREN: from *All the King's Men* ... *259*

FLANNERY O'CONNOR: "Enoch and the Gorilla" ... *263*

TRUMAN CAPOTE: from "A Christmas Memory" ... *269*

CIVIL RIGHTS

MARGARET WALKER ALEXANDER: "For My People" ... *272*

RED BARBER and ROBERT CREAMER: from *Rhubarb in the Catbird Seat* ... *282*

ROSA PARKS: from *Rosa Parks: My Story* ... *285*

Songs of the Civil Rights Movement:
"Keep Your Eyes on the Prize" ... *286*
"We Shall Overcome" ... *287*

MARTIN LUTHER KING, JR.: "I Have a Dream" ... *288*

THE SOUTH AT PLAY

TOM WOLFE: from "The Last American Hero" ... *291*

HUNTER S. THOMPSON: from "The Kentucky Derby Is Decadent and Depraved" ... *305*

WALKER PERCY: "Bourbon" ... *308*

FLORENCE KING: "The Cult of Southern Womanhood" ... *312*

CRAIG CLAIBORNE: from "A Feast Made for Laughter" ... *314*

ROY BLOUNT, JR.: "Song to Grits" ... *319*

REYNOLDS PRICE: from *Clear Pictures: First Loves, First Guides* ... *320*

THE NEWEST SOUTH

HARPER LEE: from *To Kill a Mockingbird* ... *331*

WENDELL BERRY: "The Contrariness of the Mad Farmer" ... *333*

JAMES DICKEY: "The Sheep Child" ... *334*

WILLIE MORRIS: from *North Toward Home* ... *336*

JOHN KENNEDY TOOLE: from *A Confederacy of Dunces* ... *339*

ALICE WALKER: "Everyday Use" ... *343*

PETER TAYLOR: from "In the Miro District" ... *349*

WILLIAM STYRON: from *Sophie's Choice* ... *351*

HARRY CREWS: from *A Childhood: The Biography of a Place* ... *355*

LYNYRD SKYNYRD: "Sweet Home Alabama" ... *357*

BARRY HANNAH: "Knowing He Was Not My Kind Yet I Followed" ... *359*

ALFRED UHRY: from *Driving Miss Daisy* ... *362*

INDEX ... *365*

PHOTOGRAPHY CREDITS ... *368*

INTRODUCTION

The South has been called many things. Writers and historians often want to liken it to something—usually something large and monolithic and strange. Historian David Potter said that the South "has been a kind of sphinx on the American land." Surly Baltimore journalist H. L. Mencken, writing in *The New York Evening Mail* in 1917, called the South "a Sahara of the Beaux Arts." Others have more or less thrown up their hands in futility, like Quentin Compson, the doomed young Harvard student of William Faulkner's *Absalom, Absalom!,* who takes hundreds of pages to respond to his roommate's request to *"Tell about the South,"* only to say finally, "You cant understand it. You would have to be born there."

Certainly, the South is an enigma. That it is a place worthy of scrutiny is undeniable. Mencken railed endlessly about the South because he was so fascinated by its very bereftness. The region was, he said,

> almost as sterile, artistically, intellectually, culturally, as the Sahara Desert. . . . In all that gargantuan paradise of the fourth rate there is not a single picture gallery worth going into, or a single orchestra capable of playing the nine symphonies of Beethoven, or a single opera-house, or a single theater devoted to decent plays . . . when you come to critics, musical composers, painters, sculptors, architects and the like, you will have to give it up, for there is not even a bad one between the Potomac mud-flats and the Gulf.

The South was interesting to Mencken for what he claimed was its *uninterestingness,* although one suspects he knew better, and even had a pro-Southern agenda. It is a region and a culture of high contradiction: gracious hospitality and rabid violence, heavy drinking and pious teetotalling, illiteracy and literary genius, inadequate nutrition and extraordinary cuisine, unabashed hedonism and fervent religiosity, great wealth and appalling poverty.

One reason the South is so difficult to describe is that there are many Souths: the independent upland South of the Appalachian and Ozark mountains, the exotic coastal lowcountry, the Tidewater, the rich cotton-growing Deep South, north Florida, east Texas, predominantly Catholic Louisiana. Another way to describe it would be as a region of extraordinary geophysical diversity. There are areas of seasonal changes and unabating subtropical heat, there are mountains and swamps, seacoasts and savannas, islands, caverns, powerful rivers, and anomalies of weather: tornadoes, ice storms, hurricanes. Ethnically, the South is just as diverse. Indigenous native Americans have been joined with Southerners whose roots extend to the British Isles, China, Germany, France, Spain, Italy, and Africa, and most recently to Central America and Southeast Asia.

The South as a region embraces change slowly, but has had change thrust upon it more forcefully than any other part of the country. The changes have been dramatic and bloody, but Southerners have come through them with a resilience and determination that has perhaps brought them closer to one another in the way that members of a family might inflict injury upon each other, those to whom they are closest, tightening the inextricable bond.

In spite of, or, in a converse way, *because of* the vast changes that have occurred in the South, certain continuities persist throughout Southern history. Resistance to change is in itself a thread that runs throughout Southern art and literature. Pervasive religious influence, a penchant for violence, mistrust of outsiders, reverence for the past, and a close connection to the natural world are other themes in Southern history.

In choosing a representative collection of art and literature, a collection that would speak of all these things and illustrate them, there were many difficulties, not the least of which was limiting the work to be included. This was especially true for literature, as might be expected. The South's rich literary tradition is widely acclaimed, and if literature is expanded to include oratory and song, the voice of the South perhaps is the most universally recognized form of expression in the world. What French intellectual does not know Richard Wright or William Faulkner? What Japanese teenager does not know Elvis? Who has not read *Gone with the Wind* or *Roots,* or at least seen the film versions? What people engaged in a struggle for freedom would not know the words of Martin Luther King, Jr. or Thomas Jefferson?

Why is it that the Southern literary tradition is readily acknowledged, but art is not? Perhaps Mencken was partly, but only *partly,* right. While it may seem that in the visual arts, Southerners worked in old-fashioned, derivative styles, lacked academic training, and appeared to be relatively unaware of innovative shifts in style and taste, there were reasons for this apparent lack of progress. Southerners were just as interested in keeping abreast of style and taste, but their geographical isolation (a plantation was often an island or a town unto itself) hindered the rapid spread of ideas imported from Europe in all but the most cosmopolitan ports like Charleston and New Orleans. It is also true that fewer examples of Southern art are extant, a result of a hot, humid climate that accelerates the deterioration of paintings and artifacts. The Civil War contributed to more loss, and the concomitant devastation of the economy prevented Southerners from being able to afford fine art, to create it, or to experience it in other places. There was little money for museums, patronage, conservation, or art training. In the early twentieth century, scarcely more than a generation after the war, the South was still reeling psychologically and materially.

Mencken may have had a point, at least as far as the beaux arts are concerned, but one suspects that he probably knew otherwise, and only intended his harsh indictment to make provocative copy and to goad the South into getting back on its creative feet. Academic Southern painting, sculpture, and architecture could be slavishly derivative and say more about national or European trends than about a distinctly Southern aesthetic. It may be that Mencken was looking in the wrong places with the wrong expectations. Perhaps he should have been traveling the back roads of the Appalachians or of south Mississippi instead of touring the mossy, airless postbellum museums of Richmond or Charleston. He might then have understood the uselessness of beaux arts comparisons, and seen instead the creolized beauty of the shotgun house with a lineage extending back to Haiti and Nigeria, or a carved Cherokee booger mask, an elegant wood dulcimer, or a vibrant, meticulously appliquéd album quilt. These traditional folk arts are unsurpassed in their frank beauty and are the heart of Southern art.

In recent years, there has, finally, been a vigorous defense of the fine arts in the South. Jessie Poesch's beautiful and important book, *Art of the Old South,* the Virginia Museum of Fine Arts' *Painting in the South 1564–1980,* studies by Estill Curtis Pennington and others have sought to identify a Southern aesthetic and to analyze Southern art as a phenomenon shaped by the history of the region and within a national context.

In Southern painting, some scholars have identified characteristics that define Southern art and taste. There is an exquisite quality of light similar to that which illuminates the paintings of Venice and Florence. Southerners seem particularly fond of portraiture, especially family por-

TOM MILLER. *And The Livin Is Easy.* 1989. Enamel on wood and acrylic on nylon. 68 x 45 x 45 in. Collection of Southeastern Center for Contemporary Art, Winston-Salem, NC. *African-American artists confront and lampoon stereotypical imagery about black culture, appropriating the stereotypes and thereby neutralizing their degrading effect. Tom Miller uses the minstrel's grin, cartoonish hands, and watermelon slice in a tongue-in-cheek synthesis that might be called "Afro-Deco."*

traiture, and neoclassical architecture was more enthusiastically embraced in the South than in other parts of the country. Realism has always been important in Southern art, beginning with the Etowah figures and the early naturalists, perhaps suggesting that like the Greeks (with whose ideals Southerners have long loved to associate themselves), Southerners value above all their ties with the natural world.

This connection to the natural world is one of the first threads to find expression in Southern art and literature. The South was, without a doubt, a paradise for European naturalists, whose accounts of the New World, especially of the lower southeast coast, express a stunned sensibility, an overload of stimuli ranging from interaction with exotic native people—the first Southerners—and the luxuriant vegetation, to examination of fantastic and unknown forms of animal life. Garcilaso describes the splendid temple of the powerful Cofachiqui kingdom, which symbolized the pinnacle of one civilization's achievement before it was virtually destroyed by another. John Smith, John Lawson, Mark Catesby, Philipp von Reck, and William Bartram, writing over a span of nearly two centuries, give awed accounts of their observations and explorations from insects to Indian maidens. Their written and drawn descriptions, scientific but betraying a heady amazement, show that the South was clearly regarded as a sublime new Eden, a land of innocence and fertility and promise. It was not difficult to attract new settlers, and by the eighteenth century, settlements and even cities were well established, systems of government in place, and commercial relationships developed with Europe and other parts of the world.

Colonial life in the South is revealed in the diaries and letters of men and women at the very heart of things, who, in fact, helped to shape the culture. William Byrd II's *Secret Diary* is a very intimate and detailed record—nearly hour by hour—of life, personal and otherwise, on the James River in Tidewater Virginia, while Eliza Lucas Pinckney's letterbook gives readers a glimpse of the Carolina lowcountry from the perspective of an enlightened and industrious woman. Charles Woodmason's stern admonishment to his flocks reveals a totally different Carolina experience on the backcountry frontier.

The Revolutionary War experience in the South was not essentially different from that experience in the rest of the colonies. The American struggle for liberty was quick to begin in the South, and ended there. Thomas Jefferson wrote the Declaration of Independence, and fellow Virginian Patrick Henry, the South's first rebel, gave his stirring "Liberty or Death" speech calling for Virginia patriots to arm themselves and rise up. St. George Tucker's journal entry describes events at the surrender of Lord Cornwallis at Yorktown.

Historical events and military anecdotes were subjects favored by Southern artists like William D. Washington, who painted a popular story about the Revolutionary hero Francis Marion, the Swamp Fox. Like the Romans, Southerners enjoyed not only hero worship, but also a sort of ancestor and family worship. These interests were carried out in portraiture, like the lovely portrait of Ann Hill Carter Lee and the charming Foster and Everette family groups. Portraiture often afforded Southerners, whose financial prospects were increasing and stabilizing, a means of showing off their new status and material wealth.

Many of the forces that really made the South a region distinct from the rest of the nation were rooted in earlier, seventeenth-century developments. Some of these forces were not positive ones. The slave trade had grown since Dutch traders brought the first cargo in 1619, and upon that grim system rested a thriving plantation economy. Crops like indigo, rice, and tobacco flourished in the Colonial South, as did cotton after the invention of the gin in 1793. More than a million slaves were kidnapped in West and Central Africa and brought to the Southern United States to forcibly work these crops. Alex Haley, in his novel *Roots,* has written a terrifying account of how men and women like his African ancestor were abducted and shipped across the Atlantic by slavers like John Newton, who marks his repentance in the old hymn "Amazing Grace." Will D. Campbell describes the heartbreaking Indian removal, during which approximately 50,000 native Southerners were forced west on the "Trail of Tears" to live on reservations, a drama which breaks the naive notion of a harmonious (although paternalistic) peaceable kingdom as portrayed in the painting of what is probably Benjamin Hawkins with the Creek Indians.

If the roots of Southern distinctiveness are in the seventeenth and eighteenth centuries, the region is firmly defined in the first part of the nineteenth. The Old South is a period of high contrast. The antebellum years were years of great prosperity and, even today in the minds of many white Southerners, represent the culmination of all the good things the South stood for: gracious living, chivalrous ways, beautiful homes and furnishings, and a few generations of ancestors—enough to constitute a heritage.

For other Southerners—slaves and poor whites (only about one percent of the South's population actually was well-to-do slaveowners)—it was a different South, and one that represented anything but gentility and flush times. Since few slaves were literate (in many places it was illegal to teach them to read or write), most were unable to record their perspectives on the antebellum years. Fortunately, there are exceptions. Slave narratives such as Frederick Douglass's are eloquent personal testimonies to the shocking realities of "the peculiar institution." Spirituals like "Go Down, Moses" passed along the slaves' feelings in an equally eloquent fashion. For many years it was believed that slavery stripped African-Americans of their culture, but scholarship has shown otherwise. Harriet Powers's narrative quilt shows clear connections to an old textile tradition of Benin, and ceramic face vessels from the Edgefield district of South Carolina evoke West African sculpture. Slaves carried familiar traditions and aesthetics in their hearts and heads and passed them down; not even the crushing oppression of slavery could eradicate them.

Popular literature of the day reflected the white Southerners' need to defend themselves against narratives like Douglass's—common enough in the Northern and English press—and against such books as *Uncle Tom's Cabin,* published in 1852. A whole genre developed—the plantation romance—based on the formula of the kind, generous, and benevolent master and his gentle family who fall into difficulties and are assisted or saved by slaves who have

UNKNOWN SLAVE. *Face Jug.* Monkey Form. c. 1862. One loop handle attached across upper body; wide band or collar, rolled band rim; olive glaze; applied facial features: kaolin eyes and teeth (incised). 8 $^5/_{16}$ x 19 $^{15}/_{16}$ x 4 in. Davies Pottery, Bath, SC. Collection of Tony and Marie Shank. Photograph courtesy of the McKissick Museum, University of South Carolina. *Nineteenth century face vessels from the Edgefield District, South Carolina, raise interesting questions about their makers' influences: African, European, or both? Alkaline glazing was distinctly Southern and probably developed in Edgefield around 1820.*

eschewed freedom to remain loyal to their white owners. J. P. Kennedy's *Swallow Barn* is a series of fictional vignettes in this vein. Artists illustrated this rosy picture with paintings like Lucien Powell's *The Old Log Cabin*. Other paintings, like Eastman Johnson's *The Ride for Liberty—The Fugitive Slaves* or John Antrobus's *Plantation Burial,* showed the situation in a darker light.

Life in the Old South fascinated outsiders—other Americans and foreign visitors alike. Most visitors did not fail to lash out against slavery in their writings—Fanny Kemble, Frederick Law Olmsted, and Charles Dickens were appalled—but all seemed to find many things about the South that were charming or intriguing and sometimes amusing. Southern pugnacity interested Alexis de Tocqueville, and Olmsted witnessed a charismatic religious revival. Dickens became acquainted with a dignified and articulate Choctaw on a steamboat ride, and Kemble struggled to see beauty and good in her newly acquired role as mistress of a rice plantation. Bostonian Henry Adams is merciless in his musings about the differences between New Englanders and Virginians. Artists like Robert Brammer and Augustus von Smith were charmed by the leisure activities of the Old South, like horseracing. Other artists like Hippolyte Sebron were interested in painting steamboats and the excitement they generated up and down the waterways of the South.

This affluent, romantic period ended with the Civil War. Although little publishing or art emerged from the South during the war, a great deal was certainly generated by it. The most important writing of the war was the diaries and letters—contemporary eyewitness accounts of Southerners in battle, protecting their homes and possessions, and tending the wounded and dying. Mary Boykin Chesnut, a sort of Confederate *grande dame,* records the atmosphere in Charleston at the start of the war, Caroline Seabury describes her tragic duties caring for those who had fallen at Shiloh, and Dolly Burge describes an encounter with Yankee stragglers. John Jackman and Jeremiah Gage both see action, Jackman at Shiloh and Gage at Gettysburg. One survives, the other does not.

Artists for both Union and Confederate armies recorded action at the front as well as the tedium of everyday camp life. John Ross Key captures the bombardment of Fort Sumter, Conrad Wise Chapman renders the ill-fated submarine *H. L. Hunley,* and Henri Lovie describes the chaos of Shiloh. Photography, however, revolutionized war reportage forever, as anyone who has viewed Mathew Brady's grisly battlefield photographs would agree. For the first time, people were able to see and understand the realities of war with a heart-stopping clarity that no painting or sketch could elicit.

In the war's aftermath, the suffering of the South was excruciating. White Southerners were bereaved, their hearts broken. Terrible times were ahead, especially for black Southerners, who were free but without prospects or resources, unaccustomed to supporting themselves. The grief of white Southerners evolved into a kind of civil religion—the Lost Cause. Katharine Du Pre Lumpkin, born into a typical white Georgia family, recollects the ways that many white Southerners, overwhelmed by the destruction and disintegration of the world they had known, clung to their old ideas:

> My father put it this way. He would say of his own children with tender solemnity, "Their mother teaches them their prayers. I teach them to love the Lost Cause." And surely his chosen family function in his eyes ranked but a little lower than the angels. He would say: "Men of the South, let your children hear the old stories of the South; let them hear them by the fireside, in the schoolroom, everywhere, and they will preserve inviolate the sacred honor of the South."

The "old stories" were perpetuated in art as well. Alongside the poems of Henry Timrod and Father Ryan, white Southerners were tacking up prints of E. B. D. Julio's *Last Meeting of Lee and Jackson* and flocking to view William D. Washington's *Burial of Latané*. Children cut their teeth on these instructive images that were intended to help them learn to "preserve inviolate the sacred honor of the South," and to pass them to their children as well.

War stories and odes were not the only "old stories" that were passed along. In the late nineteenth century, Southern writers like Joel Chandler Harris wanted to preserve and give "a glimpse of plantation life in the South before the war." It was Harris's intention to capture the plantation scene in its entirety—"old times dar em not forgotten"—and he was wholly cognizant of the fact that the most interesting dimension of plantation life was the slave presence. Of recording African-American folktales like "The Wonderful Tar-baby," Harris said that none of the stories was "cooked": "They are given in the simple but picturesque language of the Negroes, just as the Negroes tell them." In the late twentieth century, the Uncle Remus stories have been looked upon as racist, but it should be remembered that these tales were a medium for communication, solidarity, moral support, and education among slaves, who preserved them in an oral tradition. Harris, by writing them down, has made them accessible to all of us, thereby educating all of us.

Other local color writers sought to describe and preserve their Souths—mountain culture in east Tennessee and the Ozarks, the landscape of the Georgia hills, the bayou country of Louisiana, life along the Mississippi River. Americans, perhaps lately aware of European romanticism, were interested in seeing the different regions of the country. River panoramas were popular. Sweeping landscapes, detailed cityscapes, and views of natural wonders were available because of the development of the chromolithographic process, making color reproductions inexpensive and accessible. As photography developed, interest in painted portraiture declined, and Southerners seemed to prefer paintings that were more realistic in technique than in content, like genre scenes of poor but contented blacks, steamboats (especially wrecked ones), and leisure activities like horseracing, hunting, and fishing. Painters emigrated from England, France, and Germany, like T. A. Richards, Regis Gignoux, and Meyer Straus, who painted exotic swampscapes. Others only wintered, attracted by the tropical beauty of the St. John's River of Florida and the endless opportunity to paint *en plein air*. Europeans seemed comfortable in Charleston and New Orleans. Edgar Degas came to New Orleans to visit his mother's family in 1872–1873 and was charmed by "rosy white children in black arms, charabancs or omnibuses drawn by mules, the tall funnels of the steamboats towering at the end of the main street."

The folk culture of the South is perhaps its greatest achievement. If folk arts are the heart of the culture, the music is its soul, although it is even yet to be fully recognized. Music that we think of as American—blues, gospel, jazz, country, bluegrass, rhythm and blues, rock 'n' roll— is all rooted in the South's incredibly rich folk music traditions. Even rap musicians point to Georgia rhythm and blues singer James Brown as the original inspiration for today's rap music. In the folk music of the South are the echoes of many places—England, Scotland,

Ireland, France, Africa—the thrilling medium for expressing the passion of the people, whether the passion is religious, sexual, familial, or political. Ida Cox's "Southern Woman's Blues" speaks of disappointment and hard times in love and life, and Florence Reece and James Farmer vent their anger over the plight of Kentucky coal miners in "Which Side Are You On?" Hank Williams celebrates the spiciness of Cajun culture in "Jambalaya," and Thomas A. Dorsey expresses his sorrow and faith in "Take My Hand, Precious Lord."

Until very recently, little has been said of the remarkable flowering of painting, sculpture, and sacred art by self-taught artists in this century. Mencken and others may have failed to discern an identifiable body of Southern art with a truly Southern aesthetic, but their vision was simply misdirected. Mencken was born too soon to experience this blossoming, and it is interesting that at the same time he was condemning the South as a cultural wasteland a new generation of artists was developing whose work symbolizes the essence of the Southern experience. While the question of whether or not the creations of self-taught artists are folk or fine art is problematic, that discussion is not important here. The Paradise Garden of Howard Finster, James Harold Jennings's and David Butler's painted sculpture, and the drawings of Bill Traylor and other artists have been labelled in many ways—idiosyncratic, grass roots, transmitters, isolates, or outsiders (the current voguish term)—and their work is often perceived as crude, childlike, and devoid of intellectual content, but it is precisely this lack of sophistication that gives the art its power. Much of this art—the paintings of Sister Gertrude Morgan or Minnie Evans—is divinely inspired, steeped in the strong evangelical Protestantism of the South and created with a mystical passion few of us will ever experience. Wassily Kandinsky, the great Russian painter and one of the heroes of Western art, recognized this power in the mythological and religious folk art of his country and drew inspiration from it. He insisted that all art must spring from the depths of the soul, and that its function must be spiritual. It may be that in the closing years of the twentieth century, in a world so out of touch with spiritual things, Southern self-taught artists serve a shamanistic function and provide a glimpse into a time long forgotten, when art and magic were the same. In not too many more years, we will recognize that work by self-taught artists represents as significant a cultural phenomenon as the Southern literary renaissance of the 1920s. Like blues music, this art is quintessentially Southern: a potent blend of tradition, history, environment, religion, and individual expression. It may be that in this kind of art are the last vestiges of many things that people want to recognize as good about their culture. As James Hampton, creator of the magnificent tin foil environment *Throne of the Third Heaven of the Nations Millennium General Assembly,* believed, paraphrasing Proverbs 29:18, "Where there is no vision the people perish."

As the twentieth century turned, Southerners were faced with questions about that vision—questions that perhaps no other region was called upon to answer. What would be the role of the South in the modern world? How was the South perceived? Allen Tate, the Fugitive writer, spoke of "entering the world" after World War I, when for the first time the South virtually rejoined the Union. Southerners fought on foreign shores as Americans and began again to think of themselves as Americans. William Alexander Percy's *Lanterns on the Levee* might be the best example of the South at this juncture: one foot still on the plantation, the other attempting to forge ahead into the twentieth century. In the late nineteenth century, Henry Grady had exhorted the South to become new, to go to industry, to build up its factories and railroads, and to leave sectional differences behind. But the New South never really happened, and by 1938 Franklin Delano Roosevelt had said that "the South was the nation's number one economic problem."

In spite of, or *because of* its impoverishment, at precisely the time that the South was at such a low economic ebb, it became incredibly rich with writers. The amazing efflorescence of writing that began in the 1920s continues today. Exactly why the so-called Southern literary renaissance occurred will long be discussed, but the elements identified in this introduction—a fairy-tale land of lush beauty and abundance, a volatile confluence of complex cultures, cataclysmic defeat in war—readily provided the highly-charged conditions in which a great literary culture could germinate, take root, and grow. Put simply, Southern writers in the first half of the twentieth century were compelled to tell the South's story and, like modern writers anywhere, their own stories within that context. Richard Wright, William Faulkner, and Thomas

COLORPLATE I

ETOWAH INDIAN. *Human Figures.* A.D. 1200–1400 (Mississippian period). Georgia Department of Natural Resources, Etowah Mounds Museum. *This impressive marble couple was found near Cartersville, Georgia, in a tomb containing four individuals of high rank. The figures were originally painted with decorations, and Spanish accounts indicate that Indians in the Southeast placed carved wood and stone portraits of chiefs in their mortuary temples.*

Within the drawing:

Their rype corne

Their greene corne

Corne newly sprong

The place of solemne prayer

Their sitting at meate

The house wherin the Tombe of their Herounds standeth

SECOTON

A Ceremony in their prayers ye strange testius and sones dansing abowt posts carued on the topps lyke mens faces.

COLORPLATE 2

JOHN WHITE. *Indian Village of Secoton.* Late 1500s. Drawing. 12 ³/₄ x 7 ³/₄ in. British Museum, London. *While with the 1585 Sir Walter Raleigh expedition, White documented the flora and fauna and the customs of the native Americans at Roanoke Island. This delicate composite drawing illustrates aspects of Secotan life: eating, caring for the dead, cultivating corn, dancing. White, later governor of the mysterious "lost" colony at Roanoke, lost his daughter and granddaughter, Eleanor and Virginia Dare, with the other settlers.*

COLORPLATE 3

DE BRY. *Corn Raising in Carolina.* Lithograph. Bettmann Archives.

COLORPLATE 4

JACQUES LE MOYNE DE MORGUES. *René de Laudonniere and the Indian Chief Athore Visit Ribaut's Column.* After 1564. Watercolor on vellum. The New York Public Library, Astor, Lenox and Tilden Foundations. Bequest of James Hazen Hyde, Print Collection, Miriam and Ira D. Wallach Division of Art, Prints and Photographs. *In 1562, Huguenot Jean Ribaut explored the coastal Southeast, claiming the St. John's River area of Florida for France and erecting two stone columns in what is now Beaufort County, South Carolina. Jacques Le Moyne De Morgues arrived two years later with a second expedition and later painted more than forty-two watercolors of his memories of the trip. Here the French commander visits one of the stone columns with the Timucuan chief, whose tribe worshipped the monument.*

In the portrait, the inscriptions read:

MATOAKA ALS REBECCA FILIA POTENTISS : PRINC : POWHATANI IMP : VIRGINIÆ

Ætatis suæ 21. Aᵒ. 1616.

Matoaks als Rebecka daughter to the mighty Prince
Powhatan Emperour of Attanoughkomouck als Virginia
converted and baptized in the Christian faith, and
Wife to the Worꟙⁱ Mʳ Tho: Rolff.

COLORPLATE 5

ARTIST UNKNOWN. *Pocahontas*. Before 1899. Oil on canvas. 30 x 25 in. United States Capitol. *Pocahontas was the daughter of Powhatan, the Algonkian chief who formed an alliance with Captain John Smith. She married a Jamestown colonist, John Rolfe, had a son, and traveled to England, where she was widely celebrated and presented at court.*

L Flaminco

COLORPLATE 6

JOHN WHITE. *Flamingo.* c. 1585. British Library. *This delicate flamingo, one of the "sondry things collected and counterfeited according to the truth," is perhaps White's finest bird drawing and must have amazed his English patrons.*

COLORPLATE 7

JOHN DRAYTON (1710–1779). *Crowned Crane*. c. 1733. Watercolor on paper. 10 3/4 x 8 3/4 in. Roger Houston Ogden Collection, New Orleans.

COLORPLATE 8

MARK CATESBY. *Magnolia*. University of Mississippi, Special Collections, University, Mississippi. *This deeply colored rendering of the flower that stands as a symbol of the South is unusual because of its dark, full-page presentation.*

Wolfe wrote about individuals who embraced—or were ensnared by—the Souths they came up in. These stories reflect sorrow, bitterness, longing, and alienation, but also strength and humor and tenacity—as Faulkner said, man's "puny inexhaustible voice, still talking" in the face of an uncertain century. It seems enough to say that it did happen—is still happening—and that its occurrence is quite wonderful, and its continuation remarkable.

As Southern writers entered the world, Southern artists, many of them, turned inward and continued to explore and celebrate the region's distinctiveness. Artists like Charles Shannon and John McCrady, both of whom worked hard to promote art in the South by establishing local art groups, understood that much of what set the South apart and gave it its exotic flavor was African-American culture. As the regionalist painter Thomas Hart Benton said,

> In your childhood they taught you the language by which you express yourself, they made your songs, your jokes, and all else that will stand in your civilization as unique and characterful. They made your political theories, in that it was their peculiar position among you that was responsible for them....Nearly everything you have can be traced to their influence except your architecture, and that is borrowed.

Many talented African-American artists also emerged in the first part of the century. Some, like Beauford Delaney and William Johnson, found it necessary to train and live in the North and in Europe, and others left and eventually returned. Still others, like Romare Bearden, returned to the South only spiritually, relying on images and the sense of place that had shaped them. Sometimes the shape was warm and nurturing, sometimes the grim reality of life in the Jim Crow and segregated South was what inspired their work.

After fighting in two world wars, African-Americans expected to participate more fully and equally in American life and began to unite to work toward this common goal. The civil rights era was a watershed period in America. Everyone suffered, but for black Southerners it was a terrifying time of humiliation and anguish. It was also a time of great courage and compassion and enlightenment, as the words of Margaret Walker Alexander, Red Barber, Rosa Parks, and Martin Luther King, Jr. show.

In opposition to the South's dark side has been its great good humor and playfulness. Red Grooms's wild constructions, Roy Blount's poem about the joys of grits, Hunter Thompson's kinky account of the Kentucky Derby all testify to the *funniness* that (strange bedfellow to introspective gloominess and *contrariness*) is at the bottom of the modern Southern artistic sensibility. Storytelling, jokes, toasts and dozens, and ironic parables are fundamental forms in the Southern literary and artistic traditions and perhaps have been the South's salvation throughout many years of struggle, ugliness, and impoverishment.

Since the middle of the century, Southern writers and artists such as Barry Hannah and Ron Dale continue to work with old themes, but gradually have come to work with them on their own terms, less as apologies or explication, and more as an affirmation of what Southerners have become—the sum total of the good and the bad—better off, a richer, deeper culture for all that has gone before. In a way, there is a redefining of the region. A new South has emerged—not a freakishly distinctive region ("It's better than theatre, isn't it."), but one that is still different—very much in the world, but with a past that has marked it and not been forgotten.

Non-Southerners seem envious. Southerners might still have possession of something the rest of the country has lost. Americans love to read about Harry Crews's childhood in Georgia, or Alice Walker's and Peter Taylor's stories of very different Southern upbringings. People flock to nightclubs all over the world to hear Southern musicians like Wynton Marsalis, B. B. King, or Wynonna Judd, and fashionable TriBeCa galleries feature the work of Southern self-taught artists like Bill Traylor and Howard Finster. The last faint pulse of a rudimentary and vital America still beats in the South, a region that not long ago was pitied or belittled. Writer Willie Morris has said, "America is the South writ large," and so, perhaps the converse is true: the South is America writ small.

In the waning days of the twentieth century, Southern writers and artists may be seers, warning the world to avoid the trouble they have seen. Inextricably bound in so many ways to the natural environment, they warn us that we can lose it all, as they say, in a New York minute, if care is not taken. Photographer John McWilliams, painter Don Cooper, and writer Wendell Berry make this warning a central theme in their work. Others—William Styron and Maya Angelou—caution us that we cannot backslide, that history does not necessarily *have* to repeat itself.

Largely, though, the message is positive, the outlook hopeful. A few years ago, while he was still governor of Arkansas, William Jefferson Clinton declared the South "halfway home with a long way to go." Perhaps a home, not perfect, but sweet, is on the horizon, and as poet Maya Angelou said, reciting her powerful poem "On the Pulse of Morning" at the 1993 inauguration of two sons of the South:

> The horizon leans forward,
> Offering you space to place new steps of
>   change.
> Here, on the pulse of this fine day
> You may have the courage
> To look up and out and upon me, the
> Rock, the River, the Tree, your country.
> No less to Midas than the mendicant.
> No less to you now than the mastodon then.
>
> Here, on the pulse of this new day
> You may have the grace to look up and out
> And into your sister's eyes, and into
> Your brother's face, your country
> And say simply
> Very simply
> With hope—
> Good morning.

The reader should remember that this book is a treasury and not an exhaustive collection of Southern art and literature. There is simply too much to make selection easy, and the more one sees and reads, the more one wants to include. Inevitably, there are omissions—someone's favorite will not be here. And nothing in editing is so painful as excerpting writing that one loves. A balance was sought between well-known classic selections and more obscure but revealing ones. For instance, Walker Percy's wonderful essay on bourbon is most assuredly not his best-known work, but booze absolutely had to be represented in any book on Southern culture, and it is hoped that Dr. Percy would not have minded being the one to do it.

In the case of art, selection was so difficult because there are many relatively unknown but excitingly rich art collections in the South, and the temptation is to publish the new and "undiscovered" work. Some art could not be located, and in some cases permission for publication could not be secured from museums or individuals.

There is much work to be done in scholarship and preservation of the arts of the South. We have only begun. Without benefit of the work of Jessie Poesch, Estill Curtis Pennington, Robert Farris Thompson, John Michael Vlach, and others who blazed the trail, like Lucy, Reynolds Price's errant hound, this dog wouldn't hunt.

Lisa Howorth
Center for the Study of Southern Culture
The University of Mississippi
Oxford, Mississippi
25 April 1993

A NEW EDEN

GARCILASO DE LA VEGA

From *The Florida of the Inca*

This account, one of four that chronicle Hernando de Soto's expedition across the Southeast in 1539–1543, was written by "the Inca," Garcilaso de la Vega, so-called because he was the son of a Peruvian conquistador and an Indian princess. While in Peru and Spain, Garcilaso encountered veterans of the four-year entrada, *and his book is a compilation of their eyewitness accounts. The following passage attests to the impressive material achievement of native Americans before de Soto. The imposing temple described here, although unverified, probably was built near Camden, South Carolina.*

---

*The splendors found in the temple and burial
place of the lords of Cofachiqui*

The Castilians found no people in Talomeco because the previous pestilence had been more rigorous and devastating in this town than in any other of the whole province, and the few Indians who had escaped had not yet reclaimed their homes; hence our men paused but a short time in these houses before proceeding to the temple. Now this temple was large, being more than a hundred feet in length and forty in width. Its walls were high, conforming to the vault of the room, and its roof also was very lofty and drafty, for since the Indians had not discovered tile, they found it necessary to raise their roofs a great deal in order to keep the houses from leaking. The roof of the temple revealed that it was constructed of reeds and very thin canes split in half. With this material these Indians make neat and well-woven mats much like those of the Moors, and by throwing four, five or six of them on top of each other, they fashion a roof which is useful as well as beautiful both on the exterior and the interior, for neither sun nor water can penetrate it. From now on within this province the Indians for the greater part use cane mats instead of straw to cover their houses.

Over the roof of the temple many large and small shells of different marine animals had been arranged. The Spaniards did not learn how they had been brought inland, but it may be that they too are produced in the rivers of that land which are so numerous and so full of water. These shells had been placed with the inside out so as to show their greatest luster, and they included many conch shells of strange magnificence. Between them, spaces had been left, for each had been placed in its particular order and count; and in these spaces there were large strands (some of pearls and some of seed pearls) half a fathom in length which hung from the roof and descended in a graduated manner so that where some left off others began. The temple was covered on the outside with all these things, and they made a splendid sight in the brilliance of the sun.

To enter the temple, they opened some large doors which were in proportion to the size of the building. Close to these portals were twelve giants, carved in wood and copied from life with so much ferocity and vigor of posture that the Castilians paused and took a stand where they might examine them with care; and they were amazed to discover in such barbarous lands works which would have been prized exceedingly both for their grandeur and perfection had they been found in the most famous temples of Rome at the time of its greatest strength and empire. These giants were placed so as to guard and defend the entrance against those who

De Soto and his company landing in Florida. The Bettmann Archive.

might wish to come through it. Six were stationed on each side, one standing behind the other and all descending gradually from the largest to the smallest, for the first were four yards high, the second somewhat less, and so on down until the last.

In their hands the giants bore various weapons made in proportion to their bodies. The first two, which were the largest, stood on opposite sides and carried massive clubs, the upper fourth of which was spiked with diamond points and trimmed with strips of copper. They were constructed exactly like those seen in paintings of Hercules, and it would seem that they were copied from these paintings or vice versa. The giants held them upraised in both hands as if threatening to strike whoever might enter the door, and their gesture was so ferocious and so savage as to cause fright. The second giants, which likewise stood opposite each other (for this is the arrangement they all followed) carried broadswords made of wood in the same shape as those made in Spain of iron and steel. The third had sticks a fathom and a half in length, which were unlike clubs and more in the manner of small swingles used to brake flax, the first two-thirds of them being round and the end widening little by little until it assumed the shape of a shovel. The fourth group in the line held large battle-axes which were in conformity with their own stature. One of these weapons had a head of brass with a long and well constructed blade, on the back of which was a four-cornered point a handbreadth in length. The other had a head with exactly the same point and blade, but to the greater amazement and admiration of the Spaniards, it was made of flint. The fifth giants, in turn, held bows which were the length of their bodies and were arched with arrows placed as if they were shooting them. Both bows and arrows showed the extreme neatness and perfection that these Indians possess in making them. One arrow had a head of deerhorn carved with four sides, and the other, a head of flint which in form and size was like an ordinary dagger. The sixth and last of the giants carried very large and beautiful pikes with blades of copper.

All of these giants as well as the first ones appeared to be threatening to wound anyone who attempted to enter by the door. Those with clubs were placed so as to strike down from above; those with broadswords and pikes, to pierce; those with axes, to cut; those with sticks, to strike diagonally; and those with bows and arrows, to shoot from afar. Each one of them was in the most savage and ferocious posture that the weapon in his hand permitted; and what most amazed the Spaniards was to see the naturalness and life-likeness with which these images had been copied in all respects.

The ceiling of the temple, from the walls upward, was adorned like the roof outside with designs of shells interspersed with strands of pearls and seed pearls which were stretched so as to adhere to and follow the contour of the roof. Among these decorations were great headdresses of different colors of feathers such as those made for wear, and in addition to the pearls stretched along the ceiling and the feathers nailed to it, there were many others which had been suspended by some thin, soft-colored strings that could not be seen distinctly. Thus both pearls and feathers seemed to have been placed in the air at different levels so that they would appear to be falling from the roof. In this manner the ceiling of the temple was adorned from the walls upward, and it was an agreeable sight to behold.

CAPTAIN JOHN SMITH

From "The Description of Virginia"

John Smith was born in Lincolnshire, England in 1580. A professional soldier who had participated in campaigns from the Netherlands to the Balkans, he came to the New World with the colonists who founded Jamestown in 1606. There he became president of the governing council and reported on his New World environment and experiences.

Virginia is a Country in America that lyeth betweene the degrees of 34 and 44 of the north latitude. The bounds thereof on the East side are the great Ocean. On the South lyeth Florida: on the North nova Francia. As for the West thereof, the limits are unknowne. Of all this country wee purpose not to speake, but only of that part which was planted by the English men in the yeare of our Lord, 1606. And this is under the degrees 37. 38. and 39. The temperature of this countrie doth agree well with English constitutions being once seasoned to the country. Which appeared by this, that though by many occasions our people fell sicke; yet did they recover by very small meanes and continued in health, though there were other great causes, not only to have made them sicke, but even to end their daies, etc.

The sommer is hot as in Spaine; the winter colde as in Fraunce or England. The heat of sommer is in June, Julie, and August, but commonly the coole Breeses asswage the vehemencie of the heat. The chiefe of winter is halfe December, January, February, and halfe March. The colde is extreame sharpe, but here the proverbe is true that no extreame long continueth.

In the yeare 1607 was an extraordinary frost in most of Europe, and this frost was founde as extreame in Virginia. But the next yeare for 8. or 10. daies of ill weather, other 14 daies would be as Sommer.

The windes here are variable, but the like thunder and lightning to purifie the aire, I have seldome either seene or heard in Europe. From the Southwest came the greatest gustes with thunder and heat. The Northwest winde is commonly coole and bringeth faire weather with it. From the North is the greatest cold, and from the East and South-East as from the Bermudas, fogs and raines.

Some times there are great droughts other times much raine, yet great necessity of neither, by reason we see not but that all the variety of needfull fruits in Europe may be there in great plenty by the industry of men, as appeareth by those we there planted.

There is but one entraunce by sea into this country and that is at the mouth of a very goodly Bay the widenesse whereof is neare 18. or 20. miles. The cape on the Southside is called Cape Henry in honour of our most noble Prince. The shew of the land there is a white hilly sand like unto the Downes, and along the shores great plentie of Pines and Firres.

The north Cape is called Cape Charles in honour of the worthy Duke of Yorke. Within is a country that may have the prerogative over the most pleasant places of Europe, Asia, Africa, or America, for large and pleasant navigable rivers, heaven and earth never agreed better to frame a place for mans habitation being of our constitutions, were it fully manured and inhabited by industrious people. here [*sic*] are mountaines, hils, plaines, valleyes, rivers and brookes, all

JOHN SMITH. *Map of Virginia, 1612.*
Engraving by William Hole from sketches of Captain John Smith. The Bettmann
Archive. *Powhatan, chief of the
Algonkian Indians, is shown in state, in
the upper left corner. The map is
oriented with north to the right.*

running most pleasantly into a faire Bay compassed but for the mouth with fruitfull and
delightsome land. In the Bay and rivers are many Isles both great and small, some woody,
some plaine, most them low and not inhabited. This Bay lieth North and South in which the
water floweth neare 200 miles and hath a channell for 140 miles, of depth betwixt 7 and 15
fadome, holding in breadth for the most part 10 or 14 miles. From the head of the Bay at the
north, the land is mountanous, and so in a manner from thence by a Southwest line; So that the
more Southward, the farther off from the Bay are those mounetaines. From which fall certaine
brookes which after come to five principall navigable rivers. These run from the Northwest
into the Southeast, and so into the west side of the Bay, where the fall of every River is within
20 or 15 miles one of an other.

The mountaines are of diverse natures for at the head of the Bay the rockes are of a compo-
sition like milnstones. Some of marble, etc. And many peeces of christall we found as throwne
downe by water from the mountaines. For in winter these mountaines are covered with much
snow, and when it dissolveth the waters fall with such violence, that it causeth great inunda-
tions in the narrow valleyes which yet is scarce perceived being once in the rivers. These
waters wash from the rocks such glistering tinctures that the ground in some places seemeth as
guilded, where both the rocks and the earth are so splendent to behold, that better judgements
then ours might have beene perswaded, they contained more then probabilities. The vesture of
the earth in most places doeth manifestly prove the nature of the soile to be lusty and very rich.
The colour of the earth we found in diverse places, resembleth *bole Armoniac, terra sigillata*
and *lemnia,* Fullers earth marle and divers other such appearances. But generally for the most
part the earth is a black sandy mould, in some places a fat slimy clay, in other places a very
barren gravell. But the best ground is knowne by the vesture it beareth, as by the greatnesse of
trees or abundance of weedes, etc.

The country is not mountanous nor yet low but such pleasant plaine hils and fertle
valleyes, one prettily crossing an other, and watered so conveniently with their sweete brookes
and christall springs, as if art it selfe had devised them. By the rivers are many plaine marishes
containing some 20 some 100 some 200 Acres, some more, some lesse. Other plaines there are
fewe, but only where the Savages inhabit: but all overgrowne with trees and weedes being a
plaine wildernes as God first made it.

On the west side of the Bay, wee said were 5. faire and delightfull navigable rivers, of
which wee will nowe proceed to report. The first of those rivers and the next to the mouth of
the Bay hath his course from the West and by North. The name of this river they call Powhatan
according to the name of a principall country that lieth upon it. The mouth of this river is neere

three miles in breadth, yet doe the shoules force the Channell so neere the land that a Sacre will overshoot it at point blanck. This river is navigable 100 miles, the shouldes and soundings are here needlesse to bee expressed. It falleth from Rockes farre west in a country inhabited by a nation that they call Monacan. But where it commeth into our discoverie it is Powhatan. In the farthest place that was diligently observed, are falles, rockes, showles, etc. which makes it past navigation any higher. Thence in the running downeward, the river is enriched with many goodly brookes, which are maintained by an infinit number of smal rundles and pleasant springs that disperse themselves for best service, as doe the vaines of a mans body. From the South there fals into this river: First the pleasant river of Apamatuck: next more to the East are the two rivers of Quiyoughcohanocke. A little farther is a Bay wherein falleth 3 or 4 prettie brookes and creekes that halfe intrench the Inhabitants of Warraskoyac then the river of Nandsamund, and lastly the brooke of Chisapeack. From the North side is the river of Chickahamania, the backe river of James Towne; another by the Cedar Isle, where we lived 10 weekes upon oisters, then a convenient harbour for fisher boats or small boats at Kecoughtan, that so conveniently turneth it selfe into Bayes and Creeks that make that place very pleasant to inhabit, their cornefields being girded therein in a manner as Peninsulaes. The most of these rivers are inhabited by severall nations, or rather families, of the name of the rivers. They have also in every of those places some Governour, as their king, which they call *Werowances*. In a Peninsula on the North side of this river are the English planted in a place by them called James Towne, in honour of the Kings most excellent Majestie, upon which side are also many places under the Werowances.

JOHN LAWSON

From *A New Voyage to Carolina*

In 1700 John Lawson, five other Englishmen, and several Indian guides left Charleston charged with the task of surveying the interior of the Carolina territory. Although his knowledge and understanding of native Americans surpassed that of other early colonists, Lawson was kidnapped, tortured, and executed by the Tuscarora Indians in 1711. A New Voyage to Carolina was based on a daily journal recording the thousand-mile trip, and, when published in 1709, became the first natural history of the New World. The passenger pigeon described here is now extinct.

Wednesday. We went, this day, about 12 Miles, one of our Company being lame of his Knee. We pass'd over an exceeding rich Tract of Land, affording Plenty of great free Stones, and marble Rocks, and abounding in many pleasant and delightsome Rivulets. At Noon, we stay'd and refresh'd ourselves at a Cabin, where we met with one of their War-Captains, a Man of great Esteem among them. At his Departure from the Cabin, the Man of the House scratch'd this War-Captain on the Shoulder, which is look'd upon as a very great Compliment among them. The Captain went two or three Miles on our way, with us, to direct us in our Path. One of our Company gave him a Belt, which he took very kindly, bidding us call at his House, (which was in our Road) and stay till the lame Traveller was well, and speaking to the *Indian,* to order his Servant to make us welcome. Thus we parted, he being on his Journey to the *Congerees,* and *Savannas,* a famous, warlike, friendly Nation of *Indians,* living to the *South*-End of *Ashly* River. He had a Man-Slave with him, who was loaded with *European* Goods, his Wife and Daughter being in Company. He told us, at his Departure, that *James* had sent Knots to all the *Indians* thereabouts, for every Town to send in 10 Skins, meaning Captain *Moor,* then

Governour of *South-Carolina.* The Towns being very thick hereabouts, at Night we took up our Quarters at one of the chief Mens Houses, which was one of the Theaters I spoke of before. There ran, hard-by this Town, a pleasant River, not very large, but, as the *Indians* told us, well stor'd with Fish. We being now among the powerful Nation of *Esaws,* our Landlord entertain'd us very courteously, shewing us, that Night, a pair of Leather-Gloves, which he had made; and comparing them with ours, they prov'd to be very ingeniously done, considering it was the first Tryal.

Thursday. In the Morning, he desired to see the lame Man's affected Part, to the end he might do something, which (he believ'd) would give him Ease. After he had viewed it accordingly, he pull'd out an Instrument, somewhat like a Comb, which was made of a split Reed, with 15 Teeth of Rattle-Snakes set at much the same distance, as in a large Horn-Comb: With these he scratch'd the place where the Lameness chiefly lay, till the Blood came, bathing it, both before and after Incision, with warm Water, spurted out of his Mouth. This done, he ran into his Plantation, and got some *Sassafras* Root, (which grows here in great plenty) dry'd it in the Embers, scrap'd off the outward Rind, and having beat it betwixt two Stones, apply'd it to the Part afflicted, binding it up well. Thus, in a day or two, the Patient became sound. This day, we pass'd through a great many Towns, and Settlements, that belong to the *Sugeree-Indians,* no barren Land being found amongst them, but great plenty of Free-Stone, and good Timber. About three in the Afternoon, we reach'd the *Kadapau* King's House, where we met with one *John Stewart,* a *Scot,* then an Inhabitant of *James*-River in Virginia, who had traded there for many Years. Being alone, and hearing that the *Sinnagers (Indians* from *Canada)* were abroad in that Country, he durst not venture homewards, till he saw us, having heard that we were coming, above 20 days before. It is very odd, that News should fly so swiftly among these People. Mr. *Stewart* had left *Virginia* ever since the *October* before, and had lost a day of the Week, of which we inform'd him. He had brought seven Horses along with him, loaded with *English* Goods for the *Indians*; and having sold most of his Cargo, told us, if we would stay two Nights, he would go along with us. Company being very acceptable, we accepted the Proposal.

Friday. The next day, we were preparing for our Voyage, and baked some Bread to take along with us. Our Landlord was King of the *Kadapau Indians*, and always kept two or three trading Girls in his Cabin. Offering one of these to some of our Company, who refus'd his Kindness, his Majesty flew into a violent Passion, to be thus slighted, telling the *Englishmen*, they were good for nothing. Our old Gamester, particularly, hung his Ears at the Proposal, having too lately been a Loser by that sort of Merchandize. It was observable, that we did not see one Partridge from the *Waterrees* to this place, tho' my Spaniel-Bitch, which I had with me in this Voyage, had put up a great many before.

Saturday. On *Saturday* Morning, we all set out for *Sapona*, killing, in these Creeks, several Ducks of a strange Kind, having a red Circle about their Eyes, like some Pigeons that I have seen, a Top-knot reaching from the Crown of their Heads, almost to the middle of their Backs, and abundance of Feathers of pretty Shades and Colours. They prov'd excellent Meat. Likewise, here is good store of Woodcocks, not so big as those in *England*, the Feathers of the Breast being of a Carnation-Colour, exceeding ours for Delicacy of Food. The Marble here is of different Colours, some or other of the Rocks representing most Mixtures, but chiefly the white having black and blue Veins in it, and some that are red. This day, we met with seven heaps of Stones, being the Monuments of seven *Indians*, that were slain in that place by the *Sinnagers*, or *Troquois*. Our *Indian* Guide added a Stone to each heap. We took up our Lodgings near a Brook-side, where the *Virginia* Man's Horses got away; and went back to the *Kadapau's*.

Sunday. This day, one of our Company, with a *Sapona Indian*, who attended *Stewart*, went back for the Horses. In the mean time, we went to shoot Pigeons, which were so numerous in these Parts, that you might see many Millions in a Flock; they sometimes split off the Limbs of Stout Oaks, and other Trees, upon which they roost o' Nights. You may find several *Indian* Towns, of not above 17 Houses, that have more than 100 Gallons of Pigeons Oil, or Fat; they using it with Pulse, or Bread, as we do Butter, and making the Ground as white as a Sheet with their Dung. The *Indians* take a Light, and go among them in the Night, and bring away some thousands, killing them with long Poles, as they roost in the Trees. At this time of the Year, the Flocks, as they pass by, in great measure, obstruct the Light of the day.

Mark Catesby

From *The Natural History of Carolina, Florida, and the Bahama Islands*

Bugs

The English naturalist Mark Catesby made two visits to America, the second in 1722 to document the flora and fauna of the lower Southeast. From 1731–1743, he published his two-volume work, The Natural History of Carolina, Florida, and the Bahama Islands, *which remained the most significant work on American ornithology for many years. In the following notes, Catesby describes some all-too-familiar Southern acquaintances.*

———————

Pulex *minimus, cutem penetrans, Americanus.*

The Chego.

It is a very small kind of Flea, that is found only in warm climates: it is a very troublesome Insect, especially to Negroes and others that go bare-foot. . . . They penetrate the skin, under which they lay a bunch or bag of eggs, which swell to the bigness of a small Pea or Tare, and give great pain till it is taken out; to perform which, great care is required for fear of breaking the bag, which endangers a mortification, and the loss of a leg, and sometimes life itself. This Insect, in its natural size, is not above a fourth part so big as the common Flea, but magnified by a microscope it appeared of the size of the figure here represented. From the mouth issued a hollow tube, like that of the common Flea, between a pair of antennae. It had six jointed legs, and something resembling a tail, under which is represented one of its eggs, the size of which is so small that it can hardly be discerned by the naked eye; but magnified by a glass, appeared as here represented. These Chegoes are a nuisance to most parts of *America* between the Tropicks.

Scarabaeus *capricornus minimus cutem penetrans.*

In the year 1725, I being at the house of his Excellency Mr. *Phinney,* then Governor of the *Bahama* Islands, who, as he was searching of his feet for Chegoes, at the time we were viewing them through a microscope, produced an odd Insect on the point of his needle . . . which he then picked out of his foot. I shewed it to Negroes and others, and none of them had seen the like. The natural size of this Insect was that of the spot over its head; but magnified, it appeared of the size and form here exhibited. I think it may be called as above.

Blatta Americana.

The COCKROACH.

These are very troublesome and destructive Vermin, and are so numerous and voracious, that it is impossible to keep victuals of any kind from being devoured by them, without close covering. They are flat, and so thin, that few chests or boxes can exclude them. They eat not only leather, parchment, and woollen, but linen and paper. They disappear in winter, and appear most numerous in the hottest days in summer. It is at night they commit their depredations, and bite people in their beds, especially children's fingers that are greasy. They lay innumerable

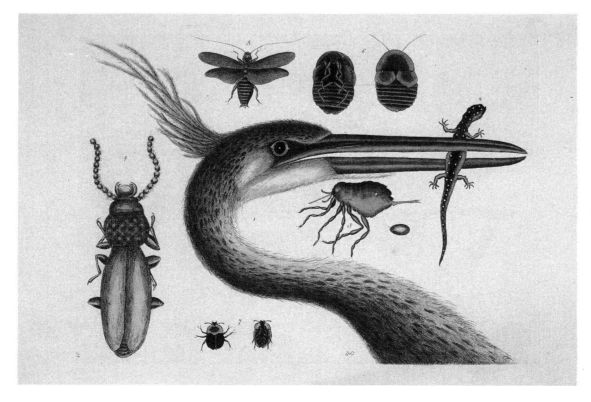

MARK CATESBY. *Insects.* 18th century. Watercolor. From *The Natural History of Carolina, Florida, and the Bahama Islands.* University of Mississippi Special Collections.

eggs, creeping into the holes of old walls and rubbish, where they lie torpid all the winter. Some have wings, and others are without, perhaps of different sexes.

Blatta maxima fusca peltata.

This is three times bigger than the common Cockroach. The head and part of the thorax were covered with an hemispherical shining hard shield; from under which proceeded two other membranes of the like consistence, which covered part of the abdomen. The abdomen was crossed with eight annuli of a shining brown colour. The face of it had somewhat the resemblance of a Monkey. The antennae were about an inch long. It had six legs, each having three joints, the lowermost joint set with sharp prickles, and crooked claws at their ends. They are found in *Carolina*. What they subsist on, and in what manner they are propagated, I know not, having seen but this one of the kind.

WILLIAM BARTRAM
From *The Travels of William Bartram*
Strawberry Hunt

The naturalist William Bartram traveled through the Southeast from 1773–1777, keeping detailed field journals for his London patron. This entry, one of the most sensuous in early American literature, describes a pastoral scene that probably took place in North Carolina, not far from the Georgia border.

After riding near two miles through Indian plantations of Corn, which was well cultivated, kept clean of weeds and was well advanced, being near eighteen inches in height, and the Beans planted at the Corn-hills were above ground; we leave the fields on our right, turning towards the mountains and ascending through a delightful green vale or lawn, which conducted us in amongst the pyramidal hills and crossing a brisk flowing creek, meandering through the meads which continued near two miles, dividing and branching in amongst the hills; we then mounted their steep ascents, rising gradually by ridges or steps one above another, frequently crossing narrow, fertile dales as we ascended; the air feels cool and animating, being charged with the fragrant breath of the mountain beauties, the blooming mountain cluster Rose, blushing Rhododendron and fair Lilly of the valley: having now attained the summit of this very elevated ridge, we enjoyed a fine prospect indeed; the enchanting Vale of Keowe, perhaps as celebrated for fertility, fruitfulness and beautiful prospects as the Fields of Pharsalia or the Vale of Tempe: the town, the elevated peeks of the Jore mountains, a very distant prospect of the Jore village in a beautiful lawn, lifted up many thousand feet higher than our present situation, besides a view of many other villages and settlements on the sides of the mountains, at various distances and elevations; the silver rivulets gliding by them and snow white cataracts glimmering on the sides of the lofty hills; the bold promontories of the Jore mountain stepping into the Tanase river, whilst his foaming waters rushed between them.

After viewing this very entertaining scene we began to descend the mountain on the other side, which exhibited the same order of gradations of ridges and vales as on our ascent, and at length rested on a very expansive, fertile plain, amidst the towering hills, over which we rode a long time, through magnificent high forests, extensive green fields, meadows and lawns. Here

WILLIAM BARTRAM.
Strawberry. c. late 1700s.
Pen and ink drawing.
British Museum of
Natural History. From the
Fothergill Album.

had formerly been a very flourishing settlement, but the Indians deserted it in search of fresh planting land, which they soon found in a rich vale but a few miles distance over a ridge of hills. Soon after entering on these charming, sequestered, prolific fields, we came to a fine little river, which crossing, and riding over fruitful strawberry beds and green lawns, on the sides of a circular ridge of hills in front of us, and going round the bases of this promontory, came to a fine meadow on an arm of the vale, through which meandered a brook, its humid vapours bedewing the fragrant strawberries which hung in heavy red clusters over the grassy verge; we crossed the rivulet, then rising a sloping, green, turfy ascent, alighted on the borders of a grand forest of stately trees, which we penetrated on foot a little distance to a horse-stamp, where was a large squadron of those useful creatures, belonging to my friend and companion, the trader, on the sight of whom they assembled together from all quarters; some at a distance saluted him with shrill neighings of gratitude, or came prancing up to lick the salt out of his hand; whilst the younger and more timorous came galloping onward, but coyly wheeled off, and fetching a circuit stood aloof, but as soon as their lord and master strewed the crystalline salty bait on the hard beaten ground, they all, old and young, docile and timorous, soon formed themselves in ranks and fell to licking up the delicious morsel.

It was a fine sight; more beautiful creatures I never saw; there were of them of all colours, sizes and dispositions. Every year as they became of age he sends off a troop of them down to Charleston, where they are sold to the highest bidder.

Having paid our attention to this useful part of the creation, who, if they are under our dominion, have consequently a right to our protection and favour. We returned to our trusty servants that were regaling themselves in the exuberant sweet pastures and strawberry fields in sight, and mounted again; proceeding on our return to town, continued through part of this high forest skirting on the meadows; began to ascend the hills of a ridge which we were under the necessity of crossing, and having gained its summit, enjoyed a most enchanting view, a vast expanse of green meadows and strawberry fields; a meandering river gliding through, saluting in its various turnings the swelling, green, turfy knolls, embellished with parterres of flowers and fruitful strawberry beds; flocks of turkeys strolling about them; herds of deer prancing in the meads or bounding over the hills; companies of young, innocent Cherokee virgins, some busily gathering the rich fragrant fruit, others having already filled their baskets, lay reclined under the shade of floriferous and fragrant native bowers of Magnolia, Azalea, Philadelphus, perfumed Calycanthus, sweet Yellow Jessamine and cerulian Glycine frutescens, disclosing their beauties to the fluttering breeze, and bathing their limbs in the cool fleeting streams; whilst other parties, more gay and libertine, were yet collecting strawberries or wantonly chasing their companions, tantalising them, staining their lips and cheeks with the rich fruit.

This sylvan scene of primitive innocence was enchanting, and perhaps too enticing for hearty young men long to continue idle spectators.

In fine, nature prevailing over reason, we wished at least to have a more active part in their delicious sports. Thus precipitately resolving, we cautiously made our approaches, yet undiscovered, almost to the joyous scene of action. Now, although we meant no other than an innocent frolic with this gay assembly of hamadryades, we shall leave it to the person of feeling and sensibility to form an idea to what lengths our passions might have hurried us, thus warmed and excited, had it not been for the vigilance and care of some envious matrons who lay in ambush, and espying us gave the alarm, time enough for the nymphs to rally and assemble together; we however pursued and gained ground on a group of them, who had incautiously strolled to a greater distance from their guardians, and finding their retreat now like to be cut off, took shelter under cover of a little grove, but on perceiving themselves to be discovered by us, kept their station, peeping through the bushes; when observing our approaches, they confidently discovered themselves and decently advanced to meet us, half unveiling their blooming faces, incarnated with the modest maiden blush, and with native innocence and cheerfulness, presented their little baskets, merrily telling us their fruit was ripe and sound.

We accepted a basket, sat down and regaled ourselves on the delicious fruit, encircled by the whole assembly of the innocently jocose sylvan nymphs; by this time the several parties under the conduct of the elder matrons, had disposed themselves in companies on the green, turfy banks.

My young companion, the trader, by concessions and suitable apologies for the bold intrusion, having compromised the matter with them, engaged them to bring their collections to his house at a stipulated price, we parted friendly.

And now taking leave of these Elysian fields, we again mounted the hills, which we crossed, and traversing obliquely their flowery beds, arrived in town in the cool of the evening.

THE EMERGING SOUTH

WILLIAM BYRD

From *The Secret Diary of William Byrd of Westover*

William Byrd II (1674–1744) was born on his father's James River plantation. Educated in England, he was a lawyer, planter, businessman, member of the Royal Society and the Virginia House of Burgesses, as well as a meticulous and earthy chronicler of life in the eighteenth-century Tidewater region and the Southern colonial frontier.

July 1710.

25. I rose at 5 o'clock and read a chapter in Hebrew and a little Greek in Thucydides. I wrote letters to my overseers above. I said no prayers this morning but ate milk and apples for breakfast. Then I went to the store and opened some things there. I sent 15 hogsheads more of tobacco on board Captain Burbydge. I ate dry beef for dinner. In the afternoon my sloop returned and was loaded again with 15 hogsheads to send to Captain Bradby. There happened a gust very violent but it did no damage. I settled my books again. In the evening Mr. C-s took a walk

about the plantation. My wife was out of humor this evening for nothing, which I bore very well and was willing to be reconciled. I neglected to say my prayers but had good thoughts, good humor, and good health, thank God Almighty.

26. I rose at 7 o'clock and read two chapters in Hebrew and some Greek in Thucydides. It rained very much. I said my prayers and ate bread and butter for breakfast, which made me very [dull]. I settled my books in the library. The Indian was better, thank God, and so were all that were sick. I ate hashed pork for dinner. In the afternoon I settled my library again and read some Latin. In the evening my wife and I took a walk about the plantation and were good friends. Mr. C-s went to Mrs. Harrison's. I said my prayers and had good health, good thoughts, and good humor, thanks be to God Almighty. I gave my wife a flourish.

27. I rose at 5 o'clock and read a chapter in Hebrew and some Greek in Thucydides. I said my prayers and ate milk for breakfast. I danced my dance. Colonel Hill came this morning and stayed about an hour. Then came Colonel Randolph who was just recovered of a dangerous sickness. My sloop came from Sandy Point and I sent more tobacco on board Captain Bradby. I ate boiled pork for dinner. In the afternoon I received letters from Falling Creek, where all was well, thank God. Our maid Moll was taken sick and so was Tom, to both whom I gave vomits which worked very well. About 5 o'clock Colonel Randolph went away. Then I wrote several letters to my overseer above. In the evening Mr. C-s and I took a walk about the plantation. I neglected to say my prayers but had good health, good thoughts, and indifferent good humor, thank God Almighty.

28. I rose at 5 o'clock and read two chapters in Hebrew and some Greek in Thucydides. I said my prayers and ate milk for breakfast. I danced my dance. Moll continued sick but Tom was better. I wrote several letters to Barbados and sent Mr. C-s a present of bacon, cherries, and apples. Mr. Will Eppes came to see me but went away before dinner. I ate boiled mutton for dinner. In the afternoon my wife and I had a little quarrel because she moved my letters. Captain Burbydge came to see us and told me my great sloop was come round. I sent ten hogsheads more on board him. I walked with him some part of the way towards Mrs. Harrison's. When we came home my wife was pleased to be out of humor. I neglected to say my prayers but had good health, good thoughts, and good humor, thanks be to God Almighty. Ned Chamberlayne came over this evening.

29. I rose at 5 o'clock and read a chapter in Hebrew and a little Greek in Thucydides. I said my prayers and ate milk for breakfast. It rained this morning till 10 o'clock. I went to the store to put up some things to send to Williamsburg and gave John some rope for the press. About 1 o'clock Captain Broadwater came over in my sloop and dined with us. I ate some stewed pigeon. In the afternoon the Captain agreed to depart from his charter and take £10 per ton. I

UNKNOWN. *The Plantation.* c. 1825. Oil on wood. 19 1/8 x 29 1/2 in. The Metropolitan Museum of Art, Gift of Edgar William and Bernice Chrysler Garbisch, 1963.

persuaded him to take my sloop with him and do some necessary things to her. I loaded my small sloop with 15 hogsheads for Captain Harvey. In the evening we took a walk about the plantation. I neglected to say my prayers but had good health, good thoughts, and good humor, thank God Almighty.

30. I rose at 5 o'clock and wrote a letter to Major Burwell about his boat which Captain Broadwater's people had brought round and sent Tom with it. I read two chapters in Hebrew and some Greek in Thucydides. I said my prayers and ate boiled milk for breakfast. I danced my dance. I read a sermon in Dr. Tillotson and then took a little [nap]. I ate fish for dinner. In the afternoon my wife and I had a little quarrel which I reconciled with a flourish. Then she read a sermon in Dr. Tillotson to me. It is to be observed that the flourish was performed on the billiard table. I read a little Latin. In the evening we took a walk about the plantation. I neglected to say my prayers but had good health, good thoughts, and good humor, thanks be to God. This month there were many people sick of fever and pain in their heads; perhaps this might be caused by the cold weather which we had this month, which was indeed the coldest that ever was known in July in this country. Several of my people have been sick, but none died, thank God.

31. I rose at 5 o'clock and read two chapters in Hebrew and some Greek in Thucydides. I said my prayers and ate boiled milk for breakfast. I danced my dance. My daughter was taken sick of a fever this morning and I gave her a vomit which worked very well and brought away great curds out of her stomach and made her well again. My people were all well again, thank God. I went to the store and unpacked some things. About 12 o'clock Captain Burbydge and Captain Broadwater came over. The first went away to Colonel Randolph's; the other stayed to dine with us. I ate hashed mutton for dinner. In the afternoon Dick Randolph came from Williamsburg and brought me the bad news that much of my wine was run out. God's will be done. In the evening Mrs. Harrison and her daughter came over. However I took a little walk. I said a short prayer and had good health, good thoughts, and good humor, thanks be to God Almighty.

Eliza Lucas Pinckney

From *The Letterbook of Eliza Lucas Pinckney*

A Lady's Labors

A remarkable woman for any era, Eliza Lucas Pinckney was a successful businesswoman who managed her family and three indigo plantations. In 1739 she began keeping her letterbook, which is a perceptive and literate reflection of life in colonial South Carolina. In this entry, Pinckney details her industrious and active days. Her plan to instruct her slaves how to teach others to read was only one of her ideas that was far ahead of its time.

[1742]

Dr. Miss B

I was much concerned to hear by our man Togo Mrs. Pinckney was unwell, but as you did not mention it in your letter I am hopeful it was but a slight indisposition.

Why, my dear Miss B, will you so often repeat your desire to know how I triffle away my time in our retirement in my fathers absence. Could it afford you advantage or pleasure I

Indigo Plant. 1753. Print.

should not have hesitated, but as you can expect neither from it I would have been excused: however, to show you my readiness in obeying your commands, here it is.

In general then I rise at five o'Clock in the morning, read till Seven, then take a walk in the garden or field, see that the Servants are at their respective business, then to breakfast. The first hour after breakfast is spent at my musick, the next is constantly employed in recolecting something I have learned least for want of practise it should be quite lost, such as French and short hand. After that I devote the rest of the time till I dress for dinner to our little Polly and two black girls who I teach to read, and if I have my paps's approbation (my Mamas I have got) I intend [them] for school mistres's for the rest of the Negroe children—another scheme you see. But to proceed, the first hour after dinner as the first after breakfast at musick, the rest of the afternoon in Needle work till candle light, and from that time to bed time read or write. 'Tis the fashion here to carry our work abroad with us so that having company, without they are great strangers, is no interruption to that affair; but I have particular matters for particular days, which is an interruption to mine. Mondays my musick Master is here. Tuesdays my friend Mrs. Chardon (about 3 mile distant) and I are constantly engaged to each other, she at our house one Tuesday—I at hers the next and this is one of the happiest days I spend at Woppoe. Thursday the whole day except what the necessary affairs of the family take up is spent in writing, either on the business of the plantations, or letters to my friends. Every other Fryday, if no company, we go a vizeting so that I go abroad once a week and no oftener.

Now you may form some judgment what time I can have to work my lappets. I own I never go to them with a quite easey conscience as I know my father has an aversion to my

COLORPLATE 9

JUSTUS ENGLEHARDT KUHN. *Henry Darnall III, as a child.* c. 1710. Oil on canvas. Maryland Historical Society, Baltimore. Bequest of Miss Ellen C. Daingerfield. *Justus Kuhn came from Germany and settled in Annapolis. This painting is one of the first American paintings to include a black person. The formal landscape in the background is almost certainly imagined or copied from a European source.*

COLORPLATE 10

PHILIPP GEORG FRIEDRICH VON RECK. *A War Dance.* Royal Library, Copenhagen. *Von Reck's drawings of native Americans provide an extremely valuable record of the culture and language of Creek and Yuchi Indians. Von Reck apparently familiarized himself with Indian languages, since many sketches bear captions in Yuchi and Creek. This sketch carefully describes a Yuchi war dance, usually performed on the eve of a planned assault.*

COLORPLATE 11 (opposite, above)

PHILIPP GEORG FRIEDRICH VON RECK. *Alligator.* Royal Library, Copenhagen. *Philipp Georg Friedrich von Reck was leader of a group of German Protestants expelled from Salzburg in 1732 who founded settlements, Ebenezer and New Ebenezer, about twenty miles north of Savannah. In order to recruit new colonists, von Reck prepared many watercolor sketches such as these to provide "ocular proof" of the environment.*

COLORPLATE 12 (opposite, below)

JOHN WHITE. *Catfish.* c. 1585. British Museum, London. *Although there are a few inaccuracies in this drawing, this is possibly the white catfish,* Ictalurus catus. *From other drawings of White's, catfish appear to have been a regular feature in the Indians' diet.*

Keetrauk. Some 2. foote and a halfe in length.

COLORPLATE 13

ARTIST UNKNOWN. *Twilight at Mount Vernon*. c. 1790. Oil on canvas. 23 x 35 ¹/₈ in. Gift of Edgar William and Bernice Chrysler Garbisch. Copyright 1992 National Gallery of Art, Washington, D.C.

COLORPLATE 14 (opposite)

JOHN TRUMBULL. *George Washington*. 1791. Oil on canvas. 90 ¹/₂ x 63 in. Collection of City Hall, Charleston, South Carolina.

COLORPLATE 15

CHARLES PEALE POLK (1767–1822). *Portrait of Thomas Jefferson.* 1799. Oil on canvas. 27 1/4 x 24 in. Robert M. Hicklin, Jr., Inc. Spartanburg, South Carolina. *Charles Peale Polk was raised by his uncle, Charles Willson Peale. His style is closer to that of a limner than it is to the polished style of his uncle. Sometimes labeled "folk," Polk's paintings are more properly called "plain" paintings. This portrait, painted at Monticello just before Thomas Jefferson became president, nonetheless captures Jefferson's character.*

COLORPLATE 16

ARTIST UNKNOWN. *Ann Hill Carter Lee.* c. 1795. Oil on canvas. 28 1/2 x 23 1/2 in. Washington/ Custis/Lee Collection, Washington and Lee University, Lexington, Virginia. *Ann Hill Carter Lee was the second wife of the Revolutionary war hero Light-Horse Harry Lee, the mother of Robert E. Lee, and the grandmother of Henry Adams's Harvard friend, Roony Lee.*

COLORPLATE 17

ARTIST UNKNOWN. *Colonel William Washington at the Battle of Cowpens, January 17, 1781*. 1781. Chicago Historical Society. *The Battle of Cowpens, South Carolina, was a brilliant American victory over the British. Colonel Washington himself clashed with Colonel Banastre Tarleton, and according to legend Washington's life was saved by his courageous slave.*

COLORPLATE 18

BENJAMIN HENRY LATROBE. *View of Norfolk from Town Point.* 1796. Pencil, pen and ink, watercolor on paper.
6 5/16 x 10 5/16 in. Maryland Historical Society, Baltimore. *From one of Latrobe's fourteen sketchbooks of accurate and fresh (if somewhat amateurish) sketches, this watercolor was rendered twenty years after Norfolk was destroyed by fire. It is the earliest known illustration of Norfolk.*

employing my time in that poreing work, but they are begun and must be finished. I hate to undertake any thing and not go thro' with it; but by way of relaxation from the other I have begun a piece of work of a quicker sort which requires nither Eyes nor genius—at least not very good ones. Would you ever guess it to be a shrimp nett? For so it is.

O! I had like to forgot the last thing I have done a great while. I have planted a large figg orchard with design to dry and export them. I have reckoned my expence and the prophets to arise from these figgs, but was I to tell you how great an Estate I am to make this way, and how 'tis to be laid out you would think me far gone in romance. Your good Uncle I know has long thought I have a fertile brain at schemeing. I only confirm him in his opinion; but I own I love the vegitable world extremly. I think it an innocent and useful amusement. Pray tell him, if he laughs much at my project, I never intend to have my hand in a silver mine and he will understand as well as you what I mean.

Our best respects wait on him and Mrs. Pinckney. If my Eyes dont deceive me you in your last [letter] talk of coming very soon by water to see how my oaks grow. Is it really so, or only one of your unripe schemes. While 'tis in your head put it speedily into execution and you will give great pleasure to

Ymos

E. Lucas

Reverend Charles Woodmason
"On Correct Behavior in Church"

After serving as justice of the peace in Charleston, Woodmason became an itinerant Anglican minister in the South Carolina backcountry. His literate and passionate appeals on behalf of his disfranchised and impoverished parishioners show him to be a champion of the Regulator movement, although, as the following remonstrance reveals, he could also be an angry and cynical figure of paternalism. Here is an extract from a sermon given at the High Hills and at Rafting Creek in July of 1770.

Always contrive to come before Service begins—Which You may do, as We begin so late. 'Tis but putting and getting things in Order over Night—Whereas many will hardly set about it till Sunday Morning. Contrive too, to go as early as possible to rest on Saturday Night so that You may rise early and refresh'd on the Lords day and not be hurry'd in dressing, and ordering Matters. The coming late to Sermon discourages People, for lack of Company—and coming in after Service is begun is very troublesome—Disturb both me and ev'ry One and should be avoided as much as possible—But if it is unavoidable, pray enter leisurely—tread softly—nor disturb any who are on their Knees or are intent on their Devotions. Bring no Dogs with You—they are very troublesome—and I shall ~~fine~~ inform the Magistrate of those who do it, for it is an Affront to the Divine Presence which We invoke, to be in the midst of Us, and to hear our Prayers, to mix unclean things with our Services.

When You are seated—do not whisper, talk, gaze about—shew light Airs, or Behaviour—for this argues a wandering Mind and Irreverence towards God; is unbecoming Religion, and may give Scandal and Offence to weak Christians:—Neither sneeze or Cough, if You can avoid it—and do not practise that unseemly, rude, indecent Custom of Chewing or of spitting, which is very ridiculous and absurd in Public, especially in Women and in Gods House. If you are thirsty—Pray drink before you enter or before Service begins, not to go out in midst of Prayer, nor be running too and fro like Jews in their Synagogues—except Your necessary

Occasions should oblige You—Do You see anything like it in Charles Town or among Well bred People. Keep Your Children as quiet as possible. If they will be fractious, Carry them out at once for I will not have Divine Worship *now* consider'd by You, as if I was officiating in a private House.

Those among you who have not the tunes we do now, or shall sing, and are desirous of them, I will write them out for. . . . Many among you possibly prefer Extempore Sermons, to those which are Premeditated, and may call my Mode of Delivery, rather *Reading* than *Preaching*. 'Tis true, extempore Discourses have their peculiar Merit—but there is hardly one Man in the World, but will speak better and more useful Sense, premediately than Extempore. . . .

Ev'ry Sunday Afternoon, I purpose catechising as Many of You, Young and old, as can possibly attend. . . .

When Banns are published—Don't make it a Matter of Sport; but let it stir You up to put up a Petition to Heav'n for a Blessing of God upon the Parties.

PATRICK HENRY

Liberty or Death Speech

Patrick Henry was one of the greatest orators in American history. A failed planter and businessman, he read for the law independently and was so successful as a colonial advocate that he was elected to the Virginia House of Burgesses and was the Virginia delegate to the First Continental Congress of 1774. On March 23, 1775 in a revolutionary meeting in St. John's Church, Richmond, Henry gave this highly charged speech arguing openly for armed rebellion. Rough, awkward, and defiant, Patrick Henry was perhaps the first Southern rebel.

———————

Mr. President, it is natural to man to indulge in the illusions of hope. We are apt to shut our eyes against a painful truth—and listen to the song of that siren, till she transforms us into beasts. Is this the part of wise men, engaged in a great and arduous struggle for liberty? Were we disposed to be of the number of those, who having eyes, see not, and having ears, hear not, the things which so nearly concern their temporal salvation? For his part, whatever anguish of spirit it might cost, *he* was willing to know the whole truth; to know the worst, and to provide for it.

He had but one lamp by which his feet were guided: and that was the lamp of experience. He knew of no way of judging of the future but by the past. And judging by the past, he wished to know what there had been in the conduct of the British ministry for the last ten years, to justify those hopes with which gentlemen had been pleased to solace themselves and the house? Is it that insidious smile with which our petition has been lately received? Trust it not, sir; it will prove a snare to your feet. Suffer not yourselves to be betrayed with a kiss. Ask yourselves how this gracious reception of our petition comports with those warlike preparations which cover our waters and darken our land. Are fleets and armies necessary to a work of love and reconciliation? Have we shown ourselves so unwilling to be reconciled, that force must be called in to win back our love? Let us not deceive ourselves, sir. These are the implements of war and subjugation—the last arguments to which kings resort. I ask gentlemen, sir, what means this martial array, if its purpose be not to force us to submission? Can gentlemen assign any other possible motive for it? Has Great Britain any enemy in this quarter of the world, to call for all this accumulation of navies and armies? No, sir, she has none. They are meant for us: they can be meant for no other. They are sent over to bind and rivet upon us those chains which the British ministry have been so long forging. And what have we oppose to them? Shall we try argument? Sir, we have been trying that for the last ten years. Have we any thing new to offer upon the subject? Nothing. We have held the subject up in every light of which it is capable; but it has been all in vain. Shall we resort to entreaty and humble supplication? What terms shall we find, which have not been already exhausted? Let us not, I beseech you, sir, deceive ourselves longer. Sir, we have done every thing that could be done, to avert the storm which is now coming on. We have petitioned—we have remonstrated—we have supplicated—we have prostrated ourselves before the throne, and have implored its interposition to arrest the tyrannical hands of the ministry and parliament. Our petitions have been slighted; our remonstrances have produced additional violence and insult; our supplications have been disregarded; and we have been spurned, with contempt, from the foot of the throne. In vain, after these things, may we indulge the fond hope of peace and reconcilation. *There is no longer any room for hope.* If we wish to be free—if we mean to preserve inviolate those inestimable privileges for which we have been so long contending—if we mean not basely to abandon the noble struggle in which we have been so long engaged, and which we have pledged ourselves never to abandon, until the glorious object of our contest shall be obtained—we must fight!—I repeat it, sir, we must fight!! An appeal to arms and to the God of hosts, is all that is left us!

They tell us, sir, that we are weak—unable to cope with so formidable an adversary. But when shall we be stronger. Will it be the next week or the next year? Will it be when we are totally disarmed, and when a British guard shall be stationed in every house? Shall we gather strength by irresolution and inaction? Shall we acquire the means of effectual resistance by lying supinely on our backs, and hugging the delusive phantom of hope, until our enemies shall have bound us hand and foot? Sir, we are not weak, if we make a proper use of those means which the God of nature hath placed in our power. Three millions of people armed in the holy cause of liberty and in such a country as that which we possess, are invincible by any force which our enemy can send against us. Besides, sir, we shall not fight our battles alone. There is a just God who presides over the destinies of nations, and who will raise up friends to fight our battles for us. The battle, sir, is not to the strong alone; it is to the vigilant, the active, the brave. Besides, sir, we have no election. If we were base enough to desire it, it is now too late to retire from the contest. There is no retreat but in submission and slavery! Our chains are forged. Their clanking may be heard on the plains of Boston! The war is inevitable—and let it come!! I repeat it, sir, let it come!!!

It is vain, sir, to extenuate the matter. Gentlemen may cry, peace, peace—but there is no peace. The war is actually begun! The next gale that sweeps from the north will bring to our ears the clash of resounding arms! Our brethren are already in the field! Why stand we here

idle? What is it that gentlemen wish? What would they have? Is life so dear, or peace so sweet, as to be purchased at the price of chains and slavery? Forbid it, Almighty God—I know not what course others may take; but as for me, give me liberty, or give me death!

ELIZA WILKINSON

From *Letters of Eliza Wilkinson*

A Day of Terror

Eliza Yonge Wilkinson, a widow living on Yonge's Island, near Charleston, South Carolina, wrote a number of letters to a friend, Mary Porcher, in 1781 and 1782. This letter recalls the invasion of the lowcountry by the British in 1779.

Well, now comes the day of terror—the 3d of June. (I shall never love the anniversary of that day.) In the morning, fifteen or sixteen horsemen rode up to the house; we were greatly terrified, thinking them the enemy, but from their behavior, were agreeably deceived, and found them friends. They sat a while on their horses, talking to us; and then rode off, except two, who tarried a minute or two longer, and then followed the rest, who had nearly reached the gate. One of the said two must needs jump a ditch—to show his activity I suppose; for he might as well, and better, have gone in the road. However, he got a sad fall; we saw him, and sent a boy to tell him, if he was hurt, to come up to the house, and we would endeavor to do something for him. He and his companion accordingly came up; he look'd very pale, and bled much; his gun somehow in the fall, had given him a bad wound behind the ear, from whence the blood flowed down his neck and bosom plentifully: we were greatly alarmed on seeing him in this situation, and had gathered around him, some with one thing, some with another, in order to give him assistance. We were very busy examining the wound, when a negro girl ran in, exclaiming—"O! the king's people are coming, it must be them, for they are all in red." Upon this cry, the two men that were with us snatched up their guns, mounted their horses, and made off; but had not got many yards from the house, before the enemy discharged a pistol at them. Terrified almost to death as I was, I was still anxious for my friends' safety; I tremblingly flew to the window, to see if the shot had proved fatal: when, seeing them both safe, "Thank heaven," said I, "they've got off without hurt!" I'd hardly utter'd this, when I heard the horses of the inhuman Britons coming in such a furious manner, that they seemed to tear up the earth, and the riders at the same time bellowing out the most horrid curses imaginable; oaths and imprecations, which chilled my whole frame. Surely, thought I, such horrid language denotes nothing less than death; but I'd no time for thought—they were up to the house—entered with drawn swords and pistols in their hands; indeed, they rushed in, in the most furious manner, crying out, "Where're these women rebels?" (pretty language to ladies from the *once famed Britons!*) That was the first salutation! The moment they espied us, off went our caps, (I always heard say none but women pulled caps!) And for what, think you? why, only to get a paltry stone and wax pin, which kept them on our heads; at the same time uttering the most abusive language imaginable, and making as if they'd hew us to pieces with their swords. But it's not in my power to describe the scene: it was terrible to the last degree; and, what augmented it, they had several armed negroes with them, who threatened and abused us greatly. They then began to plunder the house of every thing they thought valuable or worth taking; our trunks were split to pieces, and each mean, pitiful wretch crammed his bosom with the contents, which were our apparel, &c. &c. &c.

I ventured to speak to the inhuman monster who had my clothes. I represented to him the times were such we could not replace what they'd taken from us, and begged him to spare me only a suit or two; but I got nothing but a hearty curse for my pains; nay, so far was his callous heart from relenting, that, casting his eyes towards my shoes, "I want them buckles," said he, and immediately knelt at my feet to take them out, which, while he was busy about, a brother villain, whose enormous mouth extended from ear to ear, bawled out "Shares there, I say; shares." So they divided my buckles between them. The other wretches were employed in the same manner; they took my sister's ear-rings from her ears; hers, and Miss Samuells's buckles; they demanded her ring from her finger; she pleaded for it, told them it was her wedding ring, and begged they'd let her keep it; but they still demanded it, and, presenting a pistol at her, swore if she did not deliver it immediately, they'd fire. She gave it to them, and, after bundling up all their booty, they mounted their horses. But such despicable figures! Each wretch's bosom stuffed so full, they appeared to be all afflicted with some dropsical disorder; had a party of rebels (as they called us) appeared, we should soon have seen their circumference lessen.

They took care to tell us, when they were going away, that they had favored us a great deal—that we might thank our stars it was no worse. But I had forgot to tell you, that, upon their first entering the house, one of them gave my arm such a violent grasp, that he left the print of his thumb and three fingers, in black and blue, which was to be seen, very plainly, for several days after. I showed it to one of our officers, who dined with us, as a specimen of British cruelty. If they call this *favor*, what must their cruelties be? It must want a name. To be brief; after a few words more, they rode off, and glad was I. "Good riddance of bad rubbish," and indeed such rubbish was I never in company with before. One of them was an officer too! a sergeant, or some such, for he had the *badge of honor on his shoulders!* After they were gone, I began to be sensible of the danger I'd been in, and the thoughts of the vile men seemed worse (if possible) than their presence; for they came so suddenly up to the house, that I'd no time for thought; and while they staid, I seemed in amaze! Quite stupid! I cannot describe it. But when they were gone, and I had time to consider, I trembled so with terror, that I could not support myself. I went into the room, threw myself on the bed, and gave way to a violent burst of grief, which seemed to be some relief to my full-swollen heart.

ANONYMOUS

"The Dance"

This anonymous song to the tune of "Yankee Doodle" appeared soon after the surrender of Cornwallis in 1781.

———————————

Cornwallis led a country dance,
    The like was never seen, sir,
Much retrograde and much advance,
    And all with General Greene, sir.

They rambled up and rambled down,
    Join'd hands, then off they run, sir,
Our General Greene to Charlestown,
    The earl to Wilmington, sir.

JOHN VANDERLYN.
Washington and Lafayette.
Oil. The Bettmann Archive.

Greene, in the South, then danc'd a set,
    And got a mighty name, sir,
Cornwallis jigg'd with young Fayette,
    But suffer'd in his fame, sir.

Then down he figur'd to the shore,
    Most like a lordly dancer,
And on his courtly honor swore,
    He would no more advance, sir.

Quoth he, my guards are weary grown
    With footing country dances,
They never at St. James's shone,
    At capers, kicks or prances.

Though men so gallant ne'er were seen,
    While sauntering on parade, sir,
Or wriggling o'er the park's smooth green,
    Or at a masquerade, sir.

Yet are red heels and long-lac'd skirts,
    For stumps and briars meet, sir?
Or stand they chance with hunting-shirts,
    Or hardy veteran feet, sir?

Now hous'd in York he challeng'd all,
    At minuet or all 'amande,
And lessons for a courtly ball,
    His guards by day and night conn'd.

This challenge known, full soon there came,
    A set who had the bon ton,
De Grasse and Rochambeau, whose fame
Fut brillant pour un longtemps.

And Washington, Columbia's son,
    Whom easy nature taught, sir,
That grace which can't by pains be won,
    Or Plutus' gold be bought, sir.

Now hand in hand they circle round,
    This ever-dancing peer, sir;
Their gentle movements, soon confound
    The earl, as they draw near, sir.

His music soon forgets to play—
    His feet can no more move, sir,
And all his bands now curse the day,
    They jiggèd to our shore, sir.

Now Tories all, what can ye say?
    Come—is not this a griper,
That while your hopes are danc'd away,
    'Tis you must pay the piper.

St. George Tucker

From "St. George Tucker's Journal of the Siege of Yorktown, 1781"

Born in Bermuda in 1752, Tucker served as a lieutenant colonel at Yorktown. His account of the siege of Yorktown (where he was also wounded) which marked the end of the American Revolution on October 19, 1781, was meticulous and detailed, and is the only surviving eyewitness account by a resident of the Yorktown area.

Wednesday 17. As we have heard a very smart or rather incessant Cannonade last night and this Morning I take it for granted that all or the greater part of our Batteries are opened by this time. This Forenoon a Flag from York brought a Letter couch'd nearly in the following Terms—

> Sir, I propose a Cessation of Hostilities for twenty four Hours, and that two
> Officers be appointed from both sides to meet at Mr. Moores, and agree on Terms
> for the surrender of the posts of York & Gloucester—I have the Honor to be your
> Excellency's most obedt. & most hble Servant—Cornwallis
> Directed
>   To his Excellency
> General Washington, Comdr. in Chief of the combined Forces of France &
> America.

The Answer was to the following purport.
> Sir, I have recieved [*sic*] your Favor of this Morning. Regard to humanity induces
> me to agree to a suspension of hostilities for two hours that your Lordship may
> propose the Terms on which you choose to surrender, &ca

I am now ordered on Duty, & with more Sanguine hopes than ever filld the Mind of Man I now set out for the Trenches.

Thursday 18th. Lord Cornwallis being allow'd but two hours sent out another Flag to request further time to digest his proposals—It has been granted and Hostilities have ceased ever since five OClock. It was pleasing to contrast the last night with the preceeding—A solemn stillness prevailed—the night was remarkably clear & the sky decorated with ten thousand stars—numberless Meteors gleaming thro' the Atmosphere afforded a pleasing resemblance to the Bombs which had exhibited a noble Firework the night before, but happily divested of all their Horror. At dawn of day the British gave us a serenade with the Bag pipe, I believe, & were answered by the French with the Band of the Regiment of deux ponts. As Soon as the Sun rose one of the most striking pictures of War was display'd that Imagination can paint— From the point of Rock Battery on one side our Lines compleatly mann'd and our Works crowded with soldiers were exhibited to view—opposite these at the Distance of two hundred yards you were presented with a sight of the British Works; their parapets crowded with officers looking at those who were assembled at the top of our Works—the Secretary's house with one of the Corners broke off, & many large holes thro' the Roof & Walls part of which seem'd tottering with their Weight afforded a striking Instance of the Destruction occasioned by War—Many other houses in the vicinity contributed to accomplish the Scene—On the Beach of York directly under the Eye hundreds of busy people might be seen moving to & fro—At a small distance from the Shore were seen ships sunk down to the Waters Edge— further out in the Channel the Masts,

Surrender of Cornwallis at Yorktown. Undated engraving by Chapin. The Bettmann Archive.

Yards & even the top gallant Masts of some might be seen, without any vestige of the hulls. On the opposite of the river the remainder of the shipping drawn off as to a place of security. Even here the Guadaloupe sunk to the Waters Edge shew'd how vain the hope of such a place. On Gloster point the Fortifications and Encampment of the Enemy added a further Variety to the scene which was compleated by the distant View of the french Ships of War, two of which were at that time under sail—A painter need not to have wish'd for a more compleat subject to imploy his pencil without any expence of Genius.

This was the Scene which ushered in the Day when the pride of Britain was to be humbled in a greater Degree than it had ever been before, unless at the Surrender of Burgoyne—It is remarkable that the proposals for a surrender of Lord Cornwallis's Army were made on the Anniversary of that important Event—At two o Clock the Surrender was agreed on & Commissioners appointed to draw up the Articles of Capitulation—They are now employed on that Business—

The Guadaloupe or some other Frigate was sunk two night ago—we know not whether by Design or Accident—

I can not omit one Anecdote which happened during the Siege—Baron Viominit at the Attack on the Enemy's redoubts on Monday Evening observing two Sargeants distinguish themselves by their Intrepidity, sent for them to dine with him the next Day & placed them at his right hand where he treated them with the highest Respect and Attention—

[Marginal note] *Fryday*—This Morning at nine oClock the Articles of Capitulation were signed and exchanged—At retreat beating last night the British play'd the Tune of "Welcome Brother Debtor"—to their conquerors the tune was by no means disagreeable—

Fryday 19th. At two OClock to day a Detachmt. of American Light Infantry and French Grenadiers took possession of the horn-work on the East End of York town— Our Army was drawn up in a Line on each side of the road extending from our front parallel to the Forks of the Road at Hudson Allen's the Americans on the right, the French on the left. Thro' these Lines the whole British Army march'd their Drums in Front beating a slow March. Their Colours furl'd and Cased. I am told they were restricted by the capitulation from beating a French or American march. General Lincoln with his Aids conducted them—Having passed thro' our whole Army they grounded their Arms & march'd back again thro' the Army a second Time into the Town—The sight was too pleasing to an American to admit of Description—

THOMAS JEFFERSON

From *The Domestic Life of Thomas Jefferson*
Excerpt from A Letter to the Comtesse de Tesse

Although Thomas Jefferson wrote the Declaration of Independence and was the third president of the United States, he wished also to be remembered as "father of the University of Virginia," which he designed. His significant contribution to the architectural environment of the South is generally overlooked. This letter to a friend illustrates Jefferson's intoxication with neoclassical structures he visited in Europe, which then inspired his designs for his own home, Monticello, and the Virginia State Capitol.

———————————

Nismes, March 20th, 1787.

Here I am, Madam, gazing whole hours at the Maison Quarrée, like a lover at his mistress. The stocking-weavers and silk-spinners around it consider me as a hypochondriac Englishman, about to write with a pistol the last chapter of his history. This is the second time I have been

THOMAS JEFFERSON. *Virginia Capitol, Richmond; front elevation.* Architectural drawing. Massachusetts Historical Society, Boston. *While in Paris as the Minister to France, Jefferson designed the Virginia State Capitol with the assistance of the architect and scholar, Charles-Louis Clerisseau. The building, begun in 1786, was completed in 1798.*

in love since I left Paris. The first was with a Diana at the Château de Laye-Epinaye in Beaujolais, a delicious morsel of sculpture, by M. A. Slodtz. This, you will say, was in rule, to fall in love with a female beauty; but with a house! It is out of all precedent. No, Madam, it is not without a precedent in my own history. While in Paris, I was violently smitten with the Hôtel de Salm, and used to go to the Tuileries almost daily to look at it. The *loueuse des chaises*—inattentive to my passion—never had the complaisance to place a chair there, so that sitting on the parapet, and twisting my neck around to see the object of my admiration, I generally left it with a *torti-colli.*

From Lyons to Nismes I have been nourished with the remains of Roman grandeur. They have always brought you to my mind, because I know your affection for whatever is Roman and noble.

Martha Laurens Ramsay

From *Memoirs of the Life of Martha Laurens Ramsay*

A Letter to Her Son at Princeton College

Some things are constant, a mother's advice being one. Martha Laurens Ramsay was the daughter of Henry Laurens, a Charleston merchant and patriot who had been incarcerated in the Tower of London and was eventually exchanged for Lord Cornwallis. David Ramsay was en route by ship to Princeton College, then a popular choice for young Southern men, when his mother wrote this letter.

Charleston, May 7, 1810.

The first thing I did when you left me, dear David, was to retire for a few moments to your chamber, and relieve my labouring heart, by commending you solemnly and affectionately to the good Providence of our heavenly Father. I composed myself as soon as possible, and set about my accustomed domestic duties. Soon after Dr. Abeel came in; he passed a parting half hour with us, and began his journey the same evening. I should be glad that my wishes and my hopes about the perfect recovery of this excellent and interesting man, held at all equal pace. But I confess that I wish more than I dare hope.

While I was in your chamber, I discovered the little treatise (Dr. Waterhouse's lecture to the students of the university of Cambridge on smoking tobacco) which your father had requested you to read, and which, in the main, I approve of so highly that I have given away half a dozen to persons in whom I am much less interested than in you. I sent it after you by Cooney, who says you received it safely. I hope its contents will not be lost upon you, nor the book itself lost by you. While we were in church on Friday afternoon, there came up a severe thunderstorm; and while Mr. Palmer was in the act of praying for you and your fellow passengers, the flashes of lightning and peals of thunder added not a little to the solemn feeling of many persons in the church, interested most tenderly in the fate of the mixed multitude on board the Pennsylvania.

I shall be counting the days till I hear from you. It will be no disappointment to me, or rather it will give me no pain to learn that you have not entered the junior class: to whatever class you belong, do your duty in it. Be respectful to your superiors, live affectionately with your equals; make yourself a party in no broils; but mind your own business; give dignity to the Carolinian name; write to me accurately on every subject which concerns you. Be not ashamed of religion; read your Bible diligently; it will not only make you wise unto salvation, but you will find in it excellent directions for your conduct in the affairs of this life. Your grandfather, Laurens, used to say, if men made a good use of only the book of Proverbs, there would be no bankruptcies, no failures in trade; no family dissentions; none of those wide spreading evils which, from the careless conduct of men in the common concerns of life, desolate human society; and I can assure you, the more you read this divine book, the more you will love and value it. I long to hear from you, and with tender affection subscribe myself, your friend and mother.

M. L. Ramsay.

ALEX HALEY

From *Roots*

The Capture

Alex Haley, who also wrote The Autobiography of Malcolm X, *spent twelve years researching his family's history, tracing it all the way back to Africa. The resultant novel,* Roots, *was a best seller in 1976, and the twelve-hour television adaptation attracted 130 million viewers. In this excerpt, Haley reconstructs the capture of Kunta Kinte, his African ancestor.*

The familiar perfumes of wild flowers filled Kunta's nostrils as he ran, wetting his legs, through grass glistening with dew in the first rays of sunshine. Hawks circled overhead looking for prey, and the ditches beside the fields were alive with the croaking of frogs. He veered away from a tree to avoid disturbing a flock of blackbirds that filled its branches like shiny black leaves. But he might have saved himself the trouble, for no sooner had he passed by than an angry, raucous cawing made him turn his head in time to see hundreds of crows bullying the blackbirds from their roost.

Breathing deeply as he ran, but still not out of breath, he began to smell the musky aroma of the mangroves as he neared the low, thick underbrush that extended far back from the banks of the bolong. At the first sight of him, a sudden snorting spread among the wild pigs, which in turn set off a barking and snarling among the baboons, whose big males quickly pushed their females and babies behind them. When he was younger, he would have stopped to imitate them, grunting and jumping up and down, since this never failed to annoy the baboons, who would always shake their fists and sometimes throw rocks. But he was no longer a boy, and he had learned to treat all of Allah's creatures as he himself wished to be treated: with respect.

Fluttering white waves of egrets, cranes, storks, and pelicans rose from their sleeping places as he picked his way through the tangled mangrove down to the bolong. Kunta's wuolo dog raced ahead chasing watersnakes and big brown turtles down their mudslides into the water, where they left not even a ripple.

As he always did whenever he felt some need to come here after a night's lookout duty, Kunta stood awhile at the edge of the bolong, today watching a gray heron trailing its long, thin legs as it flew at about a spear's height above the pale green water, rippling the surface with each downbeat of its wings. Though the heron was looking for smaller game, he knew that this was the best spot along the bolong for kujalo, a big, powerful fish that Kunta loved to catch for Binta, who would stew it for him with onions, rice, and bitter tomatoes. With his stomach already rumbling for breakfast, it made him hungry just to think of it.

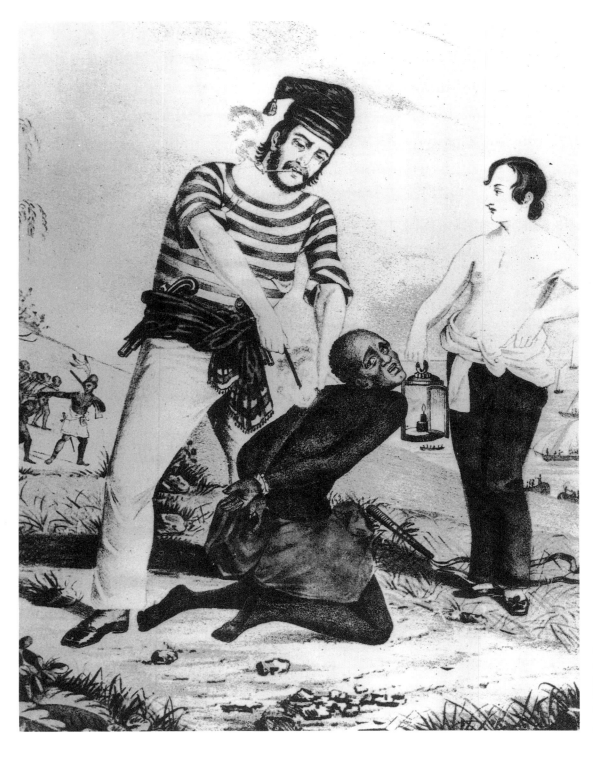

Branding slaves on the coast of Africa, previous to embarkation. Lithograph by Currier and Ives. The Bettmann Archive.

A little farther downstream, Kunta turned away from the water's edge along a path he himself had made to an ancient mangrove tree that he thought must know him, after countless visits, as well as he knew it. Pulling himself up into the lowest branch, he climbed all the way to his favorite perch near the top. From here, in the clear morning, with the sun warm on his back, he could see all the way to the next bend in the bolong, still carpeted with sleeping waterfowl, and beyond them to the women's rice plots, dotted with their bamboo shelters for nursing babies. In which one of them, he wondered, had his mother put him when he was little? This place in the early morning would always fill Kunta with a greater sense of calm, and wonder, than anywhere else he knew of. Even more than in the village mosque, he felt here how totally were everyone and everything in the hands of Allah; and how everything he could see and hear and smell from the top of this tree had been here for longer than men's memories, and would be here long after he and his sons and his sons' sons had joined their ancestors.

Trotting away from the bolong toward the sun for a little while, Kunta finally reached the head-high grass surrounding the grove where he was going to pick out and chop a section of

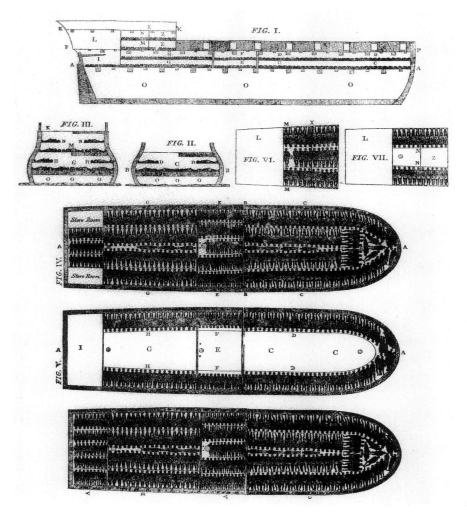

Plan of a slave ship. Schematic drawing.

tree trunk just the right size for the body of his drum. If the green wood started drying and curing today, he figured it would be ready to hollow out and work on in a moon and a half, about the time he and Lamin would be returning from their trip to Mali. As he stepped into the grove, Kunta saw a sudden movement out of the corner of his eye. It was a hare, and the wuolo dog was after it in a flash as it raced for cover in the tall grass. He was obviously chasing it for sport rather than for food, since he was barking furiously; Kunta knew that a hunting wuolo never made noise if he was really hungry. The two of them were soon out of earshot, but Kunta knew that his dog would come back when he lost interest in the chase.

Kunta headed forward to the center of the grove, where he would find more trees from which to choose a trunk of the size, smoothness, and roundness that he wanted. The soft, mossy earth felt good under his feet as he walked deeper into the dark grove, but the air here was damp and cold, he noticed, the sun not being high enough or hot enough yet to penetrate the thick foliage overhead. Leaning his weapons and ax against a warped tree, he wandered here and there, occasionally stooping, his eyes and fingers examining for just the right trunk, one just a little bit larger—to allow for drying shrinkage—than he wanted his drum to be.

He was bending over a likely prospect when he heard the sharp crack of a twig, followed quickly by the squawk of a parrot overhead. It was probably the dog returning, he thought in the back of his mind. But no grown dog ever cracked a twig, he flashed, whirling in the same instant. In a blur, rushing at him, he saw a white face, a club upraised; heard heavy footfalls behind him. *Toubob!* His foot lashed up and caught the man in the belly—it was soft and he heard a grunt—just as something hard and heavy grazed the back of Kunta's head and landed like a treetrunk on his shoulder. Sagging under the pain, Kunta spun—turning his back on the man who lay doubled over on the ground at his feet—and pounded with his fists on the faces of two black men who were lunging at him with a big sack, and at another toubob swinging a short, thick club, which missed him this time as he sprang aside.

His brain screaming for any weapon, Kunta leaped into them—clawing, butting, kneeing, gouging—hardly feeling the club that was pounding against his back. As three of them went down with him, sinking to the ground under their combined weight, a knee smashed into Kunta's lower back, rocking him with such pain that he gasped. His open mouth meeting flesh, his teeth clamped, cut, tore. His numb fingers finding a face, he clawed deeply into an eye, hearing its owner howl as again the heavy club met Kunta's head.

Dazed, he heard a dog's snarling, a toubob screaming, then a sudden piteous yelp. Scrambling to his feet, wildly twisting, dodging, ducking to escape more clubbing, with blood streaming from his split head, he saw one black cupping his eye, one of the toubob holding a bloody arm, standing over the body of the dog, and the remaining pair circling him with raised clubs. Screaming his rage, Kunta went for the second toubob, his fists meeting and breaking the force of the descending club. Almost choking with the awful toubob stink, he tried desperately to wrench away the club. Why had he not *heard* them, *sensed* them, *smelled* them?

Just then the black's club smashed into Kunta once again, staggering him to his knees, and the toubob sprang loose. His head ready to explode, his body reeling, raging at his own weakness, Kunta reared up and roared, flailing blindly at the air, everything blurred with tears and blood and sweat. He was fighting for more than his life now. Omoro! Binta! Lamin! Suwadu! Madi! The toubob's heavy club crashed against his temple. And all went black.

JOHN NEWTON
"Amazing Grace"

John Newton (1725–1807) was an English seaman who became first mate of a slave ship, rejecting the position of captain. He eventually gave up his life at sea, became a minister, and wrote hymns. "Amazing Grace" is a favorite of many Americans and is sung to different tunes, but was first introduced in its most familiar form in William Walker's shape-note tunebook, The Southern Harmony, *in 1835.*

Amazing grace! how sweet the sound,
That saved a wretch like me!
I once was lost, but now I'm found,
Was blind but now I see.

'Twas grace that taught my heart to fear,
And grace my fears relieved;
How precious did that grace appear
The hour I first believed.

Thro' many dangers, toils and snares,
I have already come;
'Tis grace has brought me safe thus far,
And grace will lead me home.

The Lord has promised good to me,
His word my hope secures;
He will my shield and portion be
As long as life endures.

Yea, when this flesh and heart shall fail,
And mortal life shall cease,
I shall possess, within the veil,
A life of joy and peace.

The earth shall soon dissolve like snow,
The sun forbear to shine;
But God, who called me here below,
Will be forever mine.

WILL D. CAMPBELL

From *Providence*

On the Expulsion of the Choctaws

*Although the Choctaws were generally loyal to the new American republic and in fact support-
ed Andrew Jackson in the War of 1812, they were the first major tribe of native Americans to
be removed to Oklahoma. The 1830 Treaty of Dancing Rabbit Creek allowed a few Choctaws
to remain in Mississippi, but most were forced west. Thousands died from exposure, starvation,
and disease on the long trip or in detention camps.*

Now they were standing on a loading dock in Vicksburg, on the opposite side of the river
where the legendary chiefs, Cahta and Cikasah, seeing the talismanic pole still leaning east-
ward, had built rafts to reach the land of Nanih Waiya, fleeing persecution then as now. Cows,
hogs, horses, and teams of oxen, yoked and hitched to iron-wheeled wagons, stood in serpentine formation waiting to be loaded. Behind them were scores of men, women, and children, all
scantily dressed for this cold beginning of a bitter journey. They were huddled close together,
the children squatting, men and women encircling them to stay the fierce winds. Many of
the women were crying. The men did not weep. But from their ranks Jesse and Luther could
hear the most doleful lamentations, deep dissonant groans and muffled sounds of indignation
and abdication.

Luther had found Ficik and was feeding her acorns he had picked up on the long trek from
Section Thirteen to the Mississippi River at Vicksburg. He and Jesse were patting and rubbing
the aging mare affectionately. A young but sickly ox had just died, still in its yoke, and two
other oxen were dragging it by the neck to the edge of the bluff where it would be rolled into
the dark waters of the mighty river. One of its horns dug into the ground, leaving a deep gash
in the earth, making the pulling more difficult, resisting even in death. Luther and Jesse
blocked the scene from Ficik's view. Throughout the trip they had tried to act casual, as if
they were on a journey everyone had made, as if what was happening was not the calamitous
thing it was.

All efforts to rescind the oppressive terms of the treaty made where the rabbits danced had
ceased. The proud and mighty Choctaws were defeated. Heartbroken and weary, they had prepared themselves for the removal journey as best they could, packing the few meager possessions they were allowed, selling to the eager settlers what they could not carry. They did not
know what lay in store, knew nothing of the land to which they would be taken by the soldiers.
They knew only that the last hope of remaining with the bones of their ancestors was no more.

Luther's old teacher, friend, and mentor, Cyrus Kingsbury, had gone west with an earlier

COLORPLATE 19

"Ehre Vater Artist." *Birth and Baptismal Certificate for Hanna Elisabeth Clodfelder.* c. 1810. Watercolor on paper. Abby Aldrich Rockefeller Folk Art Center, Williamsburg, Virginia. *Settlers of German ancestry began migrating from Pennsylvania into North Carolina and Virginia around 1723, bringing with them the folk art of fraktur. The same "fractured" lettering, primary colors, geometric designs, and floral and bird motifs that are displayed on this North Carolina example can be seen on German manuscripts that are hundreds of years old.*

COLORPLATE 20

THOMAS CORAM. *View of Mulberry Plantation (House and Street).* Oil on paper. The Gibbes Museum of Art/Carolina Art Association, Charleston, South Carolina. *Mulberry Plantation, built in 1714 for Thomas Broughton, still stands on the Cooper River in South Carolina. The "big house" may show the influence of French or Dutch architecture, while the small slave dependencies may recall some African architectural traditions.*

COLORPLATE 21

Artist unknown. *Benjamin Hawkins and the Creek Indians*. c. 1800–1810. Oil on canvas. 49 7/8 x 35 7/8 in.
Greenville County Museum of Art, Greenville, South Carolina. *Although it is uncertain who created this painting,
it is a fascinating document of late eighteenth-early nineteenth-century life centered around a trading post in the
Chattahoochee/Apalachicola area of North Florida. The grazing livestock, the abundant harvest, the friendly dog, and
the nursing mother all suggest a fecund, peaceable kingdom where native Americans and newer Americans lived in
harmony much of the time.*

COLORPLATE 22

RALPH ELEAZER WHITESIDE EARL. *Mr. and Mrs. Ephraim Hubbard Foster and their Children.* c. 1825. Cheekwood Fine Arts Center, Nashville, Tennessee. *Earl, the son of New England painter Ralph Earl, traveled through the Middle and Deep South painting portraits, including many of his wife's uncle, Andrew Jackson. Ephraim Hubbard Foster, whose charming family is shown here, was Jackson's color-bearer in the Battle of New Orleans. The warm informality, rank vegetation, balmy atmosphere, and sense of humor create the quintessential Southern family portrait.*

COLORPLATE 23

JOSHUA JOHNSON. *Mrs. Thomas Everette and Children.* 1818. Oil on canvas. Maryland Historical Society, Baltimore. *Joshua Johnson (or Johnston), one of the earliest known African-American painters, may have trained with Charles Peale Polk, although he described himself in a Baltimore newspaper advertisement in 1798 as "a self-taught genius" who had "experienced many insurpassable obstacles in the pursuit of his studies. . . ." Rebecca Myring Everette and her children were probably painted a year after the death of Mr. Everette.*

COLORPLATE 24

CHARLES BIRD KING. *Mistipee.* 1825. Oil on canvas. Collection of the Museum of Early Southern Decorative Arts, Winston-Salem, North Carolina. *Charles Bird King was commissioned by the Bureau of Indian Affairs to paint the native American chiefs visiting Washington. This portrait of Mistipee, a Creek warrior, was one of approximately 140 portraits King painted, making his gallery a popular tourist attraction.*

COLORPLATE 25

CHARLES BIRD KING. *Pushmataha*. The Warner Collection of Gulf States Paper Corporation, Tuscaloosa, Alabama. *Pushmataha, a famous warrior in his younger days, at seventy was the senior delegate of an 1824 Choctaw delegation that went to Washington to negotiate land treaties. He died during negotiations and was given a full military funeral.*

COLORPLATE 26

CHRISTIAN MAYR. *Officers of Volunteer Fire Department, 1841*. 1841. Oil on canvas. 48 ¹/₂ x 72 ¹/₂ in. Collection of City Hall, Charleston, South Carolina. *Mayr, a German-born artist working in Charleston and New Orleans, often painted what were sometimes referred to as "fancy pieces," that is, paintings that were charming to look at but not especially provocative. This scene is very like the "corporation" portraits painted by seventeenth-century Dutch painters.*

GEORGE CATLIN. *Mosholatubee (Or, He Who Puts Out and Kills), Chief of Choctaw Indian tribe when it was removed to Oklahoma.* Oil on canvas. The Bettmann Archive. *In the age before photography, George Catlin created an incredible body of information about native Americans in the nineteenth century. Between 1830 and 1836 he traveled from the Mississippi to the Rocky Mountains and as far as North Dakota, painting scenes documenting Indian life. More than 607 paintings formed Catlin's famous Indian Gallery, which was widely exhibited in the United States, England, and France.*

party. He had assured his students a new school would be built and they could continue to learn. He again encouraged Luther to prepare to go to Brown University when things were more settled, told him he carried a letter of admission with him.

Luther had asked him to get a job for Jesse as assistant escort with the cavalry on the overland trip to Vicksburg. They had ridden together on the week-long journey.

These were their final moments, each glance and gesture brimming with pangs of affection. The grizzly steamboat had moved into place to receive its human cargo. The animals were being loaded onto barges. For a moment Luther thought of paintings he had seen in Bibles at Eliot Mission School of the loading of Noah's ark. The mounted troops moved nervously, sympathetically, around the area, a peculiar advocate for, "We hold these truths to be self evident . . .," giving more commands to each other than to the vanquished and desolate mortals awaiting a fate imposed by a people they had befriended for three centuries. Strange or not, it would be the soldiers who would show the greatest degree of clemency, salvaging such dignity as they could for their doomed charges.

The steamboat *Brandywine* sounded a long blast of its whistle, brusque as the sound of hell's nurses. Bolokta came to where they were standing, said something in Choctaw, and moved back to the group.

"He says it is time to go," Luther said.

Each one stood gazing intently at the face of the other, as if studying and memorizing every marking, each blemish and line wrought ahead of its time, as if some last-minute epiphany would reveal something of the other they had not known before. The very air between them was the breathing of mercy and grace. They did not cry. They had been taught.

"Stay," Jesse pleaded, taking him by the arm. "We can hide you." They had heard the stories of some of the Choctaws hiding in the wilderness, refusing at the last to leave. And they had witnessed a number of men, and sometimes whole families, breaking ranks and deserting the caravan, disappearing into the heavy thickets, chancing survival like wild animals in these woods they knew rather than face the 550-mile jaunt through wilds unknown.

"No," Luther said, his eyes still fixed, voice resolute. "My people are going. *Chahta hapia hoke*. I will go with them."

Jesse made no further protest. "Then good-bye, my dear friend," he said, and extended his hand.

He was not aware and Luther did not notice that Jesse's enunciation was perfect. What Luther did notice was that Jesse seemed suddenly taller. Their hands clasped on a level. As if in this moment of parting some long-sought miracle had, without notice, made its visitation, unleashing a stunted growth.

They shook hands like old men at a graveside, firm, somber, and immutable. Luther turned and joined the shuffling line moving toward the gangplank. He was as quiet now as the others. As if he wanted these moments with his friend to be the last thing he remembered as he took the final step from his homeland.

When he moved away, Jesse went methodically about the chores assigned him, preparing for the return trip to Leflore's district. His eyes did not follow Luther. He fixed his mind on the little dog Cito his father had permitted him to keep. He tried to think of nothing else.

A large crowd of white settlers from the Choctaw Nation, men, women, and children of dubious bloodlines, had gathered to view the leaving of these of a near-pure breed. Jesse heard them break into a wild hurrah, slapping each other on the back, some throwing hats in the air, when the *Brandywine* weighed anchor and began the slow movement into the Mississippi's current, straining against the flow as it made its way upstream toward the Arkansas River. He knew that Luther was hearing what he was hearing, the muted echo of sadness. He hoped he could not hear the cheers.

The Choctaws were gone. Their land remained. And even as the last whistle sounded and the last smoke of the *Brandywine* disappeared in the dark February clouds, the jubilant throng dispersed to stake their claims. Section Thirteen was part of the bounty.

Luther and Jesse never saw each other again. Two months before the removal party reached its assigned destination, Luther Cashdollar died in a cypress swamp in Arkansas. A soldier Jesse had known when he worked for the cavalry told him about it ten months later, when the troops came back to conduct the last group to the West. The soldier was not sure whether it was of cholera or exposure. He said they had to wade for thirty miles through waist-deep water, their bodies sometimes breaking thin layers of ice as they went. Many people were sick. He did not know where Luther was buried. Or if he had been buried at all. Sometimes, he said, the dead had to be left to sink in the jungle of cypress knees where they died.

The soldier told Jesse he was sorry.

GEORGE CATLIN. *Ball play of the Choctaw — Ball Up.* 1834–1835. Oil on canvas. 19 ½ x 27 ½ in. National Museum of American Art, Smithsonian Institution, Washington, DC. Gift of Mrs. Joseph Harrison, Jr.

THE OLD SOUTH

T. ADDISON RICHARDS

From "The Landscape of the South"

Although he admitted that travel in the South did present difficulties, artist and writer T. Addison Richards took every opportunity to extol the virtues and beauties of the Southern landscape. In this essay originally published in Harper's New Monthly Magazine *in 1853, Richards describes the dramatic and picturesque scenery of the mountainous regions of Georgia and the Carolinas.*

But little has yet been said, either in picture or story, of the natural scenery of the Southern States; so inadequately is its beauty known abroad or appreciated at home. This ignorance is not likely to be enlightened by the reports of tourists led hastily by business errands over highways which happen for the most part to traverse the least interesting regions—the intervals in Nature's inspirations; neither will the indifference pass away in the censurable blindness which overlooks the near in its reverence for the remote.

The Great Artist in his lavish adornment of our happy land has been unmindful of no part; least of all of that of which we now write. None of the fair sisterhood of States may boast more winning charms than those of the sunny land; or if perchance they be wanting in certain features, they possess compensating beauties peculiar to themselves alone. Proud mountain heights lift their voice of praise to Heaven; the thunders of Niagara are echoed by Tallulah; as the gentler prattle of Kaaterskill and Trenton, is answered by Ammicalolah and Toccoa. For the verdant meadows of the North, dotted with cottages and grazing herds, the South has her broad savannas, calm in the shadow of the palmetto and the magnolia: for the magnificence of the Hudson, the Delaware and the Susquehanna, are her mystic lagunes, in whose stately arcades of cypress, fancy floats at will through all the wilds of past and future. In exchange for the fairy lakes of the north, she has the loveliest of valleys, composed and framed like the dream of the painter—turf-covered Horicons and Winnepisseogees. Above her are skies soft and glowing in the genial warmth of summer suns and beneath lie mysterious caverns, whose secrets are still unread.

We shall speak briefly of the various types of landscape beauty in the South, instancing the most memorable examples of each. The distinguishing mark of the mountain scenery of the Southern States as contrasted with that of the North, is its greater picturesqueness and variety of form and quantity. The grand ranges of the Catskills and the Adirondacs and the peaks of the Green and the White Mountains, are but outer links of that mighty Alleghanian chain which, centering in Virginia, rears its most famed summits in Georgia and the Carolinas. The Alleghanies in the Northern States move on in stately and unbroken line, like saddened exiles, whose stern mood is ever the same, and whose cold features are never varied with a smile; while in their home in the South, every step is free and joyous. Here they are grouped in the happiest and most capricious humor, now sweeping along in graceful outline, daintily crossing each other's path, or meeting in cordial embrace; here gathered in generous rivalry, and there breaking away sullenly in abrupt and frowning precipice. All is Alpine variety, intricacy and surprise. Seen from the general level, the mountains are ever sufficiently irregular in form and course to offer grateful contrasts; here and there in their unstudied meetings, leaving vistas of the world of hill and dale beyond; while the panoramic views command vast assemblages of

Umbrella Rock, Lookout Mountain. 19th century. Engraving. *Lookout Mountain is an Appalachian ridge extending from Tennessee across Georgia to Alabama, and is the site of some of the South's most popular natural wonders, like Ruby Falls and Rock City.*

ridge and precipice, varied in every characteristic—the large in opposition to the small, the barren in contrast with the wooded, the formal and the eccentric, the horizontal and the perpendicular; while a fairy valley in which the Abyssinian Prince might have rambled, a winding river, a glimpse of road-side or a distant hamlet, lend repose without monotony to the landscape.

It is in the existence of this variety, so essential an element of the picturesque, that is found the superior charm of the Southern mountain region over that of the North; this subtle characteristic, so completely felt by the poor peasant who refused to sell, though to provide for his necessities, one of his three cows, upon the sole ground that two would not group well; and so happily illustrated in that charming fiction of Venus' cestus, in which Juno, however beautiful, had no captivating charms before she had put on the magic girdle; in other words, until she had exchanged her formal and stately dignity for playfulness and coquetry.

* * *

The chief objects of interest in the mountain scenery of South Carolina, are the Table Rock and the neighboring peaks of Caesar's Head and Bald Mountain. Table Rock is a noble line of palisades, rising nearly a thousand feet from the crown of a majestic hill, and reaching an elevation above the sea of four thousand three hundred feet. The northern front, over half a mile in extent, is perpendicular, while the opposite side admits of easy ascent. A grand fête in honor of the statesman Calhoun, who lived hard by, was once celebrated on the summit of Table Rock, on which occasion cannon proclaimed the *vivats* of the people to the giant hills below. A flight of well-secured wooden steps leads up the eastern declivity. The top of the rock is comparatively level; much of it is covered with noble trees, while other portions are stony and unproductive. Near the centre of this haughty domain are the *débris* of a hut, built as a kitchen to an unachieved hotel. On the left of the rock is a conical spur called the "Stool," from a legend which makes it the seat of the Great Spirit, when in other days his convenience led him to lunch upon the respectable mahogany of the Table Rock. At the base of this mountain is the fair vale of Saluda, watered by the meanderings of the crystal river of the same name; and upon the opposite side of this valley are the feathery cascades of Slicking. These falls drop from a succession of rocky terraces, the highest of which overlooks the adjoining valley, and commands a noble view of the Table Mountain and the surrounding spurs. Not far from this locality, which is one of great resort, is King's Mountain, a spot of Revolutionary association; and Grassy Mountain, a singular, smooth cone of rock; barren, with the exception of a stunted growth on the crown, after the fashion of the scalp lock of the Indian.

We must not leave the hills without a mention of the famous Yonah, Currahee, Look-out, Cahutta, and Rock Mountain, in Georgia. Yonah, or the Great Bear, is a brave peak, looking down upon one of the sweetest valleys of the Pine State, and is associated with tales of that scene which, in proper place, we have yet to tell.

Currahee is cherished by Georgians, as much from the fact that it is their first mountain love, rising in solitary grandeur far to the south of the great galaxy of hills, as for its own pictorial charms. Currahee is a special resort of the sportsman—of the lover of venison above all others.

Look-out Mountain unites on its crown the States of Tennessee, Georgia, and Alabama, and while not of surpassing attraction itself, serves to unfold, for leagues in all directions, the matchless landscape around it. The Cahutta is a link midway between the hill region of the eastern and western corners of Georgia. It occupies the centre of the ancient Cherokee domain. A disused turnpike, which we once explored with fearful risk, scales its rocky acclivities. The Rock Mountain is chiefly remarkable for its singularly isolated position—no kith or kin are near, to cheer its solitude. It is a vast rock, six miles in circumference, embedded in the earth to a depth architecturally proportionate to its total magnitude, and so complete is the absence of all continuing strata, that its presence is as rationally accounted for by supposing it to have dropped from the heavens, as by any other theory.

Rock Mountain is a spot of so much visitation, that an Observatory, 165 feet in height, has been erected upon its summit; but even with this additional elevation, the view obtained is monotonous—so far has the lonely mountain wandered from its proper home. An enraptured tourist thus sums up his emotions in the album of the Rock Mountain Hotel.

> "Oh, mercy! sich a pile of stones
> Was never seed by John A. Jones!"

J. P. KENNEDY

From *Swallow Barn, or Sojourn in the Old Dominion*

"The Quarter"

J. P. Kennedy, the son of an Irish immigrant, served with the Maryland militia, practiced law, and held political offices in addition to writing satirical essays and historical romances. Swallow Barn is representative of the plantation literature of the time that sought to defend and uphold the cavalier ethic and the plantation system. The plantation is portrayed here as a warm and nurturing environment created by a benevolent and generous master.

Having despatched these important matters at the stable, we left our horses in charge of the servants, and walked towards the cabins, which were not more than a few hundred paces distant. These hovels, with their appurtenances, formed an exceedingly picturesque landscape. They were scattered, without order, over the slope of a gentle hill; and many of them were embow-

Slave Quarters on a Plantation. 19th century. Drawing. The Bettmann Archive.

ered under old and majestic trees. The rudeness of their construction rather enhanced the attractiveness of the scene. Some few were built after the fashion of the better sort of cottages; but age had stamped its heavy traces upon their exterior; the green moss had gathered upon the roofs, and the course [*sic*] weatherboarding had broken, here and there, into chinks. But the more lowly of these structures, and the most numerous, were nothing more than plain log-cabins, compacted pretty much on the model by which boys build partridge traps; being composed of the trunks of trees, still clothed with their bark, and knit together at the corners with so little regard to neatness that the timbers, being of unequal lengths, jutted beyond each other, sometimes to the length of a foot. Perhaps, none of these latter sort were more than twelve feet square, and not above seven in height. A door swung upon wooden hinges, and a small window of two narrow panes of glass were, in general, the only openings in the front. The intervals between the logs were filled with clay; and the roof, which was constructed of smaller timbers, laid lengthwise along it and projecting two or three feet beyond the side or gable walls, heightened, in a very marked degree, the rustic effect. The chimneys communicated even a droll expression to these habitations. They were, oddly enough, built of billets of wood, having a broad foundation of stone, and growing narrower as they rose, each receding gradually from the house to which it was attached, until it reached the height of the roof. These combustible materials were saved from the access of the fire by a thick coating of mud; and the whole structure, from its tapering form, might be said to bear some resemblance to the spout of a tea kettle; indeed, this domestic implement would furnish no unapt type of the complete cabin.

From this description, which may serve to illustrate a whole species of habitations very common in Virginia, it will be seen, that on the score of accommodation, the inmates of these dwellings were furnished according to a very primitive notion of comfort. Still, however, there were little garden-patches attached to each, where cymblings, cucumbers, sweet potatoes, water-melons and cabbages flourished in unrestrained luxuriance. Add to this, that there were abundance of poultry domesticated about the premises, and it may be perceived that, whatever might be the inconveniences of shelter, there was no want of what, in all countries, would be considered a reasonable supply of luxuries.

Nothing more attracted my observation than the swarms of little negroes that basked on the sunny sides of these cabins, and congregated to gaze at us as we surveyed their haunts. They were nearly all in that costume of the golden age which I have heretofore described; and showed their slim shanks and long heels in all varieties of their grotesque natures. Their predominant love of sunshine, and their lazy, listless postures, and apparent content to be silently looking abroad, might well afford a comparison to a set of terrapins luxuriating in the genial warmth of summer, on the logs of a mill-pond.

And there, too, were the prolific mothers of this redundant brood,—a number of stout negro-women who thronged the doors of the huts, full of idle curiosity to see us. And, when to these are added a few reverend, wrinkled, decrepit old men, with faces shortened as if with drawing-strings, noses that seemed to have run all to nostril, and with feet of the configuration of a mattock, my reader will have a tolerably correct idea of this negro-quarter, its population, buildings, external appearance, situation and extent.

Meriwether, I have said before, is a kind and considerate master. It is his custom frequently to visit his slaves, in order to inspect their condition, and where it may be necessary, to add to their comforts or relieve their wants. His coming amongst them, therefore, is always hailed with pleasure. He has constituted himself into a high court of appeal, and makes it a rule to give all their petitions a patient hearing, and to do justice in the premises. This, he tells me, he considers as indispensably necessary;—he says, that no overseer is entirely to be trusted; that there are few men who have the temper to administer wholesome laws to any population, however small, without some omissions or irregularities; and that this is more emphatically true of those who administer them entirely at their own will. On the present occasion, in almost every house where Frank entered, there was some boon to be asked; and I observed, that in every case, the petitioner was either gratified or refused in such a tone as left no occasion or disposition to murmur. Most of the women had some bargains to offer, of fowls or eggs or other commodities of household use, and Meriwether generally referred them to his wife, who, I found, relied almost entirely on this resource, for the supply of such commodities; the negroes being regularly paid for whatever was offered in this way.

One old fellow had a special favour to ask,—a little money to get a new padding for his saddle, which, he said, "galled his cretur's back." Frank, after a few jocular passages with the veteran, gave him what he desired, and sent him off rejoicing.

"That, sir," said Meriwether, "is no less a personage than Jupiter. He is an old bachelor, and has his cabin here on the hill. He is now near seventy, and is a kind of King of the Quarter. He has a horse, which he extorted from me last Christmas; and I seldom come here without finding myself involved in some new demand, as a consequence of my donation. Now he wants a pair of spurs which, I suppose, I must give him. He is a preposterous coxcomb, and Ned has administered to his vanity by a present of a *chapeau de bras*—a relic of my military era, which he wears on Sundays with a conceit that has brought upon him as much envy as admiration—the usual condition of greatness."

The air of contentment and good humor and kind family attachment, which was apparent throughout this little community, and the familiar relations existing between them and the proprietor struck me very pleasantly. I came here a stranger, in great degree, to the negro character, knowing but little of the domestic history of these people, their duties, habits or temper, and somewhat disposed, indeed, from prepossessions, to look upon them as severely dealt with, and expecting to have my sympathies excited towards them as objects of commiseration. I have had, therefore, rather a special interest in observing them. The contrast between my preconceptions of their condition and the reality which I have witnessed, has brought me a most agreeable surprise. I will not say that, in a high state of cultivation and of such self-dependence as they might possibly attain in a separate national existence, they might not become a more respectable people; but I am quite sure they never could become a happier people than I find them here.

FREDERICK DOUGLASS

From *Narrative of the Life of Frederick Douglass, An American Slave*

Frederick Douglass, who escaped slavery and became a famous orator and abolitionist writer, published his Narrative *in 1845. It was instantly popular in the North, and eleven thousand copies were printed within three years. Of all the slave narratives that exist, it is the most widely known today. In this selection, Douglass describes his master's unchristian behavior.*

I have now reached a period of my life when I can give dates. I left Baltimore, and went to live with Master Thomas Auld, at St. Michael's, in March, 1832. It was now more than seven years since I lived with him in the family of my old master, on Colonel Lloyd's plantation. We of course were now almost entire strangers to each other. He was to me a new master, and I to him a new slave. I was ignorant of his temper and disposition; he was equally so of mine. A very short time, however, brought us into full acquaintance with each other. I was made acquainted with his wife not less than with himself. They were well matched, being equally mean and cruel. I was now, for the first time during a space of more than seven years, made to feel the painful gnawings of hunger—a something which I had not experienced before since I left Colonel Lloyd's plantation. It went hard enough with me then, when I could look back to no period at which I had enjoyed a sufficiency. It was tenfold harder after living in Master Hugh's family, where I had always had enough to eat, and of that which was good. I have said Master Thomas was a mean man. He was so. Not to give a slave enough to eat, is regarded as the most aggravated development of meanness even among slaveholders. The rule is, no matter how coarse the food, only let there be enough of it. This is the theory; and in the part of Maryland from which I came, it is the general practice,—though there are many exceptions. Master Thomas gave us enough of neither coarse nor fine food. There were four slaves of us in the kitchen—my sister Eliza, my aunt Priscilla, Henny, and myself; and we were allowed less than a half of a bushel of corn-meal per week, and very little else, either in the shape of meat or vegetables. It was not enough for us to subsist upon. We were therefore reduced to the wretched necessity of living at the expense of our neighbors. This we did by begging and stealing, whichever came handy in the time of need, the one being considered as legitimate as the other. A great many times have we poor creatures been nearly perishing with hunger, when food in abundance lay mouldering in the safe and smoke-house, and our pious mistress was aware of the fact; and yet that mistress and her husband would kneel every morning, and pray that God would bless them in basket and store!

Bad as all slaveholders are, we seldom meet one destitute of every element of character commanding respect. My master was one of this rare sort. I do not know of one single noble act ever performed by him. The leading trait in his character was meanness; and if there were any other element in his nature, it was made subject to this. He was mean; and, like most other mean men, he lacked the ability to conceal his meanness. Captain Auld was not born a slaveholder. He had been a poor man, master only of a Bay craft. He came into possession of all his slaves by marriage; and of all men, adopted slaveholders are the worst. He was cruel, but cowardly. He commanded without firmness. In the enforcement of his rules, he was at times rigid, and at times lax. At times, he spoke to his slaves with the firmness of Napoleon and the fury of a demon; at other times, he might well be mistaken for an inquirer who had lost his way. He did nothing of himself. He might have passed for a lion, but for his ears. In all things noble which he attempted, his own meanness shone most conspicuous. His airs, words, and actions, were the airs, words, and actions of born slaveholders, and, being assumed, were awkward enough. He was not even a good imitator. He possessed all the disposition to deceive, but

Frederick Douglass. 1856. Ambrotype. 4 3/16 x 3 3/8 in. National Portrait Gallery, Smithsonian Institution, Washington, DC. Gift of an anonymous donor.

wanted the power. Having no resources within himself, he was compelled to be the copyist of many, and being such, he was forever the victim of inconsistency; and of consequence he was an object of contempt, and was held as such even by his slaves. The luxury of having slaves of his own to wait upon him was something new and unprepared for. He was a slaveholder without the ability to hold slaves. He found himself incapable of managing his slaves either by force, fear, or fraud. We seldom called him "master"; we generally called him "Captain Auld," and were hardly disposed to title him at all. I doubt not that our conduct had much to do with making him appear awkward, and of consequence fretful. Our want of reverence for him must have perplexed him greatly. He wished to have us call him master, but lacked the firmness necessary to command us to do so. His wife used to insist upon our calling him so, but to no purpose. In August, 1832, my master attended a Methodist camp-meeting held in the Bay-side, Talbot county, and there experienced religion. I indulged a faint hope that his conversion would lead him to emancipate his slaves, and that, if he did not do this, it would, at any rate, make him more kind and humane. I was disappointed in both these respects. It neither made him to be humane to his slaves, nor to emancipate them. If it had any effect on his character, it made him more cruel and hateful in all his ways; for I believe him to have been a much worse man after his conversion than before. Prior to his conversion, he relied upon his own depravity to shield and sustain him in his savage barbarity; but after his conversion, he found religious sanction and support for his slaveholding cruelty. He made the greatest pretensions to piety. His house was the house of prayer. He prayed morning, noon, and night. He very soon distinguished himself among his brethren, and was soon made a class-leader and exhorter. His activity in revivals was great, and he proved himself an instrument in the hands of the church in converting many souls. His house was the preachers' home. They used to take great pleasure in coming there to put up; for while he starved us, he stuffed them. We have had three or four preachers there at a time. The names of those who used to come most frequently while I lived there, were Mr. Storks, Mr. Ewery, Mr. Humphry, and Mr. Hickey. I have also seen Mr. George

Cookman at our house. We slaves loved Mr. Cookman. We believed him to be a good man. We thought him instrumental in getting Mr. Samuel Harrison, a very rich slaveholder, to emancipate his slaves; and by some means got the impression that he was laboring to effect the emancipation of all the slaves. When he was at our house, we were sure to be called in to prayers. When the others were there, we were sometimes called in and sometimes not. Mr. Cookman took more notice of us than either of the other ministers. He could not come among us without betraying his sympathy for us, and, stupid as we were, we had the sagacity to see it.

While I lived with my master in St. Michael's, there was a white young man, a Mr. Wilson, who proposed to keep a Sabbath school for the instruction of such slaves as might be disposed to learn to read the New Testament. We met but three times, when Mr. West and Mr. Fairbanks, both class-leaders, with many others, came upon us with sticks and other missiles, drove us off, and forbade us to meet again. Thus ended our little Sabbath school in the pious town of St. Michael's.

I have said my master found religious sanction for his cruelty. As an example, I will state one of many facts going to prove the charge. I have seen him tie up a lame young woman, and whip her with a heavy cowskin upon her naked shoulders, causing the warm red blood to drip; and, in justification of the bloody deed, he would quote this passage of Scripture—"He that knoweth his master's will, and doeth it not, shall be beaten with many stripes."

Master would keep this lacerated young woman tied up in this horrid situation four or five hours at a time. I have known him to tie her up early in the morning, and whip her before breakfast; leave her, go to his store, return at dinner, and whip her again, cutting her in the places already made raw with his cruel lash. The secret of master's cruelty toward "Henny" is found in the fact of her being almost helpless. When quite a child, she fell into the fire, and burned herself horribly. Her hands were so burnt that she never got the use of them. She could do very little but bear heavy burdens. She was to master a bill of expense; and as he was a mean man, she was a constant offence to him. He seemed desirous of getting the poor girl out of existence. He gave her away once to his sister; but, being a poor gift, she was not disposed to keep her. Finally, my benevolent master, to use his own words, "set her adrift to take care of herself." Here was a recently-converted man, holding on upon the mother, and at the same time turning out her helpless child to starve and die! Master Thomas was one of the many pious slaveholders who hold slaves for the very charitable purpose of taking care of them.

My master and myself had quite a number of differences. He found me unsuitable to his purpose. My city life, he said, had had a very pernicious effect upon me. It had almost ruined me for every good purpose, and fitted me for every thing which was bad. One of my greatest faults was that of letting his horse run away, and go down to his father-in-law's farm, which was about five miles from St. Michael's. I would then have to go after it. My reason for this kind of carelessness, or carefulness, was, that I could always get something to eat when I went there. Master William Hamilton, my master's father-in-law, always gave his slaves enough to eat. I never left there hungry, no matter how great the need of my speedy return. Master Thomas at length said he would stand it no longer. I had lived with him nine months, during which time he had given me a number of severe whippings, all to no good purpose. He resolved to put me out, as he said, to be broken; and, for this purpose, he let me for one year to a man named Edward Covey. Mr. Covey was a poor man, a farm-renter. He rented the place upon which he lived, as also the hands with which he tilled it. Mr. Covey had acquired a very high reputation for breaking young slaves, and this reputation was of immense value to him. It enabled him to get his farm tilled with much less expense to himself than he could have had it done without such a reputation. Some slaveholders thought it not much loss to allow Mr. Covey to have their slaves one year, for the sake of the training to which they were subjected, without any other compensation. He could hire young help with great ease, in consequence of this reputation. Added to the natural good qualities of Mr. Covey, he was a professor of religion—a pious soul—a member and a class-leader in the Methodist church. All of this added weight to his reputation as a "nigger-breaker." I was aware of all the facts, having been made acquainted with them by a young man who had lived there. I nevertheless made the change gladly; for I was sure of getting enough to eat, which is not the smallest consideration to a hungry man.

BENJAMIN HENRY LATROBE. *An Overseer Doing His Duty.* 1798. Watercolor on paper. Maryland Historical Society. *Author, architect, engineer, and naturalist, Latrobe came to America in 1795, recording all that he saw as he traveled throughout the South. His observations have been preserved in fourteen sketchbooks. Latrobe's thinly disguised sarcasm and distaste for slavery is evident in this sketch.*

From the *West Tennessee Democrat*

To Catch a Runaway Slave

Since slaves were expensive items of personal property, slave owners were willing to pay the "paterollers" for the return of their possessions.

BLOOD-HOUNDS.—I have TWO of the FINEST DOGS for CATCHING NEGROES in the Southwest. They can take the trail TWELVE HOURS after the NEGRO HAS PASSED, and catch him with ease. I live just four miles southwest of Boliver, on the road leading from Boliver to Whitesville. I am ready at all times to catch runaway negroes.—March 2, 1853.
                                        DAVID TURNER.

ANONYMOUS

"Go Down, Moses"

First printed in 1872 with twenty-five verses, "Go Down, Moses" is an old spiritual that illus- trates the slaves' identification with the Old Testament plight of the Jews in Egypt.

Go down, Moses,
'Way down in Egypt land,
Tell ole Pharaoh,
To let my people go.

Go down, Moses,
'Way down in Egypt's land,
Tell ole Pharaoh,
To let my people go.

When Israel was in Egypt's land;
Let my people go,
Oppressed so hard they could not stand,
Let my people go.

Go down, Moses,
'Way down in Egypt land,
Tell ole Pharaoh,
To let my people go.
O let my people go.

"Thus spoke the Lord," bold Moses said;
Let my people go,
If not I'll smite your first born dead,
Let my people go.

Go down, Moses.
'Way down in Egypt land,
Tell ole Pharaoh,
To let my people go.
O let my people go.

Sunny South.
19th century. Lithograph
by Calvert Company. The
Bettmann Archive. *Birds-
eye-view of large planta-
tion along the Mississippi
with steamboat, workers
in the field, Southern mansion in the background.*

DANIEL DECATUR EMMETT
"Dixie"

Daniel Decatur Emmett wrote the music and lyrics for this song, which was first performed in New York in 1859 by Bryant's Minstrel Troupe. The song became popular throughout the Confederacy, and today, although it is somewhat controversial, the rousing strains of "Dixie" still stir many Southerners.

I wish I was in de land ob cotton,
Old times dar am not forgotten;
   Look away! Look away! Look away! Dixie Land!
In Dixie Land whar I was born in,
Early on one frosty mornin'
   Look away! Look away! Look away! Dixie Land!

Chorus:
   Den I wish I was in Dixie! Hooray! Hooray!
   In Dixie's Land we'll take our stand, to lib an' die in Dixie.
   Away! away! away down South in Dixie.
   Away! away! away down South in Dixie.

Ole missus marry "Will-de-weaber";
Willum was a gay deceaber;
   Look away, look away, look away, Dixie Land!
But when he put his arm around her,
He smiled as fierce as a forty-pounder;
   Look away, look away, look away, Dixie Land!

His face was sharp as a butcher's cleaber;
But dat did not seem to greab her;
   Look away, look away, look away, Dixie Land!
Ole missus acted de foolish part,
And died for a man dat broke her heart;
   Look away, look away, look away, Dixie Land!

Now here's a health to de next ole missus,
An' all the gals dat want to kiss us;
   Look away, look away, look away, Dixie Land!
But if you want to drive away sorrow,
Come and hear dis song tomorrow;
   Look away, look away, look away, Dixie Land!

Dar's buckwheat cakes and Injun batter,
Makes you fat or a little fatter;
   Look away, look away, look away, Dixie Land!
Den hoe it down an' scratch your grabble,
To Dixie's land I'm bound to trabble;
   Look away, look away, look away, Dixie Land!

OUTSIDERS VIEW THE OLD SOUTH

ALEXIS DE TOCQUEVILLE

From *Journey to America*

On Southern Justice

The Frenchman Alexis de Tocqueville's comments on American culture remain some of the most respected and insightful in our history. During his famous visit to America in 1831–1832, he kept notebooks that he used when writing his classic, Democracy in America. *De Tocqueville thought that this conversation with an Alabama lawyer revealed a penchant for violence in the South.*

Conversation with a lawyer from
Montgomery (Alabama) (6th January 1832)

I travelled for two days with this young man. I have forgotten his name which anyhow is very obscure. But I think I ought to note the conversation down. It is stamped with much practical good sense. Besides what he says is corroborated by several pieces of subsequent information:

The erroneous opinion is spreading daily more and more among us, he said, that the people can do everything and is capable of ruling almost directly. From that springs an unbelievable weakening of anything that could look like executive power; it is the outstanding characteristic and the capital defect of our Constitution, and of those of all the new States in the South-West of the Union. That has grave consequences. Thus, we did not wish to give the Governor the right of appointing the judges; that was entrusted to the Legislature. What results? That responsibility for the choice is divided; that little coteries and little, local intrigues are all-powerful, and that instead of calling competent men to our tribunals, we put there little party leaders who control the elections in the districts and whom the members of the Legislature wish to attract or reward. Our magistrates are completely incompetent; the mass of the people feels it as we do. So no one is disposed to appeal to regular justice. This state of affairs which is common to the States of Kentucky, Tennessee, Mississippi and even Georgia, is, to my way of thinking, the chief factor causing these fierce manners for which the inhabitants of those States are justly blamed.

Is it then true that the ways of the people of Alabama are as violent as is said?

Yes. There is no one here but carries arms under his clothes. At the slightest quarrel, knife or pistol comes to hand. These things happen continually; it is a semi-barbarous state of society.

Q. But when a man is killed like that, is his assassin not punished?

A. He is always brought to trial, and always acquitted by the jury, unless there are greatly aggravating circumstances. I cannot remember seeing a single man who was a little known, pay with his life for such a crime. This violence has become accepted. Each juror feels that he might, on leaving the court, find himself in the same position as the accused, and he acquits.

UNKNOWN. *Students staging a fist fight at the University of Mississippi.* c. 1852. Photograph. University Archives, University of Mississippi.

Note that the jury is chosen from all the free-holders, however small their property may be. So it is the people that judges itself, and its prejudices in this matter stand in the way of its good sense. Besides, my informant added, I have been no better myself than another in my time; look at the scars that cover my head (we did see the marks of four or five deep cuts). Those are knife blows I have been given.

    Q. But you went to law?

    A. My God! No. I tried to give as good in return.

FRANCES ANNE KEMBLE

From *Journal of a Residence on a Georgia Plantation*

Touring the Plantation

Fanny Kemble was an English actress who married South Carolina planter Pierce Butler and went to live on his rice plantation. Her journal, kept during the years 1838–1839, records her impressions in a very honest and graphic fashion. Although much of her journal describes her shock and frustration at the conditions she found, this passage shows how she was charmed by the lowcountry culture and landscape.

THOMAS SULLY. *Frances Anne Kemble.* Oil on canvas.
1834. White House Collection, Washington, DC. *One of
the most accomplished American portraitists, Sully was
born in England and grew up in a theatrical family in
Richmond, Norfolk, and Charleston. Sully painted at least
thirteen portraits of the popular English actress
Fanny Kemble.*

Dear E———,— We had a species of fish this morning for our breakfast which deserves more
glory than I can bestow upon it. Had I been the ingenious man who wrote a poem upon fish,
the white mullet of the Altamaha should have been at least my heroine's cousin. 'Tis the heav-
enliest creature that goes upon fins. I took a long walk this morning to Settlement No. 3, the
third village on the island. My way lay along the side of the canal, beyond which, and only
divided from it by a raised narrow causeway, rolled the brimming river, with its girdle of glittering evergreens, while on my other hand a deep trench marked the line of the rice fields. It
really seemed as if the increase of merely a shower of rain might join all these waters together,
and lay the island under its original covering again. I visited the people and houses here. I
found nothing in any respect different from what I have described to you at Settlement No. 1.
During the course of my walk, I startled from its repose in one of the rice fields a huge blue
heron. You must have seen, as I often have, these creatures stuffed in museums; but 'tis another
matter, and far more curious, to see them stalking on their stilts of legs over a rice field, and
then, on your near approach, see them spread their wide heavy wings, and throw themselves
upon the air, with their long shanks flying after them in a most grotesque and laughable manner. They fly as if they did not know how to do it very well; but standing still, their height
(between four and five feet) and peculiar color, a dusky, grayish blue, with black about the
head, render their appearance very beautiful and striking.

In the afternoon I and Jack rowed ourselves over to Darien. It is Saturday—the day of the
week on which the slaves from the island are permitted to come over to the town to purchase
such things as they may require and can afford, and to dispose, to the best advantage, of their
poultry, moss, and eggs. I met many of them paddling themselves singly in their slight canoes,
scooped out of the trunk of a tree, and parties of three and four rowing boats of their own
building, laden with their purchases, singing, laughing, talking, and apparently enjoying their
holiday to the utmost. They all hailed me with shouts of delight as I pulled past them, and

COLORPLATE 27

GEORGE COOKE. *Tallulah Falls.* 1834–1849. 35 ¹/₄ x 28 ¹/₄ in. Georgia Museum of Art, The University of Georgia, Athens, Georgia. Gift of Mrs. Will Moss. *George Cooke traveled through Georgia in 1840, describing Tallulah Falls, the "Niagara of the South," in the most poetic terms for an article in the* Southern Literary Messenger. *Cooke includes himself sketching in the painting, perhaps to confirm for the viewer that the scene has been accurately recorded. This particular view from Devil's Pulpit no longer exists; in 1914 the river was diverted for hydroelectric power.*

COLORPLATE 28

ROBERT BRAMMER (1811–1853). *Mississippi Panorama*. c.1850. Oil on canvas. 25 x 30 in. Roger Houston Ogden Collection, New Orleans.

COLORPLATE 29

REGIS GIGNOUX (1816–1882). *Sunset on Dismal Swamp.* c. 1848. Oil on canvas. 12 x 18 in. Roger Houston Ogden Collection, New Orleans. *Regis Gignoux came to the United States from France to paint the Great Dismal Swamp on a commission from Lord Ellesmere in England. His paintings are often compared to those of the Hudson River School because of their romantic, luminous effects.*

COLORPLATE 30

M. L. PILSBURY. *Louisiana Plantation Scene.* c. 1880. Oil on canvas. 20 x 27 in. Roger Houston Ogden Collection, New Orleans.

COLORPLATE 3I

ROBERT BRAMMER AND AUGUSTUS VON SMITH. *Oakland House and Race Course, Louisville, Kentucky*. c. 1840. Oil on canvas. 35 3/4 x 28 1/4 in. Collection of the J. B. Speed Art Museum, Louisville, Kentucky. *This lively scene shows a popular Louisville racecourse the year after a nationally famous race between a Kentucky horse and one from Tennessee and Louisiana. The painters, of whom little is known, worked in Louisville and New Orleans, specializing in landscapes and miniatures.*

COLORPLATE 32

ADRIEN PERSAC. *The Asylum for the Deaf and Dumb—Baton Rouge.* 1859. Gouache on paper. 18 x 23 ¹/₂ in. Louisiana State University Museum of Art, Baton Rouge. Gift: Friends of the Museum.

COLORPLATE 33

JOHN BLAKE WHITE. *Arrival of the Mail/Perspective of Broad Street.* 1837. Collection of City Hall, Charleston, South Carolina.

COLORPLATE 34

ARTIST UNKNOWN. *Fox Hunt.* c. 1800. Oil on canvas. 34 1/2 x 53 7/8 in. Gift of Edgar William and Bernice Chrysler Garbisch. Copyright 1993 National Gallery of Art, Washington, D.C.

many were the injunctions bawled after Jack to "mind and take good care of missis!" We returned home through the glory of a sunset all amber-colored and rosy, and found that one of the slaves, a young lad for whom Mr. ——— has a particular regard, was dangerously ill. Dr. H——— was sent for; and there is every probability that he, Mr. ———, and Mr. O——— will be up all night with the poor fellow. I shall write more to-morrow. To-day being Sunday, dear E———, a large boat full of Mr. ———'s people from Hampton came up, to go to church at Darien, and to pay their respects to their master, and see their new "missis." The same scene was acted over again that occurred on our first arrival. A crowd clustered round the house door, to whom I and my babies were produced, and with every individual of whom we had to shake hands some half a dozen times. They brought us up presents of eggs (their only wealth), beseeching us to take them; and one young lad, the son of head man Frank, had a beautiful pair of chickens, which he offered most earnestly to S———. We took one of them, not to mortify the poor fellow, and a green ribbon being tied round its leg, it became a sacred fowl, "little missis's chicken." By-the-by, this young man had so light a complexion, and such regular straight features, that, had I seen him any where else, I should have taken him for a southern European, or, perhaps, in favor of his tatters, a gipsy; but certainly it never would have occurred to me that he was the son of negro parents. I observed this to Mr. ———, who merely replied, "He is the son of head man Frank and his wife Betty, and they are both black enough, as you see." The expressions of devotion and delight of these poor people are the most fervent you can imagine. One of them, speaking to me of Mr. ———, and saying that they had heard that he had not been well, added, "Oh! we hear so, missis, and we not know what to do. Oh! missis, massa sick, all him people *broken!*"

CHARLES DICKENS

From *American Notes and Pictures from Italy*

A Pleasant Encounter on the Way to Louisville

Charles Dickens toured America in 1842. Here he describes a steamboat journey from Cincinnati to Louisville, and his meeting with a fellow passenger who had been in Washington, D.C. representing the Choctaws on official business.

———————

Leaving Cincinnati at eleven o'clock in the forenoon, we embarked for Louisville in "The Pike" steamboat, which, carrying the mails, was a packet of a much better class than that in which we had come from Pittsburg. As this passage does not occupy more than twelve or thirteen hours, we arranged to go ashore that night: not coveting the distinction of sleeping in a state-room, when it was possible to sleep anywhere else.

There chanced to be on board this boat, in addition to the usual dreary crowd of passengers, one Pitchlynn, a chief of the Choctaw tribe of Indians, who *sent in his card* to me, and with whom I had the pleasure of a long conversation.

He spoke English perfectly well, though he had not begun to learn the language, he told me, until he was a young man grown. He had read many books; and Scott's poetry appeared to have left a strong impression on his mind: especially the opening of the Lady of the Lake, and the great battle scene in Marmion, in which, no doubt from the congeniality of the subjects to his own pursuits and tastes, he had great interest and delight. He appeared to understand correctly all he had read; and whatever fiction had enlisted his sympathy in its belief, had done so keenly and earnestly. I might almost say fiercely. He was dressed in our ordinary every-day

GEORGE CATLIN. *Snapping Turtle, a half-breed Choctaw.* 1834. Watercolor on paper. 29 x 24 in. 1834. 0226.1573. The Thomas Gilcrease Institute of American History and Art, Tulsa, OK. *Snapping Turtle was probably the Choctaw with whom Charles Dickens conversed.*

costume, which hung about his fine figure loosely, and with indifferent grace. On my telling him that I regretted not to see him in his own attire, he threw up his right arm, for a moment, as though he were brandishing some heavy weapon, and answered, as he let it fall again, that his race were losing many things besides their dress, and would soon be seen upon the earth no more: but he wore it at home, he added proudly.

He told me that he had been away from his home, west of the Mississippi, seventeen months: and was now returning. He had been chiefly at Washington on some negotiations pending between his Tribe and the Government: which were not settled yet (he said in a melancholy way), and he feared never would be: for what could a few poor Indians do, against such well-skilled men of business as the whites? He had no love for Washington; tired of towns and cities very soon; and longed for the Forest and the Prairie.

I asked him what he thought of Congress? He answered, with a smile, that it wanted dignity, in an Indian's eyes.

He would very much like, he said, to see England before he died; and spoke with much interest about the great things to be seen there. When I told him of that chamber in the British Museum wherein are preserved household memorials of a race that ceased to be, thousands of years ago, he was very attentive, and it was not hard to see that he had a reference in his mind to the gradual fading away of his own people.

This led us to speak of Mr. Catlin's gallery, which he praised highly: observing that his own portrait was among the collection, and that all the likenesses were "elegant." Mr. Cooper, he said, had painted the Red Man well; and so would I, he knew, if I would go home with him and hunt buffaloes, which he was quite anxious I should do. When I told him that supposing I went, I should not be very likely to damage the buffaloes much, he took it as a great joke and laughed heartily.

He was a remarkably handsome man; some years past forty, I should judge; with long black hair, an aquiline nose, broad cheek-bones, a sunburnt complexion, and a very bright, keen, dark, and piercing eye. There were but twenty thousand of the Choctaws left, he said, and their number was decreasing every day. A few of his brother chiefs had been obliged to become civilised, and to make themselves acquainted with what the whites knew, for it was their only chance of existence. But they were not many; and the rest were as they always had been. He dwelt on this: and said several times that unless they tried to assimilate themselves to their conquerors, they must be swept away before the strides of civilised society.

When we shook hands at parting, I told him he must come to England, as he longed to see the land so much: that I should hope to see him there, one day: and that I could promise him he would be well received and kindly treated. He was evidently pleased by this assurance, though he rejoined with a good-humoured smile and an arch shake of his head, that the English used to be very fond of the Red Men when they wanted their help, but had not cared much for them, since.

He took his leave; as stately and complete a gentleman of Nature's making, as ever I beheld; and moved among the people in the boat, another kind of being. He sent me a lithographed portrait of himself soon afterwards; very like, though scarcely handsome enough; which I have carefully preserved in memory of our brief acquaintance.

FREDERICK LAW OLMSTED

From *A Journey in the Seaboard Slave States*
Attending a Religious Service

A fairly objective observer of Southern culture, Frederick Law Olmsted toured the South reporting for the New York Daily Times, *and his articles resulted in several books about the region. Later in life Olmsted turned to landscape architecture, designing at Biltmore in Asheville, North Carolina, and Druid Hills in Atlanta. This account of a revival reveals the somewhat informal, charismatic style of evangelical Protestant churches in the South.*

In the house were some fifty white people, generally dressed in homespun, and of the class called "crackers," though I was told that some of them owned a good many negroes, and were by no means so poor as their appearance indicated. About one-third of the house, at the end opposite the desk, was covered by a gallery or cock-loft, under and in which, distinctly separated from the whites, was a dense body of negroes; the men on one side, the women on another. The whites were seated promiscuously in the body of the house. The negroes present outnumbered the whites, but the exercises at this time seemed to have no reference to them; there were many more waiting about the doors outside, and they were expecting to enjoy a meeting to themselves, after the whites had left the house.

* * *

During all the exercises, people of both classes were frequently going out and coming in; the women had brought their babies with them, and these made much disturbance. A negro girl

Revival scene in the rural South. 19th century. Engraving. University Archives, University of Mississippi.

would sometimes come forward to take a child out; perhaps the child would prefer not to be taken out and would make loud and angry objections; it would then be fed. Several were allowed to crawl about the floor, carrying handfuls of corn-bread and roast potatoes about with them; one had a fancy to enter the pulpit; which it succeeded in climbing into three times, and was as often taken away, in spite of loud and tearful expostulations, by its father. Dogs were not excluded; and outside, the doors and windows all being open, there was much neighing and braying, unused as were the mules and horses to see so many of their kind assembled.

The preliminary devotional exercises—a Scripture reading, singing, and painfully irreverential and meaningless harangues nominally addressed to the Deity, but really to the audience—being concluded, the sermon was commenced by reading a text, with which, however, it had, so far as I could discover, no further association. Without often being violent in his manner, the speaker nearly all the time cried aloud at the utmost stretch of his voice, as if calling to some one a long distance off; as his discourse was extemporaneous, however, he sometimes returned with curious effect to his natural conversational tone; and as he was gifted with a strong imagination, and possessed of a good deal of dramatic power, he kept the attention of the people very well. There was no argument upon any point that the congregation were likely to have much difference of opinion upon, nor any special connection between one sentence and another; yet there was a constant, sly, sectarian skirmishing, and a frequently recurring cannonade upon French infidelity and socialism, and several crushing charges upon Fourier, the Pope of Rome, Tom Paine, Voltaire, "Roosu," and Jo Smith. The audience were frequently reminded that the preacher did not want their attention, for any purpose of his own; but that he demanded a respectful hearing as "the Ambassador of Christ." He had the habit of frequently repeating a phrase, or of bringing forward the same idea in a slightly different form, a great many times. The following passage, of which I took notes, presents an example of this, followed by one of the best instances of his dramatic talent that occurred. He was leaning far over the desk, with his arm stretched forward, gesticulating violently, yelling at the highest key, and catching breath with an effort:

"A—ah! why don't you come to Christ? ah! what's the reason? ah! Is it because he was of *lowly birth?* ah! Is that it? *Is it* because he was born in a manger? ah! Is it because he was of a humble origin? ah! Is it because he was lowly born? a-ha! Is it because, ah!—is it because, ah!—because he was called a Nazarene? Is it because he was born in a stable?—or is it because—because he was of humble origin? Or is it—is it because"—He drew back, and after a moment's silence put his hand to his chin, and began walking up and down the platform of the pulpit, soliloquizing. "It can't be—it can't be—?"—then lifting his eyes and gradually turning towards the audience, while he continued to speak in a low, thoughtful tone: "perhaps you don't like the messenger—is that the reason? I'm the Ambassador of the great and glorious King; it's his invitation, 'taint mine. You mustn't mind me. I ain't no account. Suppose a ragged, insignificant little boy should come running in here and tell you, 'Mister, your house's a-fire!' would you mind the ragged, insignificant little boy, and refuse to listen to him, because he didn't look respectable?"

At the end of the sermon he stepped down from the pulpit, and, crossing the house towards the negroes, said, quietly, as he walked, "I take great interest in the poor blacks; and this evening I am going to hold a meeting specially for you." With this, he turned back, and without reentering the pulpit, but strolling up and down before it, read a hymn, at the conclusion of which, he laid his book down, and, speaking for a moment, with natural emphasis, said:

"I don't want to create a tumultuous scene, now;—that isn't my intention. I don't want to make an excitement,—that ain't what I want,—but I feel that there's some here that I may never see again, ah! and, as I may never have another opportunity, I feel it my duty as an Ambassador of Jesus Christ, ah! before I go————" By this time he had returned to the high key and whining yell. Exactly what he felt it his duty to do, I did not understand; but evidently to employ some more powerful agency of awakening, than arguments and appeals to the understanding; and, before I could conjecture, in the least, of what sort this was to be, while he was yet speaking calmly, deprecating excitement, my attention was attracted to several men, who had previously appeared sleepy and indifferent, but who now suddenly began to sigh, raise their heads, and *shed tears*—some standing up, so that they might be observed in doing this by the whole congregation—the tears running down their noses without any interruption. The speaker, presently, was crying aloud, with a mournful, distressed, beseeching shriek, as if he was himself suffering torture: "Oh, any of you fond parents, who know that any of your dear, sweet, little ones may be, oh! at any moment snatched right away from your bosom, and cast into hell fire, oh! there to suffer torment forever and ever, and ever and ever—Oh! come out here and help us pray for them! Oh, any of you wives that has got an unconverted husband, that won't go along with you to eternal glory, but is set upon being separated from you, oh! and taking up his bed in hell—Oh! I call upon you, if you love him, now to come out here and jine us in praying for him. Oh, if there's a husband here, whose wife is still in the bond of iniquity," etc., through a long category.

It was immediately evident that a large part of the audience understood his wish to be the reverse of what he had declared, and considered themselves called upon to assist him; and it was astonishing to see with what readiness the faces of those who, up to the moment he gave the signal, had appeared drowsy and stupid, were made to express agonizing excitement, sighing, groaning, and weeping. Rising in their seats, and walking up to the pulpit, they grasped each other's hands agonizingly, and remained, some kneeling, others standing, with their faces towards the remainder of the assembly. There was great confusion and tumult, and the poor children, evidently impressed by the terrified tone of the howling preacher, with the expectation of some immediately impending calamity, shrieked, and ran hither and thither, till negro girls came forward, laughing at the imposition, and carried them out.

At length, when some twenty had gathered around the preacher, and it became evident that no more could be drawn out, he stopped a moment for breath, and then repeated a verse of a hymn, which being sung, he again commenced to cry aloud, calling now upon all the unconverted, who were *willing* to be saved, to kneel. A few did so, and another verse was sung, followed by another more fervent exhortation. So it went on; at each verse his entreaties, warnings, and threats, and the responsive groans, sobs, and ejaculations of his coterie grew louder and stronger. Those who refused to kneel, were addressed as standing on the brink of the infernal pit, into which a diabolical divinity was momentarily on the point of satisfying the necessities of his character by hurling them off.

All this time about a dozen of the audience remained standing, many were kneeling, and the larger part had taken their seats—all having risen at the commencement of the singing. Those who continued standing were mainly wild-looking young fellows, who glanced with smiles at one another, as if they needed encouragement to brazen it out. A few young women were evidently fearfully excited, and perceptibly trembled, but for some reason dared not kneel, or compromise, by sitting. One of these, a good-looking and gayly-dressed girl, stood near, and directly before the preacher, her lips compressed, and her eyes fixed fiercely and defiantly upon him. He for some time concentrated his force upon her; but she was too strong for him, he could not bring her down. At length, shaking his finger toward her, with a terrible expression, as if he had the power, and did not lack the inclination to damn her for her resistance to his will, he said: "I tell you this is *the last call!*" She bit her lips, and turned paler, but still stood erect, and defiant of the immense magnetism concentrated upon her, and he gave it up himself, quite exhausted with the effort.

HENRY ADAMS

From *The Education of Henry Adams*
North Meets South at Harvard College

Henry Adams, grandson of John Quincy Adams and one of the most notable of American historians, was also a brilliant social critic. This passage from his classic, The Education of Henry Adams *(1907) is a wickedly humorous sketch of Roony Lee, son of Robert E. Lee. Adams comments further on North and South when he contrasts the Harvard Virginians as a whole with the Bostonians: "The habits of neither were good; both were apt to drink hard and to live low lives; but the Bostonian suffered less than the Virginian."*

This was Harvard College incarnate, but even for Harvard College, the Class of 1858 was somewhat extreme. Of unity this band of nearly one hundred young men had no keen sense, but they had equally little energy of repulsion. They were pleasant to live with, and above the average of students—German, French, English, or what not—but chiefly because each individual appeared satisfied to stand alone. It seemed a sign of force; yet to stand alone is quite natural when one has no passions; still easier when one has no pains.

Into this unusually dissolvent medium, chance insisted on enlarging Henry Adams's education by tossing a trio of Virginians as little fitted for it as Sioux Indians to a treadmill. By some further affinity, these three outsiders fell into relation with the Bostonians among whom Adams as a schoolboy belonged, and in the end with Adams himself, although they and he knew well how thin an edge of friendship separated them in 1856 from mortal enmity. One of the Virginians was the son of Colonel Robert E. Lee, of the Second United States Cavalry; the two others who seemed instinctively to form a staff for Lee, were town-Virginians from Petersburg. A fourth outsider came from Cincinnati and was half Kentuckian, N. L. Anderson, Longworth on the mother's side. For the first time Adams's education brought him in contact with new types and taught him their values. He saw the New England type measure itself with another, and he was part of the process.

Lee, known through life as "Roony," was a Virginian of the eighteenth century, much as Henry Adams was a Bostonian of the same age. Roony Lee had changed little from the type of his grandfather, Light Horse Harry. Tall, largely built, handsome, genial, with liberal Virginian openness towards all he liked, he had also the Virginian habit of command and took leadership as his natural habit. No one cared to contest it. None of the New Englanders wanted command. For a year, at least, Lee was the most popular and prominent young man in his class, but then seemed slowly to drop into the background. The habit of command was not enough, and the Virginian had little else. He was simple beyond analysis; so simple that even the simple New England student could not realize him. No one knew enough to know how ignorant he was; how childlike; how helpless before the relative complexity of a school. As an animal, the Southerner seemed to have every advantage, but even as an animal he steadily lost ground.

The lesson in education was vital to these young men, who, within ten years, killed each other by scores in the act of testing their college conclusions. Strictly, the Southerner had no mind; he had temperament. He was not a scholar; he had no intellectual training; he could not analyze an idea, and he could not even conceive of admitting two [*sic*]; but in life one could get along very well without ideas, if one had only the social instinct. Dozens of eminent statesmen were men of Lee's type, and maintained themselves well enough in the legislature, but college was a sharper test. The Virginian was weak in vice itself, though the Bostonian was hardly a master of crime. The habits of neither were good; both were apt to drink hard and to live low lives; but the Bostonian suffered less than the Virginian. Commonly the Bostonian would take some care of himself even in his worst stages, while the Virginian became quarrelsome and dangerous. When a Virginian had brooded a few days over an imaginary grief and substantial whiskey, none of his Northern friends could be sure that he might not be waiting, round the corner, with a knife or pistol, to revenge insult by the dry light of *delirium tremens*; and when things reached this condition, Lee had to exhaust his authority over his own staff. Lee was a gentleman of the old school, and, as every one knows, gentlemen of the old school drank almost as much as gentlemen of the new school; but this was not his trouble. He was sober even in the excessive violence of political feeling in those years; he kept his temper and his friends under control.

Adams liked the Virginians. No one was more obnoxious to them, by name and prejudice; yet their friendship was unbroken and even warm. At a moment when the immediate future posed no problem in education so vital as the relative energy and endurance of North and South, this momentary contact with Southern character was a sort of education for its own sake; but this was not all. No doubt the self-esteem of the Yankee, which tended naturally to self-distrust, was flattered by gaining the slow conviction that the Southerner, with his slave-owning limitations, was as little fit to succeed in the struggle of modern life as though he were still a maker of stone axes, living in caves, and hunting the *bos primigenius,* and that every quality in which he was strong, made him weaker; but Adams had begun to fear that even in this respect one eighteenth-century type might not differ deeply from another. Roony Lee had changed little from the Virginian of a century before; but Adams was himself a good deal nearer the type of his great-grandfather than to that of a railway superintendent. He was little more fit than the Virginians to deal with a future America which showed no fancy for the past. Already Northern society betrayed a preference for economists over diplomats or soldiers— one might even call it a jealousy—against which two eighteenth-century types had little chance to live, and which they had in common to fear.

Nothing short of this curious sympathy could have brought into close relations two young men so hostile as Roony Lee and Henry Adams, but the chief difference between them as collegians consisted only in their difference of scholarship: Lee was a total failure; Adams a partial one. Both failed, but Lee felt his failure more sensibly, so that he gladly seized the chance of escape by accepting a commission offered him by General Winfield Scott in the force then being organized against the Mormons. He asked Adams to write his letter of acceptance, which flattered Adams's vanity more than any Northern compliment could do, because, in days of violent political bitterness, it showed a certain amount of good temper. The diplomat felt his profession.

THE CIVIL WAR
AND THE LOST CAUSE

MARY CHESNUT

From *The Private Mary Chesnut*

On Slaves, Slavery, and War

Mary Chesnut's candid and irreverent writing combined with her opportune vantage point have made her diaries the most fascinating personal record of the Civil War period. As wife of a senator from South Carolina who became a leading secessionist and aide to General Beauregard and President Davis, Chesnut's home served as a salon for the Confederacy. In these entries she describes an unsettling trip from Montgomery to Augusta, discusses slavery, and recounts the excitement in Charleston over the beginning of the war.

[*1861*]

[*March 18.*] Yesterday on the cars we had a mad woman raving at being separated from her daughter. It excited me so, I quickly took opium, & *that* I kept up. It enables me to retain every particle of mind or sense or brains I ever have, & so quiets my nerves that I can calmly reason & take rational views of things otherwise maddening. Then a *drunken* preacher began to console a "bereaved widow." He quoted more fluently scripture than I ever have heard it—the beast! My book (*after* the opiate) I read diligently. He misses in attempting to describe Yankee character after an elaborate trial, & his women are detestable failures. Still, it made the time *glide* rapidly for me. Here I am for Sunday & have refused to accept overtures for peace & forgiveness. After my stormy youth, I did so hope for peace & tranquil domestic happiness. There is none for me in this world. "The peace this world cannot give, which passeth all understanding."

* * *

I am afraid Mr. C will not please the democracy. He said aloud in the cars he wished we could have separate coaches like the English & get away from those whiskey drinking, tobacca chewing rascals & *rabble*. I was scared somebody might have taken it up, & now every body is armed. The night before we left Montgomery, a man was shot in the street for a trifle, & Mr. Browne expressed his English horror, but was answered—it was only a cropping out of the right temper! The Lord have mercy on our devoted land.

Mrs. Mary Anne Taylor continued her good offices to the last. Sent me a tray of good things to travel on.

I wonder if it be a sin to think slavery a curse to any land. Sumner said not one word of this hated institution which is not true. Men & women are punished when their masters & mistresses are brutes & not when they do wrong— & then we live surrounded by prostitutes. An abandoned woman is sent out of any decent house elsewhere. Who thinks any worse of a Negro or Mulatto woman for being a thing we can't name. God forgive *us*, but ours is a *monstrous* system & wrong & iniquity. Perhaps the rest of the world is as bad. This *only* I see: like the

patriarchs of old our men live all in one house with their wives & their concubines, & the Mulattoes one sees in every family exactly resemble the white children—& every lady tells you who is the father of all the Mulatto children in every body's household, but those in her own, she seems to think drop from the clouds or pretends so to think. . . . My disgust sometimes is boiling over—but they are, I believe, in conduct the purest women God ever made. Thank God for my country women—alas for the men! No worse than men every where, but the lower their mistresses, the more degraded they must be.

My mother in law told me when I was first married not to send my female servants in the street on errands. They were there tempted, led astray—& then she said placidly, "So they told *me* when I came here—& I was very particular, *but you see with what* result." Mr. Harris said it was so patriarchal. So it is—flocks & herds & slaves—& wife Leah does not suffice. Rachel must be *added,* if not *married* & all the time they seem to think themselves patterns—models of husbands & fathers.

Mrs. Davis told me "every body described my husband's father as an odd character—a Millionaire who did nothing for his son whatever, left him to struggle with poverty," &c. I replied, "Mr. Chesnut Senior thinks himself the best of fathers—& his son thinks likewise. I have nothing to say—but it is true, he has no money but what he makes as a lawyer," &c. Again I say, my countrywomen are as pure as angels—tho surrounded by another race who are—the social evil!

* * *

[*April 12.*] Anderson refused to capitulate. At dinner yesterday Theo Stark came & Miles—it was I dare say our last merry meal. Afternoon—we were frantic. Sue King rushed in for news. Said all the King family were on the Island—but Mr. Henry King. Said I was a lucky woman, happy in my husband—ought to be so grateful, &c. Mr. C came while she was here—told me he had a most interesting interview with Anderson—Capt. In. & himself—& Jeff Davis had been telegraphed—& then they would know what answer to make Anderson. The men came in. Uncle Hamilton madly rushing about—tears in his eyes—with disappointment that he is not employed. Manning in his uniform. Mr. Chesnut sent off again to Anderson. The live long night I toss about—at half past four we hear the booming of the cannon. I start up—dress & rush to my sisters in misery. We go on the house top & see the shells bursting. They say our men are wasting ammunition.

Mr. Chesnut rode about all night in a little open boat to order our batteries to open. He ordered the first gun fired & he resigned first.

These long hours the regular sound of the cannon roar—men & women rush in—prayers—imprecations. What scenes. To night a force will attempt to land. The *Harriet Lane* has attempted to get in—been shot—her wheel house ruined & she has put to sea. Proud Carolinians—you must conquer on your own soil. The enemy must not land.

HENRI LOVIE. *Troops at Pittsburg Landing.* April 1862. Pencil. New York Public Library, New York. Miriam and Ira D. Wallach Division of Arts, Prints, and Photographs. Astor, Lennox and Tilden Foundation.

JOHN S. JACKMAN

From *Diary of a Confederate Soldier*

At the Front

John Jackman left his home in Bardstown, Kentucky one September day in 1861 "to get the daily papers" and ended up going to war for three-and-a-half years. He joined the 9th Kentucky brigade and first saw action at Shiloh in April 1862. His remarkable wartime diary provides a vivid description of the aftermath of that bloody battle.

[*1862*]

April 6th. This day will long be remembered. Soon after the sun had risen, the firing of artillery became so general, and the roar of musketry could be heard so distinctly, I knew the battle had commenced. I wished to be on the field, but was not able to walk so far. The gentleman with whom I was staying had his only remaining horse caught, which I mounted. When I bade "mine hostess" good-bye, she looked very "sorrowful"—which affected me not a little & I never knew why she took such an interest in me. The gentleman walked and kept up. Four miles brought us to Monterey, and just beyond, we met some of the wounded on foot with their arms and heads bound up in bloody bandages, & I felt then that I was getting in the vicinity of "warfare." Soon we met ambulances and wagons loaded with wounded, and I could hear the poor fellows groaning and shrieking, as they were being jolted over the rough road. Met a man on horseback with a stand of captured colors. We were now in proximity of the fighting, and we met crowds of men; some crippling along, wounded in the legs or about the body; others, no blood could be seen about their persons—yet all seemed bent on getting away. I now dismounted and started on foot. I never saw the gentleman afterwards, who had kindly brought me so far on the road. Being in so much excitement, I became stronger. I met a fellow dressed in a suit of "butter-nut" jeans, who was limping, but I don't believe was scratched. He asked me, in that whining way: "Has you'ns been in the fight yet?" I thought he meant some general, and asked my "brown" interrogator what troops General "Youens" commanded. He seemed astounded, and at last made me understand him. I told him "no," and went on. I afterwards got quite familiar with the "youens" and "weens" vernacular of "Brown Jeans."

While passing a hospital on the roadside, I happened to see one of our company lying by a tent wounded. I went out to see him, and there found the brigade hospital established. There were heaps of wounded lying about, many of them I knew, and first one then another would ask me to give him water or do some other favor for him. While thus occupied, Dr. P. told me to stay with him, that I was not able to go on the field—that I would be captured. There was no one to help him, and I turned surgeon, *pro tempore*. I was not able to do much, but rendered all the assistance in my power. Part of my business was to put patients under the influence of chloroform. I kept my handkerchief saturated all the time, and was often dizzy from the effects of it myself. It was about one o'clock in the day, when I got there.

All day long the battle raged. Occasionally there would be a lull for a short time; but the cannon were never entirely hushed. They would break out in increased thunder, and the roar of musketry would roll up and down the lines, vibrating almost regularly from one extreme to the other. All day long the ambulances continued to discharge their loads of wounded. At last night set in, and the musketry ceased; but the Federal gunboats continued shelling awhile after dark. Nearly midnight when we got through with the wounded. A heavy rain set in. I was tired, sick, and all covered with blood. But I was in far better fix than many that were there. I sat on a medicine chest in the surgeon's tent, and "nodded" the long night through.

April 7th. With the dawn came the roar of battle; but the combat did not wax very warm until later in the day. Early, all the wounded that could walk, were given passes to go to the rear, and those not able to walk, were placed in wagons, and started for Corinth. Many poor fellows were not able to be moved at all. Once that morning, a body of Federal cavalry came close enough to fire on us, tearing up the tents, but fortunately hurting no one. Dr. P. and I were standing close together talking, when a ball passed between our noses, which instantly stopped our conversation. We soon hung up strips of red flannel to prevent further accidents of the kind. A little after the middle of the day, the battle raged terribly—it was the last struggle of the Confederates, ending in defeat. Soon after, I saw Gen'l Beauregard, accompanied by one or two of his staff, ride leisurely back to the rear, as cool and unperturbed as if nothing had happened. A line was being formed in the rear of us, and we had to move. Jim B. and I put the only remaining wounded of our regiment who could be moved, into a large spring wagon, and started back. We had to leave some that it would have been death to put them in wagons. We hated to do so, but we could not do otherwise. The wagon was heavy, the horses were balky, and the roads were rough and muddy—besides the driver was inexperienced—all combined, we came near not getting out. B. was strong, and would tug at the wheels—I would plan, abuse the driver, and try to cheer up the horses. At last we came up with brother Jo. who was slightly wounded, and he assisted us. I believe if it had not been for him, we never would have gotten out. Night overtook us before we got far, and we drove off to the side of the road to wait till morning. The rain commenced pouring down, and continued all night. The road was in a perfect slush, and the shattered colums were plouting [plodding] over it all night. As luck would have it, a tent fly was in the wagon, and we cut bows and stretched it over the wagon-bed. I crept in, and with my feet propt up across Adjt Bell, managed to sleep a little.

CAROLINE SEABURY

From *The Diary of Caroline Seabury*
Tending the Wounded and the Dying

Caroline Seabury came to Mississippi to teach French at the Columbus Female Institute. When the sick and wounded came pouring into Columbus after the Battle of Shiloh, she became a volunteer nurse. Here, in a very touching diary entry, she describes her tragic duties.

[*1862*]

April 6th—Again we hear of the two great armies in battle at Shiloh—but little more than 100 miles from here—Still fighting on Sunday—"the day of battles"—"Our side completely victorious" is the last dispatch—Gens. Beauregard & Grant commanding—The suspense is heart-rending. Who can lie down & sleep quietly while such awful scenes are being enacted so near us—

7th—The death of Gen. A. S. Johnston is just announced and a more guarded account of our success—To-night there are many throbbing hearts fearing that the worst is not known—

10th—The truth has come—It was ["]a retreat of the Confederate forces—in good order"—which ended the battle of two days—& we are told that Columbus must be the hospital station—as it is the nearest safe point for the wounded & sick—The new hotel, our school building, the basements of all the churches—are at once to be fitted up with cots for the men to be brought as fast as possible on the railroad—Not a preparation has been made of either sheets, bandages, or beds—All hearts heads and hands will be full of work for many a day—With the energy of woman's nature when fully roused by distress—everybody is enlisted—

14th—The intense heat of today and the exciting scenes with which the town is filled—have left me exhausted—too much for sleep, but with no one to share my thoughts save my pen & paper—It is still outside—the moon has risen as calmly as though this earth were only smiling back her soft light. What far different sights we have just left—Agony in every conceivable form, & even worse than positive pain, the dull apathy of hopeless sickness, when all suffering is forever past, & all hope—Crowded together in the new hotel were about 800—needing everything—with the same clothes on in which they fought more than a week ago—haggard—filthy beyond description, utterly repulsive except as suffering humanity must excite our pity, a large proportion of them with vacant expressionless faces—with wounds whose only dressing since the battle has been the blessed rains from heaven—their hollow cheeks, & glaring eyes mutely asking relief—The good face of Dr. Eve was seen here & there, he trying to bring some order out of utter confusion—From the room devoted to surgical operations came shrieks & groans, some faint as from the lips of the dying, others with the strength of intense suffering—up three flights of stairs through crowds of miserable objects—lying along the sides of the halls, we went to the fever ward—which was filled to overflowing. As none of the building had been plastered, we could see through the different rooms—and, who can ever forget it. The ladies were asked to distribute some nourishment—and how the poor wasted hands stretched out for it as we passed along—some were too weak even for that & must be fed like children, here was a mere boy, grasping a piece of bread—in the next cot, a gray-haired withered old man—with nothing but rags for clothing—his glassy eyes told too plainly that death had marked him—Not far along was a man of middle age—large frame with hands which bore the marks of hard labor, he had battled with the world in times of peace & had conquered—war

had taken him from home, & now wasting sickness had destroyed the strong man—His dying words my friend could not understand. Knowing how often I had listened for the last whisper she called me, telling him I could hear them. He roused all the strength left & whispered, "I want my body sent to my wife. I promised her—tell her I am willing to go—my pay is due for six months—she'll need it"—["]will you write for me & tell her this"—his voice stopped in half an hour he was in the dead room—I learned the address of his wife from another member of his company—& my promise has tonight been kept—We passed the "bunk" of one tall black eyed young man without speaking to him—He lay perfectly quiet—but the surgeon said there is one of the sickest men—& we turned back—He was a lieutenant in a Louisiana caval-ry company—wasted to a skeleton but retained the marks of a true gentleman in his wan face & his manner—I had a rose in my hand & involuntarily laid it on his pillow—he smiled—& turned towards it. The nurse said he had been talking that morning early about the sweet shrubs in his mother's yard & wondering if they had come. I happened to have some in my pocket—handed them to him. He could only say—"thank you, I love them." I told him he should have fresh ones everyday. When we passed his place this evening it was vacant—he lived only six hours after we saw him—but kept hold of the flowers the nurse said even in death—They found quite an amount of gold about his person—he told us—As the surgeon walked on with us—a light-haired sunburnt boy of about 17—raised up, & said, "Dr. don't you know me, I'm so glad to see you"—In vain he tried to think who the boy was—at last when told—he could hardly be made to believe it—that the son of his old friend was there—As we went on—he said wiping tears from his eyes—"I have known that boy from a baby—His father is a wealthy

EASTMAN JOHNSON. *The Letter Home.* 1867. Oil on compo-sition board. 23 x 27 ¹/₂ in. Museum of Fine Arts, Boston. M. and M. Karolik Collection.

planter, & he an only child—what would his poor mother say to see him now"—"I thank God no responsibility of this war rests on my shoulders."

Just as we passed into one room—there lay one with the sheet over his face—waiting to be carried out—His companions around were talking as though no one of their number had just left—or any of them might soon follow. In one corner was one giving orders for battle—his eyes glaring wildly about—now & then he would level an imaginary gun—& exclaim—"there's one more———Yankee gone." He had been three days & nights thus raving—No one knew him—& he had nothing by which he could be identified, about his person. In the hurried retreat companies had become divided, many had "straggled"—The poor fellow screamed to Mrs. Long—"there mother, I knew you would come & see me"—then—the most violent exertions to come to her, but his feet were tied—Some poor mother may be grieving now for him, longing for some tidings of her dear boy—and he ere long will fill a grave over which will be placed on a plain board— "Unknown"—A pretty little curly headed drummer boy looked so wishfully at us—I asked the doctor about him—He can't speak a word of English—was his reply—He is a French boy from New Orleans—I said only "avez-vous une mère" when he sprang up and commenced an autobiography at once—His mother was in France, had sent him to an uncle in N. Orleans for a business education—He had run away—was 15 yrs. old but very delicate—"Oh, mlle" ["]ma pavore mère," he would often repeat. I told him I would send him a pretty French story to read—& he would soon get better—His tears dried away soon—& he seemed quite happy as I say—bon jour je reviens une autre fois—

JEREMIAH GAGE

A Dying Soldier's Letter to His Mother

At twenty-one, University of Mississippi student Jeremiah Gage enlisted in the University Greys, a Confederate unit that fought in the battles of First Manassas, Seven Pines, and Gaines' Mill. On the afternoon of July 3, 1863, Gage was one of the first to fall on the battlefield at Gettysburg. Before he died, he was able to write a last letter to his mother.

Gettysburg Penn.
July 3rd

My dear Mother

This is the last you may ever hear from me. I have time to tell you that I died like a man. Bear my loss as best you can. Remember that I am true to my country and my greatest regret at dying is that she is not free and that you and my sisters are robbed of my worth whatever that may be. I hope this will reach you and you must not regret that my body can not be obtained. It is a mere matter of form anyhow.

This is for my sisters too as I can not write more. Send my dying release to Miss Mary . . . you know who.

J. S. Gage
Co. A, 11th Miss.

Mrs. P. W. Gage
Richland,
Holmes County,
Miss.

(This letter is stained with my blood.)

SHELBY FOOTE

From *The Civil War: A Narrative*
The Fate of the *Hunley*

Shelby Foote (b. 1916) published five novels before writing his three-volume history of the Civil War, a masterpiece that took twenty years to complete (1974). Of the difference between writing fiction and history, Foote has said, "it doesn't much matter if facts come out of documents or out of your head, they are still things you work with and respect. You are looking for the truth, and, . . . it's the same truth." The following excerpt, which describes the events surrounding the fate of the world's first submarine, H. L. Hunley, *demonstrates a mastery of the historian's respect for the facts and a writer's talent for animated narrative.*

Inside the harbor, Beauregard was about as deep in the doldrums as were the blue-clad sailors beyond the bar. Disappointed that he had not been ordered west to resume command of the army Bragg had inherited from him, privately he was telling friends that his usefulness in the war had ended, and he predicted defeat for the Confederacy no later than spring or summer. He gave as the cause for both of these disasters "the persistent inability and obstinacy of our rulers." Primarily he meant Davis, of whom he said: "The curse of God must have been on our people when we chose him out of so many noble sons of the South, who would have carried us safely through this Revolution."

In addition to the frustration proceeding from his belief that presidential animosity, as evidenced by slights and snubs, had cost him the western command he so much wanted, the Creole's gloom was also due to the apparent failure of a new weapon he had predicted would accomplish, unassisted, the lifting of the Union blockade by the simple process of sinking the

CONRAD WISE CHAPMAN. *Submarine Torpedo Boat H. L. Hunley, December 6, 1863. 1864.* Oil on board. 11 1/2 x 15 1/2 in. Museum of the Confederacy, Richmond. Photo by Katherine Wetzel. *Chapman, trained by his father, Virginia artist John Gadsby Chapman, was a member of the staff of General P. G. T. Beauregard. Part of his charge was to record the fortifications of the city of Charleston, and this is one of thirty-one sketches Chapman made in 1863 and 1864.*

RUDOLPH T. LUX. *Portrait of Judah P. Benjamin.* 1861. Gilt and polychrome enamel on porcelain. 7 ¹/₄ in diameter. Robert M. Hicklin, Jr. Inc., Spartanburg, SC. *Lux, a German artist, painted gilded porcelain portraits in New Orleans between 1856 and 1868. Confederate Secretary of War and Secretary of State Judah P. Benjamin was a member of a well-respected Jewish family in Louisiana.*

blockaders. There had arrived by rail from Mobile in mid-August, disassembled and loaded on two flatcars, a cigar-shaped metal vessel about thirty feet in length and less than four feet wide and five feet deep. Put back together and launched in Charleston harbor, she resembled the little *David*-class torpedo boats whose low silhouette made them hard for enemy lookouts to detect. Actually, though, she had been designed to carry this advantage a considerable step further, in that she was intended to travel under as well as on the water, and thus present no silhouette at all. She was, in short, the world's first submarine. Christened the *H. L. Hunley* for one of her builders, who had come from Alabama with her to instruct the Carolinians in her use, she was propeller-driven but had no engine, deriving her power from her eight-man crew, posted at cranks along her drive shaft, which they turned on orders from her coxswain-captain. Water was let into ballast tanks to lower her until she was nearly awash; then her two hatches were bolted tight from inside, and as she moved forward the skipper took her down by depressing a pair of horizontal fins, which were also used to level and raise her while in motion. To bring her all the way up, force pumps ejected the water from her tanks, decreasing her specific gravity; or in emergencies her iron keel could be jettisoned in sections by disengaging the bolts that held it on, thus causing her to bob corklike to the surface. A glass port in the forward hatch enabled the steersman to see where he was going while submerged, and interior light was supplied by candles, which also served to warn of the danger of asphyxiation by guttering when the oxygen ran low. Practice dives in Mobile Bay had demonstrated that the *Hunley* could stay down about two hours before coming up for air, and she had proved her effectiveness as an offensive weapon by torpedoing and sinking two flatboats there. Her method of attack was quite as novel as her design. Towing at the end of a 200-foot line a copper cylinder packed with ninety pounds of powder and equipped with a percussion fuse, she would dive as she approached the target, pass completely under it, then elevate a bit and drag the towline across the keel of the enemy ship until the torpedo made contact and exploded, well astern of the submarine, whose crew would be cranking hard for a getaway, still underwater, and a return to port for a new torpedo to use on the next victim. Beauregard looked the strange craft over, had her workings explained to him by Hunley, and predicted an end to the Yankee blockade as soon as her newly volunteered crew learned to handle her well enough to launch their one-boat offensive against the U.S. Navy.

Such high hopes were often modified by sudden disappointments, and the *Hunley* was no exception to the general application of the rule. Certain drawbacks were soon as evident here

COLORPLATE 35

ARTIST UNKNOWN. *The Old Plantation.* Possibly 1790–1800. Watercolor on laid paper. 11 ¹¹/₁₆ x 17 ⅞ in. Abby Aldrich Rockefeller Folk Art Center, Williamsburg, Virginia. *This fascinating watercolor was probably made near Charleston, South Carolina. The instruments shown are similar to Yoruba instruments (the stringed instrument, or molo, is an ancestor to the banjo), and it is possible that the dance with a cane and scarves also reflects African roots.*

COLORPLATE 36

WILLIAM HENRY BROWN. *Hauling the Whole Week's Picking.* c. 1842. Watercolor and paper mounted to cardboard. 19 1/4 x 28 1/8 in; 19 3/8 x 24 7/8 in. The Historic New Orleans Collection, acc. nos. 1975.93.1; 1975.93.2. *For thirty years William Henry Brown was a silhouettist whose subjects included Abraham Lincoln, among many other statesmen. This cutout, interesting for its use of colors and paint, was part of a five-foot strip he made to amuse a family he was visiting.*

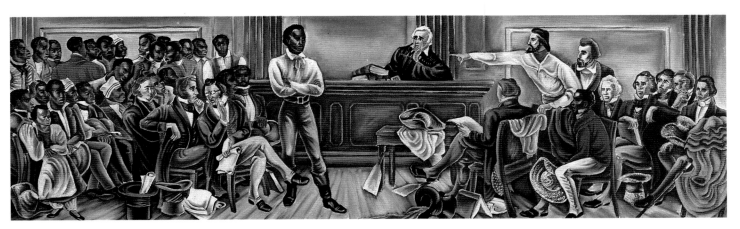

COLORPLATE 37

HALE ASPACIO WOODRUFF. *Trial of the Captive Slaves.* c. 1940. Oil on canvas studies for murals at Talladega College, Alabama. 40 x 12 ¹/₈ in. New Haven Colony Historical Society, New Haven, Connecticut. *African-American painter Hale Woodruff studied with Henry Ossawa Tanner in Paris and with Diego Rivera in Mexico. In 1938 he was commissioned to paint a mural for the Talladega College library depicting The Amistad mutiny, the 1839 slave rebellion that occurred when slaves on a Spanish slave ship took command of the ship, demanding to be returned to Africa. The sensational trial that followed eventually resulted in the return of the slaves to their homeland.*

COLORPLATE 38

CURRIER AND IVES. *Low water on the Mississippi.* Lithograph. Bettmann Archives.

COLORPLATE 39

JOHN MCCRADY. *Steamboat 'Round the Bend.* Delmonico's Restaurant, New Orleans, Louisiana. *John McCrady's Mississippi River panorama shows how the artist shared the objectives of midwestern Regionalist painters like Thomas Hart Benton, John Steuart Curry, and Grant Wood, but McCrady applied them to the region he knew best: the rural Deep South.*

COLORPLATE 40

WILLIAM D. WASHINGTON. *Marion's Camp*. 1859. University of South Carolina, Columbia. *Washington, a Washington, D.C. artist who received training in Dusseldorf, seems to have based this painting on William Gilmore Simms's romantic account of the popular legend of the Swamp Fox, Francis Marion, who so charmed a British soldier with his unpretentiousness and generosity that the soldier allegedly abandoned the loyalist cause.*

COLORPLATE 41 (opposite, above)

JOHN ANTROBUS. *A Plantation Burial*. 1860. Oil on canvas. 52 3/4 x 81 5/16 in. The Historic New Orleans Collection, acc. no. 1960.46. *John Antrobus, an Englishman who joined the Delhi Southrons in the Confederate Army, planned to paint a series of twelve scenes of "Southern life and nature." This melancholy scene, said to have been drawn from life, took place on the northern Louisiana plantation of Governor Tucker. Antrobus's sensitive and dignified portrayal of slave life was unusual for the time, and is underscored by the three barely distinguishable white people in the painting: an overseer on the far left, and the master and mistress on the right, all placed at shadowy and discreet distances.*

COLORPLATE 42 (opposite, below)

THOMAS MORAN. *Slaves Escaping through the Swamp*. 1863. Oil on canvas. 32 1/2 x 43 in. Philbrook Art Center.

COLORPLATE 43

CHARLES GIROUX (1828–1885). *Golden Twilight in Louisiana.* c. 1860. Oil on canvas. 14 x 23 in. Roger Houston Ogden Collection, New Orleans.

as they had been at Mobile earlier: one being that she was a good deal easier to take down than she was to bring back up, particularly if something went wrong with her machinery, and something often did. She was, in fact—as might have been expected from her combination of primitive means and delicate functions—accident-prone. On August 29, two weeks after her arrival, she was moored to a steamer tied to the Fort Johnson dock, resting her "engine" between dives, when the steamer unexpectedly got underway and pulled her over on her side. Water poured in through the open hatches, front and rear, and she went down so fast that only her skipper and two nimble seamen managed to get out before she hit the bottom. This was a practical demonstration that none of the methods providing for her return to the surface by her own devices would work unless she retained enough air to lift the weight of her iron hull; a started seam or a puncture, inflicted by chance or by enemy action while she was submerged, would mean her end, or at any rate the end of the submariners locked inside her. If this had not been clear before, it certainly was now. Still, there was no difficulty in finding more volunteers to man her, and Hunley himself, as soon as she had been raised and cleared of muck and corpses, petitioned Beauregard to let him take command. He did so on September 22 and began at once a period of intensive training to familiarize his new crew with her quirks. This lasted just over three weeks. On October 15, after making a series of practice dives in the harbor, she "left the wharf at 9.25 a.m. and disappeared at 9.35. As soon as she sank," the official post-mortem continued, "air bubbles were seen to rise to the surface of the water, and from this fact it is supposed the hole at the top of the boat by which the men entered was not properly closed." That was the end of Hunley and all aboard, apparently because someone had been careless. It was also thought to be the end of the vessel that bore his name, for she was nine fathoms down. A diver found her a few days later, however, and she was hauled back up again. Beauregard was on hand when her hatch lids were removed. "The spectacle was indescribably ghastly," he later reported with a shudder of remembrance. "The unfortunate men were contorted into all sorts of horrible attitudes, some clutching candles . . . others lying in the bottom tightly grappled together, and the blackened faces of all presented the expression of their despair and agony."

Despite this evidence of the grisly consequences, a third crew promptly volunteered for service under George E. Dixon, an army lieutenant who transferred from an Alabama regiment to the *Hunley* and was also a native of Mobile. Trial runs were renewed in early November, but the method of attack was not the same. Horrified by what he had seen when the unlucky boat was raised the second time, Beauregard had ordered that she was never again to function underwater, and she was equipped accordingly with a spare torpedo like the one her rival *David* had used against the *Ironsides,* ten days before she herself went into her last intentional dive. A surface vessel now like all the rest, except that she was still propelled by muscle power, she continued for the next three months to operate out of her base on Sullivan's Island, sometimes by day, sometimes by night. But conditions were never right for an attack; tide and winds conspired against her, and at times the underpowered craft was in danger of being swept out to sea because of the exhaustion of the men along her crankshaft. Finally though, in the early dusk of February 17, with a near-full moon to steer her by, a low-lying fog to screen her, and a strong-running ebb tide to increase her normal four-knot speed, Dixon maneuvered the *Hunley* out of the harbor and set a course for the Federal fleet, which lay at anchor in the wintry darkness, seven miles away.

At 8.45 the acting master of the 1200-ton screw sloop *Housatonic*—more than two hundred feet in length and mounting a total of nine guns, including an 11-inch rifle—saw what he thought at first was "a plank moving (toward us) in the water" about a hundred yards away. By the time he knew better and ordered "the chain slipped, engine backed, and all hands called to quarters" in an attempt to take evasive action and bring his guns to bear, it was too late; "The torpedo struck forward of the mizzen mast, on the starboard side, in line with the magazine." Still trembling from the shock, the big warship heeled to port and went down stern first. Five of her crew were killed or drowned, but fortunately for the others the water was shallow enough for them to save themselves by climbing the rigging, from which they were plucked by rescuers before the stricken vessel went to pieces.

There were no Confederate witnesses, for there were no Confederate survivors; the *Hunley* had made her first and last attack and had gone down with her victim, either because her hull had been cracked by the force of the explosion, only twenty feet away, or else because she was drawn into the vortex of the sinking *Housatonic*. In any case, searchers found what was left of the sloop and the submarine years later, lying side by side on the sandy bottom, just beyond the bar.

DOLLY LUNT BURGE

From *The Diary of Dolly Lunt Burge*
Yankee Raid

For more than a quarter of a century, Dolly Lunt Burge kept a journal of her life on a plantation in central Georgia. This account of a Yankee raid in July 1864 tells of Mrs. Burge's encounter with stragglers from Brigadier General George Stoneman's brigade, part of Sherman's destructive forces.

[*July 1864*]

29th. Last night was a sleepless one. At two o'clock I had the carriage at the door. Miss Mary took me out & showed me where she had buried the silver, then she, her brother, & Sally took the carriage for Madison, leaving me all alone again. I feel very much alarmed about them, fearing they will be molested.

All day I have walked about. Mrs. Graves & Libby came down to see if Sally had left. The Yankees left Covington for Macon headed by Stoneman to release prisoners held there. They robbed every house on their road of provisions, sometimes taking every piece of meat, blankets, & wearing apparel, silver & arms of every description. They would take silk dresses & put them under their saddles & things for which they had no use. Is this the way to make us love them & their union? Let the poor people answer whom they have deprived of every mouthful of meat & of their stock to make any. Our mills, too, they have burned, destroying an immense amount of property.

30th. Wheeler's cavalry are again in pursuit. There are not more than three thousand Yankees. Eb is sick. Dr. Chaney with him.

31st. I slept scarcely none last night. We heard the enemy were below Sandtown destroying everything & that Wheeler was in pursuit. I was looking for them all night. I could hear their cannon. Sadai had the toothache. Mr. Rakestraw came in to dinner & wanted me to send him to Rutledge. I am so very lonely, no one passing.

Monday, August 1st 1864. I have walked about all day scarcely doing anything. Indeed work of all kind is laid aside. Servants & all scarcely know what to be about. This evening learn by several of Wheeler's men who passed that the Federals were met & fought before getting into Macon & that our Cavalry with Militia captured their leader, Stoneman, who surrendered with most of his command. They say Wheeler might have got them all had he been at his post but that was three hours after the white flag was shown before the General could be found. They had two prisoners with them. Miss Shug Glass came over to spend the night with me. Our men tell us that five hundred of Stoneman's men got away & that they are endeavoring to make

Federal soldiers destroying the railroad tracks at Atlanta during Sherman's march to the sea. Oil on canvas. The Bettmann Archive.

their way back to their Army. Laid down to-night without any fear that I should be disturbed by the raiders.

2nd. Just as I got out of bed this morning Aunt Julia called me to look down the road & see the soldiers. I peeped through the blinds & there they were, sure enough, the "Yankees"—the "blue coats!" I was not dressed. The servant women came running in. "Mistress, they are coming! They are coming! They are riding into the lot! There are two coming up the steps!" I bid Rachel fasten my room door & go to the front door & ask them what they wanted. They did not wait for that but wanted to know "what the door was fastened for." She told them the White folks were not up. They said "they wanted breakfast & that quick, too."

Shug & Sadai as well as myself were greatly alarmed. As soon as I could get on my clothing I hastened to the kitchen to hurry up breakfast. Six of them were already in there talking with my women. They asked about our soldiers & passing themselves off as Wheeler's men, said:

"Have you seen any of our men go by?"

Several of Wheeler's men passed last evening. "Who are you?" said I.

"We are a portion of Wheeler's men," said one.

"You look like Yankees," said I.

"Yes," said one, stepping up to me, "we are Yankees. Did you ever see one before?"

"Not for a long time, & none such as you," I replied.

"Well, now tell us how many of Wheeler's men passed."

I told them & asked how many of them I had to get breakfast for. They said, "Twenty-six." They were in a great hurry & were so frightened that I became reassured. Breakfast was got speedily that morning. A picket was placed before my front gate, but one of my servant's ran to Jo[e] Perry's & told him that they were at my house. He informed some of the Cavalry that were camped some two miles from here & soon after they left here, which they did, taking off three of my best mules, they were captured. None of my servants went with them for which I feel very thankful. Miss Fannie Perry & Mrs. [William] Ezzard came down this evening. Oh

EVERETT B. D. JULIO. *The Last Meeting of Lee and Jackson.* 1869. Oil on canvas. 13 ft. 10 3/4 in. x 9 ft. 7 in. including frame. The Museum of the Confederacy, Richmond, Virginia. *This painting portrays a fantasized meeting between two of the South's greatest Confederate heroes on the eve of the battle of Chancellorsville. Displayed almost continuously in New Orleans from 1870 to 1879, the painting became an icon of the Lost Cause.*

how thankful I feel that they have done me no more injury. They were Ill. & Kentucky men but of German origin. To-night Captain Smith of an Alabama regiment with a squad of twenty men are camped opposite in the field. They have all supped with me & I shall breakfast them. We have spent a pleasant evening with music & talk. They have a prisoner along. I can't help feeling sorry for him.

5th. I sent for Mr. Ward & Rebecca to come back. The Yankees robbed him of his watch, pencil & shirt & seared the house where he was with Rebecca's trunk, &c., &c.

7th. Wiley, my stepson, arrived to-day. He is one of Wheeler's men. They are constantly passing.

9th. I sent for Mr. Glass to go to town with me to-day to get an order for my mules which were recaptured from the enemy. We met as many as two thousand soldiers, waggons, &c. It was a fearful ride. Upon my return home I learned that my mules were at a camp by Little River & that they would leave there that night. I immediately made ready & with Mr. Ward started for camp. It was seven miles from home & when I got there it was so dark I could not recognize my mules. Went back a little way & staid at Mr. Montgomery's. What a night it was of bustle and confusion. Thousands of soldierry all camped about.

10th. Went down to camp this morning & got two of my mules. Boys, Mose & Sanford mounted them & rode off proud enough. We hear the cannonading every day of Atlanta.

Margaret Mitchell

From *Gone with the Wind*

Scarlett's Promise

Gone with the Wind was published in 1936, the same year that Faulkner published Absalom, Absalom! *A million copies were sold during the first six months of publication, and Margaret Mitchell was awarded the Pulitzer Prize in 1937. In this scene, a starving and destitute Scarlett returns to Twelve Oaks, home of Ashley Wilkes, only to find it devastated by Sherman's troops.*

Mammy's old sunbonnet, faded but clean, hung on its peg on the back porch and Scarlett put it on her head, remembering, as from another world, the bonnet with the curling green plume which Rhett had brought her from Paris. She picked up a large split-oak basket and started down the back stairs, each step jouncing her head until her spine seemed to be trying to crash through the top of her skull.

The road down to the river lay red and scorching between the ruined cotton fields. There were no trees to cast a shade and the sun beat down through Mammy's sunbonnet as if it were made of tarlatan instead of heavy quilted calico, while the dust floating upward sifted into her nose and throat until she felt the membranes would crack dryly if she spoke. Deep ruts and furrows were cut into the road where horses had dragged heavy guns along it and the red gullies on either side were deeply gashed by the wheels. The cotton was mangled and trampled where cavalry and infantry, forced off the narrow road by the artillery, had marched through the green bushes, grinding them into the earth. Here and there in road and fields lay buckles and bits of harness leather, canteens flattened by hooves and caisson wheels, buttons, blue caps, worn socks, bits of bloody rags, all the litter left by a marching army.

She passed the clump of cedars and the low brick wall which marked the family burying ground, trying not to think of the new grave lying by the three short mounds of her little brothers. Oh, Ellen—She trudged on down the dusty hill, passing the heap of ashes and the stumpy chimney where the Slattery house had stood, and she wished savagely that the whole tribe of them had been part of the ashes. If it hadn't been for the Slatterys—if it hadn't been for that nasty Emmie, who'd had a bastard brat by their overseer—Ellen wouldn't have died.

She moaned as a sharp pebble cut into her blistered foot. What was she doing here? Why was Scarlett O'Hara, the belle of the County, the sheltered pride of Tara, tramping down this rough road almost barefoot? Her little feet were made to dance, not to limp, her tiny slippers to peep daringly from under bright silks, not to collect sharp pebbles and dust. She was born to be pampered and waited upon, and here she was, sick and ragged, driven by hunger to hunt for food in the gardens of her neighbors.

At the bottom of the long hill was the river and how cool and still were the tangled trees overhanging the water! She sank down on the low bank, and stripping off the remnants of her slippers and stockings, dabbled her burning feet in the cool water. It would be so good to sit here all day, away from the helpless eyes of Tara, here where only the rustle of leaves and the gurgle of slow water broke the stillness. But reluctantly she replaced her shoes and stockings and trudged down the bank, spongy with moss, under the shady trees. The Yankees had burned the bridge but she knew of a footlog bridge across a narrow point of the stream a hundred yards below. She crossed it cautiously and trudged uphill the hot half-mile to Twelve Oaks.

There towered the twelve oaks, as they had stood since Indian days, but with their leaves brown from fire and the branches burned and scorched. Within their circle lay the ruins of John Wilkes' house, the charred remains of that once stately home which had crowned the hill in white-columned dignity. The deep pit which had been the cellar, the blackened field-stone foundations and two mighty chimneys marked the site. One long column, half-burned, had fallen across the lawn, crushing the cape jessamine bushes.

Scarlett sat down on the column, too sick at the sight to go on. This desolation went to her heart as nothing she had ever experienced. Here was the Wilkes pride in the dust at her feet. Here was the end of the kindly, courteous house which had always welcomed her, the house where in futile dreams she had aspired to be mistress. Here she had danced and dined and flirted and here she had watched with a jealous, hurting heart how Melanie smiled up at Ashley. Here, too, in the cool shadows of the trees, Charles Hamilton had rapturously pressed her hand when she said she would marry him.

"Oh, Ashley," she thought, "I hope you are dead! I could never bear for you to see this."

Ashley had married his bride here but his son and his son's son would never bring brides to this house. There would be no more matings and births beneath this roof which she had so loved and longed to rule. The house was dead and, to Scarlett, it was as if all the Wilkes, too, were dead in its ashes.

"I won't think of it now. I can't stand it now. I'll think of it later," she said aloud, turning her eyes away.

Seeking the garden, she limped around the ruins, by the trampled rose beds the Wilkes girls had tended so zealously, across the back yard and through the ashes of the smokehouse, barns and chicken houses. The split-rail fence around the kitchen garden had been demolished and the once orderly rows of green plants had suffered the same treatment as those at Tara. The soft earth was scarred with hoof prints and heavy wheels and the vegetables were mashed into the soil. There was nothing for her here.

She walked back across the yard and took the path down toward the silent row of white-washed cabins in the quarters, calling "Hello!" as she went. But no voice answered her. Not even a dog barked. Evidently the Wilkes negroes had taken flight or followed the Yankees. She knew every slave had his own garden patch and as she reached the quarters, she hoped these little patches had been spared.

Her search was rewarded but she was too tired even to feel pleasure at the sight of turnips and cabbages, wilted for want of water but still standing, and straggling butter beans and snap beans, yellowing but edible. She sat down in the furrows and dug into the earth with hands that shook, filling her basket slowly. There would be a good meal at Tara tonight, in spite of the lack of side meat to boil with the vegetables. Perhaps some of the bacon grease Dilcey was using for illumination could be used for seasoning. She must remember to tell Dilcey to use pine knots and save the grease for cooking.

Close to the back step of one cabin, she found a short row of radishes and hunger assaulted her suddenly. A spicy, sharp-tasting radish was exactly what her stomach craved. Hardly waiting to rub the dirt off on her skirt, she bit off half and swallowed it hastily. It was old and coarse and so peppery that tears started in her eyes. No sooner had the lump gone down than her empty outraged stomach revolted and she lay in the soft dirt and vomited tiredly.

The faint niggery smell which crept from the cabin increased her nausea and, without strength to combat it, she kept on retching miserably while the cabins and trees revolved swiftly around her.

After a long time, she lay weakly on her face, the earth as soft and comfortable as a feather pillow, and her mind wandered feebly here and there. She, Scarlett O'Hara, was lying behind a negro cabin, in the midst of ruins, too sick and too weak to move, and no one in the world knew or cared. No one would care if they did know, for everyone had too many troubles of their own to worry about her. And all this was happening to her, Scarlett O'Hara, who had never raised her hand even to pick up her discarded stockings from the floor or to tie the laces of her slippers—Scarlett, whose little headaches and tempers had been coddled and catered to all her life.

As she lay prostrate, too weak to fight off memories and worries, they rushed at her, circled about her like buzzards waiting for a death. No longer had she the strength to say: "I'll think of Mother and Pa and Ashley and all this ruin later— Yes, later when I can stand it." She could not stand it now, but she was thinking of them whether she willed it or not. The thoughts cir-

Gone with the Wind. Still from the 1939 David O. Selznick film with Vivian Leigh as Scarlett O'Hara. The Bettmann Archive.

cled and swooped above her, dived down and drove tearing claws and sharp beaks into her mind. For a timeless time, she lay still, her face in the dirt, the sun beating hotly upon her, remembering things and people who were dead, remembering a way of living that was gone forever—and looking upon the harsh vista of the dark future.

When she arose at last and saw again the black ruins of Twelve Oaks, her head was raised high and something that was youth and beauty and potential tenderness had gone out of her face forever. What was past was past. Those who were dead were dead. The lazy luxury of the old days was gone, never to return. And, as Scarlett settled the heavy basket across her arm, she had settled her own mind and her own life.

There was no going back and she was going forward.

Throughout the South for fifty years there would be bitter-eyed women who looked backward, to dead times, to dead men, evoking memories that hurt and were futile, bearing poverty with bitter pride because they had those memories. But Scarlett was never to look back.

She gazed at the blackened stones and, for the last time, she saw Twelve Oaks rise before her eyes as it had once stood, rich and proud, symbol of a race and a way of living. Then she started down the road toward Tara, the heavy basket cutting into her flesh.

Hunger gnawed at her empty stomach again and she said aloud: "As God is my witness, as God is my witness, the Yankees aren't going to lick me. I'm going to live through this, and when it's over, I'm never going to be hungry again. No, nor any of my folks. If I have to steal or kill—as God is my witness, I'm never going to be hungry again."

Robert E. Lee

The General's Farewell Address to His Troops

After surrendering to Grant at Appomattox Courthouse on April 9, 1865, Robert E. Lee was surrounded by well-wishers from the Army of Northern Virginia. Moved by their loyalty, all he was able to say to them was, "Men, we have fought through the war together. I have done the best I could for you. My heart is too full to say more." According to Colonel Marshall, who drafted the official document the following day, General Order No. 9 was Lee's last order to his men.

General Order No. 9

Headquarters Army of Northern Virginia, 10th April 1865

After four years of arduous service marked by unsurpassed courage and fortitude the Army of Northern Virginia has been compelled to yield to overwhelming numbers and resources.

I need not tell the survivors of so many hard fought battles, who have remained steadfast to the last, that I have consented to this result from no distrust of them. But feeling that valor and devotion could accomplish nothing that could compensate for the loss that would have accompanied the continuance of the contest, I determined to avoid the useless sacrifice of those whose past services have endeared them to their country.

By the terms of the agreement Officers and men can return to their homes and remain there until exchanged. You will take with you the satisfaction that proceeds from the consciousness of duty faithfully performed and I earnestly pray that a merciful God will extend to you his blessing and protection.

With an unceasing admiration of your constancy and devotion to your country and a grateful remembrance of your kind and generous consideration of myself, I bid you all an affectionate farewell.

R. E. Lee
General

Father Ryan

"The Conquered Banner"

This poem, one of many highly sentimental creations of Father Abram J. Ryan, was extremely popular with Southerners after "The War Between the States."

Furl that Banner, for 'tis weary;
Round its staff 'tis drooping dreary;
    Furl it, fold it, it is best;
For there's not a man to wave it,
And there's not a sword to save it,

MATHEW BRADY. *Robert E. Lee in Richmond.* May 1865. Photograph. National Archives, Library of Congress, Washington, DC. *Brady was introduced to the daguerrotype process by the painter and inventor Samuel Morse who learned it directly from Daguerre in Paris. Brady and his assistants created for the first time a documentary record of the ravages of war. This poignant photograph was taken at Lee's home in April 1865, just after his surrender.*

And there's not one left to lave it
In the blood which heroes gave it;
And its foes now scorn and brave it;
   Furl it, hide it—let it rest!

Take that Banner down! 'tis tattered;
Broken is its staff and shattered;
And the valiant hosts are scattered
   Over whom it floated high.
Oh! 'tis hard for us to fold it;
Hard to think there's none to hold it;
Hard that those who once unrolled it
   Now must furl it with a sigh.

Furl that Banner! furl it sadly!
Once ten thousands hailed it gladly,
And ten thousands wildly, madly,
   Swore it should forever wave;
Swore that foeman's sword should never
Hearts like theirs entwined dissever,
Till that flag should float forever
   O'er their freedom or their grave!

Furl it! for the hands that grasped it,
And the hearts that fondly clasped it,
   Cold and dead are lying low;
And that Banner—it is trailing!

While around it sounds the wailing
    Of its people in their woe.
For, though conquered, they adore it!
Love the cold, dead hands that bore it!
Weep for those who fell before it!
Pardon those who trailed and tore it!
But, oh! wildly they deplore it,
    Now who furl and fold it so.

Furl that Banner! True, 'tis gory,
Yet 'tis wreathed around with glory,
And 'twill live in song and story,
    Though its folds are in the dust:
For its fame on brightest pages,
Penned by poets and by sages,
Shall go sounding down the ages—
    Furl its folds though now we must.

Furl that Banner, softly, slowly!
Treat it gently—it is holy—
    For it droops above the dead.
Touch it not—unfold it never,
Let it droop there, furled forever,
    For its people's hopes are dead!

LOCAL COLOR

JOHN JAMES AUDUBON

From *Delineations of American Scenery and Character*

"Kentucky Barbecue on the Fourth of July"

*John James Audubon, the great American naturalist, was born in Haiti in 1785, the illegiti-
mate son of a planter and a woman of mixed ancestry. Brought up in France, he came to
America at eighteen, where he failed in a frontier business venture. Audubon then traveled
throughout the eastern United States, spending a great deal of time in the South hunting, studying, and sketching wildlife, activities that culminated in the publication of the seven-volume*
Birds of America *(1840–1844), and* The Viviparous Quadrupeds of North America
*(1845–1846). He also described many of his more personal travel experiences, like this high-
spirited Fourth of July celebration.*

Beargrass Creek, which is one of the many beautiful streams of the highly cultivated and
happy State of Kentucky, meanders through a deeply shaded growth of majestic beech woods,

JOHN JAMES AUDUBON. *Wild Turkey.* Mid-19th century. The Bettmann Archive.

in which are interspersed various species of walnut, oak, elm, ash, and other trees, extending on either side of its course. The spot on which I witnessed the celebration of an anniversary of the glorious Proclamation of our Independence is situated on its banks, near the city of Louisville. The woods spread their dense tufts towards the shores of the fair Ohio on the west, and over the gently rising grounds to the south and east. Every open spot forming a plantation was smiling in the luxuriance of a summer harvest. The farmer seemed to stand in admiration of the spectacle: the trees of his orchards bowed their branches, as if anxious to restore to their mother earth the fruit with which they were laden; the flocks leisurely ruminated as they lay on their grassy beds; and the genial warmth of the season seemed inclined to favour their repose.

The free, single-hearted Kentuckian, bold, erect, and proud of his Virginian descent, had, as usual, made arrangements for celebrating the day of his country's Independence. The whole neighbourhood joined with one consent. No personal invitation was required where every one was welcomed by his neighbour, and from the governor to the guider of the plough all met with light hearts and merry faces.

It was indeed a beautiful day; the bright sun rode in the clear blue heavens; the gentle breezes wafted around the odours of the gorgeous flowers; the little birds sang their sweetest songs in the woods, and the fluttering insects danced in the sunbeams. Columbia's sons and daughters seemed to have grown younger that morning. For a whole week or more, many servants and some masters had been busily engaged in clearing an area. The undergrowth had been carefully cut down, the low boughs lopped off, and the grass alone, verdant and gay, remained to carpet the sylvan pavilion. Now the waggons were seen slowly moving along under their load of provisions, which had been prepared for the common benefit. Each denizen had freely given his ox, his ham, his venison, his turkeys, and other fowls. Here were to be seen flagons of every beverage used in the country; "La belle Rivière" had opened her finny stores; the melons of all sorts, peaches, plums and pears, would have sufficed to stock a market. In a word, Kentucky, the land of abundance, had supplied a feast for her children.

A purling stream gave its water freely, while the grateful breezes cooled the air. Columns of smoke from the newly kindled fires rose above the trees; fifty cooks or more moved to and fro as they plied their trade; waiters of all qualities were disposing the dishes, the glasses, and the punch-bowls, amid vases filled with rich wines. "Old Monongahela" filled many a barrel for the crowd. And now, the roasted viands perfume the air, and all appearances conspire to predict the speedy commencement of a banquet such as may suit the vigorous appetite of American woodsmen. Every steward is at his post, ready to receive the joyous groups that at this moment begin to emerge from the dark recesses of the woods.

Each comely fair one, clad in pure white, is seen advancing under the protection of her sturdy lover, the neighing of their prancing steeds proclaiming how proud they are of their burdens. The youthful riders leap from their seats, and the horses are speedily secured by twisting their bridles round a branch. As the youth of Kentucky lightly and gaily advanced towards the Barbecue, they resembled a procession of nymphs and disguised divinities. Fathers and mothers smiled upon them, as they followed the brilliant *cortège*. In a short time the ground was alive with merriment. A great wooden cannon, bound with iron hoops, was now crammed with home-made powder; fire was conveyed to it by means of a train, and as the explosion burst forth, thousands of hearty huzzas mingled with its echoes. From the most learned a good oration fell in proud and gladdening words on every ear, and although it probably did not equal the eloquence of a Clay, an Everett, a Webster, or a Preston, it served to remind every Kentuckian present of the glorious name, the patriotism, the courage, and the virtue, of our immortal Washington. Fifes and drums sounded the march which had ever led him to glory; and as they changed to our celebrated "Yankee Doodle," the air again rang with acclamations.

Now the stewards invited the assembled throng to the feast. The fair led the van, and were first placed around the tables, which groaned under the profusion of the best productions of the country that had been heaped upon them. On each lovely nymph attended her gay beau, who in her chance or sidelong glances ever watched an opportunity of reading his happiness. How the viands diminished under the action of so many agents of destruction I need not say, nor is it necessary that you should listen to the long recital. Many a national toast was offered and accepted, many speeches were delivered, and many essayed in amicable reply. The ladies then retired to booths that had been erected at a little distance, to which they were conducted by their partners, who returned to the table, and having thus cleared for action, recommenced a series of hearty rounds. However, as Kentuckians are neither slow nor long at their meals, all were in a few minutes replenished, and after a few more draughts from the bowl, they rejoined the ladies, and prepared for the dance.

Double lines of a hundred fair ones extended along the ground in the most shady part of the woods, while here and there smaller groups awaited the merry trills of reels and cotillions. A burst of music from violins, clarionets, and bugles, gave the welcome notice, and presently the whole assemblage seemed to be gracefully moving through the air. The "hunting-shirts" now joined in the dance, their fringed skirts keeping time with the gowns of the ladies, and the married people of either sex stepped in and mixed with their children. Every countenance beamed with joy, every heart leaped with gladness; no pride, no pomp, no affectation, were there; their spirits brightened as they continued their exhilarating exercise, and care and sorrow were flung to the winds. During each interval of rest, refreshments of all sorts were handed round, and while the fair one cooled her lips with the grateful juice of the melon, the hunter of Kentucky quenched his thirst with ample draughts of well-tempered punch.

I know, reader, that had you been with me on that day, you would have richly enjoyed the sight of this national *fête champêtre*. You would have listened with pleasure to the ingenious tale of the lover, the wise talk of the elder on the affairs of the state, the accounts of improvement in stock and utensils, and the hopes of continued prosperity to the country at large, and to Kentucky in particular. You would have been pleased to see those who did not join the dance, shooting at distant marks with their heavy rifles, or watched how they shewed off the superior speed of their high bred "old Virginia" horses, while others recounted their hunting-exploits, and at intervals made the woods ring with their bursts of laughter. With me the time sped like an arrow in its flight, and although more than twenty years have elapsed since I joined a Kentucky Barbecue, my spirit is refreshed every 4th of July by the recollection of that day's merriment.

JOEL CHANDLER HARRIS

From *Uncle Remus*

"The Wonderful Tar-Baby Story"

Joel Chandler Harris said that "literature that can be labeled Northern, Southern, Western or Eastern, is not worth labeling at all." Still, few writers have been so closely identified with a region as Harris. His many short stories and novels have preserved African-American folk tales and dialect in written form, although slaves had kept these stories, many of African origin, alive in an oral tradition. These stories were more than just entertaining tales; slaves educated their children with them, illustrating that the weak can often overcome the powerful through cunning. "The Wonderful Tar-Baby Story" is an old favorite.

Didn't the fox *never* catch the rabbit, Uncle Remus?" asked the little boy the next evening.

"He come mighty nigh it, honey, sho's you born—Brer Fox did. One day atter Brer Rabbit fool 'im wid dat calamus root, Brer Fox went ter wuk en got 'im some tar, en mix it wid some turkentime, en fix up a contrapshun wat he call a Tar-Baby, en he tuck dish yer Tar-Baby en he sot 'er in de big road, en den he lay off in de bushes fer to see wat de news wuz gwineter be. En he didn't hatter wait long, nudder, kaze bimeby here come Brer Rabbit pacin' down de road— lippity-clippity, clippity-lippity—dez ez sassy ez a jay-bird. Brer Fox, he lay low. Brer Rabbit come prancin' 'long twel he spy de Tar-Baby, en den he fotch up on his behime legs like he wuz 'stonished. De Tar-Baby, she sot dar, she did, en Brer Fox, he lay low.

"'Mawnin'!' sez Brer Rabbit, sezee—'nice wedder dis mawnin',' sezee.

"Tar-Baby ain't sayin' nothin', en Brer Fox, he lay low.

The Wonderful Tar-Baby. Pen and ink drawing from *Uncle Remus: His Songs and His Sayings.*

"'How duz yo' sym'tums seem ter segashuate?' sez Brer Rabbit, sezee.

"Brer Fox, he wink his eye slow, en lay low, en de Tar-Baby, she ain't sayin' nothin'.

"'How you come on, den? Is you deaf?' sez Brer Rabbit, sezee. 'Kaze if you is, I kin holler louder,' sezee.

"Tar-Baby stay still, en Brer Fox, he lay low.

"'Youer stuck up, dat's w'at you is,' says Brer Rabbit, sezee, 'en I'm gwineter kyore you, dat's w'at I'm a gwineter do,' sezee.

"Brer Fox, he sorter chuckle in his stummuck, he did, but Tar-Baby ain't sayin' nothin'.

"'I'm gwineter larn you howter talk ter 'specttubble fokes ef hit's de las' ack,' sez Brer Rabbit, sezee. 'Ef you don't take off dat hat en tell me howdy, I'm gwineter bus' you wide open,' sezee.

"Tar-Baby stay still, en Brer Fox, he lay low.

"Brer Rabbit keep on axin' 'im, en de Tar-Baby, she keep on sayin' nothin', twel present'y Brer Rabbit draw back wid his fis', he did, en blip he tuck 'er side er de head. Right dar's whar he broke his merlasses jug. His fis' stuck, en he can't pull loose. De tar hilt 'im. But Tar-Baby, she stay still, en Brer Fox, he lay low.

"'Ef you don't lemme loose, I'll knock you agin,' sez Brer Rabbit, sezee, en wid dat he fotch 'er a wipe wid de udder han', en dat stuck. Tar-Baby, she ain't sayin' nothin', en Brer Fox, he lay low.

"'Tu'n me loose, fo' I kick de natal stuffin' outen you,' sez Brer Rabbit, sezee, but de Tar-Baby, she ain't sayin' nothin'. She des hilt on, en den Brer Rabbit lose de use er his feet in de same way. Brer Fox, he lay low. Den Brer Rabbit squall out dat ef de Tar-Baby don't tu'n 'im loose he butt 'er cranksided. En den he butted, en his head got stuck. Den Brer Fox, he sa'ntered fort', lookin' des ez innercent ez one er yo' mammy's mockin'-birds.

"'Howdy, Brer Rabbit,' sez Brer Fox, sezee. 'You look sorter stuck up dis mawnin',' sezee, en den he rolled on de groun', en laughed en laughed twel he couldn't laugh no mo'. 'I speck you'll take dinner wid me dis time, Brer Rabbit. I done laid in some calamus root, en I ain't gwineter take no skuse,' sez Brer Fox, sezee."

Here Uncle Remus paused, and drew a two-pound yam out of the ashes.

"Did the fox eat the rabbit?" asked the little boy to whom the story had been told.

"Dat's all de fur de tale goes," replied the old man. "He mout, en den agin he moutent. Some say Jedge B'ar come 'long en loosed 'im—some say he didn't. I hear Miss Sally callin'. You better run 'long."

MARK TWAIN

From *Life on the Mississippi*

Southern Pastimes

Missourian Samuel Langhorne Clemens (1835–1910), who used the pen name Mark Twain, worked on the Mississippi River for four years. His experiences were recorded in a series of Atlantic *articles entitled "Old Times on the Mississippi," which became the first part of* Life on the Mississippi *(1883); the second part was based on his travels down the Father of Waters in 1882. As an observer of American culture, Clemens's pen was as sharp as his eye.*

In the North one hears the war mentioned, in social conversation, once a month; sometimes as often as once a week; but as a distinct subject for talk, it has long ago been relieved of duty.

CONRAD WISE CHAPMAN.
Weapons of War. 1863.
Watercolor on brown
paper. 5 1/8 x 4 5/8 in.
Valentine Museum,
Richmond, Virginia.

There are sufficient reasons for this. Given a dinner company of six gentlemen to-day, it can easily happen that four of them—and possibly five—were not in the field at all. So the chances are four to two, or five to one, that the war will at no time during the evening become the topic of conversation; and the chances are still greater that if it become the topic it will remain so but a little while. If you add six ladies to the company, you have added six people who saw so little of the dread realities of the war that they ran out of talk concerning them years ago, and now would soon weary of the war topic if you brought it up.

The case is very different in the South. There, every man you meet was in the war; and every lady you meet saw the war. The war is the great chief topic of conversation. The interest in it is vivid and constant; the interest in other topics is fleeting. Mention of the war will wake up a dull company and set their tongues going when nearly any other topic would fail. In the South, the war is what A.D. is elsewhere; they date from it. All day long you hear things "placed" as having happened since the waw; or du'in the waw; or befo' the waw; or right aftah the waw; or 'bout two yeahs or five yeahs or ten yeahs befo' the waw or aftah the waw. It shows how intimately every individual was visited, in his own person, by that tremendous episode. It gives the inexperienced stranger a better idea of what a vast and comprehensive calamity invasion is than he can ever get by reading books at the fireside.

At a club one evening, a gentleman turned to me and said, in an aside:

"You notice, of course, that we are nearly always talking about the war. It isn't because we haven't anything else to talk about, but because nothing else has so strong an interest for us. And there is another reason: In the war, each of us, in his own person, seems to have sampled all the different varieties of human experience; as a consequence, you can't mention an outside matter of any sort but it will certainly remind some listener of something that happened during the war—and out he comes with it. Of course that brings the talk back to the war. You may try all you want to, to keep other subjects before the house, and we may all join in and help, but there can be but one result: the most random topic would load every man up with war reminiscences, and *shut* him up, too; and talk would be likely to stop presently, because you can't talk pale inconsequentialities when you've got a crimson fact or fancy in your head that you are burning to fetch out."

The poet was sitting some little distance away; and presently he began to speak—about the moon.

The gentleman who had been talking to me remarked in an aside: "There, the moon is far enough from the seat of war, but you will see that it will suggest something to somebody about the war; in ten minutes from now the moon, as a topic, will be shelved."

The poet was saying he had noticed something which was a surprise to him; had had the impression that down here, toward the equator, the moonlight was much stronger and brighter than up North; had had the impression that when he visited New Orleans, many years ago, the moon—

Interruption from the other end of the room:

"Let me explain that. Reminds me of an anecdote. Everything is changed since the war, for better or for worse; but you'll find people down here born grumblers, who see no change except the change for the worse. There was an old negro woman of this sort. A young New-Yorker said in her presence, 'What a wonderful moon you have down here!' She sighed and said, 'Ah, bless yo' heart, honey, you ought to seen dat moon befo' de waw!'"

The new topic was dead already. But the poet resurrected it, and gave it a new start.

A brief dispute followed, as to whether the difference between Northern and Southern moonlight really existed or was only imagined. Moonlight talk drifted easily into talk about artificial methods of dispelling darkness. Then somebody remembered that when Farragut advanced upon Port Hudson on a dark night—and did not wish to assist the aim of the Confederate gunners—he carried no battle-lanterns, but painted the decks of his ships white, and thus created a dim but valuable light, which enabled his own men to grope their way around with considerable facility. At this point the war got the floor again—the ten minutes not quite up yet.

I was not sorry, for war talk by men who have been in a war is always interesting; whereas moon talk by a poet who has not been in the moon is likely to be dull.

We went to a cockpit in New Orleans on a Saturday afternoon. I had never seen a cock-fight before. There were men and boys there of all ages and all colors, and of many languages and nationalities. But I noticed one quite conspicuous and surprising absence: the traditional brutal faces. There were no brutal faces. With no cock-fighting going on, you could have played the gathering on a stranger for a prayer-meeting; and after it began, for a revival—provided you blindfolded your stranger—for the shouting was something prodigious.

A negro and a white man were in the ring; everybody else outside. The cocks were brought in in sacks; and when time was called, they were taken out by the two bottle-holders, stroked, caressed, poked toward each other, and finally liberated. The big black cock plunged instantly at the little gray one and struck him on the head with his spur. The gray responded with spirit. Then the Babel of many-tongued shoutings broke out, and ceased not thenceforth. When the cocks had been fighting some little time, I was expecting them momently to drop dead, for both were blind, red with blood, and so exhausted that they frequently fell down. Yet they would not give up, neither would they die. The negro and the white man would pick them up every few seconds, wipe them off, blow cold water on them in a fine spray, and take their heads

COLORPLATE 44

ADRIEN PERSAC. *St. John Plantation—St. Martin Parish.* 1863. Gouache on paper. 22 5/8 x 27 3/8 in. Louisiana State University Museum of Art, Baton Rouge. Gift: Friends of the Museum and Mrs. Ben Hamilton in memory of her mother, Mrs. Tela Meier. *Adrien Persac not only designed a map of all the plantations on the Mississippi River between Natchez and New Orleans, but he also executed an unusual series of collages of those sites for real estate purposes. The figures in this work are cut from magazines and pasted to the surface.*

COLORPLATE 45

FERDINAND RICHARDT (1819–1895). *View of Harper's Ferry.* c. 1858. Oil on canvas. 28 1/2 x 48 1/2 in. Robert M. Hicklin, Jr., Inc., Spartanburg, South Carolina.

COLORPLATE 46

DAVID JOHNSON. *Natural Bridge, Virginia.* 1860. Reynolda House, Winston-Salem, North Carolina. *The Natural Bridge of Virginia was the South's Niagara Falls, attracting many visitors and inspiring painters. Thomas Jefferson actually acquired the land in 1774, and a painting of the bridge, now unknown, is said to have been in his collection.*

COLORPLATE 47

MEYER STRAUS. *Bayou Teche*. c. 1870. Oil on canvas. 30 x 60 in. Morris Museum of Art, Augusta, Georgia 1989.03.239. *Meyer Straus painted in New Orleans from 1869 to 1872. His lush swampscapes are dramatic and ethereal and create a world out of place and time.*

COLORPLATE 48

JOHN ROSS KEY. *The Bombardment of Fort Sumter.* 1865. Oil on canvas. 29 x 69 in. Greenville County Museum of Art, Greenville, South Carolina. *John Ross Key, a descendant of Francis Scott Key, joined the Confederacy and was charged by Beauregard with creating a "military history of the siege of Charleston."*

COLORPLATE 49

HIPPOLYTE VICTOR VALENTIN SEBRON. *Giant Steamboats on the Levee at New Orleans.* 1853. Oil on canvas. Tulane University Art Collection, New Orleans. Gift of D. H. Holmes Company. *Sebron, a Frenchman, was acquainted with Daguerre and familiar with his photographic experiments. What at first might appear to be simply an interesting genre painting,* Giant Steamboats, *with its lovely light and slightly elevated perspective, reveals an exquisite photographic sensibility in Sebron's painting.*

COLORPLATE 50

MARSHALL J. SMITH. *Manchac Cabin*. 1874. Oil on canvas. 12 x 18 in. Roger Houston Ogden Collection, New Orleans. *Smith's barren bayou landscapes are somber in mood and reflect the influence of his German training.*

A. R. WAUD. *Sunday Amusements in New Orleans—The Cockpit.* Late 19th century. Pen and ink sketch. The Bettmann Archive.

in their mouths and hold them there a moment—to warm back the perishing life perhaps; I do not know. Then, being set down again, the dying creatures would totter gropingly about, with dragging wings, find each other, strike a guesswork blow or two, and fall exhausted once more.

I did not see the end of the battle. I forced myself to endure it as long as I could, but it was too pitiful a sight; so I made frank confession to that effect, and we retired. We heard afterward that the black cock died in the ring, and fighting to the last.

Evidently there is abundant fascination about this "sport" for such as have had a degree of familiarity with it. I never saw people enjoy anything more than this gathering enjoyed this fight. The case was the same with old gray-heads and with boys of ten. They lost themselves in frenzies of delight. The "cocking-main" is an inhuman sort of entertainment, there is no question about that; still, it seems a much more respectable and far less cruel sport than fox-hunting—for the cocks like it; they experience, as well as confer enjoyment; which is not the fox's case.

We assisted—in the French sense—at a mule-race, one day. I believe I enjoyed this contest more than any other mule there. I enjoyed it more than I remember having enjoyed any other animal race I ever saw.

* * *

There were thirteen mules in the first heat; all sorts of mules, they were; all sorts of complexions, gaits, dispositions, aspects. Some were handsome creatures, some were not; some were sleek, some hadn't had their fur brushed lately; some were innocently gay and frisky; some were full of malice and all unrighteousness; guessing from looks, some of them thought the matter on hand was war, some thought it was a lark, the rest took it for a religious occasion. And each mule acted according to his convictions. The result was an absence of harmony well compensated by a conspicuous presence of variety—variety of a picturesque and entertaining sort.

All the riders were young gentlemen in fashionable society. If the reader has been wondering why it is that the ladies of New Orleans attend so humble an orgy as a mule-race, the thing is explained now. It is a fashion freak; all connected with it are people of fashion.

It is great fun, and cordially liked. The mule-race is one of the marked occasions of the year. It has brought some pretty fast mules to the front. One of these had to be ruled out, because he was so fast that he turned the thing into a one-mule contest, and robbed it of one of its best features—variety. But every now and then somebody disguises him with a new name and a new complexion, and rings him in again.

The riders dress in full jockey costumes of bright-colored silks, satins, and velvets.

The thirteen mules got away in a body, after a couple of false starts, and scampered off with prodigious spirit. As each mule and each rider had a distinct opinion of his own as to how the race ought to be run, and which side of the track was best in certain circumstances, and how often the track ought to be crossed, and when a collision ought to be accomplished, and when it ought to be avoided, these twenty-six conflicting opinions created a most fantastic and picturesque confusion, and the resulting spectacle was killingly comical.

Mile heat; time, 2.22. Eight of the thirteen mules distanced. I had a bet on a mule which would have won if the procession had been reversed. The second heat was good fun; and so was the "consolation race for beaten mules," which followed later; but the first heat was the best in that respect.

I think that much the most enjoyable of all races is a steamboat race; but, next to that, I prefer the gay and joyous mule-rush. Two red-hot steamboats raging along, neck-and-neck, straining every nerve—that is to say, every rivet in the boilers—quaking and shaking and groaning from stern to stern, spouting white steam from the pipes, pouring black smoke from the chimneys, raining down sparks, parting the river into long breaks of hissing foam—this is sport that makes a body's very liver curl with enjoyment. A horse-race is pretty tame and colorless in comparison. Still, a horse-race might be well enough, in its way, perhaps, if it were not for the tiresome false starts. But then, nobody is ever killed. At least, nobody was ever killed when I was at a horse-race. They have been crippled, it is true; but this is little to the purpose.

LYLE SAXON

From "Have a Good Time While You Can"
An Impression of the Carnival in New Orleans

Louisianan Lyle Saxon wrote many stories and articles about New Orleans and Cane River plantation life. This is a colorful account of the parade of the Krewe of Rex as seen through the eyes of a young boy. The first officially sanctioned Mardi Gras in New Orleans was held in 1857, although Mobile's Mardi Gras is much older. Mardi Gras falls in February or March, before Ash Wednesday and forty days before Easter.

Canal Street was so tightly packed with people that it was impossible to move forward at more than a snail's pace. About half the crowd was masked, the others dressed in everyday garb. High above the streets the balconies, the windows and even the roofs were massed with spectators. Flags fluttered everywhere. Bedlam! A happy roar hung over the heads of the throng, a hum of voices punctuated with cries, whistles, cat-calls. And everywhere the tinkling of little bells, an undercurrent of sound infinitely strange. Color everywhere: red, purple, blue, arsenic green, and the glitter of spangles and metal head-dresses in the sunlight. There were clowns of every size and color of costume, ballet-girls all dressed alike in white and black. There were animal disguises—men wearing purple elephants' heads of papier-mâché, or huge donkeys' heads. Two men had combined to represent a comical spotted horse—two others constituted a violet cow. A man passed by, high on stilts, his pink and white striped coat-tails blowing out behind him. Two men wore black tights painted in white to represent skeletons, terrifying in

their macabre aspect. A fat woman dressed in the uniform of a United States marine accompanied them; she dragged a squalling child by one arm. "That's only your papa," she said wearily, indicating the larger of the skeletons; but the child, unimpressed, continued to yell.

Suddenly I became conscious of a swelling whisper that ran through the crowd. Necks were craned. Maskers stopped their antics and stood on tiptoe, all looking in the same direction. Robert, my black guide and guardian, shading his devil mask with white-gloved hand, tiptoed also. Then he shouted, his voice muffled behind his mask, "It's de parade!" Then, almost upon us, I saw twelve blue-coated policemen on horseback riding abreast. The crowd moved back before them, men falling over each other in their haste.

Elbows came in contact with my forehead, feet smashed down upon mine; I was buffeted about, almost thrown down. But Robert dragged me back to him, and in another moment I found myself seated with my legs around his neck, high above the heads of the others. I had the feeling of a swimmer rising upon the crest of a wave. There before me, stretched out as far as I could see, was a mass of maskers, and beyond them a series of glittering mountains was moving toward us. The carnival king was coming.

Behind the mounted police who cleared the way, were masked outriders on black horses; they wore gold plumes on their hats, and their purple velvet cloaks trailed behind them over the flanks of the horses; they wore doublet and hose and carried gleaming swords in their hands. Their masks were black. Behind them a brass band tooted lustily. Two negroes carried between them a large placard emblazoned with one word, "Rex."

The first float in the procession seemed to me the most wonderful thing I had ever seen. It was a mass of blue sky, clouds and a glittering rainbow. Under the rainbow's bridge were masked figures in fluttering silk, men and women who held uplifted golden goblets. This was the title car, and along the side was written the title of the parade—a subject which I have entirely forgotten, except that it dealt in some way with Greek mythology. The glittering float towered as high as the balconies which overhung the street from the second floors of the houses. As the gay-colored mountain came gliding past it seemed fragile for all its monumental size, and it swayed as though mounted on springs. The car was drawn by eight horses draped in white.

A blaring band followed the title car, and then came more outriders in green and gold and wearing purple masks. Behind them came a car even larger than the first. It was like a gigantic wedding-cake and at the top, on a golden throne, was Rex, king of the carnival. Such a perfect king he was, with fat legs incased in white silk tights, a round fat stomach under shimmering satin, long golden hair and a magnificent curled yellow beard. His face was covered with a simpering wax mask, benign and jovial. On his head was a crown of gold and jewels that sparkled in the sun; he carried a scepter of diamonds which he waved good-naturedly at the cheering crowd. Behind him a gold-embroidered robe swept down behind the throne, cascaded over the back part of the float and trailed almost to the ground, its golden fringe shaking with the movement of the car. There was gauze and gold-leaf everywhere and spangles glittered in the sunlight. At the feet of the monarch two blond pages stood, boys no larger than I, with long flaxen curls and white silk tights, rather wrinkly at the knees. How I envied them!

Robert and I—like every one else—were screaming with delight. I clapped my hands. The blond king, so high, yet so near me, leaned out and with his scepter pointed directly to me as I sat perched upon the shoulder of the big red devil. He said something to one of the pages, and the page with a bored smile tossed a string of green-glass beads to me. It swirled through the air over the heads of the people and dropped almost into my outstretched hands; but my clumsy fingers missed it and it fell to the ground. Immediately there was a scramble. Robert stooped; I fell from his shoulders, and found myself lying on the pavement as though swept under a stampede of cattle. Hands and feet were all around me, but somehow I managed to retrieve those beads, and triumphant I scrambled up again and Robert put me back on his shoulder.

This had taken only a moment, but during that time the king's car had moved on and another car was in its place. I could see monstrous golden pythons which twined around white columns, and there were nymphs with green hair who held up bunches of purple grapes as large as oranges, grapes which glittered in the sunshine with iridescent coloring. The car with the serpents and grapes came to a swaying halt before us. I had an opportunity to examine the snakes at close range and was relieved to find that they did not move but remained twined about the fluted columns.

Robert was pinching my leg. With the other hand he was pointing toward the carnival king whose throne was now a short distance from us. The king's back was turned, but I could see that he was greeting some one on a balcony opposite. I had not noticed this balcony before, oddly enough, but now I saw tier after tier of seats rising from the second to the third floor of the building, the seats filled with men and women, not maskers but ordinary mortals dressed in their best. At the moment their hands were stretched out in greeting and they were cheering. There in the first row on the balcony was a beautiful girl in a floppy pink hat; she stood with arms outstretched toward Rex as he sat before her. They were separated by a distance of perhaps twenty feet, but his high throne was nearly level with her. He was saluting with his scepter. And then from somewhere came a man with a high ladder which was leaned against the king's chair. Up the ladder the man ran nimbly, balancing a tray covered with a white napkin. He presented the tray to the king. A bottle opened with a loud pop, and I saw champagne poured into a wineglass, champagne that spilled over the edge of the goblet and ran down into the street below. Rex was toasting his queen. Years after, I heard the story of this, why it was done and how old the custom was; but then the small boy who looked upon it saw only another fantastic happening in that mad dream of Mardi Gras.

The ceremony was soon over, the step-ladder was whisked away and Rex on his swaying throne was drawn slowly down the street. I could hear the cheers as they grew fainter in the distance, drowned in the blare of bands. One by one the gorgeous floats passed before us, each telling some mythological story. There were satyrs, fawns, mermaids, centaurs, the like of which I had never dreamed before. Fairyland had become reality. I counted the cars as they passed; there were twenty of them, and nearly as many bands of music. And always that unreal quality, that gaudy, blatant thing that I could not define then, of course, and which I cannot define even now, except that it gave to me the feeling of seeing a thousand circuses rolled into one.

The parade had passed by, the maskers had the street to themselves again. Horns blared, tambourines banged. The dance was beginning afresh. "We got tuh leave dis place!" cried Robert, clutching my hand and beginning to make his way through the crowd.

VANCE RANDOLPH

"Pissing in the Snow"

Folklorist Vance Randolph began collecting the lore of the Ozarks in 1919 and continued until the 1960s. Bawdy tales like this one are only a part of the rich oral tradition of the Ozarks. "Obscene elements occupy a prominent place in American folklore, and should be accorded proportional representation in the literature," Randolph has said. Randolph was told the following story by Ozarkians who had heard the tale in the late nineteenth century.

One time there was two farmers that lived out on the road to Carico. They was always good friends, and Bill's oldest boy had been a-sparking one of Sam's daughters. Everything was going fine till the morning they met down by the creek, and Sam was pretty goddam mad. "Bill," says he, "from now on I don't want that boy of yours to set foot on my place."

"Why, what's he done?" asked the boy's daddy.

"He pissed in the snow, that's what he done, right in front of my house!"

"But surely, there ain't no great harm in that," Bill says.

"No harm!" hollered Sam. "Hell's fire, he pissed so it spelled Lucy's name, right there in the snow!"

"The boy shouldn't have done that," says Bill. "But I don't see nothing so terrible bad about it."

"Well, by God, I do!" yelled Sam. "There was two sets of tracks! And besides, don't you think I know my own daughter's handwriting?"

SIDNEY LANIER
"Song of the Chattahoochee"

Sidney Lanier of Georgia was the South's finest poet of the post-Civil War years. Lanier, who was also a flutist, wrote poetry which is beautifully musical and reveals his passionate feelings about the Southern landscape.

Out of the hills of Habersham,
  Down the valleys of Hall,
I hurry amain to reach the plain,
Run the rapid and leap the fall,
Split at the rock and together again,
Accept my bed, or narrow or wide,
And flee from folly on every side
With a lover's pain to attain the plain
  Far from the hills of Habersham,
  Far from the valleys of Hall.

All down the hills of Habersham,
  All through the valleys of Hall,
The rushes cried *Abide, abide,*
The willful waterweeds held me thrall,
The laving laurel turned my tide,
The ferns and the fondling grass said *Stay,*
The dewberry dipped for to work delay,
And the little reeds sighed *Abide, abide,*
  Here in the hills of Habersham,
  Here in the valleys of Hall.

High o'er the hills of Habersham,
  Veiling the valleys of Hall,
The hickory told me manifold
Fair tales of shade, the poplar tall
Wrought me her shadowy self to hold,
The chestnut, the oak, the walnut, the pine,
Overleaning, with flickering meaning and sign,
Said, *Pass not, so cold, these manifold*
  Deep shades of the hills of Habersham,
  These glades in the valleys of Hall.

And oft in the hills of Habersham,
  And oft in the valleys of Hall,
The white quartz shone, and the smooth brook-stone
Did bar me of passage with friendly brawl,
And many a luminous jewel lone
—Crystals clear or a-cloud with mist,
Ruby, garnet and amethyst—
Made lures with the lights of streaming stone
  In the clefts of the hills of Habersham,
  In the beds of the valleys of Hall.

Toccoa Falls, Georgia. 19th century. Engraving.
University Archives, University of Mississippi.

But oh, not the hills of Habersham,
   And oh, not the valleys of Hall
Avail: I am fain for to water the plain.
Downward the voices of Duty call—
Downward, to toil and be mixed with the main,
The dry fields burn, and the mills are to turn,
And a myriad flowers mortally yearn,
And the lordly main from beyond the plain
   Calls o'er the hills of Habersham,
   Calls through the valleys of Hall.

KATE CHOPIN
"The Storm"

In recent years, Kate Chopin's writing has been rediscovered and acclaimed for its enlightened views about women's lives. Far ahead of her time, Chopin wrote stories about women who struggled against the restraints of conventional society—especially conservative Creole society. "The Storm," written in 1898, was not accepted for publication in her lifetime because of its overtly sexual theme.

I

The leaves were so still that even Bibi thought it was going to rain. Bobinôt, who was accustomed to converse on terms of perfect equality with his little son, called the child's attention to certain somber clouds that were rolling with sinister intention from the west, accompanied by a sullen, threatening roar. They were at Friedheimer's store and decided to remain there till the storm had passed. They sat within the door on two empty kegs. Bibi was four years old and looked very wise.

"Mama'll be 'fraid, yes," he suggested with blinking eyes.

"She'll shut the house. Maybe she got Sylvie helpin' her this evenin'," Bobinôt responded reassuringly.

"No; she ent got Sylvie. Sylvie was helpin' her yistiday," piped Bibi.

Bobinôt arose and going across to the counter purchased a can of shrimps, of which Calixta was very fond. Then he returned to his perch on the keg and sat stolidly holding the can of shrimps while the storm burst. It shook the wooden store and seemed to be ripping great furrows in the distant field. Bibi laid his little hand on his father's knee and was not afraid.

II

Calixta, at home, felt no uneasiness for their safety. She sat at a side window sewing furiously on a sewing machine. She was greatly occupied and did not notice the approaching storm. But she felt very warm and often stopped to mop her face on which the perspiration gathered in beads. She unfastened her white sacque at the throat. It began to grow dark, and suddenly realizing the situation she got up hurriedly and went about closing windows and doors.

Out on the small front gallery she had hung Bobinôt's Sunday clothes to air and she hastened out to gather them before the rain fell. As she stepped outside, Alcée Laballière rode in at the gate. She had not seen him very often since her marriage, and never alone. She stood there with Bobinôt's coat in her hands, and the big rain drops began to fall. Alcée rode his horse under the shelter of a side projection where the chickens had huddled and there were plows and a harrow piled up in the corner.

"May I come and wait on your gallery till the storm is over, Calixta?" he asked.

"Come 'long in, M'sieur Alcée."

His voice and her own startled her as if from a trance, and she seized Bobinôt's vest. Alcée, mounting to the porch, grabbed the trousers and snatched Bibi's braided jacket that was about to be carried away by a sudden gust of wind. He expressed an intention to remain outside, but it was soon apparent that he might as well have been out in the open: the water beat in upon the boards in driving sheets, and he went inside, closing the door after him. It was even necessary to put something beneath the door to keep the water out.

"My! what a rain! It's good two years since it rain' like that," exclaimed Calixta as she rolled up a piece of bagging and Alcée helped her to thrust it beneath the crack.

She was a little fuller of figure than five years before when she married; but she had lost nothing of her vivacity. Her blue eyes still retained their melting quality; and her yellow hair, dishevelled by the wind and rain, kinked more stubbornly than ever about her ears and temples.

The rain beat upon the low, shingled roof with a force and clatter that threatened to break an entrance and deluge them there. They were in the dining room—the sitting room—the general utility room. Adjoining was her bed room, with Bibi's couch along side her own. The door stood open, and the room with its white, monumental bed, its closed shutters, looked dim and mysterious.

Alcée flung himself into a rocker and Calixta nervously began to gather up from the floor the lengths of a cotton sheet which she had been sewing.

"If this keeps up, *Dieu sait* if the levees goin' to stan' it!" she exclaimed.

"What have you got to do with the levees?"

"I got enough to do! An' there's Bobinôt with Bibi out in that storm—if he only didn' left Friedheimer's!"

"Let us hope, Calixta, that Bobinôt's got sense enough to come in out of a cyclone."

She went and stood at the window with a greatly disturbed look on her face. She wiped the frame that was clouded with moisture. It was stiflingly hot. Alcée got up and joined her at the window, looking over her shoulder. The rain was coming down in sheets obscuring the view of far-off cabins and enveloping the distant wood in a gray mist. The playing of the lightning was incessant. A bolt struck a tall chinaberry tree at the edge of the field. It filled all visible space with a blinding glare and the crash seemed to invade the very boards they stood upon.

Calixta put her hands to her eyes, and with a cry, staggered backward. Alcée's arm encircled her, and for an instant he drew her close and spasmodically to him.

"Bonté!" she cried, releasing herself from his encircling arm and retreating from the window, "the house'll go next! If I only knew w'ere Bibi was!" She would not compose herself; she would not be seated. Alcée clasped her shoulders and looked into her face. The contact of her warm, palpitating body when he had unthinkingly drawn her into his arms, had aroused all the old-time infatuation and desire for her flesh.

"Calixta," he said, "don't be frightened. Nothing can happen. The house is too low to be struck, with so many tall trees standing about. There! aren't you going to be quiet? say, aren't you?" He pushed her hair back from her face that was warm and steaming. Her lips were as red and moist as pomegranate seed. Her white neck and a glimpse of her full, firm bosom disturbed him powerfully. As she glanced up at him the fear in her liquid blue eyes had given place to a

JOSEPH R. MEEKER. *Solitary Pirogue by the Bayou.* 19th century. Oil on canvas. 17 3/4 x 30 in. Robert M. Hicklin, Jr., Spartanburg, SC. *"Every artist ought to paint what he himself loves,"* Joseph Meeker wrote, *"what he loves will be lovely."* No other artist loved the Louisiana swamps as much nor rendered them as romantically as Meeker.

drowsy gleam that unconsciously betrayed a sensuous desire. He looked down into her eyes and there was nothing for him to do but to gather her lips in a kiss. It reminded him of Assumption.

"Do you remember—in Assumption, Calixta?" he asked in a low voice broken by passion. Oh! she remembered; for in Assumption he had kissed her and kissed and kissed her; until his senses would well nigh fail, and to save her he would resort to a desperate flight. If she was not an immaculate dove in those days, she was still inviolate; a passionate creature whose very defenselessness had made her defense, against which his honor forbade him to prevail. Now— well, now—her lips seemed in a manner free to be tasted, as well as her round, white throat and her whiter breasts.

They did not heed the crashing torrents, and the roar of the elements made her laugh as she lay in his arms. She was a revelation in that dim, mysterious chamber; as white as the couch she lay upon. Her firm, elastic flesh that was knowing for the first time its birthright, was like a creamy lily that the sun invites to contribute its breath and perfume to the undying life of the world.

The generous abundance of her passion, without guile or trickery, was like a white flame which penetrated and found response in depths of his own sensuous nature that had never yet been reached.

When he touched her breasts they gave themselves up in quivering ecstasy, inviting his lips. Her mouth was a fountain of delight. And when he possessed her, they seemed to swoon together at the very borderland of life's mystery.

He stayed cushioned upon her, breathless, dazed, enervated, with his heart beating like a hammer upon her. With one hand she clasped his head, her lips lightly touching his forehead. The other hand stroked with a soothing rhythm his muscular shoulders.

The growl of the thunder was distant and passing away. The rain beat softly upon the shingles, inviting them to drowsiness and sleep. But they dared not yield.

The rain was over; and the sun was turning the glistening green world into a palace of gems. Calixta, on the gallery, watched Alcée ride away. He turned and smiled at her with a beaming face; and she lifted her pretty chin in the air and laughed aloud.

III

Bobinôt and Bibi, trudging home, stopped without at the cistern to make themselves presentable.

"My! Bibi, w'at will yo' mama say! You ought to be ashame'. You oughtn' put on those good pants. Look at 'em! An' that mud on yo' collar! How you got that mud on yo' collar, Bibi? I never saw such a boy!" Bibi was the picture of pathetic resignation. Bobinôt was the embodiment of serious solicitude as he strove to remove from his own person and his son's the signs of their tramp over heavy roads and through wet fields. He scraped the mud off Bibi's bare legs and feet with a stick and carefully removed all traces from his heavy brogans. Then, prepared for the worst—the meeting with an over-scrupulous housewife, they entered cautiously at the back door.

Calixta was preparing supper. She had set the table and was dripping coffee at the hearth. She sprang up as they came in.

"Oh, Bobinôt! You back! My! but I was uneasy. W'ere you been during the rain? An' Bibi? he ain't wet? he ain't hurt?" She had clasped Bibi and was kissing him effusively. Bobinôt's explanations and apologies which he had been composing all along the way, died on his lips as Calixta felt him to see if he were dry, and seemed to express nothing but satisfaction at their safe return.

"I brought you some shrimps, Calixta," offered Bobinôt, hauling the can from his ample side pocket and laying it on the table.

"Shrimps! Oh, Bobinôt! you too good fo' anything!" and she gave him a smacking kiss on the cheek that resounded. "*J'vous réponds,* we'll have a feas' to night! umph-umph!"

Bobinôt and Bibi began to relax and enjoy themselves, and when the three seated themselves at table they laughed much and so loud that anyone might have heard them as far away as Laballière's.

IV

Alcée Laballière wrote to his wife, Clarisse, that night. It was a loving letter, full of tender solicitude. He told her not to hurry back, but if she and the babies liked it at Biloxi, to stay a month longer. He was getting on nicely; and though he missed them, he was willing to bear the separation a while longer—realizing that their health and pleasure were the first things to be considered.

V

As for Clarisse, she was charmed upon receiving her husband's letter. She and the babies were doing well. The society was agreeable; many of her old friends and acquaintances were at the bay. And the first free breath since her marriage seemed to restore the pleasant liberty of her maiden days. Devoted as she was to her husband, their intimate conjugal life was something which she was more than willing to forego for a while.

So the storm passed and every one was happy.

HALE ASPACIO WOODRUFF. *Georgia Landscape.* c. 1934–1935. Oil on canvas. 21 1/8 x 25 5/8 in. National Museum of American Art, Smithsonian Institution. Gift of Alfred T. Morris, Jr. *Hale Woodruff's paintings show the obvious influence of expressionistic painters like Van Gogh, and may hint at the threatening mood of the Georgia countryside as perceived by an African-American artist.*

JEAN TOOMER
"Georgia Dusk"

"Georgia Dusk" is taken from Jean Toomer's book, Cane, *which is a collection of vignettes, poems, songs, and stories. Toomer, who grew up in a comfortable, middle-class black family in Washington, D.C., found his greatest inspiration in his Deep South roots. This poem, like the other pieces in* Cane, *celebrates the African-American "folk spirit" as something profoundly beautiful and meaningful, but which Toomer believed to be dying.*

The sky, lazily disdaining to pursue
　　The setting sun, too indolent to hold
　　A lengthened tournament for flashing gold,
Passively darkens for night's barbecue,

A feast of moon and men and barking hounds,
　　An orgy for some genius of the South
　　With blood-hot eyes and cane-lipped scented mouth,
Surprised in making folk-songs from soul sounds.

The sawmill blows its whistle, buzz-saws stop,
　　And silence breaks the bud of knoll and hill,
　　Soft settling pollen where plowed lands fulfill
Their early promise of a bumper crop.

Smoke from the pyramidal sawdust pile
　　Curls up, blue ghosts of trees, tarrying low
　　Where only chips and stumps are left to show
The solid proof of former domicile.

Meanwhile, the men, with vestiges of pomp,
　　Race memories of king and caravan,
　　High-priests, an ostrich, and a juju-man,
Go singing through the footpaths of the swamp.

Their voices rise . . the pine trees are guitars,
　　Strumming, pine-needles fall like sheets of rain . .
　　Their voices rise . . the chorus of the cane
Is caroling a vesper to the stars..

O singers, resinous and soft your songs
　　Above the sacred whisper of the pines,
　　Give virgin lips to cornfield concubines,
Bring dreams of Christ to dusky cane-lipped throngs.

SOUTHERN FOLK

W. C. HANDY

From *Father of the Blues*

William Christopher Handy, born in Florence, Alabama just after the Civil War, is often called "The Father of the Blues," but the following entry from his autobiography reveals that the real inspiration behind his best musical compositions was the hypnotic and irresistible force of country blues played by self-taught musicians in the Mississippi Delta.

I hasten to confess that I took up with low folk forms hesitantly. I approached them with a certain fear and trembling. Like many of the other musicians who received them with cold shoulders at first, I began by raising my eyebrows and wondering if they were quite the thing. I had picked up a fair training in the music of the modern world and had assumed that the correct manner to compose was to develop simples into grandissimos and not to repeat them monotonously. As a director of many respectable, conventional bands, it was not easy for me to concede that a simple slow-drag and repeat could be rhythm itself. Neither was I ready to believe that this was just what the public wanted. But we live to learn.

My own enlightenment came in Cleveland, Mississippi. I was leading the orchestra in a dance program when someone sent up an odd request. Would we play some of "our native music," the note asked. This baffled me. The men in this group could not "fake" and "sell it" like minstrel men. They were all musicians who bowed strictly to the authority of printed notes. So we played for our anonymous fan an old-time Southern melody, a melody more sophisticated than native. A few moments later a second request came up. Would we object if a local colored band played a few dances?

WILLIAM FAULKNER. *Red and Blue Club.* Pen and ink drawing. University of Mississippi Library Archives. *William Faulkner, (he added the "u" to his name when he applied to join the Royal Air Force) illustrated the University of Mississippi annuals from 1916 until the early 1920s with drawings such as this one of W. C. Handy's band, which often played for Ole Miss dances.*

Object! That was funny. What hornblower would object to a time-out and a smoke—on pay? We eased out gracefully as the newcomers entered. They were led by a long-legged chocolate boy and their band consisted of just three pieces, a battered guitar, a mandolin and a worn-out bass.

The music they made was pretty well in keeping with their looks. They struck up one of those over-and-over strains that seem to have no very clear beginning and certainly no ending at all. The strumming attained a disturbing monotony, but on and on it went, a kind of stuff that has long been associated with cane rows and levee camps. Thump-thump-thump went their feet on the floor. Their eyes rolled. Their shoulders swayed. And through it all that little agonizing strain persisted. It was not really annoying or unpleasant. Perhaps "haunting" is a better word, but I commenced to wonder if anybody besides small town rounders and their running mates would go for it.

The answer was not long in coming. A rain of silver dollars began to fall around the outlandish, stomping feet. The dancers went wild. Dollars, quarters, halves—the shower grew heavier and continued so long I strained my neck to get a better look. There before the boys lay more money than my nine musicians were being paid for the entire engagement. Then I saw the beauty of primitive music. They had the stuff the people wanted. It touched the spot. Their music wanted polishing, but it contained the essence. Folks would pay money for it. The old conventional music was well and good and had its place, no denying that, but there was no virtue in being blind when you had good eyes.

That night a composer was born, an *American* composer. Those country black boys at Cleveland had taught me something that could not possibly have been gained from books, something that would, however, cause books to be written. Art, in the high-brow sense, was not in my mind. My idea of what constitutes music was changed by the sight of that silver money cascading around the splay feet of a Mississippi string band. Seven years prior to this, while playing a cornet solo, Hartman's *Mia,* on the stage in Oakland, California, I had come to the conclusion, because of what happened in this eleven minute solo, that the American people wanted movement and rhythm for their money. Then too, the Broadway hits, *Yankee Grit* and *Uncle Sammy*—two steps in six-eight time that we featured in Mississippi—did not have this earthy flavor.

Once the purpose was fixed I let no grass grow under my feet. I returned to Clarksdale and began immediately to work on this type of music. Within a day or two I had orchestrated a number of local tunes, among them *The Last Shot Got Him, Your Clock Ain't Right,* and the distinctly Negroid *Make Me a Pallet on Your Floor.* My hunch was promptly justified, for the popularity of our orchestra increased by leaps and bounds.

Ida Cox

"Southern Woman's Blues"

Ida Cox, from Knoxville, Tennessee, the "Uncrowned Queen of the Blues," traveled for over fifty years in road shows, including F. S. Wolcott's Rabbit Foot Minstrels and Silas Green's Minstrels. The frank and salacious humor of blues lyrics is clear in this song.

Takes a southern woman: to sing this southern song
Lord I'm worried now: but I won't be worried long
When I was downtown: I wouldn't take no one's advice
But I ain't going to let: that same bee sting me twice

Because I'm going back: where the weather suits my clothes
Down where there ain't no snow: and the chilly winds never blow
I don't want no northerner: no northern black or brown
Southern men will stick by you: when the northern men can't be found
You ever been south: you know just what I mean
Southern men are all the same: from Kentucky to New Orleans
I'm going back south: where I can get my hambone boiled
These northern men: are about to let my poor hambone spoil.

FLORENCE REECE AND JAMES FARMER

"Which Side Are You On?"

*Protest and resistance are old Southern traditions. This song, written by Florence Reece, the
wife of a union organizer, came out of the coal fields in Harlan County, Kentucky. After the
High Sheriff J. H. Blair ransacked her cabin looking for her husband, Reece reportedly tore
a page from a calendar and wrote these lyrics to the tune of an old Baptist hymn, "Lay the
Lily Low."*

Come all of you good workers,
Good news to you I'll tell,
Of how the good old union
Has come in here to dwell.

ARTHUR ROTHSTEIN. *Coal Miners,
Alabama.* 1939. Photograph. U. S. Farm
Security Administration Collection,
Prints and Photographs Collection,
Library of Congress.

Refrain:
Which side are you on?
Which side are you on?

We've started our good battle,
We know we're sure to win,
Because we've got the gun thugs
A-lookin' very thin.

They say they have to guard us
To educate their child;
Their children live in luxury
Our children's almost wild.

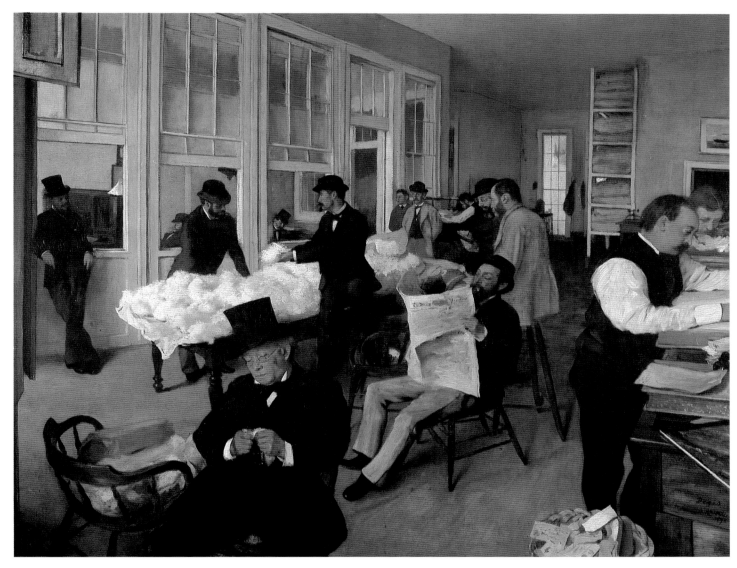

COLORPLATE 51

EDGAR DEGAS. *Portraits in an Office: The Cotton Exchange, New Orleans.* 1873. Musee des Beaux Arts, (France) Pau.
Edgar Degas was in New Orleans from 1872 to 1873, living in his uncle's home at the corner of Tonti and Esplanade.
This exquisitely composed painting of his uncle's office (the uncle is sampling cotton in the foreground) shows the bustle
of the cotton exchange. "Nothing but cotton," Degas wrote of his relative's livelihood, "one lives for cotton and
from cotton."

COLORPLATE 52

GEORGE COOKE. *Fairfax Lapsley.* 1848. Oil on canvas. 56 x 48 in. May and Frederick Hill. Berry-Hill Galleries, Inc., New York. *Posthumous portraits were not unusual in the nineteenth century, and this likeness of Joseph Fairfax Lapsley, one of five sons, was painted a year after the two-year-old died. Blended with the actual landscape of the Lapsley's Selma, Alabama, home are various personal possessions and symbols of a young life cut short: Fairfax's riderless horse and a dead tree.*

COLORPLATE 53

THOMAS SATTERWHITE NOBLE. *The Price of Blood, A Planter Selling His Son.* 1868. Oil on canvas. 39 ¹/₄ x 49 ¹/₂ in.
Morris Museum of Art, Augusta, Georgia 1989.01.155. *Noble, a Kentuckian who studied in Paris with Thomas Couture,
assembled a complex array of symbols in this painting. Here a slave trader negotiates the sale of the mulatto son of
the master.*

COLORPLATE 54

WILLIAM H. BAKER (1825–1875). *Home Regatta*. 1872. Oil on canvas. 20 x 24 in. Collection Lauren Rogers Museum of Art, Laurel, Mississippi.

COLORPLATE 55

EASTMAN JOHNSON. *The Ride for Liberty—The Fugitive Slaves.* 1862. Brooklyn Museum. *Johnson, a native of Maine, studied in Dusseldorf and other European art centers where he was influenced by the paintings of Rembrandt. Some of his most popular genre paintings dealt with life in the Old South.*

COLORPLATE 56

LOUIS GUILLAUME. *The Surrender of General Lee to General Grant at Appomattox, April 9, 1865.* 1867. Oil on canvas. 60 x 72 in. Appomattox Court House National Historic Park, Appomattox, Virginia. U.S. Department of the Interior, National Park Service, Washington, D.C. *General Grant remembers his meeting with General Lee at Appomattox Court House, April 9, 1865, this way: "Whatever his feelings, they were entirely concealed . . . but my own feelings . . . were sad and depressed. I felt like anything rather than rejoicing at the downfall of a foe who had fought so long and valiantly. . . ."*

COLORPLATE 57

GEORGE P. A. HEALY (1813–1894). *Pierre G. T. Beauregard.* Oil on canvas. 59 x 45 in. City of Charleston, South Carolina Collection. *Confederate General Pierre Gustave Toutant de Beauregard (1818–1893) commanded the attack on Fort Sumter and led forces at Bull Run, Shiloh, and Charleston.*

COLORPLATE 58

LUCIEN WHITING POWELL. *The Old Log Cabin.* c. 1865–1870. Oil on canvas. 30 x 25 in. Morris Museum of Art, Augusta, Georgia. 1989.01.155. *Lucien Powell was a member of an old and well-respected Upperville, Virginia family. His late work—mostly landscapes—reflects the influence of Moran and Turner, but early paintings like this one illustrate the standard romanticized view of black life as picturesque.*

COLORPLATE 59

HARRIET POWERS. *Pictorial Quilt.* c. 1895–1898. Pieced and appliquéd cotton, embroidered. 105 x 69 in. Bequest of
Maxim Karolik. Courtesy of the Museum of Fine Arts, Boston. *Harriet Powers, born into slavery in 1837, created this*
appliquéd quilt, one of the most famous examples of American folk art. Each block relates a Bible story, a notable local
event or local folklore, and in style and technique the quilt displays striking similarities to textiles created for centuries by
the Fon people of what is now the Republic of Benin, West Africa. An earlier, similar quilt was sold by Powers during
hard times for five dollars and now hangs in the Smithsonian Institution.

COLORPLATE 60

GEORGE F. HIGGINS (before 1859–after 1884). *Fishin' at Sunset.* c. 1880. Oil on canvas. 20 x 30 in. Roger Houston Ogden Collection, New Orleans.

COLORPLATE 61

Julius Robert Hoening. *(Allard) Plantation and Oak Tree.* 1898. Watercolor and gouache on board. 9 x 12 3/4 in. Roger Houston Ogden Collection, New Orleans.

COLORPLATE 62

WILLIAM HENRY BUCK (1840–1888). *Chinchuba to Moss Point.* 1882. Oil on canvas. 20 x 16 in. Roger Houston Ogden Collection, New Orleans.

COLORPLATE 63

F. ARTHUR CALLENDER. *New Orleans from Algiers (Point)*. 1893. Oil on canvas. 15 x 24 in. Roger Houston Ogden Collection, New Orleans.

COLORPLATE 64

ALEXANDER JOHN DRYSDALE. *Bayou Landscape.* 1916. Thinned oil on paper. 20 ¹/₄ x 30 ¹/₄ in. Robert Powell Coggins Art Trust, Morris Museum of Art COG-0352, Augusta, Georgia. *Drysdale, originally from Georgia, studied in New Orleans and at the Art Students League in New York. Using a kerosene wash technique, he was able to create an impressionistic effect that was beautifully suited to his subject matter, the bayous and marshes of Louisiana. Sometimes referred to as a tonalist, Drysdale's luxuriant landscapes are evocative and romantic. He was prolific and his work popular; by one dealer's estimate, he painted six thousand paintings.*

COLORPLATE 65

ELLIOTT DAINGERFIELD. *Moonlight.* c. 1910. Oil on canvas. 30 x 36 in. Mint Museum of Art, Charlotte, North Carolina. Gift of the Mint Museum Auxiliary. *Elliott Daingerfield personalizes the Southern landscape by imbuing his watercolors with a mysticism that is partly the result of his unusual techniques—painting from memory on sanded, sponged paper— and his admiration for German romantic and Barbizon School painters.*

COLORPLATE 66

WALTER ANDERSON. *Hummingbirds in Thistle*. 1955. Watercolor. Walter Anderson Museum of Art, Ocean Springs, Mississippi. Copyright the Estate of Walter Anderson. *Walter Anderson created hundreds of wood block prints, illustrated classics and fairy tales, and painted thousands of watercolors from the 1920s until his death in 1965. He is best known for his stylized "realizations" that capture the flora and fauna of the Gulf Coast in gorgeous watercolors.*

With pistols and with rifles
They take away our bread,
And if you miners hinted it
They'd sock you on the head.

They say in Harlan County
There are no neutrals there;
You either are a union man
Or a thug for J. H. Blair.

Oh workers, can you stand it?
Oh tell me how you can.
Will you be a lousy scab
Or will you be a man?

My daddy was a miner,
He is now in the air and sun
He'll be with you fellow workers
Until the battle's won.

JIMMIE RODGERS
"Train Whistle Blues"

Jimmie Rodgers, the legendary "Singing Brakeman," wrote this song in 1930. He was famous for his "blue yodel," and his innovative style successfully merged country blues and "hillbilly" music, both of which he was exposed to in the rural Deep South. Rodgers, also called the "Father of Country Music," was the first musician elected to the Country Music Hall of Fame in 1961.

When a woman gets the blues, she hangs her head and cries
When a woman gets the blues, she hangs her head and cries
But when a man gets the blues, he grabs a train and rides.

Every time I see that lonesome railroad train
Every time I see that lonesome railroad train
It makes me wish I was going home again.

Look a-yonder coming, coming down that railroad track
Look a-yonder coming, coming down that railroad track
With the black smoke rolling, rolling from that old smoke stack.

I've got the blues so bad till the whole round world looks blue
I've got the blues so bad till the whole round world looks blue
I ain't got a dime, I don't know what to do.

I'm weary now, I want to leave this town
I'm weary now and I want to leave this town
I can't find a job, I'm tired of hanging around.

ALBERT E. BRUMLEY

"I'll Fly Away"

Albert Brumley says the idea for this song came to him as he hummed an old prison tune while picking cotton on his father's farm. It is one of the most popular gospel songs ever written, and is still included in the repertoires of every gospel quartet, both white and black.

Some glad morning when this life is o'er
I'll fly away
To a home on God's celestial shore
I'll fly away.

I'll fly away, O glory
I'll fly away
When I die hallelujah by and by
I'll fly away.

When the shadows of this life have grown
I'll fly away
Like a bird from prison bars have flown
I'll fly away.

Just a few more weary days and then
I'll fly away
To a land where joys shall never end
I'll fly away.

Thomas Andrew Dorsey
"Take My Hand, Precious Lord"

Borrowing the tune of a nineteenth-century hymn, Thomas Andrew Dorsey wrote this gospel blues song after the unexpected deaths of his wife and newborn son in 1932. The song, translated into thirty-two languages and recorded by nearly every gospel singer, has become incredibly popular over the years. The fourteen-year-old Aretha Franklin recorded it in 1956 at her father's New Bethel Baptist Church in Detroit, and Mahalia Jackson sang it at the funeral of Martin Luther King, Jr. Dorsey, who died January 23, 1993, said of writing the inspirational song, "I became so lonely I did not feel that I could go on alone. I needed help; my friends and relations had done all they could for me. I was failing and did not see how I could live."

Precious Lord, take my hand, lead me on, let me stand
I am tired, I am weak, I am worn.
Through the storm, through the night, lead me on, to the light,
Take my hand, Precious Lord, lead me home.

When my way grows drear, Precious Lord, linger near,
When my life is almost gone,
Hear my cry, hear my call, Hold my hand lest I fall,
Take my hand, Precious Lord, lead me home.

A. P. Carter
"Can the Circle Be Unbroken?"

The Carter Family—originally A. P., Sara, and Maybelle—first began singing in the 1920s at gatherings at their home in the Clinch Mountains of Virginia. They performed and recorded energetically in the 1930s and 1940s, and became quite influential in country music. This song was first recorded by the Carter Family on May 6, 1935. Its chorus is borrowed from a gospel tune, and the tune is still widely sung.

I was standin' by the window
On one cold and cloudy day
When I saw the hearse come rolling
For to carry my mother away.

    Will the circle be unbroken, by and by, Lord, by and by?
    There's a better home a-waiting in the sky, Lord, in the sky.

Lord, I told the undertaker
"Undertaker, please drive slow
For this body you are hauling
Lord, I hate to see her go!"

I followed close behind her
Tried to hold up and be brave
But I could not hide my sorrow
When they laid her in the grave.

Went back home, Lord
My home was lonesome
All my brothers, sisters crying
What a home so sad and lone.

BILL MONROE

"Blue Moon of Kentucky"

Bill Monroe and his Blue Grass Boys performed a type of band music based on early fiddle-bands. The distinctive style became known as "bluegrass" in the late 1940s. "Blue Moon of Kentucky" was written in 1949: "Back in those days, it seems every trip we made was from Kentucky to Florida driving back and forth. I always thought about Kentucky, and I wanted to write a song about the moon we could always see over it. The best way to do this was to bring a girl into the song."

Blue moon of Kentucky, keep on shining
Shine on the one that's gone and left me blue
Blue moon of Kentucky, keep on shining
Shine on the one that's gone and left me blue
It was on one moonlight night
Stars shinin' bright
Whisper on high
Love said good-bye
Blue moon of Kentucky, keep on shining
Shine on the one that's gone and left me blue.

HANK WILLIAMS
"Jambalaya"

Hank Williams was born in Alabama in 1923, and learned about music from the Baptist church he attended and from a black street musician. His songs were so widely recorded that he really can be given credit for popularizing country music. "Jambalaya" is an infectiously fun song that nearly everyone recognizes.

Goodbye, Joe, me gotta go, me-oh, my-oh
Me gotta go pole the pirogue down the bayou
My Yvonne, the sweetest one, me-oh, my-oh
Son of a gun, we'll have big fun on the bayou.

Jambalaya and crawfish pie and filet gumbo
'Cause tonight I'm gonna see my ma chere amie-oh
Pick guitar, fill fruit jar and be gay-oh
Son of a gun, we'll have big fun on the bayou.

Thibadeaux, Fonteneaux, the place is buzzin'
Kinfolks come to see Yvonne by the dozen
Dress in style and go hog wild, me-oh, my-oh
Son of a gun, we'll have big fun on the bayou.

DORIS ULMANN. *Ainer Owensby, Gatlinburg, TN.* Undated. Photograph. Doris Ulmann Collection, #229, Special Collections, University of Oregon Library. *Doris Ulmann traveled through the Appalachian mountains in the late 1920s and early 1930s with folksong collector John Jacob Niles. Her soft, romantic portraits of the lives and arts of mountain people are in great contrast to the stark photographs made by the Farm Security Administration, suggesting that reality lies somewhere in between.*

THEODORE ROSENGARTEN

From *All God's Dangers: The Life of Nate Shaw*

Boll Weevil

Nate Shaw, whose real name was Ned Cobb, was in his mid-eighties in 1971 when he sat down in his tool shed with Theodore Rosengarten to tell the story of his humble yet remarkable life. Although illiterate, Shaw speaks eloquently about his life as a sharecropper in Alabama.

1923, I got what the boll weevil let me have—six bales. Boll weevil et up the best part of my crop. Didn't use no poison at that time, just pickin up squares. All you could do was keep them boll weevils from hatchin out and goin back up on that cotton. Couldn't kill em.

The boll weevil come into this country in the teens, between 1910 and 1912. Didn't know about a boll weevil when I was a boy comin up. They blowed in here from the western countries. People was bothered with the boll weevil way out there in the state of Texas and other states out there before we was here. And when the boll weevil hit this country, people was fully ignorant of their ways and what to do for em. Many white employers, when they discovered them boll weevils here, they'd tell their hands out on their plantations—some of em didn't have plantations, had land rented in their possession and put a farmin man out there; he was goin to gain that way by rentin land and puttin a man out there to work it; he goin to beat the nigger out of enough to more than pay the rent on it. And the white man didn't mind rentin land for a good farmer. That rent weren't enough to hurt him; he'd sub-rent it to the fellow that goin to work it or put him out there on halves. Didn't matter how a nigger workin a crop, if he worked it it's called his until it was picked out and ginned and then it was the white man's crop. Nigger delivered that cotton baled up to the white man—so they'd tell you, come out to the field to tell you or ask you when you'd go to the store, "How's your crop gettin along?" knowin the boll weevil's eatin away as he's talkin. Somebody totin news to him every day bout which of his farmers is picking up the squares and which ones aint.

"You seen any squares fallin on the ground?"

Sometimes you'd say, "Yes sir, my crop's losin squares."

He'd tell you what it was. Well, maybe you done found out. He'd tell you, "Pick them squares up off the ground, keep em picked up; boll weevil's in them squares. If you don't, I can't furnish you, if you aint goin to keep them squares up off the ground."

Boss man worryin bout his farmers heavy in debt, if he ever goin to see that money. Mr. Lemuel Tucker, when I was livin down there on Sitimachas Creek, he come to me, "You better pick them squares up, Nate, or you won't be able to pay me this year."

Don't he know I'm goin to fight the boll weevil? But fight him for my benefit. He goin to reap the reward of my labor too, but it aint for him that I'm laborin. All the time it's for myself. Any man under God's sun that's got anything industrious about him, you don't have to make him work—he goin to work. But Tucker didn't trust me to that. If a white man had anything booked against you, well, you could just expect him to ride up and hang around you to see that you worked, especially when the boll weevil come into this country. To a great extent, I was gived about as little trouble about such as that as any man. I didn't sit down and wait till the boss man seed my sorry acts in his field. I worked. I worked.

Me and my children picked up squares sometimes by the bucketsful. They'd go out to the field with little sacks or just anything to hold them squares and when they'd come in they'd have enough squares to fill up two baskets. I was industrious enough to do somethin about the boll weevil without bein driven to it. Picked up them squares and destroyed em, destroyed the weevil eggs. Sometimes, fool around there and see a old weevil himself.

WILLIAM H. JOHNSON. *Going to Market.* c. 1940. Oil on wood. 33 1/8 x 37 7/8 in. National Museum of American Art, Smithsonian Institution, Washington, DC. *Johnson, one of the leading African-American painters of the 1920s and 1930s, was quite versatile and mastered modern European styles, but he is usually remembered for his bold, painted commentaries on African-American life in the social realist style.*

I've gived my children many pennies and nickels for pickin up squares. But fact of the business, pickin up squares and burnin em—it weren't worth nothin. Boll weevil'd eat as much as he pleased. Consequently, they come to find out pickin up them squares weren't worth a dime. It was impossible to get all them squares and the ones you couldn't get was enough to ruin your crop. Say like today your cotton is illuminated with squares; come up a big rain maybe tonight, washin them squares out of the fields. Them boll weevils hatches in the woods, gets up and come right back to the field. You couldn't keep your fields clean—boll weevil schemin to eat your crop faster than you workin to get him out.

My daddy didn't know what a boll weevil was in his day. The boll weevil come in this country after I was grown and married and had three or four children. I was scared of him to an extent. I soon learnt he'd destroy a cotton crop. Yes, all God's dangers aint a white man. When the boll weevil starts in your cotton and go to depositin his eggs in them squares, that's when he'll kill you. Them eggs hatch out there in so many days, up come a young boll weevil. It don't take em but a short period of time to raise up enough out there in your field, in the spring after your cotton gets up—in a few days, one weevil's got a court of young uns hatchin. He goin to stay right in there till he's developed enough to come out of that little square, little pod; taint long, taint long, and when he comes out of there he cuts a little hole to come out. Pull the little leaves that's over that little square, pull em back out of the way and get to the natural little pod itself. Pull that pod open and there's a little boll weevil and he don't come out of there till he get developed, and then he do that hole cuttin. Cut a hole and come out of there, little sneakin devil, you look at him—he's a young fellow, looks green colored and sappy. Aint but a few days when he comes out of that square—aint but a few days stayin in there, and when he comes out of there—

I've pulled them squares open and caught em in all their stages of life: found the old egg in there, and I've found him just hatched out and he's right white like a worm, just a little spot in there, that's him; and if he's a little older he looks green-colored and sappy; and after he gets grown he's a old ashy-colored rascal, his wings is gray like ash. I've known him from the first to the last. I've picked him up and looked at him close. He's just a insect, but really, he's unusual to me. I can't thoroughly understand the nature of a boll weevil. He's a kind of insect that he'll develop in different colors right quick. He'll grow up to be, if he lives to get old enough—don't take him very long to get old—he'll grow to be as big around as a fly. He's a very short fellow, but he's bigger than a corn weevil. And he'll stick that bill in a cotton pod, then he'll shoot his tail back around there and deposit a egg—that's the way he runs his business. Then he done with that square, he done ruint it, and he hunts him another pod. And he's a very creepin fellow, he gets about, too; he'll ruin a stalk of cotton in a night's time. He crawls along gradually from one square to another; he gets on a limb where it's rolled off with blooms or young squares and he traces his way from one to the next, and he punctures every one of em just about, in a short while. Then he's creepin on, all over that stalk. Maybe he's so numerous sometime you can catch three or four, as high as half a dozen or more, that many off of one stalk of cotton.

If you meddle the boll weevil—you can see, travel amongst your cotton crop, I've done it myself, walked around amongst my cotton and looked, and you can see a boll weevil sometime stickin to a stalk and if you mess with him the least bit, he goin to fall off on the ground. And you watch him, just watch him, don't say a word. And he'll get up—he aint quick about it, but he'll get up from there and fly off, you lookin at him. Common sense teaches a man—how did he get in your cotton farm out there? He got wings, he flies. And you can get a handful of em in your hand, I have had that, and them scoundrels, if you don't bother em, they goin to eventually fly away from there.

When I seed I couldn't defeat the boll weevil by pickin up squares, I carried poison out to the field and took me a crocus sack, one of these thin crocus sacks, put my poison in there enough to poison maybe four or five rows and just walk, walk, walk; shake that sack over the cotton and when I'd look back, heaps of times, that dust flyin every whichway and the breeze blowin, that cotton would be white with dust, behind me. Get to the end, turn around and get right on the next row. Sometimes I'd just dust every other row and the dust would carry over the rows I passed. And I'd wear a mouth piece over my mouth—still that poison would get in my lungs and bother me. Now they got tractors fixed with boxes to elevate that poison out, carry poison four rows, six rows at one run.

Old weevil, he can't stand that, he goin to hit it out from there; maybe, in time, he'll take a notion to come back; you go out with your poison again. Sometimes, if the cotton's good and you keep him scared out of there and dusted out as much as you can, the boll, at that rate, gets too far advanced for him to handle it and that boll will open with healthy locks. But that's the only way to beat the devil, run him out the field.

ZORA NEALE HURSTON

From *Mules and Men*

"Formulae of Hoodoo Doctors"

Born in all-black Eatonville, Florida, Zora Neale Hurston (1903–1960) was educated at Howard University and Barnard College. At the suggestion of Franz Boas, the noted anthropologist, she studied African-American folklore in Florida and Louisiana, the result being Mules and Men, *published in 1935. Her work has preserved many aspects of black life that might have been lost, like these intriguing voodoo "receipts."*

ANNE GOLDTHWAITE. *Shoeing Mules in Alabama.* Mid-19th century. Oil on canvas. 25 ¹/₂ x 30 ¹/₂ in. Robert M. Hicklin, Jr. Inc., Spartanburg, SC. *Anne Goldthwaite was a leading supporter of women's rights as well as a leading Southern painter. One of her works was exhibited in the historic 1913 Armory Show.*

To Rent a House

Tie up some rice and sycamore bark in a small piece of goods. Tie six fig leaves and a piece of John de Conquer root in another piece. Cheesecloth is good. Boil both bundles in a quart of water at the same time. Strain it out. Now sprinkle the rice and sycamore bark mixed together in front of the house. Put the fig leaves and John de Conquer root in a corner of the house and scrub the house with the water they were boiled in. Mix it with a pail of scrub water.

For Bad Work — (Death)

Take a coconut that has three eyes. Take the name of the person you want to get rid of and write it on the paper like a coffin. (Put the name all over the coffin.) Put this down in the nut. (Pour out water.) Put beef gall and vinegar in the nut and the person's name all around the coconut. Stand nut up in sand and set one black candle on top of it. Number the days from one to fifteen days. Every day mark that coconut at twelve o'clock A.M. or P.M., and by the fifteenth day they will be gone. Never let the candle go out. You must light the new candle and set it on top of the old stub which has burnt down to a wafer.

Court Scrapes

a. Take the names of all the *good* witnesses (for your client), the judge and your client's lawyer. Put the names in a dish and pour sweet oil on them and burn a white candle each morning beside it for one hour, from nine to ten. The day of the trial when you put it upon the altar, don't take it down until the trial is over.

b. Take the names of the opponent of your client, his witnesses and his lawyer. Take all of their names on one piece of paper. Put it between two whole bricks. Put the top brick crossways. On the day of the trial set a bucket or dishpan on top of the bricks with ice in it. That's to freeze them out so they can't talk.

c. Take the names of your client's lawyer, witnesses and lawyer on paper. Buy a beef tongue and split it from the base towards the tip, thus separating top from bottom. Put the paper with names in the split tongue along with eighteen pods of hot pepper and pin it through and through with pins and needles. Put it in a tin pail with plenty of vinegar and keep it on ice until the day of court. That day, pour kerosene in the bucket and burn it, and they will destroy themselves in court.

d. Put the names of the judge and all those *for* your client on paper. Take the names of the twelve apostles after Judas hung himself and write each apostle's name on a sage leaf. Take six candles and burn them standing in holy water. Have your client wear six of the sage leaves in each shoe and the jury will be made for him.

e. Write all the enemies' names on paper. Put them in a can. Then take soot and ashes from the chimney of your client and mix it with salt. Stick pins crosswise in the candles and burn them at a good hour. Put some ice in a bucket and set the can in it. Let your client recite the One Hundred Twentieth Psalm before Court and in Court.

f. To let John the conqueror win your case; take one-half pint whiskey, nine pieces of John the Conqueror Root one inch long. Let it soak thirty-eight hours till all the strength is out. (Gather all roots before September 21.) Shake up good and drain off roots in another bottle. Get one ounce of white rose or Jockey Club perfume and pour into the mixture. Dress your client with this before going to Court.

To Kill and Harm

Get bad vinegar, beef gall, filet gumbo with red pepper, and put names written across each other in bottles. Shake the bottle for nine mornings and talk and tell it what you want it to do. To kill the victim, turn it upside down and bury it breast deep, and he will die.

Running Feet

To give anyone the running feet: Take sand out of one of his tracks and mix the sand with red pepper; throw some into a running stream of water and this will cause the person to run from place to place, until finally he runs himself to death.

To Make a Man Come Home

Take nine deep red or pink candles. Write his name three times on each candle. Wash the candles with Van-Van. Put the name three times on paper and place under the candles, and call the name of the party three times as the candle is placed at the hours of seven, nine or eleven.

To Make People Love You

Take nine lumps of starch, nine of sugar, nine teaspoons of steel dust. Wet it all with Jockey Club cologne. Take nine pieces of ribbon, blue, red or yellow. Take a dessertspoonful and put it on a piece of ribbon and tie it in a bag. As each fold is gathered together call his name. As you wrap it with yellow thread call his name till you finish. Make nine bags and place them under a rug, behind an armoire, under a step or over a door. They will love you and give you everything they can get. Distance makes no difference. Your mind is talking to his mind and nothing beats that.

To Break Up a Love Affair

Take nine needles, break each needle in three pieces. Write each person's name three times on paper. Write one name backwards and one forwards and lay the broken needles on the paper. Take five black candles, four red and three green.

Tie a string across the door from it, suspend a large candle upside down. It will hang low on the door; burn one each day for one hour. If you burn your first in the daytime, keep on in the day; if at night, continue at night. A tin plate with paper and needles in it must be placed to catch wax in.

When the ninth day is finished, go out into the street and get some white or black dog dung. A dog only drops his dung in the street when he is running and barking, and whoever you curse will run and bark likewise. Put it in a bag with the paper and carry it to running water, and one of the parties will leave town.

Doris Ulmann. *Mr. Cheevers, potter, and children, Cleveland, and Georgia.* c. 1933. Photograph. Special Collections, University of Oregon Library. *Cheevers Meaders was a second generation potter in a well-known pottery-making family in Mossy Creek, Georgia. His son, Lanier, continues the tradition, and received a National Heritage Fellowship in 1983.*

James Agee and Walker Evans

From *Let Us Now Praise Famous Men*

"Overalls"

Assigned by Fortune *magazine to write a series of articles about Southern tenant farmers, James Agee went to Hale County, Alabama, to live with three families for six weeks. Agee was accompanied by the photographer Walker Evans. Fortune* rejected their work, but it was *published as a book in 1941. What Agee and Evans had created was a poetic work that was documentary without being exploitative or sentimental and that revealed the life of the working men in great detail and with compassion and respect.*

They are pronounced overhauls.

Try—I cannot write of it here—to imagine and to know, as against other garments, the difference of their feeling against your body; drawn-on, and bibbed on the whole belly and chest, naked from the kidneys up behind, save for broad crossed straps, and slung by these straps from the shoulders; the slanted pockets on each thigh, the deep square pockets on each buttock; the complex and slanted structures, on the chest, of the pockets shaped for pencils, rulers, and watches; the coldness of sweat when they are young, and their stiffness; their sweetness to the skin and pleasure of sweating when they are old; the thin metal buttons of the fly; the lifting aside of the straps and the deep slipping downward in defecation; the belt some men use with them to steady their middles; the swift, simple, and inevitably supine gestures of dressing and of undressing, which, as is less true of any other garment, are those of harnessing and of unharnessing the shoulders of a tired and hard-used animal.

They are round as stovepipes in the legs (though some wives, told to, crease them).

In the strapping across the kidneys they again resemble work harness, and in their crossed straps and tin buttons.

And in the functional pocketing of their bib, a harness modified to the convenience of a used animal of such high intelligence that he has use for tools.

And in their whole stature: full covering of the cloven strength of the legs and thighs and of the loins; then nakedness and harnessing behind, naked along the flanks; and in front, the short, squarely tapered, powerful towers of the belly and chest to above the nipples.

And on this façade, the cloven halls for the legs, the strong-seamed, structured opening for the genitals, the broad horizontal at the waist, the slant thigh pockets, the buttons at the point of each hip and on the breast, the geometric structures of the usages of the simpler trades—the complexed seams of utilitarian pockets which are so brightly picked out against darkness when the seam-threadings, double and triple stitched, are still white, so that a new suit of overalls has among its beauties those of a blueprint: and they are a map of a working man.

THE MODERN SOUTH

HENRY WOODFIN GRADY

From "The New South"

Henry Woodfin Grady, managing editor of the Atlanta Constitution *in the 1880s, was the leading proponent behind the idea of a New South that would rise phoenix-like, overcoming sectional hostilities and racial problems. Grady made many emotional speeches like this one, given December 21, 1886 at the New England Club banquet in New York, boasting of the South's abundant natural resources and cooperative spirit, and hoping to attract Northern industry to the then destitute region.*

Let me picture to you the footsore Confederate soldier, as buttoning up in his faded gray jacket the parole which was to bear testimony to his children of his fidelity and faith, he turned his face southward from Appomattox in April, 1865. Think of him as ragged, half-starved, heavy-hearted, enfeebled by want and wounds, having fought to exhaustion, he surrenders his gun, wrings the hands of his comrades in silence, and lifting his tear-stained and pallid face for the last time to the graves that dot old Virginia hills, pulls his gray cap over his brow and begins the slow and painful journey.

What does he find—let me ask you who went to your homes eager to find, in the welcome you had justly earned, full payment for four years' sacrifice—what does he find when, having followed the battle-stained cross against overwhelming odds, dreading death not half so much as surrender, he reaches the home he left so prosperous and beautiful? He finds his house in

HENRY AMES BLOOD.
*Office of Daniel Pratt's
Cotton Gin Factory.*
Prattville, Alabama.
c. 1838–1850. Engraving.

ruins, his farm devastated, his slaves free, his stock killed, his barns empty, his trade destroyed, his money worthless, his social system, feudal in its magnificence, swept away; his people without law or legal status; his comrades slain, and the burdens of others heavy on his shoulders. Crushed by defeat, his very traditions are gone. Without money, credit, employment, material, or training; and beside all this, confronted with the gravest problem that ever met human intelligence—the establishment of a status for the vast body of his liberated slaves.

What does he do—this hero in gray with a heart of gold? Does he sit down in sullenness and despair? Not for a day. Surely God, who had stripped him of his prosperity, inspired him in his adversity. As ruin was never before so overwhelming, never was restoration swifter.

The soldier stepped from the trenches into the furrow; horses that had charged Federal guns marched before the plow, and fields that ran red with human blood in April were green with the harvest in June; women reared in luxury cut up their dresses and made breeches for their husbands, and, with a patience and heroism that fit women always as a garment, gave their hands to work. There was little bitterness in all this. Cheerfulness and frankness prevailed. "Bill Arp" struck the key-note when he said: "Well, I killed as many of them as they did of me, and now I'm going to work." So did the soldier returning home after defeat and roasting some corn on the roadside who made the remark to his comrades: "You may leave the South if you want to, but I'm going to Sandersville, kiss my wife and raise a crop, and if the Yankees fool with me any more, I'll whip 'em again."

I want to say to General Sherman, who is considered an able man in our parts, though some people think he is a kind of careless man about fire, that from the ashes he left us in 1864 we have raised a brave and beautiful city; that somehow or other we have caught the sunshine in the bricks and mortar of our homes, and have builded therein not one ignoble prejudice or memory.

But what is the sum of our work? We have found out that in the summing up the free negro counts more than he did as a slave. We have planted the schoolhouse on the hilltop and made it free to white and black. We have sowed towns and cities in the place of theories, and put business above politics. We have challenged your spinners in Massachusetts and your ironmakers in Pennsylvania. We have learned that the $400,000,000 annually received from our cotton crop will make us rich when the supplies that make it are home-raised. We have reduced the commercial rate of interest from 24 to 6 per cent., and are floating 4 per cent. bonds. We have learned that one Northern immigrant is worth fifty foreigners and have smoothed the path to Southward, wiped out the place where Mason and Dixon's line used to be, and hung out the latchstring to you and yours.

We have reached the point that marks perfect harmony in every household, when the husband confesses that the pies which his wife cooks are as good as those his mother used to bake; and we admit that the sun shines as brightly and the moon as softly as it did before the war. We have established thrift in city and country. We have fallen in love with work. We have restored comfort to homes from which culture and elegance never departed. We have let economy take root and spread among us as rank as the crab-grass which sprung from Sherman's cavalry camps, until we are ready to lay odds on the Georgia Yankee as he manufactures relics of the battlefield in a one-story shanty and squeezes pure olive-oil out of his cottonseed, against any down-easter that ever swapped wooden nutmegs for flannel sausage in the valleys of Vermont. Above all, we know that we have achieved in these "piping times of peace" a fuller independence for the South than that which our fathers sought to win in the forum by their eloquence or compel in the field by their swords.

It is a rare privilege, sir, to have had part, however humble, in this work. Never was nobler duty confided to human hands than the uplifting and upbuilding of the prostrate and bleeding South—misguided, perhaps, but beautiful in her suffering, and honest, brave, and generous always. In the record of her social, industrial, and political illustration we await with confidence the verdict of the world.

* * *

The old South rested everything on slavery and agriculture, unconscious that these could neither give nor maintain healthy growth. The new South presents a perfect democracy, the oligarchs leading in the popular movement—a social system compact and closely knitted, less splendid on the surface, but stronger at the core—a hundred farms for every plantation, fifty homes for every palace—and a diversified industry that meets the complex needs of this complex age.

The new South is enamored of her new work. Her soul is stirred with the breath of a new life. The light of a grander day is falling fair on her face. She is thrilling with the consciousness of growing power and prosperity. As she stands upright, full-statured and equal among the people of the earth, breathing the keen air and looking out upon the expanded horizon, she understands that her emancipation came because through the inscrutable wisdom of God her honest purpose was crossed, and her brave armies were beaten.

ANDREW NELSON LYTLE

From "The Hind Tit"

Tennessean Andrew Lytle, a novelist and critic, was at the heart of the Fugitives, a scholarly group centered at Vanderbilt University that sought to reconcile modernism with a Southern sensibility in art and literature. In 1930, Lytle and eleven other like-minded Southerners (Lytle was the only member who actually farmed) came together in a symposium which then launched the Agrarian movement, calling for Southerners to reject industrialization and to cling to their folk heritage and to the land. The following essay was included in the Agrarian manifesto, I'll Take My Stand.

<hr />

The Agrarian South, therefore, whose culture was impoverished but not destroyed by the war and its aftermath, should dread industrialism like a pizen snake. For the South long since finished its pioneering. It can only do violence to its provincial life when it allows itself to be forced into the aggressive state of mind of an earlier period. To such an end does bookkeeping lead. It is the numbering of a farm's resources—its stacks of fodder, bushels of corn, bales of cotton, its stock and implements, and the hundreds of things which make up its economy. And as the only reason to number them is to turn them into cash—that is, into weapons for warfare—the agrarian South is bound to go when the first page is turned and the first mark crosses the ledger.

The good-road programs drive like a flying wedge and split the heart of this provincialism—which prefers religion to science, handcrafts to technology, the inertia of the fields to the acceleration of industry, and leisure to nervous prostration. Like most demagoguery, it has been advertised as a great benefit to the farmer. Let us see just what the roads have done and who they benefit? They certainly can be of no use to the farmer who cannot afford to buy a truck. He finds them a decided drawback. The heavy automobile traffic makes it hazardous for him even to appear on the main highways. But if he has the temerity to try them, they prove most unsatisfactory. Besides being a shock to his mules' feet, it is difficult for the team to stand up on the road's hard, slick surface.

The large farmers and planting corporations who can afford to buy trucks are able to carry their produce to market with less wear and tear than if they drove over rougher dirt pikes. But this is a dubious benefit, for the question is not between trucks on good or bad roads, but between teams on passable roads and trucks on arterial highways.

But in any case the farmer receives few direct profits. Asphalt companies, motor-car companies, oil and cement companies, engineers, contractors, bus lines, truck lines, and politicians—not the farmer—receive the great benefits and the profits from good roads. But the farmer pays the bills. The states and counties float bonds and attend to the upkeep on the highways and byways, and when these states are predominantly agricultural, it is the people living on the land who mortgage their labor and the security of their property so that these super-corporations may increase incomes which are now so large that they must organize foundations to give them away.

But the great drain comes after the roads are built. Automobile salesmen, radio salesmen, and every other kind of salesman descends to take away the farmer's money. The railroad had no such universal sweep into a family's privacy. It was confined to a certain track and was constrained by its organization within boundaries which were rigid enough to become absorbed, rather than absorb. But good roads brought the motor-car and made of every individual an engineer or conductor, requiring a constant, and in some instances a daily, need for cash. The psychological pressure of such things, and mounting taxes, induce the farmer to forsake old ways and buy a ledger.

The great drain continues. The first thing he does is to trade his mules for a tractor. He has had to add a cash payment to boot, but that seems reasonable. He forgets, however, that a piece of machinery, like his mules, must wear out and be replaced; but the tractor cannot reproduce

LEWIS HINE. *Cotton Mill. North Carolina.* 1909. Photograph. George Eastman House. *In the early twentieth century, Lewis Hine traveled throughout the South documenting child abuses for the National Child Labor Committee.*

itself. He must lay aside a large sum of money against the day of replacement, whereas formerly he had only to send his brood mare to some jack for service.

The next thing it does, it throws his boys out of a job, with the possible exception of one who will remain and run it. This begins the home-breaking. Time is money now, not property, and the boys can't hang about the place draining it of its substance, even if they are willing to. They must go out somewhere and get a job. If they are lucky, some filling station will let them sell gas, or some garage teach them a mechanic's job. But the time is coming when these places will have a surfeit of farmer boys.

He next buys a truck. The gals wanted a car, but he was obdurate on that point, so he lost them. They went to town to visit kin, then gradually drifted there to marry or get a job. The time comes when the old woman succumbs to high-pressure sales talk and forces him to buy a car on the installment plan. By that time he is so far gone that one thing more seems no great matter.

He then has three vehicles which must be fed from the oil companies, several notes at the bank bearing interest, and payments, as regular as clock strokes, to be made on the car.

He finds his payment for gasoline, motor oil, and power for his tractor is tremendously higher than the few cents coal oil used to cost him. Formerly he bought it by the lampful; he now buys it by the barrelful. In fact, he no longer uses coal oil for lighting. He has installed a Delco-plant. Besides giving illumination it pumps his water, turns the churn, washes the clothes, heats the iron to press them, and cooks the victuals. If his daughters had not already moved away, he would have had to send them, for Delco has taken their place in the rural economy. The farmer's wife now becomes a drudge. As the mainstay of the structure she was content to bear the greatest burden, but now she grows restive. She has changed from a creator in a fixed culture to an assistant to machines. Her condition is miserable because her burdens are almost as great without the compensation of the highest place in the old scheme. Her services cannot be recompensed with gold, and gold has become the only currency.

* * *

When the farmer, realizing where all this is leading him, makes the attempt to find his ancient bearings, he discovers his provincialism rapidly disintegrating. The Sacred Harp gatherings, and to a less extent the political picnics and barbecues, have so far withstood the onslaught; but the country church languishes, the square dance disappears, and camp meetings are held, but they have lost their vitality. Self-consciousness has crept into the meetings, inhibiting the brothers and sisters and stifling in their bosoms the desire to shout. When shouting ceases and the mourner's bench is filled up by the curious from the rear, the camp meeting may count its days, for they are numbered.

He finds that there is a vast propaganda teaching him, but particularly his children, to despise the life he has led and would like to lead again. It has in its organization public schools, high schools, the normals, and even the most reputable universities, the press, salesmen, and all the agents of industrialism. It has set out to uplift him. It tells him that his ancestors were not cultured because they did not appreciate the fine arts; that they were illiterate because their speech was Old English; and that the South will now come to glory, to "cultural" glory, by a denial of its ancestry.

* * *

To avoid the dire consequences and to maintain a farming life in an industrial imperialism, there seems to be only one thing left for the farmer to do, and particularly for the small farmer. Until he and the agrarian West and all the conservative communities throughout the United States can unite on some common political action, he must deny himself the articles the industrialists offer for sale. It is not so impossible as it may seem at first, for, after all, the necessities they machine-facture were once manufactured on the land, and as for the bric-à-brac, let it rot on their hands. Do what we did after the war and the Reconstruction: return to our looms, our handcrafts, our reproducing stock. Throw out the radio and take down the fiddle from the wall. Forsake the movies for the play-parties and the square dances. And turn away from the liberal capons who fill the pulpits as preachers. Seek a priesthood that may manifest the will and intelligence to renounce science and search out the Word in the authorities.

COLORPLATE 67

LULU SAXON. *Uptown Street.* 1890. Oil on canvas. 90 x 68 in. Roger Houston Ogden Collection, New Orleans.

COLORPLATE 68

ELLSWORTH WOODWARD. *Wild Iris.* 1908. New Orleans Museum of Art. Bequest of Miss Lena Little, New Orleans. *Ellsworth Woodward and his brother William helped to establish the Newcomb Pottery, the Southern States Art League, and what is now the New Orleans Museum of Art, making New Orleans the art center of the South early in this century. Ellsworth Woodward's love of nature and the Louisiana landscape is reflected in this beautiful watercolor.*

COLORPLATE 69

PAUL POINCY. *Still Life with Radishes.* 1906. Oil on canvas. 8 9/16 x 11 5/8 in. The Historic New Orleans Collection, New Orleans, acc. no. 1966.9. *Paul Poincy, born in New Orleans of French parents, studied at the École des Beaux Arts in Paris, where he must have also been exposed to impressionism as the realistic subject matter and soft, indistinct areas of color in this painting reveal.*

COLORPLATE 70

Harry Nolan. *Royal Street Antique Shop.* c. 1918. Oil on fabric. 20 ¹/₂ x 26 in. Roger Houston Ogden Collection, New Orleans.

COLORPLATE 71 (opposite)

Karl Gerhardt. *624 Orleans Alley, Rear.* c. 1915. Oil on board. 13 ¹/₄ x 9 ¹/₂ in. Roger Houston Ogden Collection, New Orleans.

COLORPLATE 72

FRANK HENRY SHAPLEIGH. *In Charlotte Street, St. Augustine, Florida.* 1891. Oil on Academy Board. 7 ³/₄ x 12 ¹/₂ in.
Roger Houston Ogden Collection, New Orleans.

COLORPLATE 73

CLARENCE MILLET (1897–1959). *Melon Boats, New Orleans.* 1928. Oil on canvas. 25 x 30 in. Roger Houston Ogden Collection, New Orleans. *Louisianan Clarence Millet was one of a handful of Southern artists elected to the National Academy of Design. This painting captures the quaint, European charm of the docks and markets of New Orleans.*

COLORPLATE 74

Harold Harrington Betts (b. 1881). *On the Levee at Natchez.* 1904. Oil on canvas. 44 x 43 in. Roger Houston Ogden Collection, New Orleans.

WILLIAM ALEXANDER PERCY

From *Lanterns on the Levee*
"The Flood of 1927"

About his uncle Will, Walker Percy said, "He was the most extraordinary man I have ever known." Lanterns on the Levee: Recollections of a Planter's Son *has become a classic memoir. This excerpt describes the catastrophic flood of 1927 in Mississippi and Louisiana.*

The 1927 flood was a torrent ten feet deep the size of Rhode Island; it was thirty-six hours coming and four months going; it was deep enough to drown a man, swift enough to upset a boat, and lasting enough to cancel a crop year. The only islands in it were eight or ten tiny Indian mounds and the narrow spoil-banks of a few drainage canals. Between the torrent and the river ran the levee, dry on the land side and on the top. The south Delta became seventy-five hundred square miles of mill-race in which one hundred and twenty thousand human beings and one hundred thousand animals squirmed and bobbed.

In the thirty-six hours which the river required after its victory at Scott to submerge the country, panicky people poured out of Greenville by the last trains and by automobiles over roads axle-deep in water. These were mostly frantic mothers with their children, non-residents from the hills who regarded the river hysterically and not devotedly, and the usual run of rabbit folk who absent themselves in every emergency. During the same hours of grace panicky people poured into Greenville. These were mostly Negroes in dilapidated Fords, on the running-boards of trucks, or afoot carrying babies, leading children, and pulling cows, who are always at their worst in crises. Outside of town stock was being rushed cross-country to the levee, and Negroes were being piled into lofts, gins, and compresses by plantation managers. For thirty-

JOHN MCCRADY.
Mississippi Family. 1946.
Lithograph on paper.
8 7/8 x 12 3/4 in. Roger
Houston Ogden
Collection, New Orleans.

six hours the Delta was in turmoil, in movement, in terror. Then the waters covered everything, the turmoil ceased, and a great quiet settled down; the stock which had not reached the levee had been drowned; the owners of second-story houses with their pantries and kitchens had moved upstairs; those in one-story houses had taken to the roofs and the trees. Over everything was silence, deadlier because of the strange cold sound of the currents gnawing at foundations, hissing against walls, creaming and clawing over obstructions.

When at midnight the siren of the fire department by a long maniac scream announced to the sleepless town that the water had crowded over the town's own small protection levee, we knew the last haven of refuge had been lost. In each home the haggard family did its hysterical best to save itself and to provide for the morrow. Outside on the sidewalks you heard people running, not crying out or calling to one another, but running madly and silently to get to safety or to their loved ones. It was a sound that made you want to cry.

At home Mother, Father, and I had been waiting for that signal, like zero made audible. When it came we telephoned a few friends and then half-heartedly began dragging upstairs such furniture as we could manage and Father filled the bathtubs with water. No one knew how high the flood would rise. By breakfast time it had still not entered our neighborhood. We stood on the gallery and watched and waited. Then up the gutter of Percy Street we saw it gliding, like a wavering brown snake. It was swift and it made toward the river. It spread over a low place in the yard and covered Mother's blue larkspur. We said nothing but suddenly Mother called the terrified little Negro chauffeur and jumped into the car. She had forgotten to buy an oil stove. Our protests were useless. She was in one of those intrepid moods when Frenchwomen had best not be crossed. Up the street a truck-driver was abandoning his truck and splashing wildly home through the water. It was three months before we saw it again. When Mother and the car reappeared, it was between two flanges of spray and hub-deep. Father looked somberly over the drowning town. I think he was realizing it was the last fight he would make for his people. He was sixty-seven and though unravaged by age he was tired. But he only said: "Guess you'd better go while you can. I'll be along." I waded to relief headquarters.

Our kindly old Mayor had appointed me chairman of the Flood Relief Committee and the local Red Cross. I found myself charged with the rescuing, housing, and feeding of sixty thousand human beings and thirty thousand head of stock. To assist me in the task I had a fine committee and Father's blessing, but no money, no boats, no tents, no food. That first morning when the water reached Greenville we of the committee traipsed through the mounting flood to the poker-rooms of the Knights of Columbus, hung out a sign labeled "Relief Headquarters," installed a telephone, and called on the Lord. That calling on the Lord was a good idea, for our first job was to get people out of trees and off of roofs, which, in addition to good will and heroism, of which we had plenty, required motor boats, of which we had none. We were desperate, but the Lord, overlooking our lack of faith, performed one of His witty, whimsical miracles: out of the White River poured a daring fleet of motor boats—the bootleggers! They shot the rapids of the break and scattered into the interior. No one had sent for them, no one was paying them, no one had a good word for them—but they came. Competent, devil-may-care pariahs, they scoured the back areas, the forgotten places, across fences, over railroad embankments, through woods and brush, and never rested until there was no one left clinging to a roof or a raft or the crotch of a tree.

THOMAS WOLFE

From *Look Homeward, Angel*

Thomas Wolfe (1900–1938) used his native Asheville, North Carolina, as the setting for much of his writing. In Look Homeward, Angel *(1929), we view the world through the eyes of Eugene Gant, a young man trying to make sense of both the mountain life and the modern world that surround him. This passage is typical of Wolfe's wordy and sensuously lyrical style.*

Thus, pent in his dark soul, Eugene sat brooding on a fire-lit book, a stranger in a noisy inn. The gates of his life were closing him in from their knowledge, a vast aerial world of phantasy was erecting its fuming and insubstantial fabric. He steeped his soul in streaming imagery, rifling the book-shelves for pictures and finding there such treasures as *With Stanley in Africa,* rich in the mystery of the jungle, alive with combat, black battle, the hurled spear, vast snake-rooted forests, thatched villages, gold and ivory; or Stoddard's *Lectures,* on whose slick heavy pages were stamped the most-visited scenes of Europe and Asia; a Book of Wonder, with enchanting drawings of all the marvels of the age—Santos Dumont in his balloon, liquid air poured from a kettle, all the navies of the earth lifted two feet from the water by an ounce of radium (Sir William Crookes), the building of the Eiffel Tower, the Flatiron Building, the stick-steered automobile, the submarine. After the earthquake in San Francisco there was a book describing it, its cheap green cover lurid with crumbling towers, shaken spires, toppling many-storied houses plunging into the splitting flame-jawed earth. And there was another called *Palaces of Sin,* or *The Devil in Society,* purporting to be the work of a pious millionaire, who had drained his vast fortune in exposing the painted sores that blemish the spotless-seeming hide of great position, and there were enticing pictures showing the author walking in a silk hat down a street full of magnificent palaces of sin.

HOBSON PITTMAN. *Warm Evening.* Undated. Watercolor on paper. Approximately 17 x 23 in. The Phillips Collection, Washington, DC. *Hobson Pittman left North Carolina as a young man, but continued to paint Southern scenes and themes with stage-like settings and a dreamy, nostalgic air.*

Out of this strange jumbled gallery of pictures the pieced-out world was expanding under the brooding power of his imagination: the lost dark angels of the Doré "Milton" swooped into cavernous Hell beyond this upper earth of soaring or toppling spires, machine wonder, maced and mailed romance. And, as he thought of his future liberation into this epic world, where all the color of life blazed brightest far away from home, his heart flooded his face with lakes of blood.

He had heard already the ringing of remote church bells over a countryside on Sunday night; had listened to the earth steeped in the brooding symphony of dark, and the million-noted little night things; and he had heard thus the far retreating wail of a whistle in a distant valley, and faint thunder on the rails; and he felt the infinite depth and width of the golden world in the brief seductions of a thousand multiplex and mixed mysterious odors and sensations, weaving, with a blinding interplay and aural explosions, one into the other.

He remembered yet the East India Tea House at the Fair, the sandalwood, the turbans, and the robes, the cool interior and the smell of India tea; and he had felt now the nostalgic thrill of dew-wet mornings in Spring, the cherry scent, the cool clarion earth, the wet loaminess of the garden, the pungent breakfast smells and the floating snow of blossoms. He knew the inchoate sharp excitement of hot dandelions in young Spring grass at noon; the smell of cellars, cobwebs, and built-on secret earth; in July, of watermelons bedded in sweet hay, inside a farmer's covered wagon; of cantaloupe and crated peaches; and the scent of orange rind, bitter-sweet, before a fire of coals. He knew the good male smell of his father's sitting-room; of the smooth worn leather sofa, with the gaping horse-hair rent; of the blistered varnished wood upon the hearth; of the heated calf-skin bindings; of the flat moist plug of apple tobacco, stuck with a red flag; of wood-smoke and burnt leaves in October; of the brown tired autumn earth; of honey-suckle at night; of warm nasturtiums; of a clean ruddy farmer who comes weekly with printed butter, eggs and milk; of fat limp underdone bacon and of coffee; of a bakery-oven in the wind; of large deep-hued string beans smoking-hot and seasoned well with salt and butter; of a room of old pine boards in which books and carpets have been stored, long closed; of Concord grapes in their long white baskets.

Yes, and the exciting smell of chalk and varnished desks; the smell of heavy bread-sandwiches of cold fried meat and butter; the smell of new leather in a saddler's shop, or of a warm leather chair; of honey and of unground coffee; of barrelled sweet-pickles and cheese and all the fragrant compost of the grocer's; the smell of stored apples in the cellar, and of orchard-apple smells, of pressed-cider pulp; of pears ripening on a sunny shelf, and of ripe cherries stewing with sugar on hot stoves before preserving; the smell of whittled wood, of all young lumber, of sawdust and shavings; of peaches stuck with cloves and pickled in brandy; of pine-sap, and green pine-needles; of a horse's pared hoof; of chestnuts roasting, of bowls of nuts and raisins; of hot cracklin, and of young roast pork; of butter and cinnamon melting on hot candied yams.

Yes, and of the rank slow river, and of tomatoes rotten on the vine; the smell of rain-wet plums and boiling quinces; of rotten lily-pads; and of foul weeds rotting in green marsh scum; and the exquisite smell of the South, clean but funky, like a big woman; of soaking trees and the earth after heavy rain.

Yes, and the smell of hot daisy-fields in the morning; of melted puddling-iron in a foundry; the winter smell of horse-warm stables and smoking dung; of old oak and walnut; and the butcher's smell of meat, of strong slaughtered lamb, plump gouty liver, ground pasty sausages, and red beef; and of brown sugar melted with slivered bitter chocolate; and of crushed mint leaves, and of a wet lilac bush; of magnolia beneath the heavy moon, of dogwood and laurel; of an old caked pipe and Bourbon rye, aged in kegs of charred oak; the sharp smell of tobacco; of carbolic and nitric acids; the coarse true smell of a dog; of old imprisoned books; and the cool fern-smell near springs; of vanilla in cake-dough; and of cloven ponderous cheeses.

Yes, and of a hardware store, but mostly the good smell of nails; of the developing chemicals in a photographer's dark-room; and the young-life smell of paint and turpentine; of buckwheat batter and black sorghum; and of a negro and his horse, together; of boiling fudge; the brine smell of pickling vats; and the lush undergrowth smell of southern hills; of a slimy oyster-can, of chilled gutted fish; of a hot kitchen negress; of kerosene and linoleum; of sarsaparilla and guavas; and of ripe autumn persimmons; and the smell of the wind and the rain; and of the acrid thunder; of cold starlight, and the brittle-bladed frozen grass; of fog and the misted winter sun; of seed-time, bloom, and mellow dropping harvest.

And now, whetted intemperately by what he had felt, he began, at school, in that fecund romance, the geography, to breathe the mixed odors of the earth, sensing in every squat keg piled on a pier-head a treasure of golden rum, rich port, fat Burgundy; smelling the jungle growth of the tropics, the heavy odor of plantations, the salt-fish smell of harbors, voyaging in the vast, enchanting, but unperplexing world.

ALLEN TATE
"The Trout Map"

Allen Tate (1899–1979) was another member of the Vanderbilt Fugitive group and later of the Agrarians. A distinguished poet, critic, editor, and teacher with an international reputation, Tate has received many honors, among them the first Consultant in Poetry position at the Library of Congress and the Bollingen Prize for Poetry. In this poem we see Tate's mistrust of and disparaging resignation to a modern world dominated by technology and bureaucracy.

The Management Area of Cherokee
National Forest, interested in fish,
Has mapped Tellico and Bald Rivers
And North River, with the tributaries
Brookshire Branch and Sugar Cove Creek:
A fishy map for facile fishery

In Marvel's kind Ocean: drawn in two
Colors, blue and red—blue for the hue
Of Europe (Tennessee water is green),
Red lines by blue streams to warn
The fancy-fishmen from protected fish;
Black borders hold the Area in a cracked dish,

While other blacks, the dots and dashes, wire
The fisher's will through classic laurel
Over boar tracks to creamy pot-holes lying
Under Bald falls that thump the shying
Trout: we flew Professor, the Hackles and Worms.
(Tom Bagley and I were dotted and dashed wills.)

Up Green Cove gap from Preacher Millsap's cabin
We walked a confident hour of victory,
Sloped to the west on a trail that led us
To Bald River where map and scene were one
In seen-identity. Eight trout is the story
In three miles. We came to a rock-bridge

On which the road went left around a hill,
The river, right, tumbled into a cove;
But the map dashed the road along the stream
And we dotted man's fishiest enthymeme
With jellied feet upon understanding love
Of what eyes see not, that nourishes the will:

We were fishers, weren't we? And tried to fish
The egoed belly's dry cartograph—
Which made the government fish lie down and laugh.
(Tommy and I listened, we heard them shake
Mountain and cove because the map was fake.)
After eighteen miles our feet were clownish,

Then darkness took us into wheezing straits
Where coarse Magellan idling with his fates
Ran with the gulls for map around the Horn,
Or wheresoever the mind with tidy scorn
Revisits the world upon a dry sunbeam.
Now mapless the mountains were a dream.

WILLIAM FAULKNER

From *Absalom, Absalom!*

William Faulkner, born in New Albany, Mississippi in 1897, won the Nobel Prize in literature in 1949. Absalom, Absalom!, published in 1936, tells the story of the rise and fall of Thomas Sutpen and perhaps of the South itself. In this excerpt, Quentin Compson has been summoned by Miss Rosa Coldfield, who wants to relate her version of the Sutpen story before Quentin leaves for Harvard. Faulkner believed Absalom, Absalom! *was "the best novel yet written by an American," and many readers would still agree.*

From a little after two oclock until almost sundown of the long still hot weary dead September afternoon they sat in what Miss Coldfield still called the office because her father had called it that—a dim hot airless room with the blinds all closed and fastened for forty-three summers because when she was a girl someone had believed that light and moving air carried heat and that dark was always cooler, and which (as the sun shone fuller and fuller on that side of the house) became latticed with yellow slashes full of dust motes which Quentin thought of as being flecks of the dead old dried paint itself blown inward from the scaling blinds as wind might have blown them. There was a wistaria vine blooming for the second time that summer on a wooden trellis before one window, into which sparrows came now and then in random gusts, making a dry vivid dusty sound before going away: and opposite Quentin, Miss Coldfield in the eternal black which she had worn for forty-three years now, whether for sister, father, or nothusband none knew, sitting so bolt upright in the straight hard chair that was so tall for her that her legs hung straight and rigid as if she had iron shinbones and ankles, clear of the floor with that air of impotent and static rage like children's feet, and talking in that grim haggard amazed voice until at last listening would renege and hearing-sense self-confound and the long-dead object of her impotent yet indomitable frustration would appear, as though by outraged recapitulation evoked, quiet inattentive and harmless, out of the biding and dreamy and victorious dust.

Her voice would not cease, it would just vanish. There would be the dim coffin-smelling gloom sweet and oversweet with the twice-bloomed wistaria against the outer wall by the savage quiet September sun impacted distilled and hyperdistilled, into which came now and then the loud cloudy flutter of the sparrows like a flat limber stick whipped by an idle boy, and the rank smell of female old flesh long embattled in virginity while the wan haggard face watched him above the faint triangle of lace at wrists and throat from the too tall chair in which she resembled a crucified child; and the voice not ceasing but vanishing into and then out of the long intervals like a stream, a trickle running from patch to patch of dried sand, and the ghost mused with shadowy docility as if it were the voice which he haunted where a more fortunate one would have had a house. Out of quiet thunderclap he would abrupt (man-horse-demon) upon a scene peaceful and decorous as a schoolprize water color, faint sulphur-reek still in hair clothes and beard, with grouped behind him his band of wild niggers like beasts half tamed to walk upright like men, in attitudes wild and reposed, and manacled among them the French architect with his air grim, haggard, and tatter-ran. Immobile, bearded and hand palm-lifted the horseman sat; behind him the wild blacks and the captive architect huddled quietly, carrying in bloodless paradox the shovels and picks and axes of peaceful conquest. Then in the long una-maze Quentin seemed to watch them overrun suddenly the hundred square miles of tranquil and astonished earth and drag house and formal gardens violently out of the soundless Nothing and clap them down like cards upon a table beneath the up-palm immobile and pontific, creating the Sutpen's Hundred, the *Be Sutpen's Hundred* like the oldentime *Be Light*. Then hearing would reconcile and he would seem to listen to two separate Quentins now—the Quentin

Compson preparing for Harvard in the South, the deep South dead since 1865 and peopled with garrulous outraged baffled ghosts, listening, having to listen, to one of the ghosts which had refused to lie still even longer than most had, telling him about old ghost-times; and the Quentin Compson who was still too young to deserve yet to be a ghost but nevertheless having to be one for all that, since he was born and bred in the deep South the same as she was—the two separate Quentins now talking to one another in the long silence of notpeople in not-language, like this: *It seems that this demon—his name was Sutpen—(Colonel Sutpen)— Colonel Sutpen. Who came out of nowhere and without warning upon the land with a band of strange niggers and built a plantation—(Tore violently a plantation, Miss Rosa Coldfield says)—tore violently. And married her sister Ellen and begot a son and a daughter which— (Without gentleness begot, Miss Rosa Coldfield says)—without gentleness. Which should have been the jewels of his pride and the shield and comfort of his old age, only—(Only they destroyed him or something or he destroyed them or something. And died)—and died. Without regret, Miss Rosa Coldfield says—(Save by her) Yes, save by her. (And by Quentin Compson) Yes. And by Quentin Compson.*

"Because you are going away to attend the college at Harvard they tell me," she said. "So I dont imagine you will ever come back here and settle down as a country lawyer in a little town like Jefferson since Northern people have already seen to it that there is little left in the South for a young man. So maybe you will enter the literary profession as so many Southern gentlemen and gentlewomen too are doing now and maybe some day you will remember this and write about it. You will be married then I expect and perhaps your wife will want a new gown or a new chair for the house and you can write this and submit it to the magazines. Perhaps you will even remember kindly then the old woman who made you spend a whole afternoon sitting indoors and listening while she talked about people and events you were fortunate enough to escape yourself when you wanted to be out among young friends of your own age."

"Yessum," Quentin said. *Only she dont mean that* he thought. *It's because she wants it told.* It was still early then. He had yet in his pocket the note which he had received by the hand of a small negro boy just before noon, asking him to call and see her—the quaint, stiffly formal request which was actually a summons, out of another world almost—the queer archaic sheet of ancient good notepaper written over with the neat faded cramped script which, due to his astonishment at the request from a woman three times his age and whom he had known all his life without having exchanged a hundred words with her or perhaps to the fact that he was only twenty years old, he did not recognise as revealing a character cold, implacable, and even ruthless. He obeyed it immediately after the noon meal, walking the half mile between his home and hers through the dry dusty heat of early September and so into the house (it too somehow smaller than its actual size—it was of two storeys—unpainted and a little shabby, yet with an air, a quality of grim endurance as though like her it had been created to fit into and comple-ment a world in all ways a little smaller than the one in which it found itself) where in the gloom of the shuttered hallway whose air was even hotter than outside, as if there were pris-oned in it like in a tomb all the suspiration of slow heat-laden time which had recurred during the forty-three years, the small figure in black which did not even rustle, the wan triangle of lace at wrists and throat, the dim face looking at him with an expression speculative, urgent, and intent, waited to invite him in.

It's because she wants it told he thought *so that people whom she will never see and whose names she will never hear and who have never heard her name nor seen her face will read it and know at last why God let us lose the War: that only through the blood of our men and the tears of our women could He stay this demon and efface his name and lineage from the earth.* Then almost immediately he decided that neither was this the reason why she had sent the note, and sending it, why to him, since if she had merely wanted it told, written and even printed, she would not have needed to call in anybody—a woman who even in his (Quentin's) father's youth had already established (even if not affirmed) herself as the town's and the county's poetess laureate by issuing to the stern and meager subscription list of the county newspaper poems, ode eulogy and epitaph, out of some bitter and implacable reserve of undefeat; and

ROBERT GWATHMEY. *Reflections.* c. 1950. Oil on canvas. 26 3/4 x 32 1/2 in. Morris Museum of Art, Augusta, Georgia. © Estate of Robert Gwathmey/VAGA, New York 1993. *Robert Gwathmey often painted scenes with social commentary, although this painting is more psychological. It is difficult to ignore the literary characters evoked by this dark scene: Faulkner's Emily Grierson, Minnie Cooper, and Rosa Coldfield, and Tennessee Williams's Blanche DuBois.*

these from a woman whose family's martial background as both town and county knew consisted of the father who, a conscientious objector on religious grounds, had starved to death in the attic of his own house, hidden (some said, walled up) there from Confederate provost marshals' men and fed secretly at night by this same daughter who at the very time was accumulating her first folio in which the lost cause's unregenerate vanquished were name by name embalmed; and the nephew who served for four years in the same company with his sister's fiancé and then shot the fiancé to death before the gates to the house where the sister waited in her wedding gown on the eve of the wedding and then fled, vanished, none knew where.

It would be three hours yet before he would learn why she had sent for him because this part of it, this first part of it, Quentin already knew. It was a part of his twenty years' heritage of breathing the same air and hearing his father talk about the man; a part of the town's—Jefferson's—eighty years' heritage of the same air which the man himself had breathed between this September afternoon in 1909 and that Sunday morning in June in 1833 when he first rode into town out of no discernible past and acquired his land no one knew how and built his house, his mansion, apparently out of nothing and married Ellen Coldfield and begot his two children—the son who widowed the daughter who had not yet been a bride—and so accomplished his allotted course to its violent (Miss Coldfield at least would have said, just) end. Quentin had grown up with that; the mere names were interchangeable and almost myriad. His childhood was full of them; his very body was an empty hall echoing with sonorous defeated names; he was not a being, an entity, he was a commonwealth. He was a barracks filled with stubborn back-looking ghosts still recovering, even forty-three years afterward, from the fever which had cured the disease, waking from the fever without even knowing that it had been the fever itself which they had fought against and not the sickness, looking with stubborn recalcitrance backward beyond the fever and into the disease with actual regret, weak from the fever yet free of the disease and not even aware that the freedom was that of impotence.

RICHARD WRIGHT

From *Black Boy*

Black Boy (1945) is a "fictionalized" account of Richard Wright's early life in Mississippi and Memphis up to his immigration north to Chicago. In this selection, a young boy comes to the horrifying realization that his first job, which affords him food, reading material, and a little freedom, has been as a paperboy for the Ku Klux Klan.

In my class was a tall, black, rebellious boy who was bright in his studies and yet utterly fearless in his assertion of himself; he could break the morale of the class at any moment with his clowning and the teacher never found an adequate way of handling him. It was he who detected my plaguing hunger and suggested to me a way to earn some money.

"You can't sit in school all day and not eat," he said.

"What am I going to eat?" I asked.

"Why don't you do like me?"

"What do you do?"

"I sell papers."

"I tried to get a paper route, but they're all full," I said. "I'd like to sell papers because I could read them. I can't find things to read."

"You too?" he asked, laughing.

"What do you mean?" I asked.

"That's why I sell papers. I like to read 'em and that's the only way I can get hold of 'em," he explained.

"Do your parents object to your reading?" I asked.

"Yeah. My old man's a damn crackpot," he said.

"What papers are you selling?"

"It's a paper published in Chicago. It comes out each week and it has a magazine supplement," he informed me.

"What kind of a paper is it?"

"Well, I never read the newspaper. It isn't much. But, boy, the magazine supplement! What stories . . . I'm reading the serial of Zane Grey's *Riders of the Purple Sage.*"

I stared at him in complete disbelief.

"Riders of the Purple Sage!" I exclaimed.

"Yes."

"Do you think I can sell those papers?"

"Sure. I make over fifty cents a week and have stuff to read," he explained.

I followed him home and he gave me a copy of the newspaper and the magazine supplement. The newspaper was thin, ill-edited, and designed to circulate among rural, white Protestant readers.

"Hurry up and start selling 'em," he urged me. "I'd like to talk to you about the stories."

I promised him that I would order a batch of them that night. I walked home through the deepening twilight, reading, lifting my eyes now and then from the print in order not to collide with strangers. I was absorbed in the tale of a renowned scientist who had rigged up a mystery room made of metal in the basement of his palatial home. Prompted by some obscure motive, he would lure his victims into this room and then throw an electric switch. Slowly, with heart-racking agony, the air would be sucked from the metal room and his victims would die, turning red, blue, then black. This was what I wanted, tales like this. I had not read enough to have developed any taste in reading. Anything that interested me satisfied me.

Now, at last, I could have my reading in the home, could have it there with the approval of Granny. She had already given me permission to sell papers. Oh, boy, how lucky it was for me

MARION POST WOLCOTT.
*Negro using outside
stairway for "colored" to
enter movie theatre.*
Belzoni, Mississippi.
1939. Photograph.
U.S. Farm Security
Administration
Collection, Prints and
Photographs Collection,
Library of Congress.
*Marion Post Wolcott
joined the Farm Security
Administration in 1938.
Much of Wolcott's best
work was done in the
Deep South, where her
clear, light-filled images
seem to have had a
special and personal
sensibility.*

that Granny could not read! She had always burned the books I had brought into the house, branding them as worldly; but she would have to tolerate these papers if she was to keep her promise to me. Aunt Addie's opinion did not count, and she never paid any attention to me anyway. In her eyes, I was dead. I told Granny that I planned to make some money by selling papers and she agreed, thinking that at last I was becoming a serious, right-thinking boy. That night I ordered the papers and waited anxiously.

The papers arrived and I scoured the Negro area, slowly building up a string of customers who bought the papers more because they knew me than from any desire to read. When I returned home at night, I would go to my room and lock the door and revel in outlandish exploits of outlandish men in faraway, outlandish cities. For the first time in my life I became aware of the life of the modern world, of vast cities, and I was claimed by it; I loved it. Though they were merely stories, I accepted them as true because I wanted to believe them, because I hungered for a different life, for something new. The cheap pulp tales enlarged my knowledge of the world more than anything I had encountered so far. To me, with my roundhouse, saloon-door, and river-levee background, they were revolutionary, my gateway to the world.

I was happy and would have continued to sell the newspaper and its magazine supplement indefinitely had it not been for the racial pride of a friend of the family. He was a tall, quiet, sober, soft-spoken black man, a carpenter by trade. One evening I called at his home with the paper. He gave me a dime, then looked at me oddly.

"You know, son," he said, "I sure like to see you make a little money each week."

"Thank you, sir," I said.

"But tell me, who told you to sell these papers?" he asked.

"Nobody."

"Where do you get them from?"

"Chicago."

"Do you ever read 'em?"

"Sure. I read the stories in the magazine supplement," I explained. "But I never read the newspaper."

He was silent a moment.

"Did a white man ask you to sell these papers?" he asked.

"No, sir," I answered, puzzled now. "Why do you ask?"

"Do your folks know you are selling these papers?"

"Yes, sir. But what's wrong?"

"How did you know where to write for these papers?" he asked, ignoring my questions.

"A friend of mine sells them. He gave me the address."

"Is this friend of yours a white man?"

"No, sir. He's colored. But why are you asking me all this?"

He did not answer. He was sitting on the steps of his front porch. He rose slowly.

"Wait right here a minute, son," he said. I want to show you something."

Now what was wrong? The papers were all right; at least they seemed so to me. I waited, annoyed, eager to be gone on my rounds so that I could have time to get home and lie in bed and read the next installment of a thrilling horror story. The man returned with a carefully folded copy of the newspaper. He handed it to me.

"Did you see this?" he asked, pointing to a lurid cartoon.

"No, sir," I said. "I don't read the newspaper; I only read the magazine."

"Well, just look at that. Take your time and tell me what you think," he said.

It was the previous week's issue and I looked at the picture of a huge black man with a greasy, sweaty face, thick lips, flat nose, golden teeth, sitting at a polished, wide-topped desk in a swivel chair. The man had on a pair of gleaming yellow shoes and his feet were propped upon the desk. His thick lips nursed a big, black cigar that held white ashes an inch long. In the man's red-dotted tie was a dazzling horseshoe stickpin, glaring conspicuously. The man wore red suspenders and his shirt was striped silk and there were huge diamond rings on his fat black fingers. A chain of gold girded his belly and from the fob of his watch a rabbit's foot dangled. On the floor at the side of the desk was a spittoon overflowing with mucus. Across the wall of the room in which the man sat was a bold sign, reading:

THE WHITE HOUSE

Under the sign was a portrait of Abraham Lincoln, the features distorted to make the face look like that of a gangster. My eyes went to the top of the cartoon and I read:

> The only dream of a nigger is to be president and
> to sleep with white women! Americans, do we
> want this in our fair land? Organize and save
> white womanhood!

I stared, trying to grasp the point of the picture and the captions, wondering why it all seemed so strange and yet familiar.

"Do you know what this means?" the man asked me.

"Gee, I don't know," I confessed.

"Did you ever hear of the Ku Klux Klan?" he asked me softly.

"Sure. Why?"

"Do you know what the Ku Kluxers do to colored people?"

"They kill us. They keep us from voting and getting good jobs," I said.

"Well, the paper you're selling preaches the Ku Klux Klan doctrines," he said.

"Oh, no!" I exclaimed.

"Son, you're holding it in your hands," he said.

"I read the magazine, but I never read the paper," I said vaguely, thoroughly rattled.

"Listen, son," he said. "Listen. You're a black boy and you're trying to make a few pennies. All right. I don't want to stop you from selling these papers, if you want to sell 'em. But I've read these papers now for two months and I know what they're trying to do. If you sell 'em, you're just helping white people to kill you."

"But these papers come from Chicago," I protested naively, feeling unsure of the entire world now, feeling that racial propaganda surely could not be published in Chicago, the city to which Negroes were fleeing by the thousands.

"I don't care where the paper comes from," he said. "Just you listen to this."

He read aloud a long article in which lynching was passionately advocated as a solution for the problem of the Negro. Even though I heard him reading it, I could not believe it.

"Let me see that," I said.

MALVIN GRAY JOHNSON. *Negro Soldier.* 1934. Oil on canvas. 38 x 30 in. New York Public Library. Schomberg Center. *Malvin Gray Johnson's dignified portraits of African-Americans, which drew inspiration from spirituals and from the street, were highly praised.*

I took the paper from him and sat on the edge of the steps; in the paling light I turned the pages and read articles so brutally anti-Negro that goose pimples broke out over my skin.

"Do you like that?" he asked me.

"No, sir," I breathed.

"Do you see what you are doing?"

"I didn't know," I mumbled.

"Are you going to sell those papers now?"

"No, sir. Never again."

"They tell me that you are smart in school, and when I read those papers you were selling I didn't know what to make of it. Then I said to myself that that boy doesn't know what he's selling. Now, a lot of folks wanted to speak to you about these papers, but they were scared. They thought you were mixed up with some white Ku Kluxers and if they told you to stop you would put the Kluxers on 'em. But I said, shucks, that boy just don't know what he's doing."

I handed him his dime, but he would not take it.

"Keep the dime, son," he said. "But for God's sake, find something else to sell."

I did not try to sell any more of the papers that night; I walked home with them under my arm, feeling that some Negro would leap from a bush or fence and waylay me. How on earth could I have made so grave a mistake? The way I had erred was simple but utterly unbelievable. I had been so enthralled by reading the serial stories in the magazine supplement that I had not read a single issue of the newspaper. I decided to keep my misadventure secret, that I would tell no one that I had been unwittingly an agent for pro-Ku Klux Klan literature. I tossed the papers into a ditch and when I reached home I told Granny, in a quiet, offhand way, that the company did not want to send me any more papers because they already had too many agents in Jackson, a lie which I thought was an understatement of the actual truth. Granny did not care one way or the other, since I had been making so little money in selling them that I had not been able to help much with household expenses.

The father of the boy who had urged me to sell the papers also found out their propagandistic nature and forbade his son to sell them. But the boy and I never discussed the subject; we were too ashamed of ourselves. One day he asked me guardedly:

"Say, are you still selling those papers?"

"Oh, no. I don't have time," I said, my eyes avoiding his.

"I'm not either," he said, pulling down the corners of his mouth. "I'm too busy."

W. J. CASH

From *The Mind of the South*

Many writers have attempted to understand and interpret the South; few have done a better job than Wilbur Joseph Cash. Cash, although focusing primarily on white Southerners, debunked many of the old myths about the South such as the notion of a "Southern aristocracy," believing the South could best be understood as a frontier populated predominantly by yeomen. Echoing the suicide of Faulkner's Quentin Compson, another Southerner who attempted to "tell about the South," Cash took his own life in 1941, the year his book was published. In these brief excerpts, Cash describes the dreamy sensuality of the South, and sums up the virtues and shortcomings of the region.

Despite the unquestionable harshness of the life he led, the Southern pioneer (like his congeners elsewhere on the American frontier and in every new country) early began to exhibit a kind of mounting exultancy, which issued in a tendency to frisk and cavort, to posture, to play the slashing hell of a fellow—a notable expansion of the ego testifying at once to his rising individualism and the burgeoning of the romantic and hedonistic spirit.

Moreover, there was the influence of the Southern physical world—itself a sort of cosmic conspiracy against reality in favor of romance. The country is one of extravagant colors, of proliferating foliage and bloom, of flooding yellow sunlight, and, above all perhaps, of haze. Pale blue fogs hang above the valleys in the morning, the atmosphere smokes faintly at midday, and through the long slow afternoon cloud-stacks tower from the horizon and the earth-heat quivers upward through the iridescent air, blurring every outline and rendering every object vague and problematical. I know that winter comes to the land, certainly. I know there are days when the color and the haze are stripped away and the real stands up in drab and depressing harshness. But these things pass and are forgotten.

The dominant mood, the mood that lingers in the memory, is one of well-nigh drunken reverie—of a hush that seems all the deeper for the far-away mourning of the hounds and the far-away crying of the doves—of such sweet and inexorable opiates as the rich odors of hot earth and pinewood and the perfume of the magnolia in bloom—of soft languor creeping through the blood and mounting surely to the brain. . . . It is a mood, in sum, in which directed thinking is all but impossible, a mood in which the mind yields almost perforce to drift and in which the imagination holds unchecked sway, a mood in which nothing any more seems improbable save the puny inadequateness of fact, nothing incredible save the bareness of truth.

But I must tell you also that the sequel to this mood is invariably a thunderstorm. For days—for weeks, it may be—the land lies thus in reverie, and then . . .

* * *

It is far easier, I know, to criticize the failure of the South to face and solve its problems than it is to solve them. Solution is difficult and, for all I know, may be impossible in some cases. But it is clear at least that there is no chance of solving them until there is a leadership

which is willing to face them fully and in all their implications, to arouse the people to them, and to try to evolve a comprehensive and adequate means for coping with them. It is the absence of that leadership, and ultimately the failure of any mood of realism, the preference for easy complacency, that I have sought to emphasize here.

This analysis might be carried much farther. But the book is already too long, and so I think I shall leave it at this. The basic picture of the South is here, I believe. And it was that I started out to set down.

Proud, brave, honorable by its lights, courteous, personally generous, loyal, swift to act, often too swift, but signally effective, sometimes terrible, in its action—such was the South at its best. And such at its best it remains today, despite the great falling away in some of its virtues. Violence, intolerance, aversion and suspicion toward new ideas, an incapacity for analysis, an inclination to act from feeling rather than from thought, an exaggerated individualism and a too narrow concept of social responsibility, attachment to fictions and false values, above all too great attachment to racial values and a tendency to justify cruelty and injustice in the name of those values, sentimentality and a lack of realism—these have been its characteristic vices in the past. And, despite changes for the better, they remain its characteristic vices today.

In the coming days, and probably soon, it is likely to have to prove its capacity for adjustment far beyond what has been true in the past. And in that time I shall hope, as its loyal son, that its virtues will tower over and conquer its faults and have the making of the Southern world to come. But of the future I shall venture no definite prophecies. It would be a brave man who would venture them in any case. It would be a madman who would venture them in face of the forces sweeping over the world in the fateful year of 1940.

GAINES RUGER DONOHO. *Storm Over Loing Valley.* c. 1902. Oil on canvas. 45 x 67 ½ in. Greenville County Museum of Art, Greenville, SC. *Donoho, forced out of the South because of the Civil War, studied painting in New York and Paris. He summered near Barbizon, France, which seems to have influenced his* plein air *landscape style.*

JOSEPH MITCHELL

"I Blame It All on Mamma"

In the 1930s and 1940s, Joseph Mitchell's "Profiles" and "Reporter at Large" articles for The New Yorker *magazine "set the standard." Mitchell was born in Robeson County, North Carolina, the model for his fictional Black Ankle County. The graveyard humor he grew up with there has been a major influence on his writing, and, as he says, "it typifies my cast of mind."*

Mrs. Copenhagen Calhoun, who lives on a riverbank watermelon farm in Black Ankle County, about a mile from the town of Stonewall, is the only termagant I have ever admired. She has no fondness for authority and is opposed to all public officials, elected or appointed. Once a distinguished senator came to Stonewall and spoke in the high-school auditorium; just after he finished telling how he made it a practice to walk in the footsteps of Thomas Jefferson, she stood up and said, "Senator, you sure are getting too big for your britches." A mayor of Stonewall once tried to get her fired from her job as cook in the station restaurant of the Charleston, Pee Dee & Northern Railroad. A woman who got drunk in public, he said, was a disgrace to the town. She kept her mouth shut until he came up for reelection; then she went up and down Main Street making speeches which helped defeat him. "Why, the stuck-up old hypocrite!" she said in one of her speeches. "He goes to the country club on Saturday night and gets as drunk as a goose on ice, and Sunday morning he stands up in the Methodist choir and sings so loud the whole church echoes for a week." She believes that public officials are inclined to overlook the fact that Americans are free, and when she is brought into court for disturbing the peace she invariably begins her address to the judge by stating, "This is a free country, by God, and I got my rights." She has a long tongue, and Judge Elisha Mullet once said she could argue the legs off an iron pot. She has many bad qualities, in fact, and her husband often complains that she has made his life a hell on earth, but when I go back to Stonewall for a visit and find that she is still insisting on her rights, I always feel better about the vigor of democracy.

I was in the tenth grade when I became one of her admirers. At that time, in 1924, she was unmarried and had just come up from Charleston to cook in the station restaurant. It was the only restaurant in Stonewall; railroad men ate there, and so did people from the sawmill, the cotton gin, and the chewing-tobacco factory. After school I used to hang around the station. I would sit on a bench beside the track and watch the Negro freight hands load boxcars with bales of cotton. Some afternoons she would come out of the kitchen and sit on the bench beside me. She was a handsome, big-hipped woman with coal-black hair and a nice grin, and the station agent must have liked her, because he let her behave pretty much as she pleased. She cooked in her bare feet and did not bother to put shoes on when she came out for a breath of fresh air. "I had an aunt," she told me, "who got the dropsy from wearing shoes in a hot kitchen." Once I asked her how she came to be named Copenhagen. "Mamma named all her babies after big towns," she said. "It was one of her fancy habits. Her first was a boy and she named him New Orleans. Then my sister came along and she named her Chattanooga. Mamma was real fond of snuff, and every payday Pa would buy her a big brown bladder of Copenhagen snuff. That's where she got my name."

One Friday night, after Miss Copey had been working at the restaurant a couple of months, the station agent wrote her a pass and she went down to Charleston to see her family. When she returned Monday on the 3:30, she was so drunk the conductor had to grab her elbows and help her down the train steps. She paid no attention to him but sang "Work, for the Night Is Coming." She bustled into the kitchen, kicked off her shoes, and began throwing things. She would pick up a pot and beat time with it while she sang a verse of the hymn, and then she

COLORPLATE 75

ALICE RAVENEL HUGER SMITH. *Fields Prepared for the Planting.* c. 1936. Watercolor on paper. Gibbes Museum of Art, Charleston, South Carolina. *Alice Smith, a descendant of old South Carolina families, painted many delicate watercolors of the region. Her most widely known work was the series of romantic watercolors executed for* A Carolina Rice Plantation of the Fifties, *which illustrated all aspects of rice cultivation and daily life on a plantation in the mid-nineteenth century.*

COLORPLATE 76

WILLIAM P. SILVA. *Magic Pool.* c. 1924. Cheekwood Fine Arts Center, Nashville. *William Silva gave up a family business in Chattanooga to devote himself to painting full time. He was basically itinerant, moving throughout the South. A stay in Paris no doubt influenced his vibrant impressionistic style.*

COLORPLATE 77

CLARENCE MILLET. *Moonscape.* 1935. Oil on canvas. 22 x 26 in. Roger Houston Ogden Collection, New Orleans.
Millet often painted nocturnal scenes of well-known homes lit by bright moonlight.

COLORPLATE 78

PAUL NINAS. *Avery Island Salt Mines.* 1934. Oil on canvas. 23 x 30 ½ in. Roger Houston Ogden Collection, New Orleans. *Paul Ninas lived in Paris, where he became acquainted with Gertrude Stein's charmed circle of friends; Isadora Duncan sponsored his first one-man exhibition. This painting of Avery Island (also home to the favorite condiment of Southerners—Tabasco sauce) is clearly influenced by Cézanne with its construction of vividly colored geometric forms.*

COLORPLATE 79

ELIOT CLARK. *View of River Savannah.* 1924. Oil on canvas. 23 $^7/_{16}$ x 28 $^1/_2$ in. Collection of the Telfair Academy of Arts and Sciences. Gift of Mary Lane Morrison. *Reminiscent of a steamy Monet railway station, this painting relies on realism, loose brushwork, and the deft handling of color and light.*

COLORPLATE 80

CAROLINE DURIEUX. *Cafe Tupinamba.* 1934. Oil on canvas. 32 ¹/₂ x 40 in. Louisiana State University Museum of Art, Baton Rouge. Gift of Mr. Charles P. Manship, Jr. in memory of his parents Leora and Charles P. Manship, Sr. *Caroline Durieux spent part of her life in Havana and Mexico City, where she became acquainted with the muralist Diego Rivera. His social realist style influenced Durieux, who turned her attention to people and their everyday lives.*

COLORPLATE 81

WILLIAM R. HOLLINGSWORTH, JR. (1910–1944). *Checks.* c. 1940. Watercolor on paper. 8 x 10 in. Roger Houston Ogden Collection, New Orleans.

COLORPLATE 82

BEAUFORD DELANEY. *Portrait of a Boy.* 1934. Pastel on paper. 18 ¹/₂ x 23 ¹/₂ in. James E. Lewis Museum of Art, Morgan State University, Baltimore, Maryland. *Like many African-American artists and musicians, Beauford Delaney was an expatriate, living most of his life in Paris.*

HUBERT SHUPTRINE. *Echoes of Praise*. 1976. Watercolor on paper. 28 1/2 x 20 1/2 in. Courtesy of the artist.

would throw it. "Work till the last beam fad-eth, fad-eth to shine no more," she would sing, and then a stewpot would go sailing across the room. I stood at a window and stared. She was the first drunken woman I had ever seen and the spectacle did not disappoint me; I thought she was wonderful. finally the chief of police, who was called Old Blunderbuss by the kids in town, came and put her under arrest. Next day she was back at work. In the afternoon she came out to sit in the sun for a few minutes, and I asked her how it felt to get drunk. She gave me a slap that almost knocked me off the bench. "Why, you little shirttail boy," she said, "What do you mean asking me such a question?" I rubbed my jaw and said, "I'm sorry, Miss Copey. I didn't mean any harm."

She leaned forward and held her head in her hands like a mourner and sat that way a few minutes. Then she straightened up and said, "I'm sorry I slapped you, son, but that was a hell of a question to ask a lady. Drinking is a sad, sad thing, and I hate to talk about it. I was a liquor-head sot before I got past the third grade, and I blame it all on Mamma. I had the colic real often when I was a little girl, and to ease the pain Mamma would take Pa's jug and measure out half a cup of liquor and sweeten it with molasses and dose me with it, and I got an everlasting taste for the awful stuff. If I knew then what I know now, I would've got up from my sickbed and knocked that liquor outa my mamma's hand." She sighed and stood up. "Still and all," she said, and a broad smile came on her face, "I got to admit that it sure cured my colic."

Miss Copey had not worked at the restaurant long before she got acquainted with Mr. Thunderbolt Calhoun. He has a watermelon farm on the bank of Shad Roe River in a section of the county called Egypt. He is so sleepy and slow he has been known as Thunderbolt ever

MARION POST
WOLCOTT. *Baptism at
Triplett Creek.* 1940.
Photograph.
U.S. Farm Security
Administration
Collection, Prints and
Photographs Division,
Library of Congress.

since he was a boy; his true name is Rutherford Calhoun. He is shiftless and most of his farm work is done by a Negro hired boy named Mister. (When this boy was born his mother said, "White people claim they won't mister a Negro. Well, by God, son, they'll mister you!") Mr. Thunderbolt's fifteen-acre farm is fertile and it grows the finest Cuban Queen, Black Gipsy, and Irish Gray watermelons I have ever seen. The farm is just a sideline, however; his principal interest in life is a copper still hidden on the bank of a bay in the river swamp. In this still he produces a vehement kind of whiskey known as tanglefoot. "I depend on watermelons to pay the taxes and feed me and my mule," he says. "The whiskey is pure profit." Experts say that his tanglefoot is as good as good Kentucky bourbon, and he claims that laziness makes it so. "You have to be patient to make good whiskey," he says, yawning, "and I'm an uncommonly patient man."

After Miss Copey began buying her whiskey from him, she went on sprees more often; his whiskey did not give her hangovers or what she called "the dismals." At least once a month, usually on a Saturday afternoon, she would leave her kitchen and walk barefooted down Main Street, singing a hymn at the top of her voice, and she seldom got below Main and Jefferson before she was under arrest. Most of the town drunks meekly paid the usual fine of seven dollars and costs or went to jail, but Miss Copey always took advantage of the question "What have you got to say for yourself?" First she would claim that the right to get drunk is guaranteed by the Constitution, and then she would accuse the judge of being a hypocrite.

"I got a right to let loose a hymn when I feel like it," she would say. "That don't harm nobody. Suppose I do make a little noise? Do they put 'em in jail for blowing the whistle at the sawmill? And anyhow, I don't drink in secret. There's nothing so low-down sorry as a man that drinks in secret. You're a secret sot, Judge Mullet, and don't try to deny it."

"I like a drop now and then, to be sure," the Judge would reply, "but that don't give me the right to run up and down the highways and byways in my bare feet."

226

"Now you're trying to tell me there's one law for a judge and another for a railroad cook," Miss Copey would say triumphantly. "That's a hell of a way for a judge to talk."

Miss Copey had been cooking in the station restaurant about two years when a stovepipe crumpled up and fell down on her head, stunning her. It made her so angry she quit her job and threatened to sue the railroad for a thousand dollars. She settled out of court, however, when a claim agent offered her a check for seventy-five. "I haven't got the patience to fight a railroad," she said. She cashed the check, insisting on having the sum in one-dollar bills, and hurried out to Mr. Thunderbolt's to buy a Mason jar of tanglefoot. When he saw her roll of bills he said he felt they ought to celebrate. He drew some whiskey out of a charred-oak keg that had been buried in the swamp for five years, and they sat in rocking chairs on the front porch and began to drink to each other. After an hour or so, Mr. Thunderbolt told her he was a lonesome man and that he had grown mighty damned tired of Mister's cooking. He wound up by asking her to be his wife. Miss Copey broke down and sobbed. Then she said, "I'll make you a good wife, Thunderbolt. We better hurry to town before the courthouse closes. If we wait until you're sober, I'm afraid you'll change your mind." Mister drove them to Stonewall in Mr. Thunderbolt's old Ford truck. They stopped at Miss Copey's rooming house and picked up her trunk; then they went over to the courthouse and were married. Judge Mullet was surprised by the marriage but said he guessed Mr. Thunderbolt's star customer wanted to get closer to the source of supply. For a week the bride and groom went fishing in Shad Roe River in the morning, got drunk in the afternoon, and rode about the country in the Ford truck at night. Then, Saturday morning, Miss Copey woke up, looked out a window, and saw that the figs were ripe on the door-yard bushes; she shook her husband awake and said, "The honeymoon's over, Thunderbolt. I got to get busy and can them figs before they drop on the ground."

For a couple of months, Miss Copey was a model wife. That autumn I hunted squirrels practically every afternoon in the swamp that runs alongside Mr. Thunderbolt's farm, and I used to stop by and see her. She showed me scores of jars of watermelon-rind pickles and fig preserves she had canned and arranged on the cellar shelves. She had spaded a pit in the back yard for barbecues, and in the corncrib she had a big barrel of scuppernong grapes in ferment. She had bought four Rhode Island Red hens and four settings of eggs, and she had a yardful of biddies. She proudly told me that every night when Mr. Thunderbolt came home from the swamp, worn out after a day of squatting beside his still, he found a plate of fried chicken and a sweet-potato pie on the kitchen table waiting for him.

After a while, however, she began to get bored. "It's too damned still around here," she told me one evening. "I need some human company. Sometimes a whole day goes past and I don't get a single word out of Thunderbolt. He lived by himself so long he almost lost the use of his tongue." There is a Baptist church a half mile up the river, and one lonesome Sunday she attended a service there. She picked an unfortunate time, because there was a fight in progress in the congregation. In fact, at that period, which was the autumn of 1926, there was dissension in many rural Baptist churches in the South over the ceremony of immersion. One group believed a convert should be immersed three times face forward in the still water of a pond and the other favored a single immersion in the running water of a river. The opposing groups were called the Trine Forwardites and the Running Riverites. Miss Copey became a churchgoer merely because she wanted to sing some hymns, but she soon got mixed up in this theological wrangle. The second Sunday she attended services she was sitting in a back pew when a man got up and advocated changing the name of the church from Egypt Baptist to Still Water Trine Forward Baptist. He said any sensible person knew that a calm pond was more spiritual than the troubled waters of a river. This did not seem right to Miss Copey; she arose and interrupted him. "Jordan wa'n't no pond," she said. "It was a running river. On that rock I stand." "That's right, sister!" exclaimed a man up front. "You hit the nail on the head." He went back and asked Miss Copey to come forward and sit with the Running River faction. "Why, I'll gladly do so," Miss Copey said. "What's this all about, anyhow?"

Presently the argument between the factions grew bitter, and Miss Copey arose again and suggested singing "On Jordan's Stormy Banks," a revival hymn. The leader of her faction said, "Let's march out of this church as we sing that hymn." Thereupon seven men and women marched up the aisle. Miss Copey got up and followed them. In the yard outside, they held a meeting and decided to organize a new church and call it the Running River One Immersion Baptist. "You can meet at my house until you locate a more suitable place," Miss Copey suggested. "Let's go there now and sit on the porch and do some singing. I feel like letting loose a few hymns." The Running Riverites were pleased by this suggestion. With Miss Copey leading, they marched down the road singing "There Is a Green Hill Far Away." When Mr. Thunderbolt saw them heading up the lane, he was sitting on the porch, playing his harmonica. He leaped off the porch and fled to the swamp. Miss Copey arranged chairs on the porch and announced that her favorite hymns were "There Is a Fountain filled with Blood" and "The Old Time Religion Is Good Enough for Me." All afternoon they sang these hymns over and over. At sundown Miss Copey said, "If you're a mind to, we'll meet here again next Sunday. We'll show those Trine Forwardite heathens!" Then the meeting ended. Late that night Mr. Thunderbolt came in, raging drunk. "Listen, you old hoot owl!" he shouted. "If you bring them hymn-singers to this house again, I'll leave you and never come back!" "Don't threaten me, you drunk old sinner," Miss Copey said. "You start threatening me, I'll pull a slat out of the bed and fracture your skull."

Next Sunday afternoon the hymn-singers held another meeting on Miss Copey's porch, and that night Mr. Thunderbolt did not come home at all. Monday night he was still missing. Early Tuesday morning, Miss Copey went down to Mister's cabin and found that he was missing too. She looked in the barn and found that the Ford truck was gone. On my way home from the swamp that afternoon I stopped by to see her, and she was sitting on the front steps, moaning. There was a carving knife in her lap. "I'll cut his black heart out," she said. "I'll put my trademark on him. The wife-deserter!" I sat down and tried to comfort her. Presently two of the hymn-singers came up the lane. "How are you this fine fall day, sister?" one called out. Miss Copey ran out to meet them. "You come another step closer, you old hymn-singers," she said, "and I'll throw you in the river! You've turned a man against his wife! You've broke up a happy home!" After a while we went in the house and she made some coffee. We were sitting on the back porch drinking it when Mister drove up in the Ford truck. "Hey there, Miss Copey!" he yelled. "They got Mr. Thunderbolt in jail down in Charleston." "Why, bless his heart," said Miss Copey. She ran in the house and got her hat and her purse. "Get back in that truck," she said to Mister, "and take me to him." The three of us climbed in the seat.

In Charleston, the jailer let us go in and see Mr. Thunderbolt. He was lying in his cell playing his harmonica. He was in fine spirits. He told us the hymn-singing had made him so angry he had ordered Mister to drive him to Charleston. There was a moving-picture theatre near the place they parked the truck, and Monday night he decided to go in and see a show; he had never seen a moving picture. Mary Pickford was in it, he said, and he became so absorbed in her troubles that he crouched way forward in his seat and got a cramp in his left leg. At first he tried not to notice it, but when he could bear it no longer he decided to try the old-fashioned remedy of kicking the cramp out. He got out in the aisle, held on to an end seat, and began kicking backward, like a mule that is being shod. All the time he kept his eyes on the picture. "I didn't want to miss a thing," he said. People began to yell for him to sit down, he said, and an usher hurried up and told him to stop kicking. "Please go away and don't bother me," he told the usher. The usher got the manager and together they grabbed him. "I couldn't properly defend myself," Mr. Thunderbolt told us. "I couldn't fight them two busybodies and keep up with what was happening to Miss Mary Pickford and kick the cramp out of my foot all at the same time. It was more than any one human could do." The usher and the manager hustled him to the lobby, and when he realized he wouldn't be able to see the rest of the picture, he put all his attention on self-defense and knocked the two men flat. Then a policeman came and arrested him for disorderly conduct.

"Why, it's a damned outrage, honey," Miss Copey said. "I'm going right down and bail you out."

"Just a minute," Mr. Thunderbolt said. "You're not going to bail me out until I get your solemn promise to leave them hymn-singers alone. It's real quiet in this jail."

"Oh, hell, Thunderbolt!" said Miss Copey. "I threw them hymn-singers in the river before I left home."

TENNESSEE WILLIAMS

From *A Streetcar Named Desire*

A Streetcar Named Desire *was first presented at the Barrymore Theatre in New York on December 3, 1947. The original cast included Marlon Brando, Jessica Tandy, and Karl Malden. This is certainly one of the best-known scenes in American drama.*

[*The bathroom door opens and Stella comes out. Blanche continues talking to Mitch.*]

Oh! Have you finished? Wait—I'll turn on the radio.

[*She turns the knobs on the radio and it begins to play "Wien, Wien, nur du allein." Blanche waltzes to the music with romantic gestures. Mitch is delighted and moves in awkward imitation like a dancing bear.*

[*Stanley stalks fiercely through the portieres into the bedroom. He crosses to the small white radio and snatches it off the table. With a shouted oath, he tosses the instrument out the window.*]

TENNESSEE WILLIAMS. *Many Moons Ago.* 1980. Oil on canvas board. 18 x 24 in. Roger Houston Ogden Collection, New Orleans.

STELLA: *Drunk—drunk—animal thing, you!* [*She rushes through to the poker table*] All of you—please go home! If any of you have one spark of decency in you—

BLANCHE [*wildly*]: Stella, watch out, he's—

   [*Stanley charges after Stella.*]

MEN [*feebly*]: Take it easy, Stanley. Easy, fellow.—Let's all—

STELLA: You lay your hands on me and I'll—

[*She backs out of sight. He advances and disappears. There is the sound of a blow. Stella cries out. Blanche screams and runs into the kitchen. The men rush forward and there is grappling and cursing. Something is overturned with a crash.*]

BLANCHE [*shrilly*]: My sister is going to have a baby!

MITCH: This is terrible.

BLANCHE: Lunacy, absolute lunacy!

MITCH: Get him in here, men.

[*Stanley is forced, pinioned by the two men, into the bedroom. He nearly throws them off. Then all at once he subsides and is limp in their grasp.*

They speak quietly and lovingly to him and he leans his face on one of their shoulders.]

Stella [*in a high, unnatural voice, out of sight*]: I want to go away, I want to go away!

MITCH: Poker shouldn't be played in a house with women.

   [*Blanche rushes into the bedroom*]

BLANCHE: I want my sister's clothes! We'll go to that woman's upstairs!

MITCH: Where is the clothes?

BLANCHE [*opening the closet*]: I've got them! [*She rushes through to Stella*] Stella, Stella, precious! Dear, dear little sister, don't be afraid!

[*With her arms around Stella, Blanche guides her to the outside door and upstairs.*]

STANLEY [*dully*]: What's the matter; what's happened?

MITCH: You just blew your top, Stan.

PABLO: He's okay, now.

STEVE: Sure, my boy's okay!

MITCH: Put him on the bed and get a wet towel.

PABLO: I think coffee would do him a world of good, now.

THOMAS HART BENTON. *Poker Night* (from *A Streetcar Named Desire*). 1948. Tempera and oil on panel. 36 x 48 in. Collection of the Whitney Museum of American Art, New York. Mrs. Percy Uris Bequest.

STANLEY [*thickly*]: I want water.

MITCH: Put him under the shower!

[*The men talk quietly as they lead him to the bathroom.*]

STANLEY: Let the rut go of me, you sons of bitches!

[*Sounds of blows are heard. The water goes on full tilt.*]

STEVE: Let's get quick out of here!

[*They rush to the poker table and sweep up their winnings on their way out.*]

MITCH [*sadly but firmly*]: Poker should not be played in a house with women.

[*The door closes on them and the place is still. The Negro entertainers in the bar around the corner play "Paper Doll" slow and blue. After a moment Stanley comes out of the bathroom dripping water and still in his clinging wet polka dot drawers.*]

STANLEY: Stella! [*There is a pause*] My baby doll's left me!

[*He breaks into sobs. Then he goes to the phone and dials, still shuddering with sobs.*]

Eunice? I want my baby! [*He waits a moment; then he hangs up and dials again*] Eunice! I'll keep on ringin' until I talk with my baby!

[*An indistinguishable shrill voice is heard. He hurls phone to floor. Dissonant brass and piano sounds as the rooms dim out to darkness and the outer walls appear in the night light. The "blue piano" plays for a brief interval.*

[*Finally, Stanley stumbles half-dressed out to the porch and down the wooden steps to the pavement before the building. There he throws back his head like a baying hound and bellows his wife's name: "Stella! Stella, sweetheart! Stella!"*]

STANLEY: Stell-*lahhhhh!*

EUNICE [*calling down from the door of her upper apartment*]: Quit that howling out there an' go back to bed!

STANLEY: I want my baby down here. Stella, Stella!

EUNICE: She ain't comin' down so you quit! Or you'll git th' law on you!

STANLEY: Stella!

EUNICE: You can't beat on a woman an' then call 'er back! She won't come! And her goin' t' have a baby! . . . You stinker! You whelp of a Polack, you! I hope they do haul you in and turn the fire hose on you, same as the last time!

STANLEY [*humbly*]: Eunice, I want my girl to come down with me!

EUNICE: Hah! [*She slams the door.*]

STANLEY [*with heaven-splitting violence*]: STELL-LAHHHHH!

[*The low-tone clarinet moans. The door upstairs opens again. Stella slips down the rickety stairs in her robe. Her eyes are glistening with tears and her hair loose about her throat and shoulders. They stare at each other. Then they come together with low, animal moans. He falls to his knees on the steps and presses his face to her belly, curving a little with maternity. Her eyes go blind with tenderness as she catches his head and raises him level with her. He snatches the screen door open and lifts her off her feet and bears her into the dark flat.*]

CARSON MCCULLERS

From "The Heart Is a Lonely Hunter"

Born Lula Carson Smith in Columbus, Georgia, Carson McCullers published The Heart Is a Lonely Hunter *in 1940, when she was only twenty-three. In this passage from the novel, Mick Kelley has had to give up her plans to study music in order to help support her family. As a teenager, McCullers had also hoped for a career as a concert pianist.*

———————————

What good was it? That was the question she would like to know. What the hell good it was. All the plans she had made, and the music. When all that came of it was this trap—the store, then home to sleep, and back at the store again. The clock in front of the place where Mister Singer used to work pointed to seven. And she was just getting off. Whenever there was overtime the manager always told her to stay. Because she could stand longer on her feet and work harder before giving out than any other girl.

The heavy rain had left the sky a pale, quiet blue. Dark was coming. Already the lights were turned on. Automobile horns honked in the street and the newsboys hollered out the

headlines in the papers. She didn't want to go home. If she went home now she would lie down on the bed and bawl. That was how tired she was. But if she went into the New York Café and ate some ice cream she might feel O.K. And smoke and be by herself a little while.

The front part of the café was crowded, so she went to the very last booth. It was the small of her back and her face that got so tired. Their motto was supposed to be "Keep on your toes and smile." Once she was out of the store she had to frown a long time to get her face natural again. Even her ears were tired. She took off the dangling green earrings that pinched the lobes of her ears. She had bought the earrings the week before—and also a silver bangle bracelet. At first she had worked in Pots and Pans, but now they had changed her to Costume Jewelry.

"Good evening, Mick," Mister Brannon said. He wiped the bottom of a glass of water with a napkin and set it on the table.

"I want me a chocolate sundae and a nickel glass of draw beer."

"Together?" He put down a menu and pointed with his little finger that wore a lady's gold ring. "See—here's some nice roast chicken or some veal stew. Why don't you have a little supper with me?"

"No, thanks. All I want is the sundae and the beer. Both plenty cold."

Mick raked her hair from her forehead. Her mouth was open so that her cheeks seemed hollow. There were these two things she could never believe. That Mister Singer had killed himself and was dead. And that she was grown and had to work at Woolworth's.

She was the one found him. They had thought the noise was a backfire from a car, and it was not until the next day that they knew. She went in to play the radio. The blood was all over his neck and when her Dad came he pushed her out the room. She had run from the house. The shock wouldn't let her be still. She had run into the dark and hit herself with her fists. And then the next night he was in a coffin in the living-room. The undertaker had put rouge and lipstick on his face to make him look natural. But he didn't look natural. He was very dead. And mixed with the smell of flowers there was this other smell so that she couldn't stay in the room. But through all those days she held down the job. She wrapped packages and handed them across the counter and rung the money in the till. She walked when she was supposed to walk and ate when she sat down to the table. Only at first when she went to bed at night she couldn't sleep. But now she slept like she was supposed to, also.

Mick turned sideways in the seat so that she could cross her legs. There was a run in her stocking. It had started while she was walking to work and she had spit on it. Then later the run had gone farther and she had stuck a little piece of chewing-gum on the end. But even that didn't help. Now she would have to go home and sew. It was hard to know what she could do about stockings. She wore them out so fast. Unless she was the kind of common girl that would wear cotton stockings.

She oughtn't to have come in here. The bottoms of her shoes were clean worn out. She ought to have saved the twenty cents toward a new half-sole. Because if she kept on standing on a shoe with a hole in it what would happen? A blister would come on her feet. And she would have to pick it with a burnt needle. She would have to stay home from work and be fired. And then what would happen?

"Here you are," said Mister Brannon. "But I never heard of such a combination before."

He put the sundae and the beer on the table. She pretended to clean her fingernails because if she noticed him he would start talking. He didn't have this grudge against her any more, so he must have forgotten about the pack of gum. Now he always wanted to talk to her. But she wanted to be quiet and by herself. The sundae was O.K., covered all over with chocolate and nuts and cherries. And the beer was relaxing. The beer had a nice bitter taste after the ice cream and it made her drunk. Next to music beer was best.

But now no music was in her mind. That was a funny thing. It was like she was shut out from the inside room. Sometimes a quick little tune would come and go—but she never went into the inside room with music like she used to do. It was like she was too tense. Or maybe because it was like the store took all her energy and time. Woolworth's wasn't the same as school. When she used to come home from school she felt good and was ready to start working on the music. But now she was always too tired. At home she just ate supper and slept and then ate breakfast and went off to the store again. A song she had started in her private notebook two months before was still not finished. And she wanted to stay in the inside room but she didn't know how. It was like the inside room was locked somewhere away from her. A very hard thing to understand.

Mick pushed her broken front tooth with her thumb. But she did have Mister Singer's radio. All the installments hadn't been paid and she took on the responsibility. It was good to have something that had belonged to him. And maybe one of these days she might be able to set aside a little for a second-hand piano. Say two bucks a week. And she wouldn't let anybody touch this private piano but her—only she might teach George little pieces. She would keep it in the back room and play on it every night. And all day Sunday. But then suppose some week she couldn't make a payment. So then would they come to take it away like the little red bicycle? And suppose like she wouldn't let them. Suppose she hid the piano under the house. Or else she would meet them at the front door. And fight. She would knock down both the two men so they would have shiners and broke noses and would be passed out on the hall floor.

Mick frowned and rubbed her fist hard across her forehead. That was the way things were. It was like she was mad all the time. Not how a kid gets mad quick so that soon it is all over—but in another way. Only there was nothing to be mad at. Unless the store. But the store hadn't asked her to take the job. So there was nothing to be mad at. It was like she was cheated. Only nobody had cheated her. So there was nobody to take it out on. However, just the same she had that feeling. Cheated.

But maybe it would be true about the piano and turn out O.K. Maybe she would get a chance soon. Else what the hell good had it all been—the way she felt about music and the plans she had made in the inside room? It had to be some good if anything made sense. And it was too and it was too and it was too and it was too. It was some good.

All right!

O.K.!

Some good.

EUDORA WELTY
"Why I Live at the P.O."

Eudora Welty (b. 1909) has lived most of her life in Jackson, Mississippi. An ardent observer of life in the Deep South, she writes with an eye for detail and an ear for the Southern vernacular as is evident in this piece, first published in 1941 in The Atlantic Monthly *and written, she has said, "to show how people talked."*

I was getting along fine with Mama, Papa-Daddy and Uncle Rondo until my sister Stella-Rondo just separated from her husband and came back home again. Mr. Whitaker! Of course I went with Mr. Whitaker first, when he first appeared here in China Grove, taking "Pose Yourself" photos, and Stella-Rondo broke us up. Told him I was one-sided. Bigger on one side than the other, which is a deliberate, calculated falsehood: I'm the same. Stella-Rondo is exact-

UNKNOWN. *William Faulkner and Eudora Welty.* Photograph. University Archives, University of Mississippi. *William Faulkner and Eudora Welty on the occasion of Faulkner's receiving the National Institute of Arts and Letters Gold Medal for Fiction in May 1962.*

ly twelve months to the day younger than I am and for that reason she's spoiled.

She's always had anything in the world she wanted and then she'd throw it away. Papa-Daddy gave her this gorgeous Add-a-Pearl necklace when she was eight years old and she threw it away playing baseball when she was nine, with only two pearls.

So as soon as she got married and moved away from home the first thing she did was separate! From Mr. Whitaker! This photographer with the popeyes she said she trusted. Came home from one of those towns up in Illinois and to our complete surprise brought this child of two.

Mama said she like to made her drop dead for a second. "Here you had this marvelous blonde child and never so much as wrote your mother a word about it," says Mama. "I'm thoroughly ashamed of you." But of course she wasn't.

Stella-Rondo just calmly takes off this *hat,* I wish you could see it. She says, "Why, Mama, Shirley-T.'s adopted, I can prove it."

"How?" says Mama, but all I says was, "H'm!" There I was over the hot stove, trying to stretch two chickens over five people and a completely unexpected child into the bargain, without one moment's notice.

"What do you mean—H'm!'?" says Stella-Rondo, and Mama says, "I heard that, Sister."

I said that oh, I didn't mean a thing, only that whoever Shirley-T. was, she was the spit-image of Papa-Daddy if he'd cut off his beard, which of course he'd never do in the world. Papa-Daddy's Mama's papa and sulks.

Stella-Rondo got furious! She said, "Sister, I don't need to tell you you got a lot of nerve and always did have and I'll thank you to make no future reference to my adopted child whatsoever."

"Very well," I said. "Very well, very well. Of course I noticed at once she looks like Mr. Whitaker's side too. That frown. She looks like a cross between Mr. Whitaker and Papa-Daddy."

"Well, all I can say is she isn't."

"She looks exactly like Shirley Temple to me," says Mama, but Shirley-T. just ran away from her.

So the first thing Stella-Rondo did at the table was turn Papa-Daddy against me.

"Papa-Daddy," she says. He was trying to cut up his meat. "Papa-Daddy!" I was taken completely by surprise. Papa-Daddy is about a million years old and's got this long-long beard. "Papa-Daddy, Sister says she fails to understand why you don't cut off your beard."

So Papa-Daddy l-a-y-s down his knife and fork! He's real rich. Mama says he is, he says he isn't. So he says, "Have I heard correctly? You don't understand why I don't cut off my beard?"

"Why," I says, "Papa-Daddy, of course I understand, I did not say any such of a thing, the idea!"

He says, "Hussy!"

I says, "Papa-Daddy, you know I wouldn't any more want you to cut off your beard than the man in the moon. It was the farthest thing from my mind! Stella-Rondo sat there and made that up while she was eating breast of chicken."

But he says, "So the postmistress fails to understand why I don't cut off my beard. Which job I got you through my influence with the government. 'Bird's nest'—is that what you call it?"

Not that it isn't the next to smallest P.O. in the entire state of Mississippi.

I says, "Oh, Papa-Daddy," I says, "I didn't say any such of a thing, I never dreamed it was a bird's nest, I have always been grateful though this is the next to smallest P.O. in the state of Mississippi, and I do not enjoy being referred to as a hussy by my own grandfather."

But Stella-Rondo says, "Yes, you did say it too. Anybody in the world could of heard you, that had ears."

"Stop right there," says Mama, looking at *me.*

So I pulled my napkin straight back through the napkin ring and left the table.

As soon as I was out of the room Mama says, "Call her back, or she'll starve to death," but Papa-Daddy says, "This is the beard I started growing on the Coast when I was fifteen years

WALKER EVANS.
*U.S. Post Office Sprott
Alabama.* 1936.
Photograph. U.S. Farm
Security Administration
Collection, Prints and
Photographs Division,
Library of Congress.

old." He would of gone on till nightfall if Shirley-T. hadn't lost the Milky Way she ate
in Cairo.

So Papa-Daddy says, "I am going out and lie in the hammock, and you can all sit here and
remember my words: I'll never cut off my beard as long as I live, even one inch, and I don't
appreciate it in you at all." Passed right by me in the hall and went straight out and got in
the hammock.

It would be a holiday. It wasn't five minutes before Uncle Rondo suddenly appeared in the
hall in one of Stella-Rondo's flesh-colored kimonos, all cut on the bias, like something Mr.
Whitaker probably thought was gorgeous.

"Uncle Rondo!" I says. "I didn't know who that was! Where are you going?"

"Sister," he says, "get out of my way, I'm poisoned."

"If you're poisoned stay away from Papa-Daddy," I says. "Keep out of the hammock.
Papa-Daddy will certainly beat you on the head if you come within forty miles of him. He
thinks I deliberately said he ought to cut off his beard after he got me the P.O., and I've told
him and told him and told him, and he acts like he just don't hear me. Papa-Daddy must of
gone stone deaf."

"He picked a fine day to do it then," says Uncle Rondo, and before you could say "Jack Robinson" flew out in the yard.

What he'd really done, he'd drunk another bottle of that prescription. He does it every single Fourth of July as sure as shooting, and it's horribly expensive. Then he falls over in the hammock and snores. So he insisted on zigzagging right on out to the hammock, looking like a half-wit.

Papa-Daddy woke up with this horrible yell and right there without moving an inch he tried to turn Uncle Rondo against me. I heard every word he said. Oh, he told Uncle Rondo I didn't learn to read till I was eight years old and he didn't see how in the world I ever got the mail put up at the P.O., much less read it all, and he said if Uncle Rondo could only fathom the lengths he had gone to to get me that job! And he said on the other hand he thought Stella-Rondo had a brilliant mind and deserved credit for getting out of town. All the time he was just lying there swinging as pretty as you please and looping out his beard, and poor Uncle Rondo was *pleading* with him to slow down the hammock, it was making him as dizzy as a witch to watch it. But that's what Papa-Daddy likes about a hammock. So Uncle Rondo was too dizzy to get turned against me for the time being. He's Mama's only brother and is a good case of a one-track mind. Ask anybody. A certified pharmacist.

Just then I heard Stella-Rondo raising the upstairs window. While she was married she got this peculiar idea that it's cooler with the windows shut and locked. So she has to raise the window before she can make a soul hear her outdoors.

So she raises the window and says, *"Oh!"* You would have thought she was mortally wounded.

Uncle Rondo and Papa-Daddy didn't even look up, but kept right on with what they were doing. I had to laugh.

I flew up the stairs and threw the door open! I says, "What in the wide world's the matter, Stella-Rondo? You mortally wounded?"

"No," she says, "I am not mortally wounded but I wish you would do me the favor of looking out that window there and telling me what you see."

So I shade my eyes and look out the window.

"I see the front yard," I says.

"Don't you see any human beings?" she says.

"I see Uncle Rondo trying to run Papa-Daddy out of the hammock," I says. "Nothing more. Naturally, it's so suffocating-hot in the house, with all the windows shut and locked, everybody who cares to stay in their right mind will have to go out and get in the hammock before the Fourth of July is over."

"Don't you notice anything different about Uncle Rondo?" asks Stella-Rondo.

"Why, no, except he's got on some terrible-looking flesh-colored contraption I wouldn't be found dead in, is all I can see," I says.

"Never mind, you won't be found dead in it, because it happens to be part of my trousseau, and Mr. Whitaker took several dozen photographs of me in it," says Stella-Rondo. "What on earth could Uncle Rondo *mean* by wearing part of my trousseau out in the broad open daylight without saying so much as 'Kiss my foot,' *knowing* I only got home this morning after my separation and hung my negligee up on the bathroom door, just as nervous as I could be?"

"I'm sure I don't know, and what do you expect me to do about it?" I says. "Jump out the window?"

"No, I expect nothing of the kind. I simply declare that Uncle Rondo looks like a fool in it, that's all," she says. "It makes me sick to my stomach."

"Well, he looks as good as he can," I says. "As good as anybody in reason could." I stood up for Uncle Rondo, please remember. And I said to Stella-Rondo, "I think I would do well not to criticize so freely if I were you and came home with a two-year-old child I had never said a word about, and no explanation whatever about my separation."

"I asked you the instant I entered this house not to refer one more time to my adopted child, and you gave me your word of honor you would not," was all Stella-Rondo would say, and started pulling out every one of her eyebrows with some cheap Kress tweezers.

So I merely slammed the door behind me and went down and made some green-tomato pickle. Somebody had to do it. Of course Mama had turned both the niggers loose; she always said no earthly power could hold one anyway on the Fourth of July, so she wouldn't even try. It turned out that Jaypan fell in the lake and came within a very narrow limit of drowning.

So Mama trots in. Lifts up the lid and says, "H'm! Not very good for your Uncle Rondo in his precarious condition, I must say. Or poor little adopted Shirley-T. Shame on you!"

That made me tired. I says, "Well, Stella-Rondo had better thank her lucky stars it was her instead of me came trotting in with that very peculiar-looking child. Now if it had been me that trotted in from Illinois and brought a peculiar-looking child of two, I shudder to think of the reception I'd of got, much less controlled the diet of an entire family."

"But you must remember, Sister, that you were never married to Mr. Whitaker in the first place and didn't go up to Illinois to live," says Mama, shaking a spoon in my face. "If you had I would of been just as overjoyed to see you and your little adopted girl as I was to see Stella-Rondo, when you wound up with your separation and came on back home."

"You would not," I says.

"Don't contradict me, I would," says Mama.

But I said she couldn't convince me though she talked till she was blue in the face. Then I said, "Besides, you know as well as I do that that child is not adopted."

"She most certainly is adopted," says Mama, stiff as a poker.

I says, "Why, Mama, Stella-Rondo had her just as sure as anything in this world, and just too stuck up to admit it."

"Why, Sister," said Mama. "Here I thought we were going to have a pleasant Fourth of July, and you start right out not believing a word your own baby sister tells you!"

"Just like Cousin Annie Flo. Went to her grave denying the facts of life," I remind Mama.

"I told you if you ever mentioned Annie Flo's name I'd slap your face," says Mama, and slaps my face.

"All right, you wait and see," I says.

"I," says Mama, "*I* prefer to take my children's word for anything when it's humanly possible." You ought to see Mama, she weighs two hundred pounds and has real tiny feet.

Just then something perfectly horrible occurred to me.

"Mama," I says, "can that child talk?" I simply had to whisper! "Mama, I wonder if that child can be—you know—in any way? Do you realize," I says, "that she hasn't spoken one single, solitary word to a human being up to this minute? This is the way she looks," I says, and I looked like this.

Well, Mama and I just stood there and stared at each other. It was horrible!

"I remember well that Joe Whitaker frequently drank like a fish," says Mama. "I believed to my soul he drank *chemicals*." And without another word she marches to the foot of the stairs and calls Stella-Rondo.

"Stella-Rondo? O-o-o-o-o! Stella-Rondo!"

"What?" says Stella-Rondo from upstairs. Not even the grace to get up off the bed.

"Can that child of yours talk?" asks Mama.

Stella-Rondo says, "Can she what?"

"Talk! Talk!" says Mama. "Burdyburdyburdyburdy!"

So Stella-Rondo yells back, "Who says she can't talk?"

"Sister says so," says Mama.

"You didn't have to tell me, I know whose word of honor don't mean a thing in this house," says Stella-Rondo.

And in a minute the loudest Yankee voice I ever heard in my life yells out, "OE'm Pop-OE the Sailor-r-r-r Ma-a-an!" and then somebody jumps up and down in the upstairs hall. In another second the house would of fallen down.

"Not only talks, she can tap-dance!" calls Stella-Rondo. "Which is more than some people I won't name can do."

"Why, the little precious darling thing!" Mama says, so surprised. "Just as smart as she can be!" Starts talking baby talk right there. Then she turns on me. "Sister, you ought to be thoroughly ashamed! Run upstairs this instant and apologize to Stella-Rondo and Shirley-T."

"Apologize for what?" I says. "I merely wondered if the child was normal, that's all. Now that she's proved she is, why, I have nothing further to say."

But Mama just turned on her heel and flew out, furious. She ran right upstairs and hugged the baby. She believed it was adopted. Stella-Rondo hadn't done a thing but turn her against me from upstairs while I stood there helpless over the hot stove. So that made Mama, Papa-Daddy and the baby all on Stella-Rondo's side.

Next, Uncle Rondo.

I must say that Uncle Rondo has been marvelous to me at various times in the past and I was completely unprepared to be made to jump out of my skin, the way it turned out. Once Stella-Rondo did something perfectly horrible to him— broke a chain letter from Flanders Field—and he took the radio back he had given her and gave it to me. Stella-Rondo was furious! For six months we all had to call her Stella instead of Stella-Rondo, or she wouldn't answer. I always thought Uncle Rondo had all the brains of the entire family. Another time he sent me to Mammoth Cave, with all expenses paid.

But this would be the day he was drinking that prescription, the Fourth of July.

So at supper Stella-Rondo speaks up and says she thinks Uncle Rondo ought to try to eat a little something. So finally Uncle Rondo said he would try a little cold biscuits and ketchup, but that was all. So *she* brought it to him.

"Do you think it wise to disport with ketchup in Stella-Rondo's flesh-colored kimono?" I says. Trying to be considerate! If Stella-Rondo couldn't watch out for her trousseau, somebody had to.

"Any objections?" asks Uncle Rondo, just about to pour out all the ketchup.

"Don't mind what she says, Uncle Rondo," says Stella-Rondo. "Sister has been devoting this solid afternoon to sneering out my bedroom window at the way you look."

"What's that?" says Uncle Rondo. Uncle Rondo has got the most terrible temper in the world. Anything is liable to make him tear the house down if it comes at the wrong time.

MINNIE EVANS. *Untitled.* 1960–1966. Oil on canvas. Collection of Mr. and Mrs. Fries Shaffner. *Inspired in part by the profusion of flowers at the estate where she worked as gatekeeper and by her peaceful visions of a heavenly world, Evans's art is mystical and Edenic. "We talk of heaven, we think of everything is going to be white. But I believe we're going to have the beautiful rainbow colors," she has said.*

COLORPLATE 83

BOYD CRUISE. *Red Plums.* 1949. Louisiana State University Museum of Art, Baton Rouge. *Boyd Cruise grew up in Lake Charles, Louisiana. His watercolors are remarkable for their attention to detail and their lush opacity.*

COLORPLATE 84

MARION SOUCHON. *After the Show.* c. 1945. Oil on masonite. 31 ¹/₂ x 29 in. Roger Houston Ogden Collection, New Orleans. *Souchon, a surgeon, had a second career as a painter from the 1930s until his death in 1954.*

COLORPLATE 85

NELL CHOATE JONES (1879–1981). *Georgia Red Clay.* 1946. Oil on canvas. 25 x 30 in. Morris Museum of Art, Augusta, Georgia. *The daughter of a Confederate captain, Nell Choate Jones had a long and active life in art, living to the age of 101. Although much of her life was spent away from her native Georgia, that landscape and culture inspired her for many years. This painting captures the violent rawness of the land, and is a fine example of her bold, expressionistic style.*

COLORPLATE 86 (following page)

THOMAS HART BENTON. *Arts of the South.* 1932. Collection of the New Britain Museum of American Art, Connecticut. Harriet Russell Stanley Fund. Photograph courtesy Arthur Evans. © Thomas Hart Benton and Rita P. Benton Testamentary Trusts/VAGA, New York 1993. *Although Benton's art, like that of Twain, his fellow Missourian, was more American in character than distinctly Southern, he nevertheless captured the spirit of the region in many paintings and murals. Using techniques and materials he learned from studying Renaissance and Baroque paintings in The Louvre, Benton combined a classic style with humble subject matter to create art that glorified the American landscape and experience. Benton understood that the South was truly rich artistically, but that its most vital arts were those of oratory, folklore, indigenous music, and fervent religious worship.*

COLORPLATE 88

AUGUSTA OELSCHIG. *Play Ball.* c. 1955. Oil on canvas. 17 x 26 in. Morris Museum of Art, Augusta, Georgia 1989.01.146. *Augusta Oelschig, from Savannah, devoted her talents to subjects that would have been easier for her to ignore. Many of her paintings are genre scenes of black life, but some present scenes of terrible social injustice.*

COLORPLATE 87 (opposite)

CHARLES SHANNON. *Saturday Night.* 1937. Oil on canvas. 34 x 24 in. Morris Museum of Art, Augusta, Georgia 1989.01.175. *Many of Shannon's expressionistic paintings show his interest in African-American life, and it was he who encouraged the homeless, self-taught artist Bill Traylor. Shannon, of Montgomery, Alabama, was instrumental in the formation of local and regional arts organizations in the 1930s and 1940s.*

COLORPLATE 89

ROMARE BEARDEN. *Mecklenberg County: High Cotton Mother and Child.* 1978. Watercolor. 6 5/8 x 10 5/8 in. Estate of Romare Howard Bearden. *Like thousands of African-Americans in the early part of the twentieth century, Romare Bearden migrated to New York from Charlotte, North Carolina. Painting and constructing collages in an abstract style that recalls cubism and the stylized forms of African art, Bearden's work is unsurpassed in its power and originality. His two greatest influences were black music and his memories of Southern life: "This is why I've gone back to the South and to jazz. Even though you go through these terrible experiences, you come out feeling good. That's what the Blues say and that's what I believe— life will prevail."*

COLORPLATE 90

BILL TRAYLOR. *Figure/Construction with Blue Border*. Collection of Charles Shannon, Montgomery, Alabama (c/o Museum of American Folk, New York). *Bill Traylor of Montgomery, Alabama, was born into slavery in 1854 and took his master's name. He sharecropped most of his life and began drawing in 1939 at the age of eighty-five. Homeless, sleeping in a funeral parlor at night, by day Traylor would draw on discarded cardboard with pencil stubs, sticks, and poster paint.*

COLORPLATE 91

REVEREND HOWARD FINSTER (b. 1916). *World of the Happy and Free.* 1986. Mixed media construction. 34 x 24 x 5 in. Roger Houston Ogden Collection, New Orleans. *God instructed evangelical Baptist preacher Finster to "paint sacred art." Finster's "sermons in paint" followed. Finster represented the US at the 1984 Venice Biennial.*

COLORPLATE 92

WILLIAM DUNLAP. *He'll Set Your Fields on Fire.* c. 1990. Jones Troyer Fitzpatrick Gallery, Washington, D.C. *Years of driving up and down country roads have given William Dunlap, a Mississippian now living in Virginia, what he calls "an aesthetic of the road," where long vistas combine with ubiquitous man-made forms like roadside signage.*

COLORPLATE 93 (opposite)

STANLEY SPORNY. *Mardi Gras Nap.* 1988. Oil on canvas. 72 x 44 in. Roger Houston Ogden Collection, New Orleans.

COLORPLATE 94

DAVID PARRISH. *Elvis.* 1988. Oil on canvas. 74 x 104 ½ in. Courtesy Louis K. Meisel Gallery, New York. Photograph by Steve Lopez. *The most famous Southerner who ever lived, Elvis revolutionized American music by synthesizing black and white gospel music, blues, and country, and made Rockabilly palatable to white audiences. Defending the electrifying sexuality of his style, Elvis said, "The colored folk been singin' it and playin' it just the way I'm doin' now, man, for more years than I know. Nobody paid it no mind 'til I goosed it up."*

COLORPLATE 95

REVEREND MCKENDREE ROBBINS LONG. *The Deceiver of the Whole World.* 1969. Oil on canvas. 48 x 60 in. Roger Houston Ogden Collection, New Orleans. *The Reverend Long, born in North Carolina, was ordained as a Presbyterian minister in 1922. Late in his life he completed ninety paintings interpreting the Book of Revelation.*

COLORPLATE 96

TARLETON BLACKWELL. "Hog Series LXVII." *Fox Chef.* 1992. Oil on canvas. 48 x 38 in.
Courtesy of Tarleton Blackwell Studio.

COLORPLATE 97

WILLIAM EGGLESTON. *Water Valley, MS.* Color photograph. Courtesy of the artist. *In 1976 William Eggleston was given the first exhibition of color photography ever mounted at the Museum of Modern Art. Using a dye-transfer printing technique normally used in commercial photography, Eggleston is able to achieve a high degree of color saturation in his work, which, as in this photograph, reproduces with remarkable intensity. "I am at war with the obvious," Mr. Eggleston has said.*

So Stella-Rondo says, "Sister says, 'Uncle Rondo certainly does look like a fool in that pink kimono!'"

Do you remember who it was really said that?

Uncle Rondo spills out all the ketchup and jumps out of his chair and tears off the kimono and throws it down on the dirty floor and puts his foot on it. It had to be sent all the way to Jackson to the cleaners and re-pleated.

"So that's your opinion of your Uncle Rondo, is it?" he says. "I look like a fool, do I? Well, that's the last straw. A whole day in this house with nothing to do, and then to hear you come out with a remark like that behind my back!"

"I didn't say any such of a thing, Uncle Rondo," I says, "and I'm not saying who did, either. Why, I think you look all right. Just try to take care of yourself and not talk and eat at the same time," I says. "I think you better go lie down."

"Lie down my foot," says Uncle Rondo. I ought to of known by that he was fixing to do something perfectly horrible.

So he didn't do anything that night in the precarious state he was in—just played Casino with Mama and Stella-Rondo and Shirley-T. and gave Shirley-T. a nickel with a head on both sides. It tickled her nearly to death, and she called him "Papa." But at 6:30 A.M. the next morning, he threw a whole five-cent package of some unsold one-inch firecrackers from the store as hard as he could into my bedroom and they every one went off. Not one bad one in the string. Anybody else, there'd be one that wouldn't go off.

Well, I'm just terribly susceptible to noise of any kind, the doctor has always told me I was the most sensitive person he had ever seen in his whole life, and I was simply prostrated. I couldn't eat! People tell me they heard it as far as the cemetery, and old Aunt Jep Patterson, that had been holding her own so good, thought it was Judgment Day and she was going to meet her whole family. It's usually so quiet here.

And I'll tell you it didn't take me any longer than a minute to make up my mind what to do. There I was with the whole entire house on Stella-Rondo's side and turned against me. If I have anything at all I have pride.

So I just decided I'd go straight down to the P.O. There's plenty of room there in the back, I says to myself.

Well! I made no bones about letting the family catch on to what I was up to. I didn't try to conceal it.

The first thing they knew, I marched in where they were all playing Old Maid and pulled the electric oscillating fan out by the plug, and everything got real hot. Next I snatched the pillow I'd done the needlepoint on right off the davenport from behind Papa-Daddy. He went "Ugh!" I beat Stella-Rondo up the stairs and finally found my charm bracelet in her bureau drawer under a picture of Nelson Eddy.

"So that's the way the land lies," says Uncle Rondo. There he was, piecing on the ham. "Well, Sister, I'll be glad to donate my army cot if you got any place to set it up, providing you'll leave right this minute and let me get some peace." Uncle Rondo was in France.

"Thank you kindly for the cot and 'peace' is hardly the word I would select if I had to resort to firecrackers at 6:30 A.M. in a young girl's bedroom," I says back to him. "And as to where I intend to go, you seem to forget my position as postmistress of China Grove, Mississippi," I says. "I've always got the P.O."

Well, that made them all sit up and take notice.

I went out front and started digging up some four-o'clocks to plant around the P.O.

"Ah-ah-ah!" says Mama, raising the window. "Those happen to be my four-o'clocks. Everything planted in that star is mine. I've never known you to make anything grow in your life."

"Very well," I says. "But I take the fern. Even you, Mama, can't stand there and deny that I'm the one watered that fern. And I happen to know where I can send in a box top and get a packet of one thousand mixed seeds, no two the same kind, free."

"Oh, where?" Mama wants to know.

But I says, "Too late. You 'tend to your house, and I'll 'tend to mine. You hear things like that all the time if you know how to listen to the radio. Perfectly marvelous offers. Get anything you want free."

So I hope to tell you I marched in and got that radio, and they could of all bit a nail in two, especially Stella-Rondo, that it used to belong to, and she well knew she couldn't get it back, I'd sue for it like a shot. And I very politely took the sewing-machine motor I helped pay the most on to give Mama for Christmas back in 1929, and a good big calendar, with the first-aid remedies on it. The thermometer and the Hawaiian ukulele certainly were rightfully mine, and I stood on the step-ladder and got all my watermelon-rind preserves and every fruit and vegetable I'd put up, every jar. Then I began to pull the tacks out of the bluebird wall vases on the archway to the dining room.

"Who told you you could have those, Miss Priss?" says Mama, fanning as hard as she could.

"I bought 'em and I'll keep track of 'em," I says. "I'll tack 'em up one on each side the post-office window, and you can see 'em when you come to ask me for your mail, if you're so dead to see 'em."

"Not I! I'll never darken the door to that post office again if I live to be a hundred," Mama says. "Ungrateful child! After all the money we spent on you at the Normal."

"Me either," says Stella-Rondo. "You can just let my mail lie there and *rot,* for all I care. I'll never come and relieve you of a single, solitary piece."

"I should worry," I says. "And who you think's going to sit down and write you all those big fat letters and postcards, by the way? Mr. Whitaker? Just because he was the only man ever dropped down in China Grove and you got him—unfairly—is he going to sit down and write you a lengthy correspondence after you come home giving no rhyme nor reason whatsoever for your separation and no explanation for the presence of that child? I may not have your brilliant mind, but I fail to see it."

So Mama says, "Sister, I've told you a thousand times that Stella-Rondo simply got homesick, and this child is far too big to be hers," and she says, "Now, why don't you all just sit down and play Casino?"

Then Shirley-T. sticks out her tongue at me in this perfectly horrible way. She has no more manners than the man in the moon. I told her she was going to cross her eyes like that some day and they'd stick.

"It's too late to stop me now," I says. "You should have tried that yesterday. I'm going to the P.O. and the only way you can possibly see me is to visit me there."

So Papa-Daddy says, "You'll never catch me setting foot in that post office, even if I should take a notion into my head to write a letter some place." He says, "I won't have you reachin' out of that little old window with a pair of shears and cuttin' off any beard of mine. I'm too smart for you!"

"We all are," says Stella-Rondo.

But I said, "If you're so smart, where's Mr. Whitaker?"

So then Uncle Rondo says, "I'll thank you from now on to stop reading all the orders I get on postcards and telling everybody in China Grove what you think is the matter with them," but I says, "I draw my own conclusions and will continue in the future to draw them." I says, "If people want to write their inmost secrets on penny postcards, there's nothing in the wide world you can do about it, Uncle Rondo."

"And if you think we'll ever *write* another postcard you're sadly mistaken," says Mama.

"Cutting off your nose to spite your face then," I says. "But if you're all determined to have no more to do with the U. S. mail, think of this: What will Stella-Rondo do now, if she wants to tell Mr. Whitaker to come after her?"

"Wah!" says Stella-Rondo. I knew she'd cry. She had a conniption fit right there in the kitchen.

"It will be interesting to see how long she holds out," I says. "And now—I am leaving."

"Good-bye," says Uncle Rondo.

"Oh, I declare," says Mama, "to think that a family of mine should quarrel on the Fourth of July, or the day after, over Stella-Rondo leaving old Mr. Whitaker and having the sweetest little adopted child! It looks like we'd all be glad!"

"Wah!" says Stella-Rondo, and has a fresh conniption fit.

"*He* left *her*—you mark my words," I says. "That's Mr. Whitaker. I know Mr. Whitaker. After all, I knew him first. I said from the beginning he'd up and leave her. I foretold every single thing that's happened."

"Where did he go?" asks Mama.

"Probably to the North Pole, if he knows what's good for him," I says.

But Stella-Rondo just bawled and wouldn't say another word. She flew to her room and slammed the door.

"Now look what you've gone and done, Sister," says Mama. "You go apologize."

"I haven't got time, I'm leaving," I says.

"Well, what are you waiting around for?" asks Uncle Rondo.

So I just picked up the kitchen clock and marched off, without saying "Kiss my foot" or anything, and never did tell Stella-Rondo good-bye.

There was a nigger girl going along on a little wagon right in front.

"Nigger girl," I says, "come help me haul these things down the hill, I'm going to live in the post office."

Took her nine trips in her express wagon. Uncle Rondo came out on the porch and threw her a nickel.

And that's the last I've laid eyes on any of my family or my family laid eyes on me for five solid days and nights. Stella-Rondo may be telling the most horrible tales in the world about Mr. Whitaker, but I haven't heard them. As I tell everybody, I draw my own conclusions.

But oh, I like it here. It's ideal, as I've been saying. You see, I've got everything cater-cornered, the way I like it. Hear the radio? All the war news. Radio, sewing machine, book ends, ironing board and that great big piano lamp—peace, that's what I like. Butter-bean vines planted all along the front where the strings are.

Of course, there's not much mail. My family are naturally the main people in China Grove, and if they prefer to vanish from the face of the earth, for all the mail they get or the mail they write, why, I'm not going to open my mouth. Some of the folks here in town are taking up for me and some turned against me. I know which is which. There are always people who will quit buying stamps just to get on the right side of Papa-Daddy.

But here I am, and here I'll stay. I want the world to know I'm happy.

And if Stella-Rondo should come to me this minute, on bended knees, and *attempt* to explain the incidents of her life with Mr. Whitaker, I'd simply put my fingers in both my ears and refuse to listen.

ROBERT PENN WARREN

From *All the King's Men*

A poet, critic, and novelist, Robert Penn Warren was one of America's most prolific and versatile writers. All the King's Men, *a novel about a Louisiana politician named Willie Stark who closely resembles Huey Long, won a Pulitzer Prize in 1947. Here, Willie Stark shows some of the charismatic power that made him a very effective but dangerous leader.*

You come in on Number 58, and pass the cotton gin and the power station and the fringe of nigger shacks and bump across the railroad track and down a street where there are a lot of little houses painted white one time, with the sad valentine lace of gingerbread work around the eaves of the veranda, and tin roofs, and where the leaves on the trees in the yards hang straight

down in the heat, and above the mannerly whisper of your eighty-horsepower valve-in-head (or whatever it is) drifting at forty, you hear the July flies grinding away in the verdure.

That was the way it was the last time I saw Mason City, nearly three years ago, back in the summer of 1936. I was in the first car, the Cadillac, with the Boss and Mr. Duffy and the Boss's wife and son and Sugar-Boy. In the second car, which lacked our quiet elegance reminiscent of a cross between a hearse and an ocean liner but which still wouldn't make your cheeks burn with shame in the country-club parking lot, there were some reporters and a photographer and Sadie Burke, the Boss's secretary, to see they got there sober enough to do what they were supposed to do.

Sugar-Boy was driving the Cadillac, and it was a pleasure to watch him. Or it would have been if you could detach your imagination from the picture of what near a couple of tons of expensive mechanism looks like after it's turned turtle three times at eighty and could give your undivided attention to the exhibition of muscular co-ordination, satanic humor, and split-second timing which was Sugar-Boy's when he whipped around a hay wagon in the face of an oncoming gasoline truck and went through the rapidly diminishing aperture close enough to give the truck driver heart failure with one rear fender and wipe the snot off a mule's nose with the other. But the Boss loved it. He always sat up front with Sugar-Boy and looked at the speedometer and down the road and grinned to Sugar-Boy after they got through between the mule's nose and the gasoline truck. And Sugar-Boy's head would twitch, the way it always did when the words were piling up inside of him and couldn't get out, and then he'd start. "The b-b-b-b-b—" he would manage to get out and the saliva would spray from his lips like Flit from a Flit gun. "The b-b-b-b-bas-tud—he seen me c-c-c—" and here he'd spray the inside of the windshield— "c-c-com-ing." Sugar-Boy couldn't talk, but he could express himself when he got his foot on the accelerator. He wouldn't win any debating contests in high school, but then nobody would ever want to debate with Sugar-Boy. Not anybody who knew him and had seen him do tricks with the .38 Special which rode under his left armpit like a tumor.

No doubt you thought Sugar-Boy was a Negro, from his name. But he wasn't. He was Irish, from the wrong side of the tracks. He was about five-feet-two, and he was getting bald, though he wasn't more than twenty-seven or -eight years old, and he wore red ties and under the red tie and his shirt he wore a little Papist medal on a chain, and I always hoped to God it was St. Christopher and that St. Christopher was on the job. His name was O'Sheean, but they called him Sugar-Boy because he ate sugar. Every time he went to a restaurant he took all the cube sugar there was in the bowl. He went around with his pockets stuffed with sugar cubes, and when he took one out to pop into his mouth you saw little pieces of gray lint sticking to it, the kind of lint there always is loose in your pocket, and shreds of tobacco from cigarettes. He'd pop the cube in over the barricade of his twisted black little teeth, and then you'd see the thin little mystic Irish cheeks cave in as he sucked the sugar, so that he looked like an under-nourished leprechaun.

The Boss was sitting in the front seat with Sugar-Boy and watching the speedometer, with his kid Tom up there with him. Tom was then about eighteen or nineteen—I forgot which—but you would have thought he was older. He wasn't so big, but he was built like a man and his head sat on his shoulders like a man's head without that gangly, craning look a kid's head has. He had been a high-school football hero and the fall before he had been the flashiest thing on the freshman team at State. He got his name in the papers because he was really good. He knew he was good. He knew he was the nuts, as you could tell from one look at his slick-skinned handsome brown face, with the jawbone working insolently and slow over a little piece of chewing gum and his blue eyes under half-lowered lids working insolently and slow over you, or the whole damned world. But that day when he was up in the front seat with Willie Stark, who was the Boss, I couldn't see his face. I remembered thinking his head, the shape and the way it was set on his shoulders, was just like his old man's head.

Mrs. Stark—Lucy Stark, the wife of the Boss—Tiny Duffy, and I were in the back seat—Lucy Stark between Tiny and me. It wasn't exactly a gay little gathering. The temperature didn't make for chitchat in the first place. In the second place, I was watching out for the hay wagons and gasoline trucks. In the third place, Duffy and Lucy Stark never were exactly chummy. So she sat between Duffy and me and gave herself to her thoughts. I reckon she had plenty to think about. For one thing, she could think about all that had happened since she was a girl teaching her first year in the school at Mason City and had married a red-faced and red-necked farm boy with big slow hands and a shock of dark brown hair coming down over his brow (you can look at the wedding picture which has been in the papers along with a thousand other pictures of Willie) and a look of dog-like devotion and wonder in his eyes when they fixed on her. She would have had a lot to think about as she sat in the hurtling Cadillac, for there had been a lot of changes.

We tooled down the street where the little one-time-white houses were, and hit the square. It was Saturday afternoon and the square was full of folks. The wagons and the crates were parked solid around the patch of grass roots in the middle of which stood the courthouse, a red-brick box, well weathered and needing paint, for it had been there since before the Civil War, with a little tower with a clock face on each side. On the second look you discovered that the clock faces weren't real. They were just painted on, and they all said five o'clock and not eight-seventeen the way those big painted watches in front of third-string jewelry stores used to. We eased into the ruck of folks come in to do their trading, and Sugar-Boy leaned on his horn, and his head twitched, and he said, "B-b-b-b-as-tuds," and the spit flew.

We pulled up in front of the drugstore, and the kid Tom got out and then the Boss, before Sugar-Boy could get around to the door. I got out and helped out Lucy Stark, who came up from the depths of heat and meditation long enough to say, "Thank you." She stood there on the pavement a second, touching her skirt into place around her hips, which had a little more beam on them than no doubt had been the case when she won the heart of Willie Stark, the farm boy.

Mr. Duffy debouched massively from the Cadillac, and we all entered the drugstore, the Boss holding the door open so Lucy Stark could go in and then following her, and the rest of us trailing in. There were a good many folks in the store, men in overalls lined up along the soda fountain, and women hanging around the counters where the junk and glory was, and kids hanging on skirts with one hand and clutching ice-cream cones with the other and staring out over their own wet noses at the world of men from eyes which resembled painted china marbles. The Boss just stood modestly back of the gang of customers at the soda fountain, with his

JOHN McCRADY. *Political Rally.* 1935. Multi-stage oil on canvas. Courtesy Mr. and Mrs. Jack McLarty, Jackson, MS. *John McCrady painted many scenes of small-town life in Oxford, Mississippi, where he had lived. This gathering of townspeople listens to a local demagogue. The tweedy, aloof figure of William Faulkner is on the right, pipe in hand.*

hat in his hand and the damp hair hanging down over his forehead. He stood that way a minute maybe, and then one of the girls ladling up ice cream happened to see him, and got a look on her face as though her garter belt had busted in church, and dropped her ice-cream scoop, and headed for the back of the store with her hips pumping hell-for-leather under the lettuce-green smock.

Then a second later a little bald-headed fellow wearing a white coat which ought to have been in the week's wash came plunging through the crowd from the back of the store, waving his hand and bumping the customers and yelling, "It's Willie!" The fellow ran up to the Boss, and the Boss took a couple of steps to meet him, and the fellow with the white coat grabbed Willie's hand as though he were drowning. He didn't shake Willie's hand, not by ordinary standards. He just hung on to it and twitched all over and gargled the sacred syllables of *Willie.* Then, when the attack had passed, he turned to the crowd, which was ringing around at a polite distance and staring, and announced, "My God, folks, it's Willie!"

The remark was superfluous. One look at the faces rallied around and you knew that if any citizen over the age of three didn't know that the strong-set man standing there in the Palm Beach suit was Willie Stark, that citizen was a half-wit. In the first place, all he would have to do would be to lift his eyes to the big picture high up there above the soda fountain, a picture about six times life size, which showed the same face, the big eyes, which in the picture had the suggestion of a sleepy and inward look (the eyes of the man in the Palm Beach suit didn't have that look now, but I've seen it), the pouches under the eyes and the jowls beginning to sag off, and the meaty lips, which didn't sag but if you looked close were laid one on top of the other like a couple of bricks, and the tousle of hair hanging down on the not very high squarish forehead. Under the picture was the legend: *My study is the heart of the people.* In quotation marks, and signed, *Willie Stark.* I had seen that picture in a thousand places, pool halls to palaces.

Somebody back in the crowd yelled, "Hi, Willie!" The Boss lifted his right hand and waved in acknowledgment to the unknown admirer. Then the Boss spied a fellow at the far end of the soda fountain, a tall, gaunt-shanked, malarial, leather-faced side of jerked venison, wearing jean pants and a brace of mustaches hanging off the kind of face you see in photographs of General Forrest's cavalrymen, and the Boss started toward him and put out his hand. Old Leather-Face didn't show. Maybe he shuffled one of his broken brogans on the tiles, and his Adam's apple jerked once or twice, and the eyes were watchful out of that face which resembled the seat of an old saddle left out in the weather, but when the Boss got close, his hand came up from the elbow, as though it didn't belong to Old Leather-Face but was operating on its own, and the Boss took it.

"How you making it, Malaciah?" the Boss asked.

The Adam's apple worked a couple of times, and the Boss shook the hand which was hanging out there in the air as if it didn't belong to anybody, and Old Leather-Face said, "We's grabblen."

"How's your boy?" the Boss asked.

"Ain't doen so good," Old Leather-Face allowed.

"Sick?"

"Naw," Old Leather-Face allowed, "jail."

"My God," the Boss said, "what they doing round here, putting good boys in jail?"

"He's a good boy," Old Leather-Face allowed. "Hit wuz a fahr fight, but he had a lettle bad luck."

"Huh?"

"Hit wuz fahr and squahr, but he had a lettle bad luck. He stobbed the feller and he died."

"Tough tiddy," the Boss said. Then: "Tried yet?"

"Not yit."

"Tough tiddy," the Boss said.

"I ain't complainen," Old Leather-Face said. "Hit wuz fit fahr and squahr."

"Glad to seen you," the Boss said. "Tell your boy to keep his tail over the dashboard."

"He ain't complainen," Old Leather-Face said.

The Boss started to turn away to the rest of us who after a hundred miles in the dazzle were looking at that soda fountain as though it were a mirage, but Old Leather-Face said, "Willie."

"Huh?" the Boss answered.

"Yore pitcher," Old Leather-Face allowed, and jerked his head creakily toward the six-times-life-size photograph over the soda fountain. "Yore pitcher," he said, "hit don't do you no credit, Willie."

"Hell, no," the Boss said, studying the picture, cocking his head to one side and squinting at it, "but I was porely when they took it. I was like I'd had the cholera morbus. Get in there busting some sense into that Legislature, and it leaves a man worse'n the summer complaint."

"Git in thar and bust 'em, Willie!" somebody yelled from back in the crowd, which was thickening out now, for folks were trying to get in from the street.

"I'll bust 'em," Willie said, and turned around to the little man with the white coat. "Give us some cokes, Doc," he said, "for God's sake."

FLANNERY O'CONNOR
"Enoch and the Gorilla"

"Enoch and the Gorilla" became a chapter in Wise Blood, *O'Connor's first novel, published in 1952. O'Connor's work is often labelled "Southern Grotesque" or "Southern Gothic," but as she herself once said, "Whenever I'm asked why Southern writers particularly have a penchant for writing about freaks, I say it is because we are still able to recognize one."*

Enoch Emery had borrowed his landlady's umbrella and he discovered as he stood in the entrance of the drugstore, trying to open it, that it was at least as old as she was. When he finally got it hoisted, he pushed his dark glasses back on his eyes and re-entered the downpour.

The umbrella was one his landlady had stopped using fifteen years before (which was the only reason she had lent it to him) and as soon as the rain touched the top of it, it came down

with a shriek and stabbed him in the back of the neck. He ran a few feet with it over his head and then backed into another store entrance and removed it. Then to get it up again, he had to place the tip of it on the ground and ram it open with his foot. He ran out again, holding his hand up near the spokes to keep them open and this allowed the handle, which was carved to represent the head of a fox terrier, to jab him every few seconds in the stomach. He proceeded for another quarter of a block this way before the back half of the silk stood up off the spokes and allowed the storm to sweep down his collar. Then he ducked under the marquee of a movie house. It was Saturday and there were a lot of children standing more or less in a line in front of the ticket box.

Enoch was not very fond of children, but children always seemed to like to look at him. The line turned and twenty or thirty eyes began to observe him with a steady interest. The umbrella had assumed an ugly position, half up and half down, and the half that was up was about to come down and spill more water under his collar. When this happened the children laughed and jumped up and down. Enoch glared at them and turned his back and lowered his dark glasses. He found himself facing a life-size four-color picture of a gorilla. Over the goril-la's head, written in red letters was "GONGA! Giant Jungle Monarch and a Great Star! HERE IN PERSON!!!" At the level of the gorilla's knee, there was more that said, "Gonga will appear in person in front of this theater at 12 A.M. *TODAY!* A free pass to the first ten brave enough to step up and shake his hand!"

Enoch was usually thinking of something else at the moment that Fate began drawing back her leg to kick him. When he was four years old, his father had brought him home a tin box from the penitentiary. It was orange and had a picture of some peanut brittle on the outside of it and green letters that said, "A NUTTY SURPRISE!" When Enoch had opened it, a coiled piece of steel had sprung out at him and broken off the ends of his two front teeth. His life was full of so many happenings like that that it would seem he should have been more sensitive to his times of danger. He stood there and read the poster twice through carefully. To his mind, an opportunity to insult a successful ape came from the hand of Providence.

He turned around and asked the nearest child what time it was. The child said it was twelve-ten and that Gonga was already ten minutes late. Another child said that maybe the rain had delayed him. Another said, no not the rain, his director was taking a plane from Hollywood. Enoch gritted his teeth. The first child said that if he wanted to shake the star's hand, he would have to get in line like the rest of them and wait his turn. Enoch got in line. A child asked him how old he was. Another observed that he had funny-looking teeth. He ignored all this as best he could and began to straighten out the umbrella.

In a few minutes a black truck turned around the corner and came slowly up the street in the heavy rain. Enoch pushed the umbrella under his arm and began to squint through his dark glasses. As the truck approached, a phonograph inside it began to play "Tarara Boom Di Aye," but the music was almost drowned out by the rain. There was a large illustration of a blonde on the outside of the truck, advertising some picture other than the gorilla's.

The children held their line carefully as the truck stopped in front of the movie house. The back door of it was constructed like a paddy wagon, with a grate, but the ape was not at it. Two men in raincoats got out of the cab part, cursing, and ran around to the back and opened the door. One of them stuck his head in and said, "Okay, make it snappy, willya?" The other jerked his thumb at the children and said, "Get back willya, willya get back?"

A voice on the record inside the truck said, "Here's Gonga, folks, Roaring Gonga and a Great Star! Give Gonga a big hand, folks!" The voice was barely a mumble in the rain.

The man who was waiting by the door of the truck stuck his head in again. "Okay willya get out?" he said.

There was a faint thump somewhere inside the van. After a second a dark furry arm emerged just enough for the rain to touch it and then drew back inside.

"Goddamn," the man who was under the marquee said; he took off his raincoat and threw it to the man by the door, who threw it into the wagon. After two or three minutes more, the gorilla appeared at the door, with the raincoat buttoned up to his chin and the collar turned up. There was an iron chain hanging from around his neck; the man grabbed it and pulled him down and the two of them bounded under the marquee together. A motherly-looking woman was in the glass ticket box, getting the passes ready for the first ten children brave enough to step up and shake hands.

The gorilla ignored the children entirely and followed the man over to the other side of the entrance where there was a small platform raised about a foot off the ground. He stepped up on it and turned facing the children and began to growl. His growls were not so much loud as poisonous; they appeared to issue from a black heart. Enoch was terrified and if he had not been surrounded by the children, he would have run away.

"Who'll step up first?" the man said. "Come on come on, who'll step up first? A free pass to the first kid stepping up."

There was no movement from the group of children. The man glared at them. "What's the matter with you kids?" he barked. "You yellow? He won't hurt you as long as I got him by this chain." He tightened his grip on the chain and jangled it at them to show he was holding it securely.

After a minute a little girl separated herself from the group. She had long wood-shaving curls and a fierce triangular face. She moved up to within four feet of the star.

"Okay okay," the man said, rattling the chain, "make it snappy."

The ape reached out and gave her hand a quick shake. By this time there was another little girl ready and then two boys. The line re-formed and began to move up.

The gorilla kept his hand extended and turned his head away with a bored look at the rain. Enoch had got over his fear and was trying frantically to think of an obscene remark that would be suitable to insult him with. Usually he didn't have any trouble with this kind of composition but nothing came to him now. His brain, both parts, was completely empty. He couldn't think even of the insulting phrases he used every day.

EUDORA WELTY. *Side Show, State Fair, Jackson.* 1939.
Photograph. © Eudora Welty Collection—Mississippi
Department of Archives and History.

There were only two children in front of him by now. The first one shook hands and stepped aside. Enoch's heart was beating violently. The child in front of him finished and stepped aside and left him facing the ape, who took his hand with an automatic motion.

It was the first hand that had been extended to Enoch since he had come to the city. It was warm and soft.

For a second he only stood there, clasping it. Then he began to stammer. "My name is Enoch Emery," he mumbled. "I attended the Rodemill Boys' Bible Academy. I work at the city zoo. I seen two of your pictures. I'm only eighteen years old but I already work for the city. My daddy made me come . . ." and his voice cracked.

The star leaned slightly forward and a change came in his eyes: an ugly pair of human ones moved closer and squinted at Enoch from behind the celluloid pair. "You go to hell," a surly voice inside the ape-suit said, low but distinctly, and the hand was jerked away.

Enoch's humiliation was so sharp and painful that he turned around three times before he realized which direction he wanted to go in. Then he ran off into the rain as fast as he could.

In spite of himself, Enoch couldn't get over the expectation that something was going to happen to him. The virtue of hope, in Enoch, was made up of two parts suspicion and one part lust. It operated on him all the rest of the day. He had only a vague idea what he wanted, but he was not a boy without ambition: he wanted to become something. He wanted to better his condition. He wanted, some day, to see a line of people waiting to shake his hand.

All afternoon he fidgeted and fooled in his room, biting his nails and shredding what was left of the silk off the landlady's umbrella. finally he denuded it entirely and broke off the spokes. What was left was a black stick with a sharp steel point at one end and a dog's head at the other. It might have been an instrument for some specialized kind of torture that had gone out of fashion. Enoch walked up and down his room with it under his arm and realized that it would distinguish him on the sidewalk.

About seven o'clock in the evening he put on his coat and took the stick and headed for a little restaurant two blocks away. He had the sense that he was setting off to get some honor, but he was very nervous, as if he were afraid he might have to snatch it instead of receive it.

He never set out for anything without eating first. The restaurant was called the Paris Diner; it was a tunnel about six feet wide, located between a shoeshine parlor and a dry-cleaning establishment. Enoch slid in and climbed up on the far stool at the counter and said he would have a bowl of split-pea soup and a chocolate malted milkshake.

The waitress was a tall woman with a big yellow dental plate and the same color hair done up in a black hairnet. One hand never left her hip; she filled orders with the other one. Although Enoch came in every night, she had never learned to like him.

Instead of filling his order, she began to fry bacon; there was only one other customer in the place and he had finished his meal and was reading a newspaper; there was no one to eat the bacon but her. Enoch reached over the counter and prodded her hip with the stick. "Listenhere," he said, "I got to go. I'm in a hurry."

"Go then," she said. Her jaw began to work and she stared into the skillet with a fixed attention.

"Lemme just have a piece of theter cake yonder," he said, pointing to a half of pink and yellow cake on a round glass stand. "I think I got something to do. I got to be going. Set it up there next to him," he said, indicating the customer reading the newspaper. He slid over the stools and began reading the outside sheet of the man's paper.

The man lowered the paper and looked at him. Enoch smiled. The man raised the paper again. "Could I borrow some part of your paper that you ain't studying?" Enoch asked. The man lowered it again and stared at him; he had muddy unflinching eyes. He leafed deliberately through the paper and shook out the sheet with the comic strips and handed it to Enoch. It was Enoch's favorite part. He read it every evening like an office. While he ate the cake that the waitress had torpedoed down the counter at him, he read and felt himself surge with kindness and courage and strength.

When he finished one side, he turned the sheet over and began to scan the advertisements for movies that filled the other side. His eye went over three columns without stopping; then it came to a box that advertised Gonga, Giant Jungle Monarch, and listed the theaters he would visit on his tour and the hours he would be at each one. In thirty minutes he would arrive at the Victory on 57th Street and that would be his last appearance in the city.

If anyone had watched Enoch read this, he would have seen a certain transformation in his countenance. It still shone with the inspiration he had absorbed from the comic strips, but something else had come over it: a look of awakening.

The waitress happened to turn around to see if he hadn't gone. "What's the matter with you?" she said. "Did you swallow a seed?"

"I know what I want," Enoch murmured.

"I know what I want too," she said with a dark look.

Enoch felt for his stick and laid his change on the counter. "I got to be going."

"Don't let me keep you," she said.

"You may not see me again," he said, "—the way I am."

"Any way I don't see you will be all right with me," she said.

Enoch left. It was a pleasant damp evening. The puddles on the sidewalk shone and the store windows were steamy and bright with junk. He disappeared down a side street and made his way rapidly along the darker passages of the city, pausing only once or twice at the end of an alley to dart a glance in each direction before he ran on. The Victory was a small theater, suited to the needs of the family, in one of the closer subdivisions; he passed through a succession of lighted areas and then on through more alleys and back streets until he came to the business section that surrounded it. Then he slowed up. He saw it about a block away, glittering in its darker setting. He didn't cross the street to the side it was on but kept on the far side, moving forward with his squint fixed on the glary spot. He stopped when he was directly across from it and hid himself in a narrow stair cavity that divided a building.

The truck that carried Gonga was parked across the street and the star was standing under the marquee, shaking hands with an elderly woman. She moved aside and a gentleman in a polo shirt stepped up and shook hands vigorously, like a sportsman. He was followed by a boy of about three who wore a tall Western hat that nearly covered his face; he had to be pushed ahead by the line. Enoch watched for some time, his face working with envy. The small boy was followed by a lady in shorts, she by an old man who tried to draw extra attention to himself by dancing up instead of walking in a dignified way. Enoch suddenly darted across the street and slipped noiselessly into the open back door of the truck.

The handshaking went on until the feature picture was ready to begin. Then the star got back in the van and the people filed into the theater. The driver and the man who was master of ceremonies climbed in the cab part and the truck rumbled off. It crossed the city rapidly and continued on the highway, going very fast.

There came from the van certain thumping noises, not those of the normal gorilla, but they were drowned out by the drone of the motor and the steady sound of wheels against the road. The night was pale and quiet, with nothing to stir it but an occasional complaint from a hoot owl and the distant muted jarring of a freight train. The truck sped on until it slowed for a crossing, and as the van rattled over the tracks, a figure slipped from the door and almost fell, and then limped hurriedly off toward the woods.

Once in the darkness of a pine thicket, he laid down a pointed stick he had been clutching and something bulky and loose that he had been carrying under his arm, and began to undress. He folded each garment neatly after he had taken it off and then stacked it on top of the last thing he had removed. When all his clothes were in the pile, he took up the stick and began making a hole in the ground with it.

The darkness of the pine grove was broken by paler moonlit spots that moved over him now and again and showed him to be Enoch. His natural appearance was marred by a gash that ran from the corner of his lip to his collarbone and by a lump under his eye that gave him a dulled insensitive look. Nothing could have been more deceptive for he was burning with the intensest kind of happiness.

He dug rapidly until he had made a trench about a foot long and a foot deep. Then he placed the stack of clothes in it and stood aside to rest a second. Burying his clothes was not a symbol to him of burying his former self; he only knew he wouldn't need them any more. As soon as he got his breath, he pushed the displaced dirt over the hole and stamped it down with his foot. He discovered while he did this that he still had his shoes on, and when he finished, he removed them and threw them from him. Then he picked up the loose bulky object and shook it vigorously.

In the uncertain light, one of his lean white legs could be seen to disappear and then the other, one arm and then the other: a black heavier shaggier figure replaced his. For an instant, it had two heads, one light and one dark, but after a second, it pulled the dark back head over the other and corrected this. It busied itself with certain hidden fastenings and what appeared to be minor adjustments of its hide.

For a time after this, it stood very still and didn't do anything. Then it began to growl and beat its chest; it jumped up and down and flung its arms and thrust its head forward. The growls were thin and uncertain at first but they grew louder after a second. They became low and poisonous, louder again, low and poisonous again; they stopped altogether. The figure extended its hand, clutched nothing, and shook its arm vigorously; it withdrew the arm, extended it again, clutched nothing, and shook. It repeated this four or five times. Then it picked up the pointed stick and placed it at a cocky angle under its arm and left the woods for the highway. No gorilla anywhere, Africa or California or New York, was happier than he.

A man and woman sitting close together on a rock just off the highway were looking across an open stretch of valley at a view of the city in the distance and they didn't see the shaggy figure approaching. The smokestacks and square tops of buildings made a black uneven wall against the lighter sky and here and there a steeple cut a sharp wedge out of a cloud. The young man turned his neck just in time to see the gorilla standing a few feet away, hideous and black, with its hand extended. He eased his arm from around the woman and disappeared silently into the woods. She, as soon as she turned her eyes, fled screaming down the highway. The gorilla stood as though surprised and presently its arm fell to its side. It sat down on the rock where they had been sitting and stared over the valley at the uneven skyline of the city.

Truman Capote

From "A Christmas Memory"

Theora Hamblett. *Christmas Trees.* Drawing. University Museums, University of Mississippi.

Truman Streckfus Persons was born in New Orleans but spent most of his childhood in Monroeville, Alabama. His recollections of those days and the people he knew there (including his friend Harper Lee, who based the character Dill in To Kill a Mockingbird *on Capote) are the basis for stories like "A Christmas Memory."*

Imagine a morning in late November. A coming of winter morning more than twenty years ago. Consider the kitchen of a spreading old house in a country town. A great black stove is its main feature; but there is also a big round table and a fireplace with two rocking chairs placed in front of it. Just today the fireplace commenced its seasonal roar.

A woman with shorn white hair is standing at the kitchen window. She is wearing tennis shoes and a shapeless gray sweater over a summery calico dress. She is small and sprightly, like a bantam hen; but, due to a long youthful illness, her shoulders are pitifully hunched. Her face is remarkable—not unlike Lincoln's, craggy like that, and tinted by sun and wind; but it is delicate too, finely boned, and her eyes are sherry-colored and timid. "Oh my," she exclaims, her breath smoking the windowpane, "it's fruitcake weather!"

The person to whom she is speaking is myself. I am seven; she is sixty-something. We are cousins, very distant ones, and we have lived together—well, as long as I can remember. Other people inhabit the house, relatives; and though they have power over us, and frequently make us cry, we are not, on the whole, too much aware of them. We are each other's best friend. She calls me Buddy, in memory of a boy who was formerly her best friend. The other Buddy died in the 1880's, when she was still a child. She is still a child.

"I knew it before I got out of bed," she says, turning away from the window with a purposeful excitement in her eyes. "The courthouse bell sounded so cold and clear. And there were no birds singing; they've gone to warmer country, yes indeed. Oh, Buddy, stop stuffing biscuit and fetch our buggy. Help me find my hat. We've thirty cakes to bake."

It's always the same: a morning arrives in November, and my friend, as though officially inaugurating the Christmas time of year that exhilarates her imagination and fuels the blaze of her heart, announces: "It's fruitcake weather! Fetch our buggy. Help me find my hat."

The hat is found, a straw cartwheel corsaged with velvet roses out-of-doors has faded: it once belonged to a more fashionable relative. Together, we guide our buggy, a dilapidated baby carriage, out to the garden and into a grove of pecan trees. The buggy is mine; that is, it was bought for me when I was born. It is made of wicker, rather unraveled, and the wheels wobble like a drunkard's legs. But it is a faithful object; springtimes, we take it to the woods and fill it with flowers, herbs, wild fern for our porch pots; in the summer, we pile it with picnic paraphernalia and sugar-cane fishing poles and roll it down to the edge of a creek; it has its winter uses, too: as a truck for hauling firewood from the yard to the kitchen, as a warm bed for Queenie, our tough little orange and white rat terrier who has survived distemper and two rattlesnake bites. Queenie is trotting beside it now.

Three hours later we are back in the kitchen hulling a heaping buggyload of windfall pecans. Our backs hurt from gathering them: how hard they were to find (the main crop having been shaken off the trees and sold by the orchard's owners, who are not us) among the concealing leaves, the frosted, deceiving grass. Caarackle! A cheery crunch, scraps of miniature thunder sound as the shells collapse and the golden mound of sweet oily ivory meat mounts in the milk-glass bowl. Queenie begs to taste, and now and again my friend sneaks her a mite, though insisting we deprive ourselves. "We mustn't, Buddy. If we start, we won't stop. And there's scarcely enough as there is. For thirty cakes." The kitchen is growing dark. Dusk turns the window into a mirror: our reflections mingle with the rising moon as we work by the fireside in the firelight. At last, when the moon is quite high, we toss the final hull into the fire and, with joined sighs, watch it catch flame. The buggy is empty, the bowl is brimful.

We eat our supper (cold biscuits, bacon, blackberry jam) and discuss tomorrow. Tomorrow the kind of work I like best begins: buying. Cherries and citron, ginger and vanilla and canned Hawaiian pineapple, rinds and raisins and walnuts and whiskey and oh, so much flour, butter, so many eggs, spices, flavorings: why, we'll need a pony to pull the buggy home.

But before these purchases can be made, there is the question of money. Neither of us has any. Except for skinflint sums persons in the house occasionally provide (a dime is considered very big money); or what we earn ourselves from various activities: holding rummage sales, selling buckets of hand-picked blackberries, jars of homemade jam and apple jelly and peach preserves, rounding up flowers for funerals and weddings. Once we won seventy-ninth prize, five dollars, in a national football contest. Not that we know a fool thing about football. It's just that we enter any contest we hear about: at the moment our hopes are centered on the fifty-thousand-dollar Grand Prize being offered to name a new brand of coffee (we suggested "A.M."; and, after some hesitation, for my friend thought it perhaps sacrilegious, the slogan "A.M.! Amen!"). To tell the truth, our only *really* profitable enterprise was the Fun and Freak Museum we conducted in a back-yard woodshed two summers ago. The Fun was a stereopticon with slide views of Washington and New York lent us by a relative who had been to those places (she was furious when she discovered why we'd borrowed it); the Freak was a three-legged biddy chicken hatched by one of our own hens. Everybody hereabouts wanted to see that biddy: we charged grownups a nickel, kids two cents. And took in a good twenty dollars before the museum shut down due to the decease of the main attraction.

But one way and another we do each year accumulate Christmas savings, a Fruitcake Fund. These moneys we keep hidden in an ancient bead purse under a loose board under the floor under a chamber pot under my friend's bed. The purse is seldom removed from this safe location except to make a deposit, or, as happens every Saturday, a withdrawal; for on Saturdays I am allowed ten cents to go to the picture show. My friend has never been to a picture show, nor does she intend to: "I'd rather hear you tell the story, Buddy. That way I can imagine it more. Besides, a person my age shouldn't squander their eyes. When the Lord comes, let me see Him clear." In addition to never having seen a movie, she has never: eaten in a restaurant, traveled more than five miles from home, received or sent a telegram, read anything except funny papers and the Bible, worn cosmetics, cursed, wished someone harm, told a lie on purpose, let a hungry dog go hungry. Here are a few things she has done, does do: killed with a hoe the biggest rattlesnake ever seen in this county (sixteen rattles), dip snuff (secretly), tame hummingbirds (just try it) till they balance on her finger, tell ghost stories (we both believe in ghosts) so tingling they chill you in July, talk to herself, take walks in the rain, grow the prettiest japonicas in town, know the recipe for every sort of old-time Indian cure, including a magical wart-remover.

Now, with supper finished, we retire to the room in a faraway part of the house where my friend sleeps in a scrap-quilt-covered iron bed painted rose pink, her favorite color. Silently, wallowing in the pleasures of conspiracy, we take the bead purse from its secret place and spill its contents on the scrap quilt. Dollar bills, tightly rolled and green as May buds. Somber fifty-cent pieces, heavy enough to weight a dead man's eyes. Lovely dimes, the liveliest coin, the one that really jingles. Nickels and quarters, worn smooth as creek pebbles. But mostly a hateful heap of bitter-odored pennies. Last summer others in the house contracted to pay us a penny for every twenty-five flies we killed. Oh, the carnage of August: the flies that flew to heaven! Yet it was not work in which we took pride. And, as we sit counting pennies, it is as though we were back tabulating dead flies. Neither of us has a head for figures; we count slowly, lose track, start again. According to her calculations, we have $12.73. According to mine, exactly $13. "I do hope you're wrong, Buddy. We can't mess around with thirteen. The cakes will fall. Or put somebody in the cemetery. Why, I wouldn't dream of getting out of bed on the thirteenth." This is true: she always spends thirteenths in bed. So, to be on the safe side, we subtract a penny and toss it out the window.

Of the ingredients that go into our fruitcakes, whiskey is the most expensive, as well as the hardest to obtain: State laws forbid its sale. But everybody knows you can buy a bottle from Mr. Haha Jones. And the next day, having completed our more prosaic shopping, we set out for Mr. Haha's business address, a "sinful" (to quote public opinion) fish-fry and dancing café down by the river. We've been there before, and on the same errand; but in previous years our dealings have been with Haha's wife, an iodine-dark Indian woman with brassy peroxided hair and a dead-tired disposition. Actually, we've never laid eyes on her husband, though we've heard that he's an Indian too. A giant with razor scars across his cheeks. They call him Haha because he's so gloomy, a man who never laughs. As we approach his café (a large log cabin festooned inside and out with chains of garish-gay naked light bulbs and standing by the river's muddy edge under the shade of river trees where moss drifts through the branches like gray mist) our steps slow down. Even Queenie stops prancing and sticks close by. People have been murdered in Haha's café. Cut to pieces. Hit on the head. There's a case coming up in court next month. Naturally these goings-on happen at night when the colored lights cast crazy patterns and the victrola wails. In the daytime Haha's is shabby and deserted. I knock at the door, Queenie barks, my friend calls: "Mrs. Haha, ma'am? Anyone to home?"

Footsteps. The door opens. Our hearts overturn. It's Mr. Haha Jones himself! And he *is* a giant; he *does* have scars; he *doesn't* smile. No, he glowers at us through Satan-tilted eyes and demands to know: "What you want with Haha?"

For a moment we are too paralyzed to tell. Presently my friend half-finds her voice, a whispery voice at best: "If you please, Mr. Haha, we'd like a quart of your finest whiskey."

His eyes tilt more. Would you believe it? Haha is smiling! Laughing, too. "Which one of you is a drinkin' man?"

"It's for making fruitcakes, Mr. Haha. Cooking."

This sobers him. He frowns. "That's no way to waste good whiskey." Nevertheless, he retreats into the shadowed café and seconds later appears carrying a bottle of daisy-yellow unlabeled liquor. He demonstrates its sparkle in the sunlight and says: "Two dollars."

We pay him with nickels and dimes and pennies. Suddenly, as he jangles the coins in his hand like a fistful of dice, his face softens. "Tell you what," he proposes, pouring the money back into our bead purse, "just send me one of them fruitcakes instead."

"Well," my friend remarks on our way home, "there's a lovely man. We'll put an extra cup of raisins in *his* cake."

The black stove, stoked with coal and firewood, glows like a lighted pumpkin. Eggbeaters whirl, spoons spin round in bowls of butter and sugar, vanilla sweetens the air, ginger spices it; melting, nose-tingling odors saturate the kitchen, suffuse the house, drift out to the world on puffs of chimney smoke. In four days our work is done. Thirty-one cakes, dampened with whiskey, bask on window sills and shelves.

CIVIL RIGHTS

MARGARET WALKER ALEXANDER
"For My People"

Margaret Walker Alexander has won a prodigious number of awards and honors for her writing and has been a professor of literature for many years. When published in 1942, "For My People" was extremely inspirational to African-Americans. The poem recalls black history and challenges African-Americans to rise up and overcome oppression.

For my people everywhere singing their slave songs repeatedly: their
    dirges and their ditties and their blues and jubilees, praying their
    prayers nightly to an unknown god, bending their knees humbly to an
    unseen power;

For my people lending their strength to the years, to the gone years and
    the now years and the maybe years, washing ironing cooking
    scrubbing sewing mending hoeing plowing digging planting pruning
    patching dragging along never gaining never reaping never knowing
    and never understanding;

For my playmates in the clay and dust and sand of Alabama backyards
    playing baptizing and preaching and doctor and jail and soldier and
    school and mama and cooking and playhouse and concert and store
    and hair and Miss Choomby and company;

For the cramped bewildered years we went to school to learn to know
    the reasons why and the answers to and the people who and the
    places where and the days when, in memory of the bitter hours when
    we discovered we were black and poor and small and different and
    nobody cared and nobody wondered and nobody understood;

For the boys and girls who grew in spite of these things to be man and
    woman, to laugh and dance and sing and play and drink their wine
    and religion and success, to marry their playmates and bear children
    and then die of consumption and anemia and lynching;

COLORPLATE 98

ED MCGOWIN. *A Bird in the Hand.* c. 1990. Oil on canvas. 54 x 54 in. Collection of the artist. *McGowin, who draws inspiration from Delacroix and da Vinci as well as Red Grooms, finds in their work a common interest in humans facing struggle and confusion—physical and psychic. McGowin's hand-carved frames, which extend motifs from the canvas, echo the movement within his paintings.*

COLORPLATE 99

DAVID PARRISH. *Royal Chevy.* 1981. Oil on canvas. 84 x 60 in. Montgomery Museum of Fine Arts, Montgomery, Alabama. *Alabaman David Parrish once worked as a technical artist for the aerospace industry in Huntsville, and his penchant for scientific precision is evident in his photorealistic style.*

COLORPLATE 100

JONI MABE. *The Elvis Playpen with Einstein and Jesus Walking on the Water.* 1984. Mixed media. Approximately 6 x 10 ft. Joni Mabe's Traveling Museum of Obsessions, Personalities & Oddities. Nexus Contemporary Art Center, Atlanta, Georgia. Photograph by Dennis O'Kain. *Joni Mabe, a resident of Athens, Georgia, began collecting Elvis memorabilia after the death of The King in 1977. Subsequent sightings of Elvis, as reported in* The National Enquirer, *piqued her interest and have led to some interesting connections in her work between Elvis and Jesus, both powerful and charismatic icons of Southern culture.*

275

COLORPLATE 101

REBECCA DAVENPORT. *Sommers: Kettleburn.* 1982. Oil on canvas. 72 x 66 in. Collection of the artist. *"I try to portray my subjects' ugliness and their beauty, their honesty and their self-deception through my knowledge of them and through an exploration of myself,"* Davenport says of her paintings. *The writing of Flannery O'Connor has been a major influence on her work.*

COLORPLATE 102

ROMARE BEARDEN. *The Piano Lesson.* 1983. Collage and watercolor. 29 x 22 in. ACA Gallery and The Romare Howard Bearden Foundation.

COLORPLATE 103

WILLIAM CHRISTENBERRY. *Abandoned House Near Montgomery, Alabama.* 1971. Color photograph. 16 x 20 in. Courtesy of the artist. *Christenberry, who grew up in the part of Alabama photographed by Walker Evans in* Let Us Now Praise Famous Men, *returns to Hale County to redocument the same buildings, signs, and landmarks, this time in color. The ubiquitous dogtrot house, like the one pictured here, is a quintessentially Southern dwelling, perfectly suited to the Southern climate and rural lifestyle.*

COLORPLATE 104 (opposite)

MATTIE LOU O'KELLEY. *My Parent's Farm.* 1980. Oil on canvas. 58 x 42 in. Collection High Museum of Art, Atlanta, Georgia. Gift of the artist in memory of her parents, Mary Bell Cox O'Kelley and Augustus Franklin O'Kelley and their children, Willie, Lillie, Gertrude, Tom, Ben, Mattie Lou, and Johnnie, 1980.68. *Mattie Lou O'Kelley, of Georgia paints memory paintings with a bird's-eye perspective that enables her to include more detail in her domestic landscapes. Part of a poem she has written tells her story:* "Now my one room house has only me/ I never roam/ No lessons have I, But I paint/ And paint/ And stay at home."

COLORPLATE 105

H. H. SCARTABELLI. *Still Life with Orchids.* 1899. Oil on canvas. 12 ¹/₂ x 15 ¹/₂ in. Roger Houston Ogden Collection, New Orleans.

For my people thronging 47th Street in Chicago and Lenox Avenue in
New York and Rampart Street in New Orleans, lost disinherited
dispossessed and happy people filling the cabarets and taverns and
other people's pockets needing bread and shoes and milk and land and
money and something—something all our own;

For my people walking blindly spreading joy, losing time being lazy,
sleeping when hungry, shouting when burdened, drinking when
hopeless, tied and shackled and tangled among ourselves by the
unseen creatures who tower over us omnisciently and laugh;

For my people blundering and groping and floundering in the dark of
churches and schools and clubs and societies, associations and councils
and committees and conventions, distressed and disturbed and
deceived and devoured by money-hungry glory-craving leeches,
preyed on by facile force of state and fad and novelty, by false prophet
and holy believer;

For my people standing staring trying to fashion a better way from
confusion, from hypocrisy and misunderstanding, trying to fashion a
world that will hold all the people, all the faces, all the adams and
eves and their countless generations;

Let a new earth rise. Let another world be born. Let a bloody peace be
written in the sky. Let a second generation full of courage issue forth;
let a people loving freedom come to growth. Let a beauty full of
healing and a strength of final clenching be the pulsing in our spirits
and our blood. Let the martial songs be written, let the dirges
disappear. Let a race of men now rise and take control.

Jackie Robinson with Branch Rickey. Photograph.
National Baseball Library, Cooperstown, NY.

RED BARBER AND ROBERT CREAMER

From *Rhubarb in the Catbird Seat*

Walter Lanier Barber, born in Mississippi but raised in Florida, was for many years a radio sports broadcaster; first for the Brooklyn Dodgers from 1939–1953 and then for the New York Yankees. He was appreciated by a wide audience that enjoyed his folksy, intelligent, and gentlemanly broadcasts. He died in Tallahassee on October 22, 1992. In this excerpt from one of his books, Rhubarb in the Catbird Seat, *Barber describes how he was affected by the news of the impending integration of professional baseball, which he heard from Brooklyn Dodgers owner Branch Rickey.*

He looked at me. "What I am telling you is this: there is a Negro ballplayer coming to the *Dodgers,* not the Brown Dodgers. I don't know who he is, and I don't know where he is, and I don't know when he's coming. But he is *coming.* And he is coming soon, just as soon as we can find him."

Again, I didn't say a word. I couldn't.

"Needless to say," he went on, "I have taken you into my confidence in telling you this. I have talked about it only with my family. Jane is utterly opposed to my doing it. The family is dead set against it. But I have got to do it. I must do it. I will do it. I *am* doing it. And now you know it."

This was a year before I heard the name Robinson. It was a full year later—Rickey never talked to me about it again—that I picked up the paper and saw that Jackie Robinson had been signed and was going to play that season with Montreal, Brooklyn's number one farm team. I said to myself, "Well, he said he was going to do it."

I have often wondered why this man told *me* about his earth-shaking project that afternoon in Joe's Restaurant. You could argue that the thing had become so much a part of him, and the opposition of his family was so complete, and he was carrying all of this inside himself, that he had to have some human being to speak out loud to, that he had to have some other human being hear him say what was inside him. You could say he paid me a high compliment in choosing me as the human being that he would trust to listen to him and respect his confidence.

But Rickey's strength was such that he could walk his way alone. I don't think he needed me as his confessor. And, certainly, when he spoke to me about it, I gave him back no support. I gave him back 100 per cent silence, because he had shaken me. He had shaken me to my heels.

* * *

Rickey saw to it, in other words, that I had sole occupancy of the catbird seat, but he shook me that afternoon in Joe's Restaurant. He needed me in Brooklyn, or he *wanted* me in Brooklyn, which is more accurate. But he knew that the coming of a Negro ballplayer could disturb me, could upset me. I believe he told me about it so far in advance so that I could have time to wrestle with the problem, live with it, solve it. I was born in Mississippi. I grew up in Florida. My father was from North Carolina. My mother's people were long-time Mississippians. My entire heredity and environment was of the Deep South. Florida is not Deep South in the sense that Mississippi, Alabama, Georgia and South Carolina would be considered Deep South—Florida has always been a more cosmopolitan state—but make no mistake about it, it is still a southern state. So I was raised southern. I was raised by wonderful, tolerant people who taught me never to speak unkindly to anyone or to take advantage of anyone. The Negroes who came and went through our lives were always treated with the utmost respect and a great deal of warmth and a great deal of affection. But there was a line drawn, and that line was always there.

I know that it gave me great pause when I first went to Cincinnati, the first time I went north to live. I wondered how I could get along in a northern city. Well, I got along all right, because I tended strictly to my own business. But what Mr. Rickey told me in Joe's Restaurant meant that this was now part of my business. I would still be broadcasting baseball, with all its closeness and intimate friendships and back-and-forth and give-and-take, but now a Negro player would be part of all that. And if he meant one Negro player, he meant more than one. He meant that the complexion (and this is no play on words) in the dugout and the clubhouse was going to be drastically and permanently changed.

I went home that night to Scarsdale and as soon as I got in the house I told my wife what Mr. Rickey had said. (That was in no sense a violation of confidence: Rickey believed in wives and husbands sharing each other's lives.) I told her about it, and I said to her, "I'm going to quit. I don't think I want—I don't know whether I can—I'm going to quit."

She said, "Well, it's your job and you're the one who's going to have to make the decision. But it's not immediate. You don't have to do anything about it right now. Why don't we have a martini? And then let's have dinner."

So time went by and, as I said, Mr. Rickey never referred to it again. But the thing was gnawing on me. It tortured me. I finally found myself doing something I had never really done before. I set out to do a deep self-examination. I attempted to find out who I was. This did not come easily, and it was not done lightly.

* * *

But then I had to ask myself, what is it that is so upsetting about the prospect of working with a Negro ballplayer? Or broadcasting the play of a Negro ballplayer? Or traveling with a Negro ballplayer? What is it that has me so stirred up? Why did I react the way I did when Rickey told me he was bringing in a Negro player? Why did I go straight home and tell my wife I was going to quit?

* * *

And then—I don't know why the thought came to my mind—I asked myself the basic question that a human being, if he is fair, ought to ask. How much control did I have over the parents I was born to? The answer was immediate: I didn't have any. By an accident of birth I was born to Selena and William Barber, white, Protestant, in Columbus, Mississippi, February 17, 1908. . . .

Then, of course, I worked out that but for an accident of birth I could have been born to black parents. I could have been born to any parents. Then I figured out that I didn't have anything to be so proud of after all, this accident of the color of my skin.

Just about that time, the rector of the church of St. James the Less in Scarsdale asked me to do a radio talk for him out in Westchester County. You look back and you say to yourself, how marvelous it is the way things synchronize in your life, how they fit and mesh together, the timing. I had been brought up in a family that believed in religion. I had gone to Sunday School as a regular thing, and later, as a young man, I taught Sunday School briefly myself. But I lost the habit of going to church after I got involved in broadcasting, and it wasn't until after the birth of our daughter Sarah that I became interested again. My father was a Baptist and my mother was a Presbyterian, but I married an Episcopalian and when I went back to church I went back as an Episcopalian. And so, while I was trying to work out this thing of who I am, and this accident of birth, and losing a lot of false pride, the Reverend Harry Price, an Episcopal clergyman I had gotten to know, asked me to do this radio talk. The talk, built on a sentence from St. Paul, was to be called "Men and Brothers." And what the rector wanted me to talk about was a problem that was coming to a head then. It was just about the time that it was beginning to get attention, and later it got to be quite serious and it hasn't diminished. It was the problem of the relationship between the Jews and the non-Jews in the wealthy community of Scarsdale, New York. It was going pretty good—and it still is. A lot of people forgot that Jesus was a Jew. Some embarrassingly sickening things were beginning to happen. Sad things were being said. Things were being done to children. And so the rector asked me to talk about men and brothers, with the idea being that whether you were a Jew or a Christian, you were brothers. You were men, and you were men and brothers together, and you should get along together.

Well, when I worked out that talk I suddenly found that I wasn't nearly so interested in the relationship between Christians and Jews, Jews and Christians, as I was about the relationship between one white southern broadcaster and one unknown Negro ballplayer, who was coming. That talk—working it out, preparing it, giving it—I don't know how much help it gave to anyone who was listening, but it helped me a great deal. What was my job? What was my function? What was I supposed to do as I broadcast baseball games? As I worked along on that line, I remembered something about Bill Klem, the great umpire. Klem always said, "All there is to umpiring is umpiring the ball." When you think about it, that is the one thing you must tell a fellow who wants to umpire. Just umpire the ball. There are a couple of other technicalities that you have to know, of course, but the ball is the basic thing. Is the ball foul or fair? Is the ball a good pitch or a bad pitch? Did the ball get to the base before the runner did, or did it not? Did the ball stick in the fielder's glove, or did it bounce out? An umpire doesn't care anything about how big the crowd is or which team is ahead or who the runner is on third or whether this is the winning run that is approaching the plate. All he does is umpire the ball. It doesn't matter whether the man at bat is a great star or a brand new rookie. It doesn't even matter what color he is.

I took that and worked over it a little bit, and I said, "Well, isn't that what I'm supposed to do? Just broadcast the ball? Certainly, a broadcaster is concerned with who is at the plate—you're deeply concerned. You're concerned about the score, and the excitement of the crowd, and the drama of the moment. You do care if this is the winning run approaching the plate. But still, basically, primarily, beyond everything else, you broadcast the ball—*what* is happening to it. All you have to do is tell the people what is going on."

I got something else in my head then. I understood that I was not a sociologist, that I was not Mr. Rickey, that I was not building the ball club, that I was not putting players on the field, that I was not involved in a racial experiment, that I did not care what anybody else said, thought, or did about this Negro player who was coming and whose name I still did not know. All I had to do when he came—and I didn't say *if* he came, because after Mr. Rickey talked to me I *knew* he was coming—all I had to do when he came was treat him as a man, a fellow man, treat him as a ballplayer, broadcast the ball.

I had this all worked out before I ever read that Jackie Robinson was signed and going to Montreal. And when he did come, I didn't broadcast Jackie Robinson, I broadcast what Jackie Robinson did.

Rosa Parks

From *Rosa Parks: My Story*

In 1955, Rosa Parks was arrested, tried, and found guilty of violating segregation laws by refusing to give up her seat to a white person on a Montgomery, Alabama bus. Her refusal touched off a 381-day bus boycott and galvanized the civil rights movement, hurrying it to a more militant phase.

I saw a vacant seat in the middle section of the bus and took it. I didn't even question why there was a vacant seat even though there were quite a few people standing in the back. If I had thought about it at all, I would probably have figured maybe someone saw me get on and did not take the seat but left it vacant for me. There was a man sitting next to the window and two women across the aisle.

The next stop was the Empire Theater, and some whites got on. They filled up the white seats, and one man was left standing. The driver looked back and noticed the man standing. Then he looked back at us. He said, "Let me have those front seats," because they were the front seats of the black section. Didn't anybody move. We just sat right where we were, the four of us. Then he spoke a second time. "Y'all better make it light on yourselves and let me

Mrs. Rosa Parks. December 21, 1958. Photograph. The Bettmann Archive. *Mrs. Parks sits in the front of a city bus in Montgomery as a Supreme Court ruling which banned segregation on the city's public transit system took effect.*

have those seats."

The man in the window seat next to me stood up, and I moved to let him pass by me, and then I looked across the aisle and saw that the two women were also standing. I moved over to the window seat. I could not see how standing up was going to "make it light" for me. The more we gave in and complied the worse they treated us.

I thought back to the time when I used to sit up all night and didn't sleep, and my grandfather would have his gun right by the fireplace, or if he had his one-horse wagon going anywhere, he always had his gun in the back of the wagon. People always say that I didn't give up my seat because I was tired, but that isn't true. I was not tired physically, or no more tired than I usually was at the end of a working day. I was not old, although some people have an image of me as being old then. I was forty-two. No, the only tired I was, was tired of giving in.

The driver of the bus saw me still sitting there, and he asked was I going to stand up. I said, "No." He said, "Well, I'm going to have you arrested." Then I said, "You may do that." These were the only words we said to each other. I didn't even know his name, which was James Blake, until we were in court together. He got out of the bus and stayed outside for a few minutes, waiting for the police.

As I sat there, I tried not to think about what might happen. I knew that anything was possible. I could be manhandled or beaten. I could be arrested. People have asked me if it occurred to me then that I could be the test case the NAACP had been looking for. I did not think about that at all. In fact if I had let myself think too deeply about what might happen to me, I might have gotten off the bus. But I chose to remain.

Songs of the Civil Rights Movement
"Keep Your Eyes On The Prize"

This song was used very early in the freedom struggle; it was probably an outgrowth of voter education schools on Johns Island, South Carolina, in 1956.

———————

Paul and Silas, bound in jail,
Had no money for to go their bail.

Chorus:
Keep your eyes on the prize,
Hold on, hold on,
Hold on, hold on —
Keep your eyes on the prize,
    Hold on, hold on.

Paul and Silas begin to shout,
The jail door opened and they walked out.

Freedom's name is mighty sweet —
Soon one of these days we're going to meet.

Got my hand on the Gospel plow,
I wouldn't take nothing for my journey now.

The only chain that a man can stand
Is that chain of hand in hand.

The only thing that we did wrong —
Stayed in the wilderness too long.

But the one thing we did right
Was the day we started to fight.

We're gonna board that big Greyhound,
Carryin' love from town to town.

We're gonna ride for civil rights,
We're gonna ride, both black and white.

We've met jail and violence too,
But God's love has seen us through.

Haven't been to Heaven but I've been told
Streets up there are paved with gold.

"We Shall Overcome"

An adaptation of the old hymn, "I'll Be All Right," the song "We Shall Overcome" became the anthem of the civil rights movement. It originated in the 1940s with African-American textile workers who came to the Highlander Folk School at Monteagle, Tennessee, and from there folk singers like Pete Seeger and Guy Carawan introduced it to union and civil rights groups across the South.

We shall overcome,
   we shall overcome,
We shall overcome some day.
Oh, deep in my heart, I do believe,
We shall overcome some day.

Black demonstrators, Birmingham, Alabama. 1963. Photograph. The Bettmann Archive. *Barred window of a waiting paddy wagon frames Black demonstrators — some singing, some praying — as an estimated 2000 marched on the Birmingham jail May 5, 1963 in a segregation protest.*

We are not afraid,
   we are not afraid,
We are not afraid today.
Oh, deep in my heart, I do believe,
We shall overcome some day.

We are not alone,
   we are not alone,
We are not alone today.
Oh, deep in my heart, I do believe,
We shall overcome some day.

The truth will make us free,
   the truth will make us free,
The truth will make us free some day.
Oh, deep in my heart, I do believe,
We shall overcome some day.

We'll walk hand in hand,
   we'll walk hand in hand,
We'll walk hand in hand some day.
Oh, deep in my heart, I do believe,
We shall overcome some day.

The Lord will see us through,
   the Lord will see us through,
The Lord will see us through today.
Oh, deep in my heart, I do believe,
We shall overcome some day.

MARTIN LUTHER KING, JR.
"I Have a Dream"

On August 28, 1963, Martin Luther King, Jr. was one of several speakers who addressed more than 200,000 people who had come to Washington, D.C. to bring the problems of civil rights and poverty to the forefront of Congressional awareness. Dr. King's speech electrified the assembled crowd with its powerful message and stirring rhetoric, and stands as a constant reminder of his commitment to nonviolent protest and Christian doctrine.

Five score years ago, a great American, in whose symbolic shadow we stand, signed the Emancipation Proclamation. This momentous decree came as a great beacon light of hope to millions of Negro slaves who had been seared in the flames of withering injustice. It came as a joyous daybreak to end the long night of captivity.

But one hundred years later, we must face the tragic fact that the Negro is still not free. One hundred years later, the life of the Negro is still sadly crippled by the manacles of segregation and the chains of discrimination. One hundred years later, the Negro lives on a lonely island of poverty in the midst of a vast ocean of material prosperity. One hundred years later,

Martin Luther King, Jr.
1963. Photograph.
UPI/Bettmann. *With the Washington Monument in the distance, Reverend Martin Luther King, Jr. waves to participants in the march on Washington August 28, 1963, after delivering an electrifying speech.*

the Negro is still languished in the corners of American society and finds himself an exile in his own land. So we have come here today to dramatize an appalling condition.

In a sense we have come to our nation's Capital to cash a check. When the architects of our republic wrote the magnificent words of the Constitution and the Declaration of Independence, they were signing a promissory note to which every American was to fall heir. This note was a promise that all men would be guaranteed the unalienable rights of life, liberty, and the pursuit of happiness.

It is obvious today that America has defaulted on this promissory note insofar as her citizens of color are concerned. Instead of honoring this sacred obligation, America has given the Negro people a bad check; a check which has come back marked "insufficient funds." But we refuse to believe that the bank of justice is bankrupt. We refuse to believe that there are insufficient funds in the great vaults of opportunity of this nation. So we have come to cash this check—a check that will give us upon demand the riches of freedom and the security of justice.

We have also come to this hallowed spot to remind America of the fierce urgency of *now.* This is no time to engage in the luxury of cooling off or to take the tranquilizing drug of gradualism. *Now* is the time to make real the promises of democracy. *Now* is the time to rise from the dark and desolate valley of segregation to the sunlit path of racial justice. *Now* is the time to open the doors of opportunity to all of God's children. *Now* is the time to lift our nation from the quicksands of racial injustice to the solid rock of brotherhood.

It would be fatal for the nation to overlook the urgency of the moment and to underestimate the determination of the Negro. This sweltering summer of the Negro's legitimate discontent will not pass until there is an invigorating autumn of freedom and equality. Nineteen sixty-three is not an end, but a beginning. Those who hope that the Negro needed to blow off steam and will now be content will have a rude awakening if the nation returns to business as usual. There will be neither rest nor tranquility in America until the Negro is granted his citizenship rights. The whirlwinds of revolt will continue to shake the foundations of our nation until the bright day of justice emerges.

But there is something that I must say to my people who stand on the warm threshold which leads into the palace of justice. In the process of gaining our rightful place we must not be guilty of wrongful deeds. Let us not seek to satisfy our thirst for freedom by drinking from the cup of bitterness and hatred. We must forever conduct our struggle on the high plane of dignity and discipline. We must not allow our creative protest to degenerate into physical violence. Again and again we must rise to the majestic heights of meeting physical force with soul force.

The marvelous new militancy which has engulfed the Negro community must not lead us to a distrust of all white people, for many of our white brothers, as evidenced by their presence here today, have come to realize that their destiny is tied up with our destiny and their freedom is inextricably bound to our freedom. We cannot walk alone.

And as we walk, we must make the pledge that we shall march ahead. We cannot turn back. There are those who are asking the devotees of civil rights, "When will you be satisfied?"

We can never be satisfied as long as the Negro is the victim of the unspeakable horrors of police brutality.

We can never be satisfied as long as our bodies, heavy with the fatigue of travel, cannot gain lodging in the motels of the highways and the hotels of the cities.

We cannot be satisfied as long as the Negro's basic mobility is from a smaller ghetto to a larger one.

We can never be satisfied as long as a Negro in Mississippi cannot vote and a Negro in New York believes he has nothing for which to vote.

No, no, we are not satisfied, and we will not be satisfied until justice rolls down like waters and righteousness like a mighty stream.

I am not unmindful that some of you have come here out of great trials and tribulations. Some of you have come fresh from narrow jail cells. Some of you have come from areas where your quest for freedom left you battered by the storms of persecution and staggered by the winds of police brutality. You have been the veterans of creative suffering. Continue to work with the faith that unearned suffering is redemptive.

Go back to Mississippi, go back to Alabama, go back to South Carolina, go back to Georgia, go back to Louisiana, go back to the slums and ghettos of our Northern cities, knowing that somehow this situation can and will be changed. Let us not wallow in the valley of despair.

I say to you today, my friends, that in spite of the difficulties and frustrations of the moment I still have a dream. It is a dream deeply rooted in the American dream.

I have a dream that one day this nation will rise up and live out the true meaning of its creed: "We hold these truths to be self-evident; that all men are created equal."

I have a dream that one day on the red hills of Georgia the sons of former slaves and the sons of former slaveowners will be able to sit down together at the table of brotherhood.

I have a dream that one day even the state of Mississippi, a desert state sweltering with the heat of injustice and oppression, will be transformed into an oasis of freedom and justice.

I have a dream that my four little children will one day live in a nation where they will not be judged by the color of their skin but by the content of their character.

I have a dream today.

I have a dream that one day the state of Alabama, whose governor's lips are presently dripping with the words of interposition and nullification, will be transformed into a situation where little black boys and black girls will be able to join hands with little white boys and white girls and walk together as sisters and brothers.

I have a dream today.

I have a dream that one day every valley shall be exalted, every hill and mountain shall be made low, the rough places will be made plain, and the crooked places will be made straight, and the glory of the Lord shall be revealed, and all flesh shall see it together.

This is our hope. This is the faith with which I return to the South. With this faith we will be able to hew out of the mountain of despair a stone of hope. With this faith we will be able to transform the jangling discords of our nation into a beautiful symphony of brotherhood.

With this faith we will be able to work together, to pray together, to struggle together, to go to jail together, to stand up for freedom together, knowing that we will be free one day.

This will be the day when all of God's children will be able to sing with new meaning, "My country 'tis of thee, sweet land of liberty, of thee I sing. Land where my fathers died, land of the Pilgrims' pride, from every mountainside, let freedom ring."

And if America is to be a great nation, this must become true. So let freedom ring from the prodigious hilltops of New Hampshire. Let freedom ring from the mighty mountains of New York. Let freedom ring from the heightening Alleghenies of Pennsylvania!

Let freedom ring from the snowcapped Rockies of Colorado! Let freedom ring from the curvaceous peaks of California! But not only that; let freedom ring from Stone Mountain of Georgia! Let freedom ring from Lookout Mountain of Tennessee!

Let freedom ring from every hill and molehill of Mississippi. From every mountainside, let freedom ring.

When we let freedom ring, when we let it ring from every village and every hamlet, from every state and every city, we will be able to speed up that day when all of God's children, black men and white men, Jews and Gentiles, Protestants and Catholics, will be able to join hands and sing in the words of the old Negro spiritual, "Free at last! Free at last! Thank God Almighty, we are free at last!"

THE SOUTH AT PLAY

TOM WOLFE

From "The Last American Hero"

A native of Richmond and a sharp observer of American culture, Tom Wolfe has written about everything from acid to astronauts. The amazing legend of Junior Johnson, a contemporary folk hero, fascinated Americans when it was first published in Esquire *in 1965. Here Wolfe writes about stock car racing, moonshine, and guts.*

The legend of Junior Johnson! In this legend, here is a country boy, Junior Johnson, who learns to drive by running whiskey for his father, Johnson, Senior, one of the biggest copper-still operators of all time, up in Ingle Hollow, near North Wilkesboro, in northwestern North Carolina, and grows up to be a famous stock car racing driver, rich, grossing $100,000 in 1963, for example, respected, solid, idolized in his hometown and throughout the rural South. There is all this about how good old boys would wake up in the middle of the night in the apple shacks and hear a supercharged Oldsmobile engine roaring over Brushy Mountain and say, "Listen at him—there he goes!" although that part is doubtful, since some nights there were so many good old boys taking off down the road in supercharged automobiles out of Wilkes County, and running loads to Charlotte, Salisbury, Greensboro, Winston-Salem, High Point, or wherever, it would be pretty hard to pick out one. It was Junior Johnson specifically, however, who was famous for the "bootleg turn" or "about-face," in which, if the Alcohol Tax agents had a roadblock up for you or were too close behind, you threw the car up into second gear, cocked the wheel, stepped on the accelerator and made the car's rear end skid around in a complete 180-degree arc, a complete about-face, and tore on back up the road exactly the way you came from. God! The Alcohol Tax agents used to burn over Junior Johnson. Practically every good old boy in town in Wilkesboro, the county seat, got to know the agents by sight in a very short time. They would rag them practically to their faces on the subject of Junior Johnson, so that it got to be an obsession. Finally, one night they had Junior trapped on the road up toward

SUSAN LEE. *Stock car racing.* Photograph. Courtesy of the photographer.

the bridge around MIllersville, there's no way out of there, they had the barricades up and they could hear this souped-up car roaring around the bend, and here it comes—but suddenly they can hear a siren and see a red light flashing in the grille, so they think it's another agent, and boy, they run out like ants and pull those barrels and boards and sawhorses out of the way, and then—Ggghhzzzzzzzzzhhhhhhggggggzzzzzzzeeeeeong!—gawdam! there he goes again, it was him, Junior Johnson! with a gawdam agent's si-reen and a red light in his grille!

I wasn't in the South five minutes before people started making oaths, having visions, telling these hulking great stories, all on the subject of Junior Johnson. At the Greensboro, North Carolina, Airport there was one good old boy who vowed he would have eaten "a bucket of it" if that would have kept Junior Johnson from switching from a Dodge racer to a Ford. Hell yes, and after that—God-almighty, remember that 1963 Chevrolet of Junior's? Whatever happened to that car? A couple of more good old boys join in. A good old boy, I ought to explain, is a generic term in the rural South referring to a man, of any age, but more often young than not, who fits in with the status system of the region. It usually means he has a good sense of humor and enjoys ironic jokes, is tolerant and easygoing enough to get along in long conversations at places like on the corner, and has a reasonable amount of physical courage. The term is usually heard in some such form as: "Lud? He's a good old boy from over at Crozet." These good old boys in the airport, by the way, were in their twenties, except for one fellow who was a cabdriver and was about forty-five, I would say. Except for the cabdriver, they all wore neo-Brummellian clothes such as Lacoste tennis shirts, Slim Jim pants, windbreakers with the collars turned up, "fast" shoes of the winkle-picker genre, and so on. I mention these details just by way of pointing out that very few grits, Iron Boy overalls, clodhoppers or hats with ventilation holes up near the crown enter into this story. Anyway, these good old boys are talking about Junior Johnson and how he has switched to Ford. This they unanimously regard as some kind of betrayal on Johnson's part. Ford, it seems, they regard as the car symbolizing the established power structure. Dodge is kind of a middle ground. Dodge is at least a challenger, not a ruler. But the Junior Johnson they like to remember is the Junior Johnson of 1963, who took on the whole field of NASCAR (National Association for Stock Car Auto Racing) Grand National racing with a Chevrolet. All the other drivers, the drivers driving Fords, Mercurys, Plymouths, Dodges, had millions, literally millions when it is all added up, millions of dollars in backing from the Ford and Chrysler Corporations. Junior Johnson took them all on in a Chevrolet without one cent of backing from Detroit. Chevrolet had pulled out of stock car racing. Yet every race it was the same. It was never a question of whether anybody was going to *outrun* Junior Johnson. It was just a question of whether he was going to win or his car was going to break down, since, for one thing, half the time he had to make his own racing parts. God! Junior Johnson was like Robin Hood or Jesse James or Little David or something. Every time that Chevrolet, No. 3, appeared on the track, wild curdled yells, "Rebel!" yells, they still have those, would rise up. At Daytona, at Atlanta, at Charlotte, at Darlington, South Carolina, Bristol, Tennessee, Martinsville, Virginia—Junior Johnson!

And then the good old boys get to talking about whatever happened to that Chevrolet of Junior's, and the cabdriver says he knows. He says Junior Johnson is using that car to run liquor out of Wilkes County. What does he mean? For Junior Johnson ever to go near another load of bootleg whiskey again—he would have to be insane. He has this huge racing income. He has two other businesses, a whole automated chicken farm with 42,000 chickens, a road-grading business—but the cabdriver says he has this dream Junior is still roaring down from Wilkes County, down through the clay cuts, with the Atlas Arc Lip jars full in the back of that Chevrolet. It is in Junior's blood—and then at this point he puts his right hand up in front of him as if he is groping through fog, and his eyeballs glaze over and he looks out in the distance and he describes Junior Johnson roaring over the ridges of Wilkes County as if it is the ghost of Zapata he is describing, bounding over the Sierras on a white horse to rouse the peasants.

A stubborn notion! A crazy notion! Yet Junior Johnson has followers who need to keep him, symbolically, riding through nighttime like a demon. Madness! But Junior Johnson is one of the last of those sports stars who is not just an ace at the game itself, but a hero a whole people or class of people can identify with. Other, older examples are the way Jack Dempsey stirred up the Irish or the way Joe Louis stirred up the Negroes. Junior Johnson is a modern figure. He is only thirty-three years old and still racing. He should be compared to two other sports heroes whose cultural impact is not too well known. One is Antonino Rocca, the professional wrestler, whose triumphs mean so much to New York City's Puerto Ricans that he can fill Madison Square Garden, despite the fact that everybody, the Puerto Ricans included, knows that wrestling is nothing but a crude form of folk theatre. The other is Ingemar Johanssen, who had a tremendous meaning to the Swedish masses—they were tired of that old king who played tennis all the time and all his friends who keep on drinking Cointreau behind the screen of socialism. Junior Johnson is a modern hero, all involved with car culture and car symbolism in the South. A wild new thing—

* * *

Junior Johnson was over in the garden by the house some years ago, plowing the garden barefooted, behind a mule, just wearing an old pair of overalls, when a couple of good old boys drove up and told him to come on up to the speedway and get in a stock car race. They wanted some local boys to race, as a preliminary to the main race, "as a kind of side show," as Junior remembers it.

"So I just put the reins down," Junior is telling me, "and rode on over 'ere with them. They didn't give us seat belts or nothing, they just roped us in. H'it was a dirt track then. I come in second."

Junior was a sensation in dirt-track racing right from the start. Instead of going into the curves and just sliding and holding on for dear life like the other drivers, Junior developed the technique of throwing himself into a slide about seventy-five feet before the curve by cocking the wheel to the left slightly and gunning it, using the slide, not the brake, to slow down, so that he could pick up speed again halfway through the curve and come out of it like a shot. This was known as his "power slide," and—yes! of course!—every good old boy in North Carolina started saying Junior Johnson had learned that stunt doing those goddamned *about-faces* running away from the Alcohol Tax agents. Junior put on such a show one night on a dirt track in Charlotte that he broke two axles, and he thought he was out of the race because he didn't have any more axles, when a good old boy came running up out of the infield and said, "Goddamn it, Junior Johnson, you take the axle off my car here, I got a Pontiac just like yours," and Junior took it off and put it on his and went out and broke *it* too. Mother dog! To this day Junior Johnson loves dirt-track racing like nothing else in this world, even though there is not much money in it. Every year he sets new dirt track speed records, such as at Hickory, North Carolina, one of the most popular dirt tracks, last spring. As far as Junior is concerned, dirt track racing is not so much of a mechanical test for the car as those long five- and six-hundred-mile races on asphalt are. Gasoline, tire and engine wear aren't so much of a problem. It is all the driver, his skill, his courage—his willingness to mix it up with the other cars, smash and carom off of them at a hundred miles an hour or so to get into the curves first. Junior has a lot of fond recollections of mixing it up at places like Bowman Gray Stadium in Winston-Salem, one of the minor league tracks, a very narrow track, hardly wide enough for two cars. "You could always figure Bowman Gray was gonna cost you two fenders, two doors and two quarter panels," Junior tells me with nostalgia.

Anyway, at Hickory, which was a Saturday night race, all the good old boys started pouring into the stands before sundown, so they wouldn't miss anything, the practice runs or the qualifying or anything. And pretty soon, the dew hasn't even started falling before Junior Johnson and David Pearson, one of Dodge's best drivers, are out there on practice runs, just warming up, and they happen to come up alongside each other on the second curve, and–the thing is, here are two men, each of them driving $15,000 automobiles, each of them standing to make $50,000 to $100,000 for the season if they don't get themselves killed, and they meet on a curve on a goddamned practice run on a dirt track, and neither of them can resist it. Coming out of the turn they go into a wildass race down the backstretch, both of them trying to get into the third turn first, and all the way across the infield you can hear them ricocheting off each other and bouncing at a hundred miles an hour on loose dirt, and then they go into ferocious power slides, red dust all over the goddamned place, and then out of this goddamned red-dust cloud, out of the fourth turn, here comes Junior Johnson first, like a shot, with Pearson right on his tail, and the good old boys in the stands going wild, and the *qualifying* runs haven't started yet, let alone the race.

Junior worked his way up through the minor leagues, the Sportsman and Modified classifications, as they are called, winning championships in both, and won his first Grand National race, the big leagues, in 1955 at Hickory, on dirt. He was becoming known as "the hardest of the hard-chargers," power sliding, rooting them out of the groove, raising hell, and already the Junior Johnson legend was beginning.

He kept hard-charging, power sliding, going after other drivers as though there wasn't room on the track but for one, and became the most popular driver in stock car racing by 1959. The presence of Detroit and Detroit's big money had begun to calm the drivers down a little. Detroit was concerned about Image. The last great duel of the dying dog-eat-dog era of stock car racing came in 1959, when Junior and Lee Petty, who was then leading the league in points, had it out on the Charlotte raceway, Junior was in the lead, and Petty was right on his tail, but couldn't get by Junior. Junior kept coming out of the curves faster. So every chance he got, Petty would get up right on Junior's rear bumper and start banging it, gradually forcing the fender in to where the metal would cut Junior's rear tire. With only a few laps to go, Junior had a blowout and spun out up against the guardrail. That is Junior's version. Petty claimed Junior hit a pop bottle and spun out. The fans in Charlotte were always throwing pop bottles and other stuff onto the track late in the race, looking for blood. In any case, Junior eased back into the pits, had the tire changed, and charged out after Petty. He caught him on a curve and—well, whatever really happened, Petty was suddenly "up against the wall" and out of the race, and Junior won.

RED GROOMS.
Fran Tarkenton. 1979. Painted vinyl, aluminum armature and polyester stuffing. 96 x 48 x 8 in. Brooke Alexander, Inc. © 1993 Red Grooms/ ARS. Writer Willie Morris has said, "It is no doubt a cliche, yet true, that Southern football is a religion, and many Southern football heroes have achieved a sort of civil sainthood." Fran Tarkenton was born in Richmond and played for the University of Georgia.

What a howl went up. The Charlotte chief of police charged out onto the track after the race, according to Petty, and offered to have Junior arrested for "assault with a dangerous weapon," the hassling went on for weeks—

"Back then," Junior tells me, "when you got into a guy and racked him up, you might as well get ready, because he's coming back for you. H'it was dog eat dog. That straightened Lee Petty out right smart. They don't do stuff like that anymore, though, because the guys don't stand for it."

Anyway, the Junior Johnson legend kept building up and building up, and in 1960 it got better than ever when Junior won the biggest race of the year, the Daytona 500, by discovering a new technique called "drafting." That year stock car racing was full of big powerful Pontiacs manned by top drivers, and they would go like nothing else anybody ever saw. Junior went down to Daytona with a Chevrolet.

"My car was about ten miles an hour slower than the rest of the cars, the Pontiacs," Junior tells me. "In the preliminary races, the warmups and stuff like that, they was smoking me off the track. Then I remember once I went out for a practice run, and Fireball Roberts was out there in a Pontiac and I got in right behind him on a curve, right on his bumper. I knew I couldn't stay with him on the straightaway, but I came out of the curve fast, right in behind him, running flat out, and then I noticed a funny thing. As long as I stayed right in behind him, I noticed I picked up speed and stayed right with him and my car was going faster than it had ever gone before. I could tell on the tachometer. My car wasn't running no more than 6000 before, but when I got into this drafting position, I was turning 6800 to 7000. H'it felt like the car was plumb off the ground, floating along."

"Drafting," it was discovered at Daytona, created a vacuum behind the lead car and both cars would go faster than they normally would. Junior "hitched rides" on the Pontiacs most of the afternoon, but was still second to Bobby Johns, the lead Pontiac. Then, late in the race, Johns got into a drafting position with a fellow Pontiac that was actually one lap behind him and the vacuum got so intense that the rear window blew out of Johns' car and he spun out and crashed and Junior won.

This made Junior the Lion Killer, the Little David of stock car racing, and his performance in the 1963 season made him even more so.

Junior raced for Chevrolet at Daytona in February, 1963, and set the all-time stock car speed record in a hundred-mile qualifying race, 164.083 miles an hour, twenty-one miles an hour faster than Parnelli Jones's winning time at Indianapolis that year. Junior topped that at Daytona in July of 1963, qualifying at 166.005 miles per hour in a five-mile run, the fastest that anyone had ever averaged that distance in a racing car of any type. Junior's Chevrolet lasted only twenty-six laps in the Daytona 500 in 1963, however. He went out with a broken push rod. Although Chevrolet announced they were pulling out of racing at this time, Junior took his car and started out on the wildest performance in the history of stock car racing. Chevrolet wouldn't give him a cent of backing. They wouldn't even speak to him on the telephone. Half the time he had to have his own parts made. Plymouth, Mercury, Dodge and Ford, meantime, were pouring more money than ever into stock car racing. Yet Junior won seven Grand National races out of the thirty-three he entered and led most others before mechanical trouble forced him out.

All the while, Junior was making record qualifying runs, year after year. In the usual type of qualifying run, a driver has the track to himself and makes two circuits, with the driver with the fastest average time getting the "pole" position for the start of the race. In a way this presents stock car danger in its purest form. Driving a stock car does not require much handling ability, at least not as compared to Grand Prix racing, because the tracks are simple banked ovals and there is almost no shifting of gears. So qualifying becomes a test of raw nerve—of how fast a man is willing to take a curve. Many of the top drivers in competition are poor at qualifying. In effect, they are willing to calculate their risks only against the risks the other drivers are taking. Junior takes the pure risk as no other driver has ever taken it.

"Pure" risk or total risk, whichever, Indianapolis and Grand Prix drivers have seldom been willing to face the challenge of Southern stock car drivers. A. J. Foyt, last year's winner at Indianapolis, is one exception. He has raced against the Southerners and beaten them. Parnelli Jones has tried and fared badly. Driving "Southern style" has a quality that shakes a man up. The Southerners went on a tour of northern tracks last fall. They raced at Bridgehampton, New York, and went into the corners so hard the marshals stationed at each corner kept radioing frantically to the control booth: "They're going off the track. They're all going off the track!"

COLORPLATE 106

Ida Kohlmeyer. *Mythic Series #31*. 1985. Mixed media on canvas. 68 x 77 ¹/₂ in. Roger Houston Ogden Collection, New Orleans. *Kohlmeyer, born in New Orleans in 1912, studied with Mark Rothko and Hans Hofmann. Her work since the 1970s shows her continued interest in abstraction and her primary concern with color.*

COLORPLATE 107

FRANCIS X. PAVY. *Betting Money on the Cockfight.* 1990. Oil on canvas. 37 x 37 in. Morris Museum of Art, Augusta, Georgia 1990.109. *Pavy incorporates symbols of all the usual vices—sex, booze, gambling, and violence, unifying them with rhythmic musical elements and pictographic forms branded on a hot, fleshy background.*

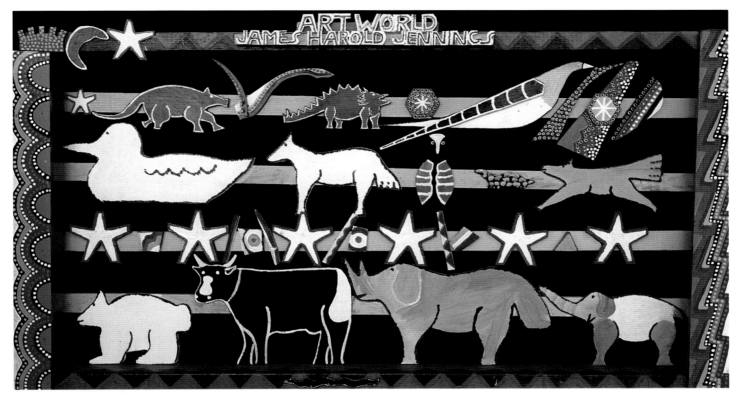

COLORPLATE 108

JAMES HAROLD JENNINGS. *Art World*. 1988. Dr. Kurt A. Gitter and Alice Rae Yelen, New Orleans. *Jennings, of Stokes County, North Carolina, constructs painted sculpture in his schoolbus workshop. He draws on a number of sources of inspiration: movies, traditional Christianity, and his own personal metaphysical ideas.*

COLORPLATE 109

Vera Dickerson. *West Virginia Madonna.* 1978. Handmade paper with watercolor, fabric, sisal, and pins. 26 x 32 in. Collection of the artist.

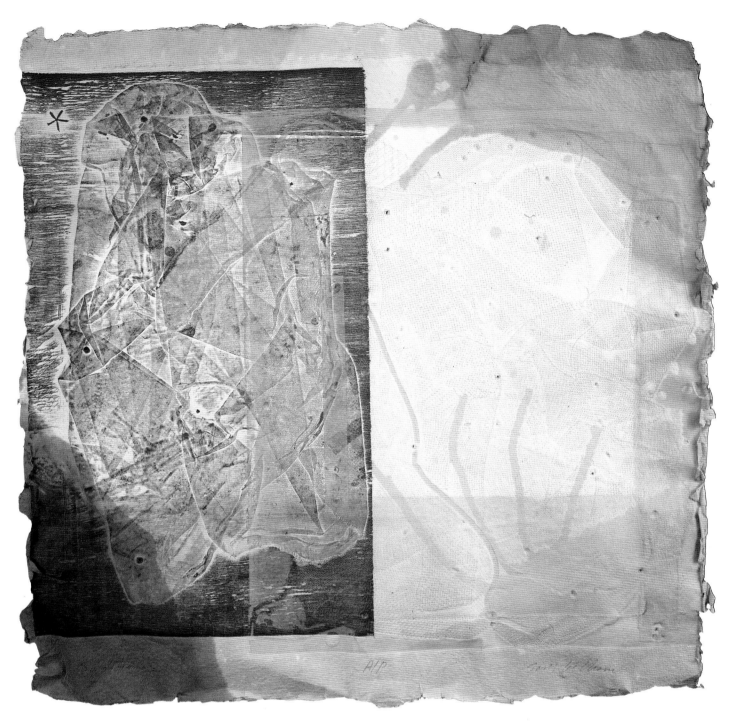

COLORPLATE 110

SAM GILLIAM. *Bardstown*. 1976. Collection of the artist, Washington, D.C. (Courtesy Nancy Drysdale Gallery, 2103 O Street, NW, Washington, D.C. 20037.) *Sam Gilliam, who grew up in Louisville, became associated in the 1960s with the Washington, D.C. color field painters, who created abstract works that rely on large, flat, poured-on or saturated areas of color.* Bardstown *is one of a collograph series called* Kentucky Towns.

COLORPLATE III

YVONNE WELLS. *Civil Rights Quilt.* 1989. Cottons and cotton blends. 66 x 68 in. Robert Cargo Folk Art Gallery, Tuscaloosa, Alabama. *Yvonne Wells is an Alabama quilter whose handwork shows how quilts are sometimes used to chronicle local history or events of significance. Among the images on this quilt are a lynching, a black student being barred from a school, a police dog attack, segregated public facilities, marching to Selma, and a black rider in the back of a bus.*

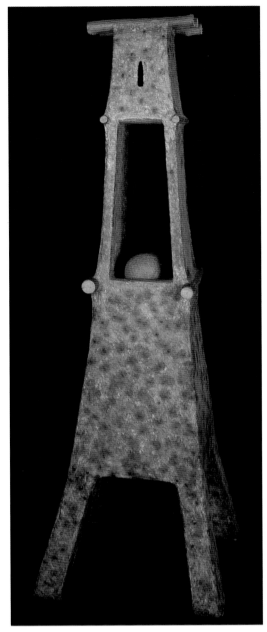

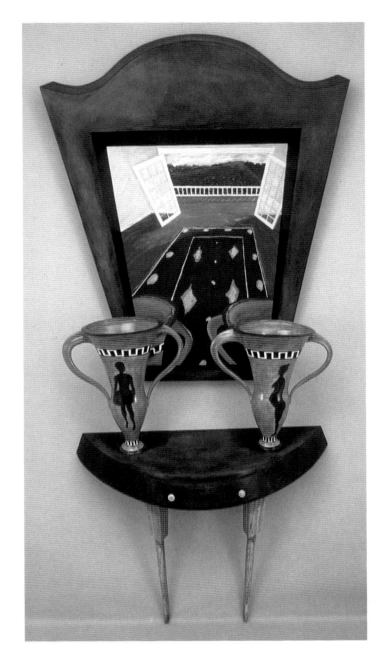

COLORPLATE 112 (left)

CLYDE CONNELL. *Pondering Place.* 1981. Mixed media sculpture. 80 x 25 x 25 in. Roger Houston Ogden Collection, New Orleans.

COLORPLATE 113 (right)

RON DALE. *Ain't Life Great? In the Big House.* Private collection, Oxford, Mississippi. *Dale, raised in Spruce Pine, North Carolina, and now living in Mississippi, feels that social criticism is a central aspect of his sculpture. Here two classical amphorae with black-figure slaves grace a pier table, and the doors of an elegant home open upon endless cotton fields worked by field hands.*

COLORPLATE 114

ROBERT RAUSCHENBERG. *Bed.* 1955.
Oil and pencil on pillow, quilt, sheet on
wood. 75 ¹/₄ x 31 ¹/₂ x 8 in. Fractional gift of
Leo Castelli in honor of Alfred H. Barr, Jr. to
The Museum of Modern Art, New York.
© Robert Rauschenberg/VAGA, New York
1993. Bed *is a painting incorporating a
traditional Log Cabin quilt given to
Rauschenberg by a fellow student at Black
Mountain College in North Carolina. Having
no canvas and no money, he simply
transformed the quilt into one of his first
"combines." The painting provoked a great
deal of controversy, but Rauschenberg said it
was "one of the friendliest pictures I've
ever painted. My fear has always been that
someone would want to crawl into it."*

HUNTER S. THOMPSON

From "The Kentucky Derby Is Decadent and Depraved"

Hunter Thompson, the Gonzo journalist (and model for the character Uncle Duke from the comic strip "Doonesbury") is from Louisville and returned there in 1970 to cover the Kentucky Derby. A pageant that began in 1875 and was patterned after England's Epsom Derby, the race is run on the first Saturday in May, and is the occasion for mint juleps, high fashion, and much revelry. Although approximately 130,000 people enjoy the Derby each year, for Thompson and English artist Ralph Steadman, the event inevitably inspired fear and loathing.

It was Saturday morning, the day of the Big Race, and we were having breakfast in a plastic hamburger palace called the Fish-Meat Village. Our rooms were just across the road in the Brown Suburban Hotel. They had a dining room, but the food was so bad that we couldn't han-

Earl of Derby with Matt Win, President of Churchill Downs. 1930. Photograph. Kinetic Corporation/Churchill Downs. The Kentucky Derby is appropriately named after the Epsom classic, a race that was conceived during a notoriously wild party at The Oaks, estate of the 12th Earl of Derby, in 1779.

The First Turn at Churchill Downs, the 100th Kentucky Derby, 1974. Photograph. Kinetic Corporation/ Churchill Downs.

dle it anymore. The waitresses seemed to be suffering from shin splints; they moved around very slowly, moaning and cursing the "darkies" in the kitchen.

Steadman liked the Fish-Meat place because it had fish and chips. I preferred the "French toast," which was really pancake batter, fried to the proper thickness and then chopped out with a sort of cookie cutter to resemble pieces of toast.

Beyond drink and lack of sleep, our only real problem at that point was the question of access to the clubhouse. finally we decided to go ahead and steal two passes, if necessary, rather than miss that part of the action. This was the last coherent decision we were able to make for the next forty-eight hours. From that point on—almost from the very moment we started out to the track—we lost all control of events and spent the rest of the weekend churning around in a sea of drunken horrors. My notes and recollections from Derby Day are somewhat scrambled.

But now, looking at the big red notebook I carried all through that scene, I see more or less what happened. The book itself is somewhat mangled and bent; some of the pages are torn, others are shriveled and stained by what appears to be whiskey, but taken as a whole, with sporadic memory flashes, the notes seem to tell the story. To wit:

Rain all nite until dawn. No sleep. Christ, here we go, a nightmare of mud and madness. . . . But no. By noon the sun burns through—perfect day, not even humid.

Steadman is now worried about fire. Somebody told him about the clubhouse catching on fire two years ago. Could it happen again? Horrible. Trapped in the press box. Holocaust. A hundred thousand people fighting to get out. Drunks screaming in the flames and the mud, crazed horses running wild. Blind in the smoke. Grandstand collapsing into the flames with us on the roof. Poor Ralph is about to crack. Drinking heavily, into the Haig & Haig.

Out to the track in a cab, avoid that terrible parking in people's front yards, $25 each, toothless old men on the street with big signs: PARK HERE, flagging cars in the yard. "That's fine, boy, never mind the tulips." Wild hair on his head, straight up like a clump of reeds.

Sidewalks full of people all moving in the same direction, towards Churchill Downs. Kids hauling coolers and blankets, teenyboppers in tight pink shorts, many blacks . . . black dudes in white felt hats with leopard-skin bands, cops waving traffic along.

The mob was thick for many blocks around the track; very slow going in the crowd, very hot. On the way to the press box elevator, just inside the clubhouse, we came on a row of soldiers all carrying long white riot sticks. About two platoons, with helmets. A man walking next to us said they were waiting for the governor and his party. Steadman eyed them nervously. "Why do they have those clubs?"

"Black Panthers," I said. Then I remembered good old "Jimbo" at the airport and I wondered what he was thinking right now. Probably very nervous; the place was teeming with cops and soldiers. We pressed on through the crowd, through many gates, past the paddock where the jockeys bring the horses out and parade around for a while before each race so the bettors can get a good look. Five million dollars will be bet today. Many winners, more losers. What the hell. The press gate was jammed up with people trying to get in, shouting at the guards, waving strange press badges: Chicago Sporting Times, Pittsburgh Police Athletic League . . . they were all turned away. "Move on, fella, make way for the working press." We shoved through the crowd and into the elevator, then quickly up to the free bar. Why not? Get it on. Very hot today, not feeling well, must be this rotten climate. The press box was cool and airy, plenty of room to walk around and balcony seats for watching the race or looking down at the crowd. We got a betting sheet and went outside.

Pink faces with a stylish Southern sag, old Ivy styles, seersucker coats and buttondown collars. "Mayblossom Senility" (Steadman's phrase) . . . burnt out early or maybe just not much to burn in the first place. Not much energy in these faces, not much *curiosity.* Suffering in silence, nowhere to go after thirty in this life, just hang on and humor the children. Let the young enjoy themselves while they can. Why not?

The grim reaper comes early in this league . . . banshees on the lawn at night, screaming out there beside that little iron nigger in jockey clothes. Maybe he's the one who's screaming. Bad DT's and too many snarls at the bridge club. Going down with the stock market. Oh Jesus, the kid has wrecked the new car, wrapped it around the big stone pillar at the bottom of the driveway. Broken leg? Twisted eye? Send him off to Yale, they can cure anything up there.

Yale? Did you see today's paper? New Haven is under siege. Yale is swarming with Black Panthers. . . . I tell you, Colonel, the world has gone mad, stone mad. Why, they tell me a goddam woman jockey might ride in the Derby today.

I left Steadman sketching in the Paddock bar and went off to place our bets on the fourth race. When I came back he was staring intently at a group of young men around a table not far away. "Jesus, look at the corruption in that face!" he whispered. "Look at the madness, the fear, the greed!" I looked, then quickly turned my back on the table he was sketching. The face he'd picked out to draw was the face of an old friend of mine, a prep school football star in the good old days with a sleek red Chevy convertible and a very quick hand, it was said, with the snaps of a 32 B brassiere. They called him "Cat Man."

But now, a dozen years later, I wouldn't have recognized him anywhere but here, where I should have expected to find him, in the Paddock bar on Derby Day . . . fat slanted eyes and a pimp's smile, blue silk suit and his friends looking like crooked bank tellers on a binge . . .

Steadman wanted to see some Kentucky Colonels, but he wasn't sure what they looked like. I told him to go back to the clubhouse men's rooms and look for men in white linen suits vomiting in the urinals. "They'll usually have large brown whiskey stains on the fronts of their suits," I said. "But watch the shoes, that's the tip-off. Most of them manage to avoid vomiting on their own clothes, but they never miss their shoes."

In a box not far from ours was Colonel Anna Friedman Goldman, *Chairman and Keeper of the Great Seal of the Honorable Order of Kentucky Colonels.* Not all the 76 million or so Kentucky Colonels could make it to the Derby this year, but many had kept the faith, and several days prior to the Derby they gathered for their annual dinner at the Seelbach Hotel.

The Derby, the actual race, was scheduled for late afternoon, and as the magic hour approached I suggested to Steadman that we should probably spend some time in the infield, that boiling sea of people across the track from the clubhouse. He seemed a little nervous about it, but since none of the awful things I'd warned him about had happened so far—no race riots, firestorms or savage drunken attacks—he shrugged and said, "Right, let's do it."

To get there we had to pass through many gates, each one a step down in status, then through a tunnel under the track. Emerging from the tunnel was such a culture shock that it took us a while to adjust. "God almighty!" Steadman muttered. "This is a . . . Jesus!" He plunged ahead with his tiny camera, stepping over bodies, and I followed, trying to take notes.

Total chaos, no way to see the race, not even the track . . . nobody cares. Big lines at the outdoor betting windows, then stand back to watch winning numbers flash on the big board, like a giant bingo game.

Old blacks arguing about bets; "Hold on there, I'll handle this" (waving pint of whiskey, fistful of dollar bills); girl riding piggyback, T-shirt says, "Stolen from Fort Lauderdale Jail." Thousands of teen-agers, group singing "Let the Sun Shine In," ten soldiers guarding the American flag and a huge fat drunk wearing a blue football jersey (No. 80) reeling around with quart of beer in hand.

No booze sold out here, too dangerous . . . no bathrooms either. Muscle Beach . . . Woodstock . . . many cops with riot sticks, but no sign of a riot. Far across the track the club-house looks like a postcard from the Kentucky Derby.

We went back to the clubhouse to watch the big race. When the crowd stood to face the flag and sing "My Old Kentucky Home," Steadman faced the crowd and sketched frantically. Somewhere up in the boxes a voice screeched, "Turn around, you hairy freak!" The race itself was only two minutes long, and even from our super-status seats and using 12-power glasses, there was no way to see what was really happening. Later, watching a TV rerun in the press box, we saw what happened to our horses. Holy Land, Ralph's choice, stumbled and lost his jockey in the final turn. Mine, Silent Screen, had the lead coming into the stretch, but faded to fifth at the finish. The winner was a 16–1 shot named Dust Commander.

Moments after the race was over, the crowd surged wildly for the exits, rushing for cabs and buses. The next day's *Courier* told of violence in the parking lot; people were punched and trampled, pockets were picked, children lost, bottles hurled. But we missed all this, having retired to the press box for a bit of post-race drinking. By this time we were both half-crazy from too much whiskey, sun fatigue, culture shock, lack of sleep and general dissolution. We hung around the press box long enough to watch a mass interview with the winning owner, a dapper little man named Lehmann who said he had just flown into Louisville that morning from Nepal, where he'd "bagged a record tiger." The sportswriters murmured their admiration and a waiter filled Lehmann's glass with Chivas Regal. He had just won $127,000 with a horse that cost him $6,500 two years ago. His occupation, he said, was "retired contractor." And then he added, with a big grin, "I just retired."

WALKER PERCY

From *Signposts in a Strange Land*

"Bourbon"

Walker Percy (1916–1990), raised by his uncle, the poet and planter William Alexander Percy, gave up the practice of medicine after a long bout with tuberculosis and pursued a quiet life of reading and writing. His first novel, The Moviegoer, *won the 1962 National Book Award for fiction. Much of Percy's later writing is nonfiction, and this selection reveals his wonderful urbanity and a spirited sense of humor.*

E. J. BELLOQ. *Woman with Striped Stockings.* c. 1912.
Photograph. Copyright E. J. Belloq by Lee Friedlander.
From Storyville Portrait. *E. J. Belloq photographed prostitutes in Storyville, the red-light district of New Orleans,
around 1912.*

This is not written by a connoisseur of Bourbon. Ninety-nine percent of Bourbon drinkers
know more about Bourbon than I do. It is about the aesthetic of Bourbon drinking in general
and in particular of knocking it back neat.

I can hardly tell one Bourbon from another, unless the other is very bad. Some bad
Bourbons are even more memorable than good ones. For example, I can recall being broke
with some friends in Tennessee and deciding to have a party and being able to afford only two-
fifths of a $1.75 Bourbon called Two Natural, whose label showed dice coming up 5 and 2. Its
taste was memorable. The psychological effect was also notable. After knocking back two or
three shots over a period of half an hour, the three male drinkers looked at each other and said
in a single voice: "Where are the women?"

I have not been able to locate this remarkable Bourbon since.

Not only should connoisseurs of Bourbon not read this article, neither should persons pre-
occupied with the perils of alcoholism, cirrhosis, esophageal hemorrhage, cancer of the palate,
and so forth—all real enough dangers. I, too, deplore these afflictions. But, as between these
evils and the aesthetic of Bourbon drinking, that is, the use of Bourbon to warm the heart, to
reduce the anomie of the late twentieth century, to cut the cold phlegm of Wednesday afternoons, I choose the aesthetic. What, after all, is the use of not having cancer, cirrhosis, and
such, if a man comes home from work every day at five-thirty to the exurbs of Montclair or
Memphis and there is the grass growing and the little family looking not quite at him but just
past the side of his head, and there's Cronkite on the tube and the smell of pot roast in the living room, and inside the house and outside in the pretty exurb has settled the noxious particles
and the sadness of the old dying Western world, and him thinking: "Jesus, is this it? Listening
to Cronkite and the grass growing?"

If I should appear to be suggesting that such a man proceed as quickly as possible to anes-
thetize his cerebral cortex by ingesting ethyl alcohol, the point is being missed. Or part of the
point. The joy of Bourbon drinking is not the pharmacological effect of C_2H_5OH on the cortex

but rather the instant of the whiskey being knocked back and the little explosion of Kentucky U.S.A. sunshine in the cavity of the nasopharynx and the hot bosky bite of Tennessee summertime—aesthetic considerations to which the effect of the alcohol is, if not dispensable, at least secondary.

By contrast, Scotch: for me (not, I presume, for a Scot), drinking Scotch is like looking at a picture of Noel Coward. The whiskey assaults the nasopharynx with all the excitement of paregoric. Scotch drinkers (not all, of course) I think of as upward-mobile Americans, Houston and New Orleans businessmen who graduate from Bourbon about the same time they shed seersuckers for Lilly slacks. Of course, by now these same folk may have gone back to Bourbon and seersucker for the same reason, because too many Houston oilmen drink Scotch.

Nothing, therefore, will be said about the fine points of sour mash, straights, blends, bonded, except a general preference for the lower proofs. It is a matter of the arithmetic of aesthetics. If one derives the same pleasure from knocking back 80-proof Bourbon as 100-proof, the formula is both as simple as $2 + 2 = 4$ and as incredible as non-Euclidean geometry. Consider. One knocks back five one-ounce shots of 80-proof Early Times or four shots of 100-proof Old Fitzgerald. The alcohol ingestion is the same:

$$5 \times 40\% = 2$$
$$4 \times 50\% = 2$$

Yet, in the case of the Early Times, one has obtained an extra quantum of joy without cost to liver, brain, or gastric mucosa. A bonus, pure and simple, an aesthetic gain as incredible as two parallel lines meeting at infinity.

An apology to the reader is in order, nevertheless, for it has just occurred to me that this is the most unedifying and even maleficent piece I ever wrote—if it should encourage potential alcoholics to start knocking back Bourbon neat. It is also the unfairest. Because I am, happily and unhappily, endowed with a bad GI tract, diverticulosis, neurotic colon, and a mild recurring nausea, which make it less likely for me to become an alcoholic than my healthier fellow Americans. I can hear the reader now: Who is he kidding? If this joker has to knock back five shots of Bourbon every afternoon just to stand the twentieth century, he's already an alcoholic. Very well. I submit to this or any semantic. All I am saying is that if I drink much more than this I will get sick as a dog for two days and the very sight and smell of whiskey will bring on the heaves. Readers beware, therefore, save only those who have stronger wills or as bad a gut as I.

The pleasure of knocking back Bourbon lies in the plane of the aesthetic but at an opposite pole from connoisseurship. My preference for the former is or is not deplorable depending on one's value system—that is to say, how one balances out the Epicurean virtues of cultivating one's sensory end organs with the greatest discrimination and at least cost to one's health, against the virtue of evocation of time and memory and of the recovery of self and the past from the fogged-in disoriented Western world. In Kierkegaardian terms, the use of Bourbon to such an end is a kind of aestheticized religious mode of existence, whereas connoisseurship, the discriminating but single-minded stimulation of sensory end organs, is the aesthetic of damnation.

Two exemplars of the two aesthetics come to mind:

Imagine Clifton Webb, scarf at throat, sitting at Cap d'Antibes on a perfect day, the little wavelets of the Mediterranean sparkling in the sunlight, and he is savoring a 1959 Mouton Rothschild.

Then imagine William Faulkner, having finished *Absalom, Absalom!,* drained, written out, pissed-off, feeling himself over the edge and out of it, nowhere, but he goes somewhere, his favorite hunting place in the Delta wilderness of the Big Sunflower River and, still feeling bad with his hunting cronies and maybe even a little phony, which he was, what with him trying to pretend that he was one of them, a farmer, hunkered down in the cold and rain after the hunt, after honorably passing up the does and seeing no bucks, shivering and snot-nosed, takes out a flat pint of any Bourbon at all and flatfoots about a third of it. He shivers again but not from the cold.

Bourbon does for me what the piece of cake did for Proust.

1926: As a child watching my father in Birmingham, in the exurbs, living next to number-

6 fairway of the New Country Club, him disdaining both the bathtub gin and white lightning of the time, aging his own Bourbon in a charcoal keg, on his hands and knees in the basement sucking on a siphon, a matter of gravity requiring cheek pressed against cement floor, the siphon getting going, the decanter ready, the first hot spurt into his mouth not spat out.

1933: My uncle's sun parlor in the Mississippi Delta and toddies on a Sunday afternoon, the prolonged and meditative tinkle of silver spoon against crystal to dissolve the sugar; talk, tinkle, talk; the talk mostly political: "Roosevelt is doing a good job; no, the son of a bitch is betraying his class."

1934: Drinking at a Delta dance, the boys in bi-swing jackets and tab collars, tough-talking and profane and also scared of the girls and therefore safe in the men's room. Somebody passes around bootleg Bourbon in a Coke bottle. It's awful. Tears start from eyes, faces turn red. "Hot damn, that's good!"

1935: Drinking at a football game in college, UNC versus Duke. One has a blind date. One is lucky. She is beautiful. Her clothes are the color of the fall leaves and her face turns up like a flower. But what to *say* to her, let alone what to do, and whether she is "nice" or "hot"—a distinction made in those days. But what to *say?* Take a drink, by now from a proper concave hip flask (a long way from the Delta Coke bottle) with a hinged top. Will she have a drink? No. But it's all right. The taste of the Bourbon (Cream of Kentucky) and the smell of her fuse with the brilliant Carolina fall and the sounds of the crowd and the hit of the linemen in a single synesthesia.

1941: Drinking mint juleps, famed Southern Bourbon drink, though in the Deep South not really drunk much. In fact, they are drunk so seldom that when, say, on Derby Day somebody gives a julep party, people drink them like cocktails, forgetting that a good julep holds at least five ounces of Bourbon. Men fall face-down unconscious, women wander in the woods disconsolate and amnesiac, full of thoughts of Kahlil Gibran and the limberlost.

Would you believe the first mint julep I had I was sitting not on a columned porch but in the Boo Snooker bar of the New Yorker Hotel with a Bellevue nurse in 1941? The nurse, a nice upstate girl, head floor nurse, brisk, swift, good-looking; Bellevue nurses, the best in the world and this one the best of Bellevue, at least the best-looking. The julep, an atrocity, a heavy syrupy Bourbon and water in a small glass clotted with ice. But good!

How could two women be more different than the beautiful languid Carolina girl and this swift handsome girl from Utica, best Dutch stock? One thing was sure. Each was to be courted, loved, drunk with, with Bourbon. I should have stuck with Bourbon. We changed to gin fizzes because the bartender said he came from New Orleans and could make good ones. He could and did. They were delicious. What I didn't know was that they were made with raw egg albumen and I was allergic to it. Driving her home to Brooklyn and being in love! What a lovely fine strapping smart girl! And thinking of being invited into her apartment where she lived alone and of her offering to cook a little supper and of the many kisses and the sweet love that already existed between us and was bound to grow apace, when on the Brooklyn Bridge itself my upper lip began to swell and little sparks of light flew past the corner of my eye like St. Elmo's fire. In the space of thirty seconds my lip stuck out a full three-quarter inch, like a shelf, like Mortimer Snerd. Not only was kissing out of the question but my eyes swelled shut. I made it across the bridge, pulled over to the curb, and fainted. Whereupon this noble nurse drove me back to Bellevue, gave me a shot, and put me to bed.

Anybody who monkeys around with gin and egg white deserves what he gets. I should have stuck with Bourbon and have from that day to this.

POSTSCRIPT: *Reader, just in case you don't want to knock it back straight and would rather monkey around with perfectly good Bourbon, here's my favorite recipe, "Cud'n Walker's Uncle Will's Favorite Mint Julep Receipt."*

You need excellent Bourbon whiskey; rye or Scotch will not do. Put half an inch of sugar in the bottom of the glass and merely dampen it with water. Next, very quickly—and here is the trick in the procedure—crush your ice, actually powder it, preferably in a towel with a wooden mallet, so quickly that it remains dry, and, slipping two sprigs of fresh mint against the inside of the glass, cram the ice in right to the brim, packing it with your hand. Finally, fill the glass, which apparently has no room left for anything else, with Bourbon, the older the better, and grate a bit of nutmeg on the top. The glass will frost immediately. Then settle back in your chair for half an hour of cumulative bliss.

FLORENCE KING

From *Southern Ladies and Gentlemen*
"The Cult of Southern Womanhood"

Southern Ladies and Gentlemen, *a collection of funny essays on the manners and mores of Southerners, was published in 1975. The following sample exposes the phenomenon of the "self-rejuvenating virgin" and other foibles and wiles of Southern "ladies."*

Novelists prefer complex women for their protagonists, which is why the Southern woman has been the heroine of so many more novels than her Northern sister. The cult of Southern womanhood endowed her with at least five totally different images and asked her to be good enough to adopt all of them. She is required to be frigid, passionate, sweet, bitchy, and scatter-brained—all at the same time. Her problems spring from the fact that she succeeds.

Antebellum Southern civilization was built upon the white woman's untouchable image. In order to keep her footing on the pedestal men had erected for her, she had to be aloof, aristocratic, and haughty. These qualities have always been required of women in societies based upon vast, entailed estates, but they were especially necessary in the South. They enabled the white woman to maintain her sanity when she saw light-skinned slave children, who were the very spit of Old Massa, running around the plantation. By being sufficiently frosty and above it all, she was able to ignore and endure the evidence of intercaste sexuality that surrounded her.

When the disregard she cultivated was mixed with the inevitable disgust she felt, the result was often frigidity. Southern men have actually been known to drink a toast to women's sexual coldness. The best of these florid paeans has been recorded by Carl Carmer in *Stars Fell on Alabama:* "To Woman, lovely woman of the Southland, as pure and chaste as this sparkling water, as cold as this gleaming ice, we lift this cup, and we pledge our hearts and our lives to the protection of her virtue and chastity."

Southernese loses a great deal in translation. Here's what the toast really means: "To Woman, without whose purity and chastity we could never have justified slavery and segregation, without whose coldness we wouldn't have had the excuse we needed for messing around down in the slave cabins and getting plenty of poontang. We pledge our hearts and our lives to the protection of her virtue and chastity because they are the best political leverage we ever did see."

As male propaganda continued through the years, Southern women came to believe these fulsome testimonials to their purity and tried to find a middle road between their normal desires and their male-manufactured image. Anything can happen in a land where men drink toasts to frigidity, so the Southern woman often decided to enjoy sex as much as possible while remaining a virgin—a compromise that won her a reputation as a sadistic flirt.

More time passed, and other American women gained greater sexual freedom, so the Southern woman evolved another compromise. It was easy for her to do this sort of thing because she was the product of a region that had spent two centuries justifying itself to the rest of the country. After performing the kind of mental gymnastics it takes to prove that slavery is

LUSTER WILLIS. *This Is It.*
c. 1970. Tempera and
glitter on plywood. 15 3/4
x 24 3/4 in. University
Museums, University of
Mississippi. Gift of Bill
Ferris. *Willis, a stick
carver and a painter, created work, some of it
enhanced with glitter, that
represents life and lore
in his small Mississippi
community.*

God's will, rationalizing mere sexual peccadilloes was child's play. She hit upon another modus vivendi, a much more swinging one this time, that would permit her to lose her virgini-ty, enjoy a regular sex life, and yet soothe her male-induced guilt. She would throw away her hot pantalets, do as she pleased, and convince herself that her hymen was still intact.

She became a self-rejuvenating virgin.

To recycle her pearl beyond price, certain ground rules had to be established. first, premed-itation was forbidden. The self-rejuvenating virgin never planned ahead, she was always "swept off her feet." If she could not make herself believe this, she engineered bizarre sexual encounters that were never quite the real thing, so that the next morning she could tell herself, "It didn't really happen because . . ."

1. I was drunk.
2. We didn't take all our clothes off.
3. We didn't do it in a bed.
4. He didn't put it all the way inside me.
5. He didn't come inside me.
6. I didn't come.
7. . . . Well, not really.

The self-rejuvenating virgin never bothered with contraceptives because that was premedi-tation. If her date wanted to use one, that was his business. They might drive past two dozen drugstores on their way to the woods, but she never said a word until the very last minute—at which point she shrieked: "Do you have something?" (He nearly always did.) Thanks to the self-rejuvenating virgin, the wallet of a Southern man in pre-pill days was likely to contain more condoms than money.

The woods, of course, was the only place a respectable self-rejuvenating virgin could go to earth. The very idea of making love in a bed threw her into conflict—it was too official, too premeditated, and too comfortable. She preferred to mortify her flesh in the woods, where she could count the chiggers and ticks as punishment.

When I was at Ole Miss in 1958, the boys were so used to self-rejuvenating virgins that they automatically headed for the woods even when a bed was available. Every car trunk con-tained both a blanket and the most Southern of all contraceptives, a bottle of warm Coca-Cola, because the self-rejuvenating virgin would walk over hot coals before she would ever buy a douche bag.

If her date failed to use a "precaution" and if the douche-that-refreshes did not work, the self-rejuvenating virgin could claim the best excuse in her rule book:

"It didn't really happen, because I'm pregnant."

This is the webby Southern mind at its best. Translation: "I let him do it to me and I enjoyed it, but now I'm being punished, which wipes out the pleasure and therefore the entire act."

Some self-rejuvenating virgins behaved themselves at home but went into a sexual frenzy on holiday trips. Their lovers were men they met in hotels and resorts. Thanks to this vacation psychology, they were able to go home and tell themselves: "It didn't really happen because . . ."

1. I'll never see him again.
2. I don't remember his name.
3. He never told me his name.
4. I didn't tell him my name.
5. It happened in New York.

The self-rejuvenating virgin might fondle a man's privates as he drove to the motel, but when he pulled up to room 102 she refused to go in.

"Let's just sit here a minute," she said, and the next minute was all over him. A steamy petting session ensued, but when they became excited to the point of adjourning to the paid-for room, she said, "Let's go somewhere!" Meaning, of course, the woods.

Sometimes she was drunk enough to enter the motel room, tear off her clothes, and fall backward onto the bed. She landed in the missionary position and promptly passed out—or pretended to. The next morning she awoke naked, next to a naked man, stared at him in horror, and then shook him awake: "Did anything happen? Tell me the truth."

Southern men always knew what to say.

"No, honey, nothin' happened, I swear it didn't."

The self-rejuvenating virgin always had a ladylike orgasm, a pelvic legerdemain that she infused with fey girlishness. When she felt it coming on, she giggled—a feat that ought to be worth an Oscar or two—and when it hit she trembled prettily in the zephyr range. Afterward, she registered an awesome combination of astonishment and innocence: "Ohhh, what happened to me?"

The birth-control pill has all but wiped the self-rejuvenating virgin and her plea of crime passionnel from the face of the South. She must now own up to the fact that she is guilty of canoodling in the first degree.

I am glad she is passing into history, but I will miss her, because she made life, particularly dormitory life, most lively and interesting. The self-rejuvenating virgin I will never forget was a Mississippi girl who, without a doubt, had the most active sex life of any woman since Pauline Bonaparte—and, of course, convinced all of her lovers that she was a virgin. Her secret weapon was an alum-spiked red mouthwash that assured her of having pucker-power.

CRAIG CLAIBORNE

From "A Feast Made for Laughter"
The Best Cook in the South

Mississippian Craig Claiborne was for many years food editor of The New York Times. *This warm and amusing account of his mother's well-managed boarding house and fine cooking shares her recipe for chicken spaghetti, a favorite Southern dish that is little-known outside the region.*

SUSUS FREDERICK VON EHREN. *Luscious Fare.* c. 1940. Watercolor on paper. 10 x 13 ¹/₄ in. Roger Houston Ogden Collection, New Orleans.

My Mother's Chicken Spaghetti

1 (3¹/₂-pound) chicken with giblets
Fresh or canned chicken broth to
*   cover*
Salt
3 cups imported Italian peeled
*   tomatoes*
7 tablespoons butter
3 tablespoons flour
¹/₂ cup heavy cream
¹/₈ teaspoon grated nutmeg
Freshly ground pepper
¹/₂ pound fresh mushrooms
2 cups finely chopped onion
1¹/₂ cups finely chopped celery

1¹/₂ cups chopped seeded green
*   pepper*
1 tablespoon or more finely minced
*   garlic*
¹/₄ pound ground beef
¹/₄ pound ground pork
1 bay leaf
¹/₂ teaspoon hot red pepper flakes,
*   optional*
1 pound spaghetti or spaghettini
¹/₂ pound Cheddar cheese, grated
*   (about 2 to 2¹/₂ cups)*
Freshly grated Parmesan cheese

1. Place the chicken with neck, gizzard, heart, and liver in a kettle and add chicken broth to cover and salt to taste. Partially cover. Bring to the boil and simmer until the chicken is tender without being dry, 35 to 45 minutes. Let cool.

2. Remove the chicken and take the meat from the bones. Shred the meat, cover, and set aside. Return the skin and bones to the kettle and cook the stock down for 30 minutes or longer. There should be 4 to 6 cups of broth. Strain and reserve the broth. Discard the skin and bones.

3. Meanwhile, put the tomatoes in a saucepan and cook down to half the original volume, stirring.

4. Melt 3 tablespoons butter in a saucepan and add the flour, stirring to blend with a wire whisk. When blended and smooth, add 1 cup of the reserved hot broth and the cream, stirring rapidly with the whisk. When thickened and smooth, add the nutmeg, salt, and pepper to taste. Continue cooking, stirring occasionally, for about 10 minutes. Set aside.

5. If the mushrooms are very small, leave them whole. Otherwise, cut them in half or quarter them. Heat 1 tablespoon of butter in a small skillet and add the mushrooms. Cook, shaking the skillet occasionally and stirring, until the mushrooms are golden brown. Set aside.

JONATHAN GREEN. *Shucking Oysters.* 1988. Oil on masonite. 32 x 24 in. Photograph courtesy of McKissick Museum. *Green's paintings are dedicated to celebrating the self-sufficiency and unique qualities of Gullah culture in the Sea Islands.*

6. Heat 3 tablespoons of butter in a deep skillet and add the onion. Cook, stirring, until wilted. Add the celery and green pepper and cook, stirring, for about 5 minutes. Do not overcook. The vegetables should remain crisp-tender.

7. Add the garlic, beef, and pork and cook, stirring and chopping down with the edge of a large metal spoon to break up the meat. Cook just until the meat loses its red color. Add the bay leaf and red pepper flakes, if desired. Add the tomatoes and the white sauce made with the chicken broth. Add the mushrooms.

8. Cook the spaghetti in 3 or 4 quarts of boiling salted water until it is just tender. Do not overcook. Remember that it will cook again when blended with the chicken and meat sauce. Drain the spaghetti and run under cold running water.

9. Spoon enough of the meat sauce over the bottom of a 5- or 6-quart casserole to cover it lightly. Add about one third of the spaghetti. Add about one third of the shredded chicken, a layer of meat sauce, and a layer of grated Cheddar cheese. Continue making layers, ending with a layer of spaghetti topped with a thin layer of meat sauce and grated Cheddar cheese.

10. Pour in up to 2 cups of the reserved chicken broth or enough to almost but not quite cover the top layer of spaghetti. At this point the dish may be left to stand, covered, for up to an hour. If the liquid is absorbed as the dish stands, add a little more chicken broth. Remember that when this dish is baked and served, the sauce will be just a bit soupy rather than thick and clinging.

11. When ready to bake, preheat the oven to 350 degrees.

12. Place the spaghetti casserole on top of the stove and bring it just to the boil. Cover and place it in the oven. Bake for 15 minutes and uncover. Bake for 15 minutes longer, or until the casserole is hot and bubbling throughout and starting to brown on top. Serve immediately with grated Parmesan cheese on the side.

YIELD: 12 or more servings.

In my childhood, it would never have occurred to anyone to analyze or categorize the kind of food we dined on from my mother's kitchen. It was simply "southern cooking." In retrospect, it fell into three categories—soul food, which is a blend of African and American Indian; creole cookery, which is a marriage of innocent Spanish and bastardized French; and pure French, desserts mostly, from the first edition of *The Boston Cooking-School Cook Book*. To my mind that book was, in its original concept, the first great cookbook in America. For years it had no peer (Mrs. Rorer's works notwithstanding) and it was my mother's kitchen bible.

My mother had an incredible aptitude in her ability to "divine" the ingredients of one dish or another. She could dine in New Orleans and come back to reproduce on her own table the likes of oysters Rockefeller, oysters Bienville, the creole version (so different from the original French) of rémoulade sauce with shrimp.

There was another advantage to the old-fashioned southern kitchen: the talent and palate of the American Negro. I am convinced that given the proper training in the kitchen of a great French restaurant, any American black with cooking in his or her soul would be outstanding.

With rare exceptions, all the servants in our kitchen arrived with a full knowledge of soul cooking, which is broad in scope. Essentially it encompasses the use of all parts of the pig, more often than not boiled, plain, or with other ingredients. Pig's feet, pig's tails, hog jowl, and that most soul of all foods, chitterlings, the small intestines of pigs. It has always amused me, since I first encountered the regional cooking of France, to know that one of that nation's most prized and delectable of sausages—called andouille or andouillettes—is nothing more than chitterlings blended with various spices, onions or shallots, white wine, and so on, and stuffed into casings. For what it's worth, a New Year's party without grilled andouillettes in my house is as unthinkable as an absence of at least a couple of bottles of champagne. Once a year in my childhood home, Mother had a chitterling supper. Chitterlings, cooked and served with vinegar and hot pepper are, to some noses, a bit odoriferous. Therefore, the boarders were advised that they were invited to the chitterling supper, but if they found the aromas less than fastidious, they were cordially invited to find another place to dine.

The standard items of soul food that appeared almost daily at my mother's table were one form of greens or another, always cooked with pieces of pork, the feet, hocks, belly, and so on, sometimes salted, sometimes smoked. The greens were of a common garden-variety, such as mustard greens, collard greens, and turnip greens. These would be put on to boil with a great quantity of water and salt and allowed to cook for hours. Once cooked, the liquid is much treasured by southern palates. It is called "pot likker" and you sip it like soup with corn bread. If you want to be fancy, you can always make corn meal dumplings to float on top of the greens. Black eye peas are also a regional treasure, some people think the finest of all staples. These, too, are cooked for a long while (preferably from a fresh state; if not, frozen; if not frozen, dried; and if none of these, canned).

One of the most distinguished roomers and boarders in my mother's house was a scholarly gentleman, well known in academic circles, the late Dr. John Dollard, a highly praised Yale psychologist and social scientist. Dr. Dollard had come to Indianola to do research on a book called *Caste and Class in a Southern Town* and with what might have been an uncanny sense of direction or perception, had chosen my house as his base of operation.

Dr. Dollard, a patient, kindly, amiable man was, of course, a Yankee and thus had a "funny accent." The other boarders did not take kindly to him for no other reason than that he was an "outsider." In the beginning he criticized the cooking of the greens, complaining that there was not a vitamin left in the lot. And as a result of his well-intentioned explanations and at the base encouragement of the other boarders, my mother willingly committed one of the most wicked acts of her life. Dr. Dollard was placed at a bridge table, covered, of course, with linen and set with sterling, and he was served a mess of raw greens that he ate with considerable and admirable composure and lack of resentment. Always the detached and critical observer, I found my mother's role in this little game almost intolerable, although I said nothing.

Odd coincidences have occurred often in my life. One day, a decade or so ago, I wandered into the photographic studio where portraits bearing the title *New York Times Studio* were taken. I glanced at an assignment sheet and saw the name John Dollard, Yale.

As I walked out, John walked in.

"John," I said, "I'm Craig Claiborne."

"How's your mother?" he asked. "She's a great woman."

With one possible exception, the dishes prepared by my mother that I liked best were the creole foods. As I have noted, to this day, like the madeleines of Proust's childhood, I can smell chopped onions, celery, and green peppers, cooking together in butter or oil. This, to my mind, is the creole base, and it is a combination that often perfumes my own kitchen.

My mother would purchase one of Mr. Colotta's (Mr. Colotta was the only fish dealer for miles around) finest red snappers from the Gulf Coast brought in that morning, encased in ice, and weighing almost twenty pounds. A fish that size would barely fit in the oven. It would be baked and basted with oil and the creole base and it was as succulent and tender as anything I ever tasted here or abroad. Her shrimp creole with the same base was robust and glorious.

It would be easy to recite the entire roster of her creole and other southern specialties. A remarkable Brunswick stew, an incredibly good barbecue sauce with tomato ketchup, Worcestershire sauce, and vinegar as a base. She made a delectable assortment of gumbos—crab, oyster, and plain okra. (The word gumbo, I was to learn in later life, derived from the Bantu word for okra.) Her deviled crab was spicy, rich, and irresistible.

There were two specialties of my home kitchen for which my mother made only the final preparation. In my earliest years, my father cured his own hams and sausages in the smokehouse out back and these she prepared with expert hands. On occasion she made country sausages, fiery hot and spiced with red pepper flakes before smoking, but more often than not she bought these from a neighbor. These sausages, for which I have developed a formula as closely paralleling the original as possible, I prepare today in a small portable smoker. Southern to the core, my mother frequently prepared beaten biscuits, one of the most curious of southern kitchen or back porch rituals.

Beaten biscuits are a blend of flour, lard, and butter that is worked together by hand. You then add enough milk to make a stiff dough, which is rolled out and literally beaten with any handy sturdy instrument. It might be a rolling pin, a shortened broom handle, even a hatchet or ax. You beat the dough, folding it over as you work, for the better part of an hour until it blisters. The dough is then rolled out, cut into small round biscuits, and pricked in the center with a fork. There are beaten biscuit cutters that cut and prick at the same time. And there are, or used to be, special beaten biscuit machines with rollers through which you roll the dough until it blisters, not unlike the old-fashioned clothes wringer.

There are dozens of dishes that come to my mind when I think of my mother's kitchen—fantastic caramels, divinity fudge, a luscious coconut cake with meringue and fresh coconut topping, the best, richest pecan pie in the world, incredible fried chicken, great shrimp rémoulade, chicken turnovers in an awesomely rich pastry served with a cream sauce—but two of the dishes that she made for very "party" occasions had a curious appeal for my childhood palate. Sunday dinner, which was served at twelve-thirty in the afternoon, was always paramount among our weekly meals and if she wished to offer the boarders an uncommon treat she would serve them as a first course toast points topped with canned, drained white asparagus spears, over which was spooned a hot tangy Cheddar cheese sauce. This dish was generally garnished with strips of pimento.

Another for which she was renowned was a three-layered salad composed of a bottom layer of lime gelatin chilled until set, a middle layer of well-seasoned cream cheese blended with gelatin and chilled until set, and a top layer of delicately firm tomato aspic. The salad was cut into cubes, garnished with greens, and topped with a dab of mayonnaise.

Years later, when I was working for the American Broadcasting Company in public relations, I knew a reporter for the old, once thriving monthly called *Liberty* magazine. Her name was Beulah Karney and she was food editor of that journal. She once asked me casually if I could name the best cook in the South and I specified my mother. Beulah traveled to Mississippi and interviewed "Miss Kathleen." In the May 1948 issue there appeared an article entitled "The Best Cook in Town" and it described my mother's boardinghouse. Pursuant to a good deal of recent research, I found that issue in the New York Public Library.

One sentence stated "the six paying guests, all bachelors, said there wasn't much point in getting married when Miss Kathleen's food was so good." Four recipes were printed, including one for Miss Kathleen's Party Salad, that three-layered affair.

ROY BLOUNT, JR.
"Song to Grits"

It would be difficult to say how long grits have been a staple in the diet of Southerners, since settlers at Jamestown were introduced to the dish by their native American neighbors. Roy Blount, Jr., who grew up in Decatur, Georgia, celebrates this most popular Southern dietary mainstay.

———————————

When my mind's unsettled,
When I don't feel spruce,
When my nerves get frazzled,
When my flesh gets loose —

What knits
Me back together's grits.

TARLETON BLACKWELL. *The Hog Series XVI (Alyce/Piggly Wiggly).* 1983. Oil on canvas. 91 x 70 3/4 in. Southeastern Center for Contemporary Art. Courtesy of the artist, Manning, South Carolina. *Tarleton Blackwell makes an interesting statement about pigs and people, poverty and plenty in his Hog Series paintings.*

Grits with gravy,
Grits with cheese.
Grits with bacon,
Grits with peas.
Grits with a minimum
Of two over-medium eggs mixed in 'em: um!

Grits, grits, it's
Grits I sing —
Grits fits
In with anything.

Rich and poor, black and white,
Lutheran and Campbellite,
Jews and Southern Jesuits,
All acknowledge buttered grits.

Give me two hands, give me my wits,
Give me forty pounds of grits.

Grits at taps, grits at reveille.
I am into grits real heavily.

True grits,
More grits,
Fish, grits and collards.
Life is good where grits are swallered.

Grits
Sits
Right.

REYNOLDS PRICE

From *Clear Pictures: First Loves, First Guides*
"An Absolute Hunter"

Reynolds Price was born in Macon, North Carolina in 1933. Price uses the rural North Carolina Piedmont as the setting for many of his stories and novels, creating there rich worlds peopled by characters whose lives are deeply entwined. Clear Pictures, *his autobiography, reveals a life and family as vivid and complex as those of his fiction. Here Price recounts hunting experiences with his cousin Mac.*

A fox hunt then in the upper South bore no resemblance to the red-coated pastime of people too rich to know better. Mac's method was typical of real country hunters with a purpose for killing, men for whom the fox is a costly enemy of domestic fowl. I'd go to Macon on a Friday night, sleep at Ida's, eat a quick breakfast and be ready when Mac came to get me at dawn. He

COLORPLATE 115

HUBERT SHUPTRINE. *The Francis Mill.* 1982. Drypoint. 15 ¹/₈ x 16 ¹/₂ in. Copyright 1982 by Hubert Shuptrine.
All rights reserved. Used with permission. In the collection of Dr. and Mrs. Lawrence H. Lassiter. *Native Tennessean
Hubert Shuptrine has illustrated writings by James Dickey, William Styron, and Willie Morris.*

COLORPLATE 116

CARROLL CLOAR. *Where the Southern Cross the Yellow Dog.* 1965. Cassein tempera on masonite. 23 x 33 3/4 in.
Memphis Brooks Museum of Art. Brooks Fine Arts Foundation Purchase 65.17. *Not at all the naive or folk artist that he
is sometimes labeled, Carroll Cloar was trained in New York and traveled in Europe before returning to Memphis to paint
scenes based on his memories of the Arkansas and Mississippi Delta. The title of this painting is taken from a popular W.
C. Handy song about the legendary Moorhead, Mississippi, railroad crossing. Writer Nancy Lemann claims that "if
[Mississippi Deltans] go somewhere, to a strange place, they stand up on a table and yell out, 'Where does the Southern
cross the Yellow Dog?' and then if someone yells out 'Moorehead,' [sic] then they know they have a friend there."*

COLORPLATE 117

THEORA HAMBLETT. *A Tiskit, A Tasket.* 1972. The University Museums, The University of Mississippi, University, Mississippi. *Many of Theora Hamblett's paintings record her dreams and visions, but others, like this one, are valuable records of childhood games played in rural Mississippi.*

COLORPLATE 118

SIMON B. GUNNING (b. 1956). *Tangled in Deep*. 1990. Oil on canvas. 43 ¹/₂ x 79 ¹/₂ in. Roger Houston Ogden Collection, New Orleans.

COLORPLATE 119

MAUD GATEWOOD. *Swinger in Summer Shade.* 1981. Mr. and Mrs. Frank P. Ward, Jr., Raleigh, North Carolina.
*Maud Gatewood of Yanceyville, North Carolina, uses dramatic lighting to contrast the intense Southern sunlight with
cool, deep shade creating a static, photographic effect.*

COLORPLATE 120

DON COOPER. *Extreme Southeast Georgia.* 1990. Oil on canvas. 60 x 70 in. Morris Museum of Art, Augusta, Georgia 1992.011. *This painting, inspired by a visit to the old Carnegie estate on Cumberland Island, Georgia, is part of a series in which Cooper superimposes Oriental elements—visual and mystical—on the landscape of the South, perhaps mourning its decay. About Cumberland Island, writer Padgett Powell has said, "A barrier island is a barrier; it is beauty, but it is rough beauty," and this painting evokes an ominous Eden just before the fall.*

COLORPLATE 121

MORGAN MONCEAUX. *Presidential Portraits (Presidents Taylor, Tyler, Polk, Jackson).* 1992. Pastel, oil pastel, and collage. Copyright 1992 Morgan Rank Gallery, East Hampton, New York. *Morgan Monceaux of Louisiana is a self-taught artist who has created presidential portraits from George Washington to Bill Clinton.*

COLORPLATE 122
BENNY ANDREWS. *The Hunters.* 1989. Oil and collage on canvas. 73 ¹/₄ x 53 ¹/₄ in. Collection of the artist.
*Benny Andrews grew up in rural Georgia, where his educational experience was not unusual for poor blacks and whites:
"I had to quit going to school in the spring when it came time to plant cotton. . . . the principal would negotiate with the
teachers to try to give me some kind of credit that had to do with drawing . . . so I drew my way through high school."*

Lamar Dodd. *Cascade.* 1948. Georgia Museum of Art, University of Georgia, Athens, Georgia. Used with permission of the artist.

was always alone; for whatever reason, Joe never hunted with us. We'd ride deeper into the country to another white tenant's house—call him Woodrow Stegall—where Mac kept his dogs.

Woody would be out by the dog pen, a good many yards on past the chickens. We'd join him there, in a wide globe of the rank clean odor of working dogs. Mac would count the dozen or fifteen smart-faced, wigglesome and ever-ready hounds; and he'd name them over with no hesitation (to my valuable instruction—that so many of any one thing deserved proper and characteristic names and got them, even from these busy men). The dogs had risen to the mere sight of Mac's truck; the sound of his voice was almost more than they could bear. So Woody would either lay down the ramp, and they'd run into the bed of the pickup; or if Mac were short of time and wanted a quick taste of dog voices, Woody would just wave them off toward the nearest woods.

If we had a few hours, we'd shut the tailgate and ride up the road to whatever spot Woody chose that day; Mac always let him run the show. Once the dogs were unloaded, they'd moil at our ankles, frantic for permission. Woody might stand stock-still for a minute, letting their hope and dread boil higher. Then he might dig into his back pocket, find a worn old foxtail and give the smartest bitch a sniff, but that was merely a teasing delay—they all knew the point so truly that their hearts nearly burst with forethought till Woody raised his stubby horn and blew a high bellow. They'd pound out of sight like a small herd of footstools, that stiff and fast. And for the next hour or more, we'd stand near the truck or go to a cluster of rocks and sit to hear the dogs. There'd be a good deal of spitting, whittling and a lot of farm and weather talk but very little else. The son for instance seldom came with us; and when he did, he was far too grandly gone at sixteen to spare a look or word my way, least of all a secret from his side of puberty that I longed to know.

And I doubt that my youth or innocence suppressed a natural bawdry in Mac—other cousins and uncles were freely ribald in my presence—but for his private reason, I never heard Mac say an obscene word or tell a blue joke. And none of his men did either in his presence, though all would say *nigger* at least once a day; and ever so often we'd meet one of those compelled poor-whites who had to say it every two or three minutes, like a wrenching tic that

329

ruined his face. I'd wince inside, knowing how my parents hated the word. Mac never flinched and would sometimes say it himself but always lightly, with a built-in grin as if he meant it as the joke it was when black people said it to one another, though I knew it was different and tried not to hear.

The hounds would be conducting the hunt. At first their cries were as foreign as Finnish; but soon I came to know the random early solos and then the business-like full-cry fugue. That wild polyphony could run for whole long minutes of chase, then crumble in an instant if the fox escaped, as it generally did every four or five minutes. Then lastly the hectic screams of the catch, the young dogs' cries of incredulous triumph. I never attained Mac's or Woody's powers of detection; they could name individual hounds by their voices—"That's old Rowlet," "Big Molly's hurting" (with senile arthritis) or "They've lost poor Stitch. I knew he was too young. Hope to God he can find his way back"—but at least I could share their vicarious pleasure. They'd give the dogs ten minutes with the corpse; then Mac would say "Woody, hail em on in."

Woody would walk to the edge of the pines and blow long wails in several directions, notes so native to our Celtic bones that even Mac would laugh and say "Ren, don't that make your damned beard stand up?"

I'd have to remind him I still wasn't shaving.

And he'd say "Thank your damned blessings then" and heist up his trousers with the sides of his arms. We'd wait awhile longer till the hounds limped one by one from the woods. Tired as they were, they came right to us and sought our eyes. Before they could rest though, they wanted our report.

Mac was manly with them; he'd never squat and scratch their ears, but he would call their names and give them short reviews of their work, "Tim, you done all right. Lucy, where *were* you? Never heard your voice. Don't expect no extra cornbread tonight."

And that satisfied them. They were far too self-respecting to cringe or to run through a round of house-pet stunts to beg an embrace from any idle human. Once they were judged, they'd haul their tails back up the ramp or, if we'd stayed at Woodrow's, on down past the chickens (whose blood arch-enemy they'd just now killed) to their own pen and a day-long nap. They knew they'd paid their room and board.

Since no masculine code of courage-near-death had ever been conveyed to me, I was never the classic spooked lad so common in fiction, trembling on the verge of manly blood-knowledge. No fox was likely to turn on me, though rabid foxes were not unknown. In the company of certified men like Mac and Woody, I could stand through hunts with no big worries about my performance. So the hyper-male obsessions that threaten so many boyhoods passed me luckily by. The exact-right killing equipment, the precise body-stance for deadly blows, the approved cast of eye, the mystic goal of oneness through death with nature and beast and a few other men—any such concerns would have thrown Mac and Woody, or any man I knew, to the ground in laughter.

If Mac and Woody could have told you why they hunted, near a village with three cheap grocery-stores, they might have said "Oh to pass a little time an dnot hurt anything anybdoy cares about more than a fox. It's good for the dogs too, lets them feel useful." And Mac might have added "It pays Woody back for feeding them good." If you'd said "Fine but it's hard on foxes," they'd have looked you over, grinned and said "How many chickens you raising, sport?"

Even so I tried to look as nearly grown as I could, to be as calm and intent as the men (I was already spitting through my front teeth so often that Mother had warned me of dehydration). And when Mac and I were alone again, and he didn't correct me on anything, I knew I'd passed with no demerit through one more almost invisible gate. I'd watched a squealing bloody pig-slaughter in Mac's yard, but I was never present at the actual death of any wild creature larger than a rabbit, so I had the luck to miss the temptation to deface with sentiment the killing of things as grand in their beastliness as deer or bear. What Mac spared me, in our strange detached hunts, was the poisonous narcissism that fuels bloodsports in well-fed societies. What he taught me was one more use of male companionship—a friend will stand with you, still and easy, while you run your dogs, whatever dogs you need to run at the time.

THE NEWEST SOUTH

HARPER LEE

From *To Kill a Mockingbird*

Nelle Harper Lee published To Kill a Mockingbird *in 1960, winning the Pulitzer Prize in 1961. Although she never wrote another book, this one has become a much loved classic and has been translated into at least ten languages. Here Scout Finch receives a lesson in manners from Calpurnia, the family's housekeeper and surrogate mother.*

——————

Catching Walter Cunningham in the schoolyard gave me some pleasure, but when I was rubbing his nose in the dirt Jem came by and told me to stop. "You're bigger'n he is," he said.

"He's as old as you, nearly," I said. "He made me start off on the wrong foot."

"Let him go, Scout. Why?"

EUDORA WELTY. *Girl on Porch. Hinds County.* 1939. Photograph. © Eudora Welty Collection—Mississippi Department of Archives and History.

"He didn't have any lunch," I said, and explained my involvement in Walter's dietary affairs.

Walter had picked himself up and was standing quietly listening to Jem and me. His fists were half cocked, as if expecting an onslaught from both of us. I stomped at him to chase him away, but Jem put out his hand and stopped me. He examined Walter with an air of speculation. "Your daddy Mr. Walter Cunningham from Old Sarum?" he asked, and Walter nodded.

Walter looked as if he had been raised on fish food: his eyes, as blue as Dill Harris's, were red-rimmed and watery. There was no color in his face except at the tip of his nose, which was moistly pink. He fingered the straps of his overalls, nervously picking at the metal hooks.

Jem suddenly grinned at him. "Come on home to dinner with us, Walter," he said. "We'd be glad to have you."

Walter's face brightened, then darkened.

Jem said, "Our daddy's a friend of your daddy's. Scout here, she's crazy—she won't fight you any more."

"I wouldn't be too certain of that," I said. Jem's free dispensation of my pledge irked me, but precious noontime minutes were ticking away. "Yeah Walter, I won't jump on you again. Don't you like butterbeans? Our Cal's a real good cook."

Walter stood where he was, biting his lip. Jem and I gave up, and we were nearly to the Radley Place when Walter called, "Hey, I'm comin'!"

When Walter caught up with us, Jem made pleasant conversation with him. "A hain't lives there," he said cordially, pointing to the Radley house. "Ever hear about him, Walter?"

"Reckon I have," said Walter. "Almost died first year I come to school and et them pecans—folks say he pizened 'em and put 'em over on the school side of the fence."

Jem seemed to have little fear of Boo Radley now that Walter and I walked beside him. Indeed, Jem grew boastful: "I went all the way up to the house once," he said to Walter.

"Anybody who went up to the house once oughta not to still run every time he passes it," I said to the clouds above.

"And who's runnin', Miss Priss?"

"You are, when ain't anybody with you."

By the time we reached our front steps Walter had forgotten he was a Cunningham. Jem ran to the kitchen and asked Calpurnia to set an extra plate, we had company. Atticus greeted Walter and began a discussion about crops neither Jem nor I could follow.

"Reason I can't pass the first grade, Mr. Finch, is I've had to stay out ever' spring an' help Papa with the choppin', but there's another'n at the house now that's field size."

"Did you pay a bushel of potatoes for him?" I asked, but Atticus shook his head at me.

While Walter piled food on his plate, he and Atticus talked together like two men, to the wonderment of Jem and me. Atticus was expounding upon farm problems when Walter interrupted to ask if there was any molasses in the house. Atticus summoned Calpurnia, who returned bearing the syrup pitcher. She stood waiting for Walter to help himself. Walter poured syrup on his vegetables and meat with a generous hand. He would probably have poured it into his milk glass had I not asked what the sam hill he was doing.

The silver saucer clattered when he replaced the pitcher, and he quickly put his hands in his lap. Then he ducked his head.

Atticus shook his head at me again. "But he's gone and drowned his dinner in syrup," I protested. "He's poured it all over—"

It was then that Calpurnia requested my presence in the kitchen.

She was furious, and when she was furious Calpurnia's grammar became erratic. When in tranquility, her grammar was as good as anybody's in Maycomb. Atticus said Calpurnia had more education than most colored folks.

When she squinted down at me the tiny lines around her eyes deepened. "There's some folks who don't eat like us," she whispered fiercely, "but you ain't called on to contradict 'em at the table when they don't. That boy's yo' comp'ny and if he wants to eat up the table cloth you let him, you hear?"

"He ain't company, Cal, he's just a Cunningham—"

"Hush your mouth! Don't matter who they are, anybody sets foot in this house's yo' comp'ny, and don't you let me catch you remarkin' on their ways like you was so high and mighty! Yo' folks might be better'n the Cunninghams but it don't count for nothin' the way you're disgracin' 'em—if you can't act fit to eat at the table you can just set here and eat in the kitchen!"

Calpurnia sent me through the swinging door to the diningroom with a stinging smack. I retrieved my plate and finished dinner in the kitchen, thankful, though, that I was spared the humiliation of facing them again. I told Calpurnia to just wait, I'd fix her: one of these days when she wasn't looking I'd go off and drown myself in Barker's Eddy and then she'd be sorry. Besides, I added, she'd already gotten me in trouble once today: she had taught me to write and it was all her fault. "Hush your fussin'," she said.

WENDELL BERRY
"The Contrariness of the Mad Farmer"

The poetry of Wendell Berry (b. 1934) often is shaped by his experience as a Kentucky farmer and his profound attachment to the land. Many of his poems deal with ecology and pacifism. Berry's witty and sometimes cantankerous style is at its best in a poem like this one.

I am done with apologies. If contrariness is my
inheritance and destiny, so be it. If it is my mission
to go in at exits and come out at entrances, so be it.
I have planted by the stars in defiance of the experts,
and tilled somewhat by incantation and by singing,
and reaped, as I knew, by luck and Heaven's favor,
in spite of the best advice. If I have been caught
so often laughing at funerals, that was because
I knew the dead were already slipping away,
preparing a comeback, and can I help it?
And if at weddings I have gritted and gnashed
my teeth, it was because I knew where the bridegroom
had sunk his manhood, and knew it would not
be resurrected by a piece of cake. "Dance," they told me,
and I stood still, and while they stood
quiet in line at the gate of the Kingdom, I danced.
"Pray," they said, and I laughed, covering myself
in the earth's brightnesses, and then stole off gray
into the midst of a revel, and prayed like an orphan.
When they said, "I know that my Redeemer liveth,"
I told them, "He's dead." And when they told me,
"God is dead," I answered, "He goes fishing every day
in the Kentucky River. I see Him often."
When they asked me would I like to contribute
I said no, and when they had collected
more than they needed, I gave them as much as I had.
When they asked me to join them I wouldn't,
and then went off by myself and did more
than they would have asked. "Well, then," they said

"go and organize the International Brotherhood
of Contraries," and I said, "Did you finish killing
everybody who was against peace?" So be it.
Going against men, I have heard at times a deep harmony
thrumming in the mixture, and when they ask me what
I say I don't know. It is not the only or the easiest
way to come to the truth. It is one way.

JAMES DICKEY

"The Sheep Child"

James Dickey became interested in poetry during the years he was a fighter pilot in the Pacific in World War II. In 1966 Buckdancer's Choice *won the National Book Award for poetry, and from 1966 to 1968, Dickey served as Consultant in Poetry at the Library of Congress. Dickey's interest in the sensational and horrific juxtaposed with a sweet and humorous style is evident in this poem.*

Farm boys wild to couple
With anything   with soft-wooded trees
With mounds of earth   mounds
Of pinestraw   will keep themselves off
Animals by legends of their own:
In the hay-tunnel dark
And dung of barns, they will
Say   I have heard tell

That in a museum in Atlanta
Way back in a corner somewhere
There's this thing that's only half
Sheep   like a woolly baby
Pickled in alcohol   because
Those things can't live   his eyes
Are open   but you can't stand to look
I heard from somebody who . . .

But this is now almost all
Gone. The boys have taken
Their own true wives in the city,
The sheep are safe in the west hill
Pasture   but we who were born there
Still are not sure. Are we,
Because we remember, remembered
In the terrible dust of museums?

Merely with his eyes, the sheep-child may

Be saying   saying

I am here, in my father's house.
I who am half of your world, came deeply
To my mother in the long grass
Of the west pasture, where she stood like moonlight
Listening for foxes. It was something like love
From another world that seized her
From behind, and she gave, not lifting her head
Out of dew, without ever looking, her best
Self to that great need. Turned loose, she dipped her face
Farther into the chill of the earth, and in a sound
Of sobbing   of something stumbling
Away, began, as she must do,
To carry me. I woke, dying,

In the summer sun of the hillside, with my eyes
Far more than human. I saw for a blazing moment
The great grassy world from both sides,
Man and beast in the round of their need,
And the hill wind stirred in my wool,
My hoof and my hand clasped each other,
I ate my one meal
Of milk, and died
Staring. From dark grass I came straight

HUBERT SHUPTRINE.
Summertime. 1983.
Watercolor on paper.
10 3/8 x 18 1/4 in. Courtesy
of the artist.

To my father's house, whose dust
Whirls up in the halls for no reason
When no one comes   piling deep in a hellish mild corner,
And, through my immortal waters
I meet the sun's grains eye
To eye, and they fail at my closet of glass.
Dead, I am most surely living
In the minds of farm boys: I am he who drives
Them like wolves from the hound bitch and calf
And from the chaste ewe in the wind.
They go into woods   into bean fields   they go
Deep into their known right hands. Dreaming of me,
They groan   they wait   they suffer
Themselves, they marry, they raise their kind.

WILLIE MORRIS

From *North Toward Home*

"New York"

Willie Morris grew up in Yazoo City, Mississippi. As editor of Harper's Magazine *from 1967 to 1971, he was able to encourage other young Southern writers and to introduce a fresh perspective on life in the South to the New York literary scene. In the following excerpt from* North Toward Home, *Morris's candid autobiography, he writes of his need to leave the South, but also of his compelling and irrevocable attachment to it.*

Our literature is filled with young people like myself who came from the provinces to the Big Cave, seeking involvement in what one always thought from the outside was a world of incomparable wonder, hoping for some vague kind of literary "fulfillment." In the 1960s, as always since New York became our literary and journalistic marketplace, there would be thousands of them clustered around the great axis of publishing, newspapering, and broadcasting, starting out at minuscule salaries, living in unfamiliar, claustrophobic walk-ups, fighting the dread and alien subways twice a day, coming to terms with the incredible noise and crowdedness. Most of them would not "make it"; the more resourceful and talented might.

Why did we come? Not because the materials for our work did not exist in those places we knew best. Not merely for fame and money and success, for these also some of us could have had, and perhaps in more civilized ways, in places far removed from New York. Not even because we wanted to try ourselves in the big time, and out of curiosity to see how good the competition was. We had always come, the most ambitious of us, because we *had* to, because the ineluctable pull of the cultural capital when the wanderlust was high was too compelling to resist.

Yet there were always secret dangers for these young people from the provinces in the city. It became dangerously easy to turn one's back on his own past, on the isolated places that nurtured and shaped him into maturity, for the sake of some convenient or fashionable "sophistication." There were temptations to be not merely careless, but dishonest, with the most distinctive things about one's self. The literary and publishing worlds of the city were perilous vantage points from which to understand the rest of America. There was a marked sense of superiority, amounting to a kind of distrust, toward other American places. This had always been true, and it was likely to become more so, as the older regionalism died in America and as the cities of the East became more and more the center of an engaged and argumentative intellection. Coming to New York for the first time, the sensitive outlander might soon find himself in a subtle interior struggle with himself, over the most fundamental sense and meaning of his own origins. It was this struggle, if fully comprehended, which finally could give New York its own peculiar and wonderful value as a place, for it tested who you are, in the deepest and most contorted way.

I spent that night with an old friend from Mississippi, in a cramped apartment high above Washington Square. He was teaching now at the New York University Law School. The last time I had seen him had been the previous summer, at the Ole Miss law school, to which he had returned from Oxford, England, to finish three courses; outside class that summer, he had spent his whole time getting drunk in front of an electric fan, either that or indulging himself in wild, uncontrollable outbursts against the young middle-class racists who were his fellow students. He was a "liberated Mississippian" who had just joined New York's burgeoning and implacable Southern expatriot community; he was the first of many Mississippi "exiles" I would see in the Big Cave — for, in truth, as I would come to understand, Mississippi may have been the only state in the Union (or certainly one of a half dozen in the South) which had produced a genuine set of exiles, almost in the European sense: alienated from home yet forever drawn back to it, seeking some form of personal liberty elsewhere yet obsessed with the texture and the complexity of the place from which they had departed as few Americans from other states could ever be. We sat talking until midnight about people we had known, about old forgotten high school football games in the delta, about Ross Barnett and James Meredith, Paul Johnson and Hodding Carter, about unusual weekend celebrations at country clubs in the hills. Then, groggy from the transcontinental Greyhound, I went off to bed.

The next morning I arose early to set out to find a job. On the recommendation of a mutual acquaintance I had made an appointment with a well-known editor — he was described to me as "tough-minded," a glowing description for anyone in those days — in a distinguished publishing firm. I strolled through Washington Square, walking past those sepulchral warehouses of NYU, the magnificent old townhouses on the north side which had yet to give in to the wrecker's hammer, the red brick apartment towers to the west. Then I sat on a bench to while away an hour, watching the old men playing chess on the concrete tables, and the bums and the beats who congregated in agitated little circles making activity out of nothing. Two young men with sandals and long hair appeared from nowhere and accosted me on my bench. "Could I have fifteen cents for a cup of coffee?" one of them asked. I forked over fifteen cents. Then the

GEORGE OHR. *Vase.*
1895–1900. Earthenware.
6 3/4 x 6 5/8 in. Courtesy
Janet Ford, Department of
Anthropology, University
of Mississippi. *When
George Ohr, the "Mad
Potter of Biloxi," stopped
making his distorted,
obscene, and violently colored ceramic vessels in
1906, he packed away
8000 pieces that were forgotten until fifty years
later. Now Ohr is recog-
nized as one of the greatest American potters.*

other said, "Could I have fifty cents for a *Partisan Review?*" When I declined, he shrugged his shoulders, whispered *square,* and he and his running-mate ambled off.

I sat there counting out my private responsibilities. Besides having to get a job to support a family, I needed to find an apartment, one with enough room for a three-year-old boy to roam around in, next to a big park perhaps, and preferably overlooking some body of water: a place with a study, and dark-oak paneling, and within walking distance of my office. I started feeling again, as I had not since my sophomore year in Austin, as Thomas Wolfe had felt, coming north to this Rock. *Only the dead know Brooklyn,* he said, and he got a book published, and he went to literary cocktail parties in Park Avenue penthouses; he stood on their terraces and heard the tinkling of the ice in the glasses of those critics and editors and authors, and watched the lights of Manhattan come on. At that point he always felt he would never die.

All of a sudden, in the middle of these harmless recollections, I saw a slightly familiar figure from the corner of my eye, from the arch at the north side of Washington Square. Be damned if it wasn't Mr. DeMent Warren, who ran the men's clothing store at the corner of Jefferson and Main in Yazoo City during my boyhood. I stood up to go and greet him, but I saw it wasn't Mr. DeMent at all — only a big balding man in a topcoat uncommonly heavy for that time of year. A few minutes later the same thing happened. Over near the fountain I saw, of all people, Earlene Whitt, a fine well-constructed beauty queen from the University of Texas in 1955. But it wasn't Earlene: only a big blond Village girl taking her beagle on a morning's walk. Within the next fifteen minutes I spotted four people I had once known: "Jap," the old yellow-skinned Negro man who had cut our yard for us when I was in grammar school; A. J. "Buddy" Reeves, an American Legionnaire from Yazoo County, who used to go out with us when we played taps for the military funerals; Bibb Falk, the baseball coach at Texas; and Wallace Miller, a rotund conservative in the Texas legislature — all apparitions! They were my first experience, all of them, of what would become my own peculiar New York eyesight. With my mind on the past, only haphazardly thinking of long-ago things, just basking lazily in old events as is my wont (even something as ephemeral as a touch football game in Lintonia Park twenty years ago, or the funeral of a friend's father in 1948) people all around me — on the sidewalks of Broadway or in a subway — would take on known shapes, tangible recognitions. All they had to do, when these moods were upon me, was to bear some vague resemblance to someone who once had had a meaning for me, in a period of my past I was thinking about, and my dastardly subconscious would toss up for me a real person! I believe the crowds did it, and the awful and unfamiliar isolation of the city when thousands of human beings are around you and none knows you nor cares. I later grew accustomed to this phenomenon that the city worked on me, and even to enjoy it, but on that day it struck me as passing strange; it made me fear the extent to which my rambling imaginings of past places that had intimately shaped me could, in this unknown and uncaring city, produce forms so tangible as to make the present itself incongruous and ghost-like. I had returned, among the smog pelts and pollution indices, to my childhood's land of seething mirages.

John Kennedy Toole

From *A Confederacy of Dunces*

Certainly one of the funniest of contemporary novels, A Confederacy of Dunces *also captures the wonderfully animated spirit of New Orleans. In this scene, Ignatius Reilly, a character whom Walker Percy has described as a "slob extraordinary, a mad Oliver Hardy, a fat Don Quixote, a perverse Thomas Aquinas—who is in revolt against the entire modern age," is peddling hot dogs when he has one of many calamitous encounters. Unable to publish this manuscript, Toole committed suicide in 1969. After his death, Toole's mother took the manuscript to Walker Percy who arranged for its publication.*

By night he was plagued by dreams and by day by the impossible route that Mr. Clyde had given him. No one in the French Quarter, it seemed, was interested in hot dogs. So his take-home pay was getting smaller, and his mother, in turn, was getting surlier. When and how would this vicious cycle end?

He had read in the morning paper that a ladies' art guild was having a hanging of its paintings in Pirate's Alley. Imagining that the paintings would be offensive enough to interest him for a while, he pushed his wagon up onto the flagstones of the Alley toward the variety of artwork dangling from the iron pickets of the fence behind the Cathedral. On the prow of the wagon, in an attempt to attract business among the Quarterites, Ignatius taped a sheet of Big Chief paper on which he had printed in crayon: TWELVE INCHES (12) OF PARADISE. So far no one had responded to its message.

The Alley was filled with well-dressed ladies in large hats. Ignatius pointed the prow of the wagon into the throng and pushed forward. A woman read the Big Chief statement and screamed, summoning her companions to draw aside from the ghastly apparition that had appeared at their art show.

"Hot dogs, ladies?" Ignatius asked pleasantly.

The ladies' eyes studied the sign, the earring, the scarf, the cutlass, and pleaded for him to move along. Rain for their hanging would have been bad enough. But *this*.

"Hot dogs, hot dogs," Ignatius said a little angrily. "Savories from the hygienic Paradise kitchens."

He belched violently during the silence that followed. The ladies pretended to study the sky and the little garden behind the Cathedral.

Ignatius lumbered over to the picket fence, abandoning the hopeless cause espoused by the wagon, and viewed the oil paintings and pastels and watercolors strung there. Although the style of each varied in crudity, the subjects of the paintings were relatively similar: camellias floating in bowls of water, azaleas tortured into ambitious flower arrangements, magnolias that looked like white windmills. Ignatius scrutinized the offerings furiously for a while all by himself, for the ladies had stepped back from the fence and had formed what looked like a protective little grouping. The wagon, too, stood forlorn on the flagstones, several feet from the newest member of the art guild.

"Oh, my God!" Ignatius bellowed after he had promenaded up and down along the fence. "How dare you present such abortions to the public."

"Please move along, sir," a bold lady said.

"Magnolias don't look like that," Ignatius said, thrusting his cutlass at the offending pastel magnolia. "You ladies need a course in botany. And perhaps geometry, too."

"You don't *have* to look at our work," an offended voice said from the group, the voice of the lady who had drawn the magnolia in question.

"Yes, I do!" Ignatius screamed. "You ladies need a critic with some taste and decency. Good heavens! Which one of you did this camellia? Speak up. The water in this bowl looks like motor oil."

"Let us alone," a shrill voice said.

"You women had better stop giving teas and brunches and settle down to the business of learning how to draw," Ignatius thundered. "First, you must learn how to handle a brush. I would suggest that you all get together and paint someone's house for a start."

"Go away."

"Had you 'artists' had a part in the decoration of the Sistine Chapel, it would have ended up looking like a particularly vulgar train terminal," Ignatius snorted.

"We don't intend to be insulted by a coarse vendor," a spokeswoman for the band of large hats said haughtily.

"I see!" Ignatius screamed. "So it is you people who slander the reputation of the hot dog vendor."

"He's mad."

"He's so common."

"So coarse."

"Don't encourage him."

"We don't want you here," the spokeswoman said tartly and simply.

"I should imagine not!" Ignatius was breathing heavily. "Apparently you are afraid of someone who has some contact with reality, who can truthfully describe to you the offenses which you have committed to canvas."

"Please leave," the spokeswoman ordered.

"I shall." Ignatius grabbed the handle of his cart and pushed off. "You women should all be on your knees begging forgiveness for what I have seen here on this fence."

"The city is certainly going down when *that's* out on the streets," a woman said as Ignatius waddled off down the Alley.

Ignatius was surprised to feel a small rock bounce off the back of his head. Angrily, he shoved the wagon along the flagstones until he was near the end of the Alley. There he parked the wagon in a little passageway so that it would be out of sight. His feet hurt, and while he was resting he didn't want anyone to bother him by asking for a hot dog. Even though business couldn't be worse, there were times when a person had to be true to himself and consider his welfare first. Much more of this vending and his feet would be bloody stumps.

RED GROOMS. *Chuck Berry.* 1978.
Color screenprint with dye cut. 18 ½ x
24 ½ in. Brooke Alexander Editions.
© 1993 Red Grooms/ARS.

Ignatius squatted uncomfortably on the side steps of the Cathedral. His recently increased weight and the bloating caused by the inoperative valve made any position other than standing or lying down somewhat awkward. Removing his boots, he began to inspect his great slabs of feet.

"Oh, dear," a voice said above Ignatius. "What am I seeing? I come out to see this dreadful, tacky art exhibit, and what do I find as Exhibit Number One? It's the ghost of Lafitte, the pirate. No. It's Fatty Arbuckle. Or is it Marie Dressler? Tell me soon or I'll die."

Ignatius looked up and saw the young man who had bought his mother's hat in the Night of Joy.

"Get away from me, you fop. Where is my mother's hat?"

"Oh, that," the young man sighed. "I'm afraid it was destroyed at a really wild gathering. Everyone dearly loved it."

"I'm sure that they did. I won't ask you just how it was desecrated."

"I wouldn't remember anyway. Too many martinis that night for little *moi.*"

"Oh, my God."

"What in God's name are you doing in that bizarre outfit? You look like Charles Laughton in drag as the Queen of the Gypsies. What *are* you supposed to be? I really want to know."

"Move along, you coxcomb," Ignatius belched, the gassy eructations echoing between the walls of the Alley. The women's art guild turned its hats toward the source of the volcanic sound. Ignatius glared at the young man's tawny velvet jacket and mauve cashmere sweater and the wave of blonde hair that fell over the forehead of his sharp, glittering face. "Get away from me before I strike you down."

"Oh, my goodness," the young man laughed in short, merry, childish breaths that made his downy jacket quiver. "You really are insane, aren't you?"

"How dare you!" Ignatius screamed. He unpinned his cutlass and began to strike the young man's calves with the plastic weapon. The young man giggled and danced about in front of Ignatius to avoid the thrusts, his lithe movements making him a difficult target. Finally he danced across the Alley and waved to Ignatius. Ignatius picked up one of his elephantine desert boots and flung it at the pirouetting figure.

"Oh," the young man squealed. He caught the shoe and threw it back at Ignatius, whom it hit squarely in the face.

"Oh, my God! I've been disfigured."

"Shut up."

"I can easily have you booked for assault."

"If I were you, I'd stay as far away from the police as possible. What do you think they'd say when they saw that outfit, Mary Marvel? And booking *me* with assault? Let's be a little realistic. I'm surprised that they're permitting you to go cruising at all in that fortune-teller's ensemble." The young man clicked his lighter open, lit a Salem, and clicked it closed. "And with those bare feet and that toy sword? Are you kidding?"

"The police will believe anything I tell them."

"Get with it, please."

"You may be locked away for several years."

"Oh, you really are on the moon."

"Well, I certainly don't have to sit here listening to you," Ignatius said, putting on his suede boots.

"Oh!" the young man shrieked happily. "That look on your face. Like Bette Davis with indigestion."

"Don't talk to me, you degenerate. Go play with your little friends. I am certain that the Quarter is crawling with them."

"How is that dear mother of yours?"

"I don't want to hear her sainted name cross your decadent lips."

"Well, since it already has, is she all right? She's so sweet and dear, that woman, so unspoiled. You're very lucky."

"I will not discuss her with you."

"If that's the way you want to be, all right. I just hope that she doesn't know that you're flouncing around the streets like some sort of Hungarian Joan of Arc. That earring. It's so Magyar."

"If you want a costume like this, then buy one," Ignatius said. "Let me alone."

"I know that something like that couldn't be bought anywhere. Oh, but it would bring the house down at a party."

"I suspect that the parties you attend must be true visions of the apocalypse. I knew that our society was coming to this. In a few years, you and your friends will probably take over the country."

"Oh, we're planning to," the young man said with a bright smile. "We have connections in the highest places. You'd be surprised."

"No, I wouldn't. Hreswitha could have predicted this long ago."

"Who in the world is that?"

"A sibyl of a medieval nun. She has guided my life."

"Oh, you're truly fantastic," the young man said gleefully. "And although I didn't think it would be possible, you've gained weight. Where will you ever end? There's something so unbelievably tacky about your obesity."

Ignatius rose to his feet and stabbed the young man in the chest with his plastic cutlass.

"Take that, you offal," Ignatius cried, digging the cutlass into the cashmere sweater. The tip of the cutlass broke off and fell to the flagstone walk.

"Oh, dear," the young man shrieked. "You'll tear my sweater, you big crazy thing."

Down the Alley the women's art guild members were removing their paintings from the fence and folding their aluminum lawn chairs like Arabs in preparation for stealing away. Their annual outdoor exhibit had been ruined.

"I am the avenging sword of taste and decency," Ignatius was shouting. As he slashed at the sweater with his broken weapon, the ladies began to dash out the Royal Street end of the Alley. A few stragglers were snatching at their magnolias and camellias in panic.

"Why did I ever stop to talk to you, you maniac?" the young man asked in a vicious and breathless whisper. "This is my very finest sweater."

"Whore!" Ignatius cried, scraping the cutlass across the young man's chest.

"Oh, isn't this horrible."

He tried to run away, but Ignatius had been holding his arm firmly with the hand that was not wielding the cutlass. Slipping a finger through Ignatius' hoop earring, the young man pulled downward, breathing to Ignatius, "Drop that sword."

ALICE WALKER

"Everyday Use"

Alice Walker, born in Eatonton, Georgia in 1944, is the daughter of a sharecropper and a woman whose strength and character she celebrates in much of her writing. Walker, who won the Pulitzer Prize in fiction for her novel The Color Purple *(1982) has said, "You look at old photographs of Southern blacks and you see it—a fearlessness, a real determination and proof of a moral center that is absolutely bedrock to the land. I think there's hope in the South, not in the North." Although Walker is one of the most influential figures in contemporary American literature, she has been one of the harshest critics of African-American culture, as this story, first published in* Harper's *in 1973, reveals.*

for your grandmama

I will wait for her in the yard that Maggie and I made so clean and wavy yesterday afternoon. A yard like this is more comfortable than most people know. It is not just a yard. It is like an extended living room. When the hard clay is swept clean as a floor and the fine sand around the edges lined with tiny, irregular grooves, anyone can come and sit and look up into the elm tree and wait for the breezes that never come inside the house.

Maggie will be nervous until after her sister goes: she will stand hopelessly in corners, homely and ashamed of the burn scars down her arms and legs, eying her sister with a mixture of envy and awe. She thinks her sister has held life always in the palm of one hand, that "no" is a word the world never learned to say to her.

You've no doubt seen those TV shows where the child who has "made it" is confronted, as a surprise, by her own mother and father, tottering in weakly from backstage. (A pleasant surprise, of course: What would they do if parent and child came on the show only to curse out and insult each other?) On TV mother and child embrace and smile into each other's faces. Sometimes the mother and father weep, the child wraps them in her arms and leans across the table to tell how she would not have made it without their help. I have seen these programs.

Sometimes I dream a dream in which Dee and I are suddenly brought together on a TV program of this sort. Out of a dark and soft-seated limousine I am ushered into a bright room

ROLAND L. FREEMAN. *Mrs. Victoria Bennett, Wilkinson County.* 1976. Photograph. Collection of the photographer. *Roland Freeman, an African-American photographer, has for many years documented black culture throughout the South. This quilt, a variation on a traditional Log Cabin pattern, shows several characteristics of African-American quiltmaking: bold, contrasting colors, asymmetry, and an improvisational pattern that has prompted some to call quilts like this "the visual equivalent of jazz."*

filled with many people. There I meet a smiling, gray, sporty man like Johnny Carson who shakes my hand and tells me what a fine girl I have. Then we are on the stage and Dee is embracing me with tears in her eyes. She pins on my dress a large orchid, even though she has told me once that she thinks orchids are tacky flowers.

In real life I am a large, big-boned woman with rough, man-working hands. In the winter I wear flannel nightgowns to bed and overalls during the day. I can kill and clean a hog as mercilessly as a man. My fat keeps me hot in zero weather. I can work outside all day, breaking ice to get water for washing; I can eat pork liver cooked over the open fire minutes after it comes steaming from the hog. One winter I knocked a bull calf straight in the brain between the eyes with a sledge hammer and had the meat hung up to chill before nightfall. But of course all this does not show on television. I am the way my daughter would want me to be: a hundred pounds lighter, my skin like an uncooked barley pancake. My hair glistens in the hot bright lights. Johnny Carson has much to do to keep up with my quick and witty tongue.

But that is a mistake. I know even before I wake up. Who ever knew a Johnson with a quick tongue? Who can even imagine me looking a strange white man in the eye? It seems to me I have talked to them always with one foot raised in flight, with my head turned in whichever way is farthest from them. Dee, though. She would always look anyone in the eye. Hesitation was no part of her nature.

"How do I look, Mama?" Maggie says, showing just enough of her thin body enveloped in pink skirt and red blouse for me to know she's there, almost hidden by the door.

"Come out into the yard," I say.

Have you ever seen a lame animal, perhaps a dog run over by some careless person rich enough to own a car, sidle up to someone who is ignorant enough to be kind to him? That is the way my Maggie walks. She has been like this, chin on chest, eyes on ground, feet in shuffle, ever since the fire that burned the other house to the ground.

Dee is lighter than Maggie, with nicer hair and a fuller figure. She's a woman now, though sometimes I forget. How long ago was it that the other house burned? Ten, twelve years? Sometimes I can still hear the flames and feel Maggie's arms sticking to me, her hair smoking and her dress falling off her in little black papery flakes. Her eyes seemed stretched open, blazed open by the flames reflected in them. And Dee. I see her standing off under the sweet gum tree she used to dig gum out of; a look of concentration on her face as she watched the last dingy gray board of the house fall in toward the red-hot brick chimney. Why don't you do a dance around the ashes? I'd wanted to ask her. She had hated the house that much.

I used to think she hated Maggie, too. But that was before we raised the money, the church and me, to send her to Augusta to school. She used to read to us without pity; forcing words, lies, other folks' habits, whole lives upon us two, sitting trapped and ignorant underneath her voice. She washed us in a river of make-believe, burned us with a lot of knowledge we didn't necessarily need to know. Pressed us to her with the serious way she read, to shove us away at just the moment, like dimwits, we seemed about to understand.

Dee wanted nice things. A yellow organdy dress to wear to her graduation from high school; black pumps to match a green suit she'd made from an old suit somebody gave me. She was determined to stare down any disaster in her efforts. Her eyelids would not flicker for minutes at a time. Often I fought off the temptation to shake her. At sixteen she had a style of her own: and knew what style was.

I never had an education myself. After second grade the school was closed down. Don't ask me why: in 1927 colored asked fewer questions than they do now. Sometimes Maggie reads to me. She stumbles along good-naturedly but can't see well. She knows she is not bright. Like good looks and money, quickness passed her by. She will marry John Thomas (who has mossy teeth in an earnest face) and then I'll be free to sit here and I guess just sing church songs to myself. Although I never was a good singer. Never could carry a tune. I was always better at a man's job. I used to love to milk till I was hooked in the side in '49. Cows are soothing and slow and don't bother you, unless you try to milk them the wrong way.

I have deliberately turned my back on the house. It is three rooms, just like the one that burned, except the roof is tin; they don't make shingle roofs any more. There are no real windows, just some holes cut in the sides, like the portholes in a ship, but not round and not square, with rawhide holding the shutters up on the outside. This house is in a pasture, too, like the other one. No doubt when Dee sees it she will want to tear it down. She wrote me once that no matter where we "choose" to live, she will manage to come see us. But she will never bring her friends. Maggie and I thought about this and Maggie asked me, "Mama, when did Dee ever *have* any friends?"

She had a few. Furtive boys in pink shirts hanging about on washday after school. Nervous girls who never laughed. Impressed with her they worshiped the well-turned phrase, the cute shape, the scalding humor that erupted like bubbles in lye. She read to them.

When she was courting Jimmy T she didn't have much time to pay to us, but turned all her faultfinding power on him. He *flew* to marry a cheap city girl from a family of ignorant flashy people. She hardly had time to recompose herself.

When she comes I will meet—but there they are!

Maggie attempts to make a dash for the house, in her shuffling way, but I stay her with my hand. "Come back here," I say. And she stops and tries to dig a well in the sand with her toe.

It is hard to see them clearly through the strong sun. But even the first glimpse of leg out of the car tells me it is Dee. Her feet were always neat-looking, as if God himself had shaped them with a certain style. From the other side of the car comes a short, stocky man. Hair is all over his head a foot long and hanging from his chin like a kinky mule tail. I hear Maggie suck in her breath. "Uhnnnh," is what it sounds like. Like when you see the wriggling end of a snake just in front of your foot on the road. "Uhnnnh."

Dee next. A dress down to the ground, in this hot weather. A dress so loud it hurts my eyes. There are yellows and oranges enough to throw back the light of the sun. I feel my whole face warming from the heat waves it throws out. Earrings gold, too, and hanging down to her shoulders. Bracelets dangling and making noises when she moves her arm up to shake the folds of the dress out of her armpits. The dress is loose and flows, and as she walks closer, I like it. I hear Maggie go "Uhnnnh" again. It is her sister's hair. It stands straight up like the wool on a sheep. It is black as night and around the edges are two long pigtails that rope about like small lizards disappearing behind her ears.

"Wa-su-zo-Tean-o!" she says, coming on in that gliding way the dress makes her move. The short stocky fellow with the hair to his navel is all grinning and he follows up with "Asalamalakim, my mother and sister!" He moves to hug Maggie but she falls back, right up against the back of my chair. I feel her trembling there and when I look up I see the perspiration falling off her chin.

"Don't get up," says Dee. Since I am stout it takes something of a push. You can see me trying to move a second or two before I make it. She turns, showing white heels through her sandals, and goes back to the car. Out she peeks next with a Polaroid. She stoops down quickly and lines up picture after picture of me sitting there in front of the house with Maggie cowering behind me. She never takes a shot without making sure the house is included. When a cow comes nibbling around the edge of the yard she snaps it and me and Maggie *and* the house. Then she puts the Polaroid in the back seat of the car, and comes up and kisses me on the forehead.

Meanwhile Asalamalakim is going through motions with Maggie's hand. Maggie's hand is as limp as a fish, and probably as cold, despite the sweat, and she keeps trying to pull it back. It looks like Asalamalakim wants to shake hands but wants to do it fancy. Or maybe he don't know how people shake hands. Anyhow, he soon gives up on Maggie.

"Well," I say. "Dee."

"No, Mama," she says. "Not 'Dee,' Wangero Leewanika Kemanjo!"

"What happened to 'Dee'?" I wanted to know.

"She's dead," Wangero said. "I couldn't bear it any longer, being named after the people who oppress me."

"You know as well as me you was named after your aunt Dicie," I said. Dicie is my sister. She named Dee. We called her "Big Dee" after Dee was born.

"But who was *she* named after?" asked Wangero.

"I guess after Grandma Dee," I said.

"And who was she named after?" asked Wangero.

"Her mother," I said, and saw Wangero was getting tired. "That's about as far back as I can trace it," I said. Though, in fact, I probably could have carried it back beyond the Civil War through the branches.

"Well," said Asalamalakim, "there you are."

"Uhnnnh," I heard Maggie say.

"There I was not," I said, "before 'Dicie' cropped up in our family, so why should I try to trace it that far back?"

He just stood there grinning, looking down on me like somebody inspecting a Model A car. Every once in a while he and Wangero sent eye signals over my head.

"How do you pronounce this name?" I asked.

"You don't have to call me by it if you don't want to," said Wangero.

"Why shouldn't I?" I asked. "If that's what you want us to call you, we'll call you."

"I know it might sound awkward at first," said Wangero.

"I'll get used to it," I said. "Ream it out again."

Well, soon we got the name out of the way. Asalamalakim had a name twice as long and three times as hard. After I tripped over it two or three times he told me to just call him Hakim-a-barber. I wanted to ask him was he a barber, but I didn't really think he was, so I didn't ask.

"You must belong to those beef-cattle peoples down the road," I said. They said "Asalamalakim" when they met you, too, but they didn't shake hands. Always too busy: feeding the cattle, fixing the fences, putting up salt-lick shelters, throwing down hay. When the white folks poisoned some of the herd the men stayed up all night with rifles in their hands. I walked a mile and a half just to see the sight.

Hakim-a-barber said, "I accept some of their doctrines, but farming and raising cattle is not my style." (They didn't tell me, and I didn't ask, whether Wangero (Dee) had really gone and married him.)

We sat down to eat and right away he said he didn't eat collards and pork was unclean. Wangero, though, went on through the chitlins and corn bread, the greens and everything else. She talked a blue streak over the sweet potatoes. Everything delighted her. Even the fact that we still used the benches her daddy made for the table when we couldn't afford to buy chairs.

"Oh, Mama!" she cried. Then turned to Hakim-a-barber. "I never knew how lovely these benches are. You can feel the rump prints," she said, running her hands underneath her and along the bench. Then she gave a sigh and her hand closed over Grandma Dee's butter dish. "That's it!" she said. "I knew there was something I wanted to ask you if I could have." She jumped up from the table and went over in the corner where the churn stood, the milk in it clabber by now. She looked at the churn and looked at it.

"This churn top is what I need," she said. "Didn't Uncle Buddy whittle it out of a tree you all used to have?"

"Yes," I said.

"Uh-huh," she said happily. "And I want the dasher, too."

"Uncle Buddy whittle that, too?" asked the barber.

Dee (Wangero) looked up at me.

"Aunt Dee's first husband whittled the dash," said Maggie so low you almost couldn't hear her. "His name was Henry, but they called him Stash."

"Maggie's brain is like an elephant's," Wangero said, laughing. "I can use the churn top as a centerpiece for the alcove table," she said, sliding a plate over the churn, "and I'll think of something artistic to do with the dasher."

347

When she finished wrapping the dasher the handle stuck out. I took it for a moment in my hands. You didn't even have to look close to see where hands pushing the dasher up and down to make butter had left a kind of sink in the wood. In fact, there were a lot of small sinks; you could see where thumbs and fingers had sunk into the wood. It was beautiful light yellow wood, from a tree that grew in the yard where Big Dee and Stash had lived.

After dinner Dee (Wangero) went to the trunk at the foot of my bed and started rifling through it. Maggie hung back in the kitchen over the dishpan. Out came Wangero with two quilts. They had been pieced by Grandma Dee and then Big Dee and me had hung them on the quilt frames on the front porch and quilted them. One was in the Lone Star pattern. The other was Walk Around the Mountain. In both of them were scraps of dresses Grandma Dee had worn fifty and more years ago. Bits and pieces of Grandpa Jarrell's Paisley shirts. And one teeny faded blue piece, about the size of a penny matchbox, that was from Great Grandpa Ezra's uniform that he wore in the Civil War.

"Mama," Wangero said sweet as a bird. "Can I have these old quilts?"

I heard something fall in the kitchen, and a minute later the kitchen door slammed.

"Why don't you take one or two of the others?" I asked. "These old things was just done by me and Big Dee from some tops your grandma pieced before she died."

"No," said Wangero. "I don't want those. They are stitched around the borders by machine."

"That'll make them last better," I said.

"That's not the point," said Wangero. "These are all pieces of dresses Grandma used to wear. She did all this stitching by hand. Imagine!" She held the quilts securely in her arms, stroking them.

"Some of the pieces, like those lavender ones, come from old clothes her mother handed down to her," I said, moving up to touch the quilts. Dee (Wangero) moved back just enough so that I couldn't reach the quilts. They already belonged to her.

"Imagine!" she breathed again, clutching them closely to her bosom.

"The truth is," I said, "I promised to give them quilts to Maggie, for when she marries John Thomas."

She gasped like a bee had stung her.

"Maggie can't appreciate these quilts!" she said. "She'd probably be backward enough to put them to everyday use."

"I reckon she would," I said. "God knows I been saving 'em for long enough with nobody using 'em. I hope she will!" I didn't want to bring up how I had offered Dee (Wangero) a quilt when she went away to college. Then she had told me they were old-fashioned, out of style.

"But they're *priceless*!" she was saying now, furiously; for she has a temper. "Maggie would put them on the bed and in five years they'd be in rags. Less than that!"

"She can always make some more," I said. "Maggie knows how to quilt."

Dee (Wangero) looked at me with hatred. "You just will not understand. The point is these quilts, *these* quilts!"

"Well," I said, stumped. "What would *you* do with them?"

"Hang them," she said. As if that was the only thing you *could* do with quilts.

Maggie by now was standing in the door. I could almost hear the sound her feet made as they scraped over each other.

"She can have them, Mama," she said, like somebody used to never winning anything, or having anything reserved for her. "I can 'member Grandma Dee without the quilts."

I looked at her hard. She had filled her bottom lip with checkerberry snuff and it gave her face a kind of dopey, hangdog look. It was Grandma Dee and Big Dee who taught her how to quilt herself. She stood there with her scarred hands hidden in the folds of her skirt. She looked at her sister with something like fear but she wasn't mad at her. This was Maggie's portion. This was the way she knew God to work.

When I looked at her like that something hit me in the top of my head and ran down to the soles of my feet. Just like when I'm in church and the spirit of God touches me and I get happy and shout. I did something I never had done before: hugged Maggie to me, then dragged her on into the room, snatched the quilts out of Miss Wangero's hands and dumped them into Maggie's lap. Maggie just sat there on my bed with her mouth open.

"Take one or two of the others," I said to Dee.

But she turned without a word and went out to Hakim-a-barber.

"You just don't understand," she said, as Maggie and I came out to the car.

"What don't I understand?" I wanted to know.

"Your heritage," she said. And then she turned to Maggie, kissed her, and said, "You ought to try to make something of yourself, too, Maggie. It's really a new day for us. But from the way you and Mama still live you'd never know it."

She put on some sunglasses that hid everything above the tip of her nose and her chin.

Maggie smiled; maybe at the sunglasses. But a real smile, not scared. After we watched the car dust settle I asked Maggie to bring me a dip of snuff. And then the two of us sat there just enjoying, until it was time to go in the house and go to bed.

PETER TAYLOR

From "In the Miro District"
Grandfather's Visits

Peter Taylor (b. 1917) was steeped in the Southern literary tradition, having studied under Allen Tate, John Crowe Ransom, Robert Penn Warren, and Cleanth Brooks. His writing is subtle and reserved and explores the complicated relationships that exist in "good" old Southern families in a modern world.

My grandfather, when I first remember him, lived over in the next county from us, forty miles west of Nashville. But he was always and forever driving over for those visits of his—visits of three or four days, or longer—transporting himself back and forth from Hunt County to Nashville in his big tan touring car, with the canvas top put back in almost all weather, and usually wearing a broad-brimmed hat—a straw in summer, a felt in winter—and an ankle-length gabardine topcoat no matter what the season was.

He was my maternal grandfather and was known to everyone as Major Basil Manley. Seeing Major Manley like that at the wheel of his tan touring car, swinging into our driveway, it wasn't hard to imagine how he had once looked riding horseback or muleback through the wilds of West Tennessee when he was a young boy in Forrest's cavalry, or how he had looked, for that matter, in 1912, nearly half a century after he had ridden with General Forrest, at the time when he escaped from a band of hooded nightriders who had kidnapped him then—him and his law partner (and who had murdered his law partner before his eyes, on the banks of Bayou du Chien, near Reelfoot Lake).

Even when I was a very small boy, I always dreaded the sight of him out there in our driveway in his old car when he was arriving for a visit. I hated the first sound of his tires in the gravel as he came wheeling up to the house and then suddenly bore down on the brakes at the foot of our front porch steps. I dreaded him not because I was frightened by his coming or by the history of his violent exploits, which I knew about from an early time, but because I was aware always of the painful hours that he and I, who had nothing in common and for whom all our encounters were a torture, would be expected to put in together.

The old man had always had a way of turning up, you see—even when I was little more than an infant—just when it suited *me* least, when I had *other* plans which might include almost anything else in the world but the presence of a grandfather with whom it was intended

WILL H. STEVENS. *Sevierville, Tennessee.* Oil on canvas. 30 x 36 in. Robert M. Hicklin, Jr. Inc., Spartanburg, SC. *Will Stevens spent a great deal of time painting near Gatlinburg, Tennessee until its development drove him deeper into the Great Smoky mountains. His wonderful landscapes mix elements of cubism, expressionism, and a fauvist love of color.*

I should be companionable. Sometimes he would go directly into our back yard, if it were summertime, without even removing his hat or his gabardine coat. He would plant one of the canvas yard chairs on the very spot where I had been building a little airfield or a horse farm in the grass. Then he would throw himself down into the chair and undo his collar button and remove his starched collar—he seldom wore a tie in those days—and next he would pull his straw hat down over his face and begin his inevitable dialogue with me without our having exchanged so much as a glance or a how-do-you-do. It used to seem to me he only knew I was there with him because he knew I was required to be there. "I guess you've been behaving yourself," he said from under his hat, "the way a Nashville boy ought to behave himself." . . . And, of course, I knew well enough what was meant by that. It meant I was some kind of effeminate city boy who was never willing to visit his grandfather alone in the country and who could never comprehend what it would be to ride muleback through the wilds of West Tennessee—either in pursuit of Yankee marauders or in flight from hooded nightriders. Looking up at the old man from the grass beside his chair (or from the carpet beside his platform rocker if we were settled in his downstairs bedroom), I thought to myself—thought this, or something like it—Someday you and I will have to have it out between us. I shall have to show you how it is with me and how I could never be what you are. . . . I often looked up at him, wanting—I know now—to say something that would insult him and make him leave me alone or make him take his walking stick to me. The trouble was, of course—and I seemed to have sensed this before I was school age even—that we couldn't understand or care anything about each other. Something in each of us forbade it. It was as though we faced each other across the distasteful present, across a queer, quaint world that neither of us felt himself a part of.

When I looked up at him while we were talking, often out in the back yard but more often in his room, I could never think exactly what it was about him that I hated or if I really hated him at all. Yet many a time I had that shameful feeling of wanting to insult him. And so I got into the habit of trying to see him as my two parents saw him. That's the awful part, really. I would look at him until I saw him as I knew they saw him: an old country granddaddy who came to town not wearing a tie and with only a bright gold collar button shining where a tie ought to have been in evidence. It seems shocking to me nowadays how well I knew at that tender age just how my parents did surely see such an old man and, indeed, how they saw all else in the world about us. They saw everything in terms of Acklen Park in the city of Nashville in the Nashville Basin in Middle Tennessee in the old Miro District as it had come to be in the first quarter of the twentieth century. I suppose it was my knowing how Mother and Father saw the other grandfathers who did actually live with *their* families in the Acklen Park neighborhood that made me know for certain how they saw Major Basil Manley. To them, those other grandfathers seemed all elegance while he seemed all roughness. Those others lived quietly with their sons and daughters while he insisted upon living apart and in a county that was only on the periphery of Middle Tennessee. Those other grandfathers were a part of the families who had taken them in. (They had managed to become so or perhaps had always been so.) When you saw one of those other grandfathers out walking with a little grandson along West End Avenue, it was apparent at once that the two of them were made of the same clay or at least that their mutual aim in life was to make it appear to the world that they were. Sometimes the old man and the little boy walked along West End hand in hand or sometimes with their arms about each other, the old man's arm on the little boy's shoulder, the little boy's arm about the old man's waist. It is a picture that comes into my mind almost every day that I live.

WILLIAM STYRON

From *Sophie's Choice*

Novelist William Styron's work has been heavily influenced by his Virginia upbringing as well as by contemporary European intellectual ideas. Sophie's Choice *(1979) brings a traditional Southern perspective to the concerns of a larger world—New York and Europe. In this scene, Nathan turns on his friend Stingo, insisting that as a Southerner Stingo should answer for all the injustices of the South.*

Beneath all the jollity, the tenderness, the solicitude, I sensed a disturbing tension in the room. I don't mean that the tension at that moment directly involved the two lovers. But there was tension, an unnerving strain, and most of it seemed to emanate from Nathan. He had become distracted, restless, and he got up and fiddled with the phonograph records, replaced the Handel with Vivaldi again, in obvious turmoil gulped a glass of water, sat down and drummed his fingers against his pants leg in rhythm to the celebrant horns.

Then swiftly he turned to me, peering at me searchingly with his troubled and gloomy eyes, and said, "Just an old briar-hopper, ain't you?" After a pause and with a touch of the bogus drawl he had baited me with before, he added, "You know, you Confederate types interest me. You-all"—and here he bore down on the "all"—"you-*all* interest me very, very much."

I began to do, or undergo, or experience what I believe is known as a slow burn. This Nathan was incredible! How could he be so clumsy, so unfeeling—such a *creep?* My euphoric haze evaporated like thousands of tiny soap bubbles all at once. This swine! I thought. He had actually trapped me! How otherwise to explain this sly change in mood, unless it was to try to edge me into a corner? It was either clumsiness or craft: there was no other way to fathom such words, after I had so emphatically and so recently made it a condition of our amity—if such it might be called—that he would lay off his heavy business about the South. Once more indignation rose like a regurgitated bone in my gorge, though I made a last attempt to be patient. I turned up the butane under my Tidewater accent and said, "Why, Nathan ole hoss, you Brooklyn folks interest us boys down home, too."

This had a distinctly adverse effect on Nathan. He was not only unamused, his eyes flashed warfare; he glowered at me with implacable mistrust, and for an instant I could have sworn I saw in those shining pupils the freak, the redneck, the alien he knew me to be.

"Oh, fuck it," I said, starting to rise to my feet. "I'll just be going—"

But before I could set down my glass and get up he had clutched me by the wrist. It was not a rough or painful grasp, but he bore down strongly nonetheless, and insistently, and his grip held me fast in the chair. There was something desperately importunate in that grip which chilled me.

"It's hardly a joking matter," he said. His voice, though restrained, was, I felt, charged with turbulent emotion. Then his next words, spoken with deliberate, almost comical slowness, were like an incantation. "Bobby . . . Weed . . . *Bobby Weed!* Do you think Bobby Weed is worthy of nothing more than your attempt . . . at . . . humor?"

"It wasn't *I* who started that cotton-picking accent," I retorted. And I thought: *Bobby Weed!* Oh shit! Now he's going to get on Bobby Weed. Let me out of here.

Then at this moment Sophie, as if sensing the perhaps sinister shift in Nathan's mood, hurried to his side and touched his shoulder with a fluttery, nervously placating hand. "Nathan," she said, "no more about Bobby Weed. Please, Nathan! It will just disturb you when we were having such a lovely time." She cast me a look of distress. "All week he's been talking about Bobby Weed. I can't get him to stop." To Nathan again she begged, "Please, darling, we were having such a lovely time!"

But Nathan was not to be deflected. "What about Bobby Weed?" he demanded of me.

"Well, what *about* him, for Christ's sake?" I groaned, and pulled myself upward out of his grasp. I had begun to eye the door and the intervening furniture, and quickly schemed out the best way of immediate exit. "Thanks for the beer," I muttered.

"*I'll* tell you what about Bobby Weed," Nathan persisted. He was not about to allow me off the hook, and dumped more foaming beer into the glass which he pressed into my hand. His expression still seemed calm enough but was betrayed by inner excitement in the form of a waggling, hairy, didactic forefinger which he thrust into my face. "I'll tell you something about Bobby Weed, Stingo my friend. And that is *this!* You Southern white people have a lot to answer for when it comes to such bestiality. You deny that? Then listen. I say this as one whose people have suffered the death camps. I say this as a man who is deeply in love with one who survived them." He reached up and surrounded Sophie's wrist with his hand while the forefinger of his other hand still made its vermiform scrawl in the air above my cheekbone. "But mainly I say this as Nathan Landau, common citizen, research biologist, human being, witness to man's inhumanity to man. I say that the fate of Bobby Weed at the hands of white Southern Americans is as bottomlessly barbaric as any act performed by the Nazis during the rule of Adolf Hitler! Do you agree with me?"

I bit the inside of my mouth in an effort to keep my composure. "What happened to Bobby Weed, Nathan," I replied, "was horrible. Unspeakable! But I don't see any point in trying to equate one evil with another, or to assign some stupid scale of values. They're *both* awful! Would you mind taking your finger out of my face?" I felt my brow growing moist and feverish. "And I damn well question this big net you're trying to throw out to catch all of what you call *you Southern white people.* Goddamnit, I'm not going to swallow that line! I'm *Southern* and I'm *proud* of it, but I'm not one of those pigs—those *troglodytes* who did what they did to Bobby Weed! I was born in Tidewater Virginia, and if you'll pardon the expression, I regard myself as a gentleman! Also, if you'll pardon me, this simplistic nonsense of yours, this *ignorance* coming from somebody so obviously intelligent as yourself truly *nauseates* me!" I heard my voice climb, quavering, cracked and no longer under control, and I feared another disastrous coughing fit as I watched Nathan calmly rising to his full height, so that in effect we were confronting each other. Despite the now rather threatful forward-thrusting nature of his stance and the fact that he outmanned me in bulk and stature, I had the powerful urge to punch him in the jaw. "Nathan, let me tell *you* something. You are now dealing in the cheapest kind of New York-liberal, hypocritical horseshit! What gives you the right to pass judgment on millions of people, most of whom would die before they'd harm a Negro!"

"Ha!" he replied. "See, it's even in your speech pattern. *Nig*-ro! I find that *so* offensive."

"It's the way we *say* it down there. It's not *meant* to offend. All right—*Knee-grow.* Anyway," I went on impatiently, "what gives you the right to pass judgment? I find *that* so offensive."

"As a Jew, I regard myself as an authority on anguish and suffering." He paused and as he gazed at me now I thought I saw for the first time contempt in his look, and mounting disgust. "As for this 'New York-liberal' evasion, this 'hypocritical horseshit'—I consider that a laughably feeble, insubstantial comeback to an honest accusation. Aren't you able to perceive the simple truth? Aren't you able to discern the truth in its awful outlines? And that is that your refusal to admit responsibility in the death of Bobby Weed is the same as that of those Germans who disavowed the Nazi party even as they watched blandly and unprotestingly as the thugs vandalized the synagogues and perpetrated the *Kristallnacht.* Can't you see the truth about yourself? About the South? After all, it wasn't the citizens of New York State who destroyed Bobby Weed."

Most of what he was saying—especially about *my* "responsibility"—was lopsided, irrational, smug and horrendously wrong, yet to my nearly total chagrin at that point, I found that I could not answer. I was momentarily demoralized. I made an odd chirping sound in the back of my throat and moved in a sort of weak-kneed graceless lurch toward the window. Feeble, impotent though inwardly raging, I struggled for words that would not come. I swilled at a gulp the larger part of a glass of beer, looking through eyes bleared with frustration down at the sunny pastoral lawns of Flatbush, the rustling sycamores and maples, decorous streets all gently astir with Sunday-morning motion: shirt-sleeved ball-throwers, churning bicycles, sun-dappled strollers on the walks. The scent of new-mown grass was rank, sweet, warmly green to the nostrils, reminding me of countryside prospects and distances—fields and lanes perhaps not too different from those once meandered upon by the young Bobby Weed, whom Nathan had implanted like a pulsing lesion in my brain. And as I thought of Bobby Weed, I was overtaken by bitter, disabling despair. How could this infernal Nathan summon up the shade of Bobby Weed on such a ravishing day?

I listened to Nathan's voice behind me, high now, hectoring, reminiscent of that of a squat, half-hysteric Communist youth organizer with a mouth like a torn pocket I had once heard screaming up at the empty empyrean over Union Square. "The South today has abdicated any right to connection with the human race," Nathan harangued me. "Each white Southerner is accountable for the tragedy of Bobby Weed. No Southerner escapes responsibility!"

I shivered violently, my hand jerked, and I watched my beer slosh greasily in its glass. Nineteen forty-seven. One, nine, four, seven. In that summer, twenty years almost to the month before the city of Newark burned down, and Negro blood flowed incarnadine in the gutters of Detroit, it was possible—if one was Dixie-born and sensitive and enlightened and aware of one's fearsome and ungodly history—to smart beneath such a tongue-lashing, even when one knew that it partook heavily of renascent abolitionist self-righteousness, ascribing to itself moral superiority so hygienic as to provoke tolerant though mirthless amusement. In less violent form, in subtle digs and supercilious little drawing-room slanders, Southerners who had ventured north were to endure such exploitative assaults upon their indwelling guilt during an era of unalleviated discomfort which ended officially on a morning in August, 1963, when on North Water Street in Edgartown, Massachusetts, the youngish, straw-haired, dimple-kneed wife of the yacht-club commodore, a prominent Brahmin investment banker, was seen brandishing a copy of James Baldwin's *The Fire Next Time* as she uttered to a friend, in tones of clamp-jawed desolation, these words: "My dear, it's going to happen to *all* of us!"

This understatement could not have seemed quite so omniscient to me back then in 1947. At that time the drowsing black behemoth, although beginning to stir, was still not regarded as much of a Northern problem. Perhaps for this very reason—although I might honestly have bridled at the intolerant Yankee slurs that had sometimes come my way (even good old Farrell had gotten in a few mildly caustic licks)—I *did* feel at my heart's core a truly burdensome

WILLIAM DUNLAP. *Object Lesson Series: Lights Out: 1939–1945.* 1991. Construction. Courtesy of the artist. Photograph by David Diaz Guerrero. *About his constructions, William Dunlap says, "I, too, can paint objects, but its just as satisfying to find them and then incorporate them into a larger, more grandiloquent work. I'm trying to jog people's memories."*

shame over the kinship I was forced to acknowledge with those solidly Anglo-Saxon subhumans who were the torturers of Bobby Weed. These Georgia backwoodsmen—denizens, as it so happened, of that same piney coast near Brunswick where my savior Artiste had toiled and suffered and died—had made sixteen-year-old Bobby Weed one of the last and certainly one of the most memorably wiped-out victims of lynch justice the South was to witness. His reputed crime, very much resembling that of Artiste, had been so classic as to take on the outlines of a grotesque cliché: he had ogled, or molested, or otherwise interfered with (actual offense never made clear, though falling short of rape) the simpleton daughter, named Lula—another cliché! but true: Lula's woebegone and rabbity face had sulked from the pages of six metropolitan newspapers—of a crossroads storekeeper, who had instigated immediate action by an outraged daddy's appeal to the local rabble.

I had read of the peasantry's medieval vengeance only a week before, while standing on an uptown Lexington Avenue local, squashed between an enormously fat woman with an S. Klein shopping bag and a small Popsicle-licking Puerto Rican in a busboy's jacket whose gardenia-ripe brilliantine floated sweetishly up to my nose as he mooned over my *Mirror,* sharing with me its devil's photographs. While he was still alive Bobby Weed's cock and balls had been hacked off and thrust into his mouth (this feature not displayed), and when near death, though reportedly aware of all. had by a flaming blowtorch received the brand on his chest of a serpentine "L"—representing what? "Lynch?" "Lula?" "Law and Order?" "Love?" Even as Nathan raved at me, I recalled having semi-staggered out of the train and up into the bright summer light of Eighty-sixth Street, amid the scent of wienerwurst and Orange Julius and scorched metal from the subway gratings, moving blindly past the Rossellini movie I had traveled that far to see. I did not go to the theatre that afternoon. Instead, I found myself at Gracie Square on the promenade by the river, gazing as if in a trance at the municipal hideousness of the river islands, unable to efface the mangled image of Bobby Weed from my mind even as I kept murmuring—endlessly it seemed—lines from Revelation I had memorized as a boy: *And God shall wipe away all tears from their eyes. And there shall be no more death, neither sorrow nor crying, neither shall there be any more pain. . . .* Perhaps it had been an overreaction, but—ah God, even so, *I* could not weep.

Nathan's voice, still badgering me, swam back into hearing. "Look, in the *concentration camps* the brutes in charge would not have stooped to *that* bestiality!"

Would they? Would they not? It seemed hardly to matter, and I was sick of the argument, sick of the fanaticism I was unable to counter or find shelter from, sick with the vision of Bobby Weed and—despite feeling no complicity whatever in the Georgia abomination—suddenly sick with a past and a place and a heritage I could neither believe in nor fathom. I had the idle urge now—at risk of a broken nose—to heave the rest of my beer in Nathan's face. Restraining myself, I tensed my shoulders and said in tones of frosty contempt, "As a member of a race which has been unjustly persecuted for centuries for having allegedly crucified Christ, *you*—yes, *you,* goddamnit!—should be aware of how inexcusable it is to condemn any single *people for anything!*" And then I found myself so enraged that I blurted out something which to Jews, in that tormented bygone year scant months removed from the crematoriums, was freighted with enough incendiary offensiveness to make me regret the words as soon as they escaped my lips. But I didn't take them back. "And that goes for *any* people," I said, "by God, even the Germans!"

HARRY CREWS

From *A Childhood: The Biography of a Place*

Eating Possum

Harry Crews, who now lives in Florida, is the son of a Georgia sharecropper. He has written many books, essays, and stories, but his autobiography (1978) is particularly powerful. Crews has said that the South is "a neighborhood," and this excerpt illustrates the close ties that often existed between Southerners and that transcended questions of race.

But Willalee was not entirely helpless, and he gave back about as good as he got. He once took a crabapple and cut the core out of it, put some cow plop down in the bottom of the hole, and then covered it over all around the top with some blackberry jam his mama had canned.

"Jam in a apple?" I said.

"Bes thing *you* ever put in your mouth," he said.

My brother, who had seen him fix the apple, stood there and watched him offer it to me, did in fact encourage me to take it.

"Had one myself," he said. "That thing is some goooood eatin."

"I ain't had nair one with jam in it," I said.

"Take you a great big bite," said Willalee.

I not only took a great big bite, I took *two* great big bites, getting right down to the bottom. Anybody else would have known what he was eating after the first bite. It took me two. Even then, I did not so much taste it as I smelled it.

"I believe this thing is ruint," I said.

"Nawwwww," said Willalee.

"Nawwwww," said my brother.

"It smells just like . . . like. . . ." And then I knew what he had fed me.

Willalee was laughing when he should have been running. I got him around the neck and we both went into the dust, where we wallowed around for a while before my brother got tired of watching it and pulled us apart. No matter what we did to one another, though, Willalee and I never stayed angry at each other for more than an hour or two, and I always felt welcome at his family's house. Whatever I am, they had a large part in making. More, I am convinced Willalee's grandma, Auntie, made the best part of me. She was thin and brittle with age, and her white hair rode her fleshless face like a cap. From daylight to dark she kept a thick cud of snuff working in her caving, toothless mouth, and she was expert at sending streams of brown spit great distances into tin cans.

The inside of their tiny house was dark on the brightest day and smelled always of ashes, even in the summer. Auntie did not like much light inside the house, so most of the time she kept the curtains drawn, curtains she had made from fertilizer sacks and decorated with bits of colored cloth. Bright light was for the outside, she said, and shade—the more the better—was for the inside.

I ate with them often, as often as mama would let me, and the best thing I ever got from their table was possum, which we *never* got at home because mama would not cook it. She said she knew it would taste like a wet dog smells. But it did not. Auntie could cook it in a way that would break your heart. Willalee and I would stand about in her dark, ash-smelling little kitchen and watch her prepare it. She would scald and scrape it just like you would scald and scrape a hog, gut it, remove the eyes, which she always carefully set aside in a shallow dish. The head, except for the eyes, would be left intact. After she parboiled it an hour and a half, she would take out the teeth, stuff the little body with sweet potatoes, and then bake the whole thing in the oven for two hours.

The reason mama would never cook a possum, of course, was because a possum is just like a buzzard. It will eat anything that is dead. The longer dead the better. It was not unusual to come across a cow that had been dead in the woods for three or four days and see a possum squeezing out of the swollen body after having eaten a bellyful of rotten flesh. But it never occurred to me to think of that when we all sat down to the table and waited for Willalee's daddy to say the only grace he ever said: "Thank the Lord for this food."

The first possum I ever shared with them was in that first summer in my memory of myself, and with the possum we had fresh sliced tomatoes and steamed okra—as well as fried okra—and corn on the cob, butter beans, fried pork, and biscuits made out of flour and water and lard.

Because I was company, Auntie gave me the best piece: the head. Which had a surprising amount of meat on it and in it. I ate around on the face for a while, gnawing it down to the cheekbones, then ate the tongue, and finally went into the skull cavity for the brains, which Auntie had gone to some pains to explain was the best part of the piece.

After we finished the possum, Willalee and Lottie Mae and I stayed at the table sopping cane syrup with biscuits. Will and Katie had gone out on the front porch to rest, and we were left alone with Auntie, who was already working over the table, taking plates to the tin tub where she would wash them, and putting whatever food had been left over into the screen-wire safe.

Finally, she came to stand beside where I sat at the table. "Come on now, boy," she said, "an ole Auntie'll show you."

"Show me what?" I said.

She was holding the little shallow saucer with the possum's eyes in it. The eyes were clouded in a pink pool of diluted blood. They rolled on the saucer as I watched.

"Nem mind," she said. "Come on."

We followed her out the back door into the yard. We didn't go but a step or two before she squatted down and dug a hole. The rear of the house was almost covered with stretched and nailed hides of squirrels and rabbits and coons and even a fox which Willalee's daddy had trapped. I would find out later that Auntie had tanned the hides by rubbing the animals' hides on the flesh side with their own brains. It caused the hair to fall out of the hide and left it soft and pliable.

"You eat a possum, you bare its eyes," she said, still squatting beside the little hole she had dug.

I motioned toward Sam where he stood at my heels. "You gone bury it," I said, "you better bury it deeper'n that. Don't he'll dig it up. You might as well go on and give it to'm now."

"Won't dig up no possum's eyes," she said. "Sam's got good sense."

Sam did not, either.

"Know how come you got to barum?" she said.

"How come?" I said.

"Possums eat whatall's dead," she said. Her old, cracked voice had gone suddenly deep and husky. "You gone die too, boy."

"Yes," I said, stunned.

"You be dead an in the ground, but you eat this possum an he gone come lookin for you. He ain't ever gone stop lookin for you."

I could not now speak. I watched as she carefully took the two little clouded eyes out of the dish and placed them in the hole, arranging them so they were looking straight up toward the cloudless summer sky. They seemed to watch me where I was.

Auntie smiled, showing her snuff-colored gums. "You ain't got to think on it, boy. See, we done put them eyes looking up. But you gone be *down*. Ain't never gone git you. Possum be looking for you up, an you gone be six big feets under the ground. You gone allus be all right, you put the eyes lookin up."

Auntie made me believe we live in a discoverable world, but that most of what we discover is an unfathomable mystery that we can name—even defend against—but never understand.

LYNYRD SKYNYRD

"Sweet Home Alabama"

Bands like The Allman Brothers, The Marshall Tucker Band, and Lynyrd Skynyrd, a Jacksonville, Florida group that took its name from a despised high school gym teacher, formed the core of a Southern rock movement in the early 1970s. Hard living and hard drinking, Lynyrd Skynyrd celebrated Southern life in aggressive, unapologetic, hard rock songs like "Sweet Home Alabama."

Big wheels keep on turnin'
Carryin' me home to see my kin
Singin' songs about the Southland
I miss ol' Bamy once again, and I think it's a sin

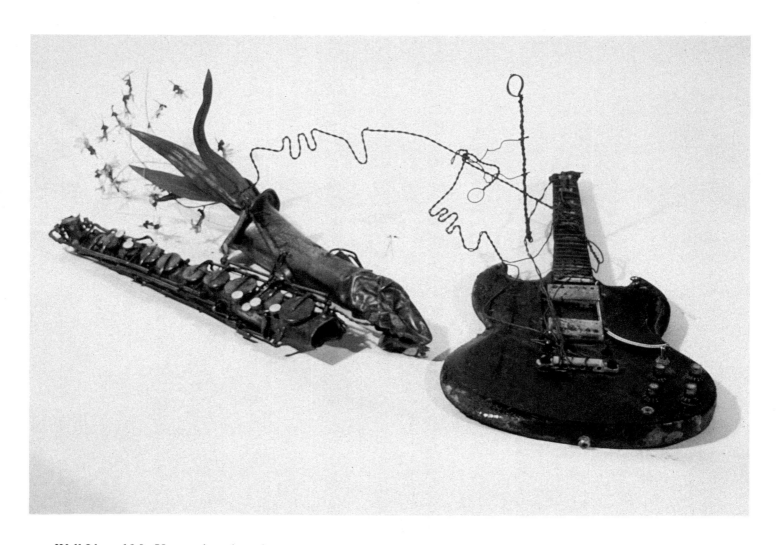

Well I heard Mr. Young sing about her
Well, I heard ol' Neil put her down
Well I hope Neil Young will remember
A Southern man don't need him around anyhow

    Chorus:
    Sweet Home Alabama
    Where the sky's always blue
    Sweet Home Alabama
    Lord I'm comin' home to you

In Birmingham, they love the governor (Boo, boo, boo)
Now we all did what we could do
Now Watergate does not bother me
Does your conscience bother you, tell the truth

    (Chorus)

Now Muscle Shoals has got the swampers
And they been known to pick a song or two
Lord, they get me off so much
They pick me up when I'm feelin' blue, now how about you

    (Chorus)

LONNIE HOLLEY.
The Music Lives After the Instruments Is Destroyed. c. 1980. Mixed media. 33 x 36 x 13 in. Collection of William Arnett, Atlanta, Georgia.

BARRY HANNAH

From *Airships*

"Knowing He Was Not My Kind Yet I Followed"

Barry Hannah's innovative stories and extraordinary use of language have placed him, according to James Dickey, "in the very first rank of American literary artists." Hannah will sometimes reach back to the Civil War to give an old story a new twist although he said, "I don't like historical siobs, you know, who just live in it forever." In this excerpt from Airships *(1978), a homosexual cavalryman expresses his love and admiration for the heroic Confederate general Jeb Stuart.*

It makes me sick when we kill them or ride horses over them. My gun is blazing just like the rest of them, but I hate it.

One day I rode up on a fellow in blue and we were both out of ammunition. He was trying to draw his saber and I was so outraged I slapped him right off his horse. The horseman behind me cheered. He said I'd broken the man's neck. I was horrified. Oh, life, life—you kill what you love. I have seen such handsome faces with their mouths open, their necks open to the Pennsylvania sun. I love stealing for forage and food, but I hate this murdering business that goes along with it.

Some nights I amble in near the fire to take a cup with the boys, but they chase me away. I don't scold, but in my mind there are the words: All right, have your way in this twinkling mortal world.

Our Jeb Stuart is never tired. You could wake him with a message any time of night and he's awake on the instant. He's such a bull. They called him "Beauty" at West Point. We're fighting and killing all his old classmates and even his father-in-law, General Philip St. George Cooke. Jeb wrote about this man once when he failed to join the Confederacy: "He will regret it but once, and that will be continuously."

Gee, he can use the word, Jeb can. I was with him through the ostrich feathers in his hat and the early harassments, when we had nothing but shotguns and pretty horses. He was always a fool at running around his enemy. I was with him when we rode down a lane around a confused Yank picket, risking the Miniés. But he's a good family man too, they say.

I was with him when he first went around McClellan and scouted Porter's wing. That's when I fell in love with burning and looting. We threw ourselves on railroad cars and wagons, we collected carbines, uniforms and cow steaks that we roasted on sticks over the embers of the rails. Jeb passed right by when I was chewing my beef and dipping water out of the great tank. He had his banjo man and his dancing nigger with him. Jeb has terrific body odor along with his mud-spattered boots, but it rather draws than repels, like the musk of a woman.

When we were celebrating in Richmond, even I was escorted by a woman out into the shadows and this is why I say this. She surrendered to me, her hoop skirt was around her eyebrows, her white nakedness lying under me if I wanted it, and I suppose I did, because I went laboring at her, head full of smoke and unreason. I left her with her dress over her face like a tent and have no clear notion of what her face was like, though my acquaintance Ruppert Longstreet told me in daylight she was a troll.

That was when young Pelham set fire to the Yank boat in the James with his one Napoleon cannon. We whipped a warship from the shore. Pelham was a genius about artillery. I loved that too.

It's killing close up that bothers me. Once a blue-suited man on the ground was holding his hands out after his horse fell over. This was at Manassas. He seemed to be unclear about whether this was an actual event; he seemed to be asking for directions back to his place in a stunned friendly way. My horse, Pardon Me, was rearing way high and I couldn't put the muzzle of my shotgun at him. Then Jeb rode in, plumes shivering. He slashed the man deep in the shoulder with his saber. The man knelt down, closing his eyes as if to pray. Jeb rode next to me. What a body odor he had. On his horse, he said:

"Finish that poor Christian off, soldier."

My horse settled down and I blew the man over. Pardon Me reared at the shot and tore away in his own race down a vacant meadow—fortunate for me, since I never had to look at the carnage but only thought of holding on.

After McClellan placed himself back on the York, we slipped through Maryland and here we are in Pennsylvania. We go spying and cavorting and looting. I'm wearing out. Pardon Me, I think, feels the lunacy even in this smooth countryside. We're too far from home. We are not defending our beloved Dixie anymore. We're just bandits and maniacal. The gleam in the men's eyes tells this. Everyone is getting crazier on the craziness of being simply too far from home for decent return. It is like Ruth in the alien corn, or a troop of men given wings over the terrain they cherished and taken by the wind to trees they do not know.

Jeb leads us. Some days he has the sneer of Satan himself.

Nothing but bad news comes up from home, when it comes.

Lee is valiant but always too few.

All the great bullies I used to see out front are dead or wounded past use.

The truth is, not a one of us except Jeb Stuart believes in anything any longer. The man himself the exception. There is nobody who does not believe in Jeb Stuart. Oh, the zany purposeful eyes, the haggard gleam, the feet of his lean horse high in the air, his rotting flannel shirt under the old soiled grays, and his heroic body odor! He makes one want to be a Christian. I wish I could be one. I'm afraid the only things I count on are chance and safety.

The other night I got my nerve up and asked for him in his tent. When I went in, he had his head on the field desk, dead asleep. The quill was still in his hand. I took up the letter. It was to his wife, Flora. A daguerreotype of her lay next to the paper. It was still wet from Jeb's tears. At the beginning of the letter there was small talk about finding her the black silk she'd always wanted near Gettysburg. Then it continued: "After the shameful defeat at Gettysburg," etc.

I was shocked. I always thought we won at Gettysburg. All the fellows I knew thought we had won. Further, he said:

"The only thing that keeps me going on my mission is the sacred inalienable right of the Confederacy to be the Confederacy, Christ Our Lord, and the memory of your hot hairy jumping nexus when I return."

I placed the letter back on the table. This motion woke him.

I was incredulous that he knew my first name. He looked as if he had not slept a second.

The stories were true.

"Corporal Deed Ainsworth," he said.

"Sorry to wake you, General."

"Your grievance?" he said.

"No one is my friend," I mumbled.

"Because the Creator made you strange, my man. I never met a chap more loyal in the saddle than you. God made us different and we should love His differences as well as His likenesses."

"I'd like to kiss you, General," I said.

"Oh, no. He made me abhor that. Take to your good sleep, my man. We surprise the railroad tomorrow."

"Our raids still entertain you?" I asked.

"Not so much. But I believe our course has been written. We'll kill ten and lose two. Our old Bobbie Lee will smile when we send the nigger back to him with the message. I'll do hell for Lee's smile."

The nigger came in the tent about then. He was high-falutin, never hardly glanced at me. They had a magnificent bay waiting for the letters. Two soldiers came in and took an armload

of missives from General Stuart's trunk, pressing them into the saddlebags. The nigger, in civilian clothes, finally looked at me.

"Who dis?" he said.

"Corporal Deed Ainsworth; shake hands," said General Stuart.

I have a glass shop in Biloxi. I never shook hands with any nigger. Yet the moment constrained me to. He was Jeb's best minstrel. He played the guitar better than anything one might want to hear, and the banjo. His voice singing "All Hail the Power" was the only feeling I ever had to fall on my knees and pray. But now he was going back down South as a rider with the messages.

"Ain't shaking hands with no nancy," said the nigger. "They say he lay down with a Choctaw chief in Mississip, say he lick a heathen all over his feathers."

"You're getting opinions for a nigger, George," said Jeb, standing. "I don't believe Our Lord has room for another nigger's thoughts. You are tiring God when you use your mouth, George."

"Yessuh," said George.

"Do you want to apologize to Corporal Ainsworth?"

"I real sorry. I don't know what I say," the nigger said to me. "General Jeb taught me how to talk and sometimes I justs go on talking to try it out."

"Ah, my brother George," Jeb suddenly erupted.

He rushed to the nigger and threw his arms around him. His eyes were full of tears. He embraced the black man in the manner of my dreams of how he might embrace me.

"My chap, my chum. Don't get yourself killed," said Jeb to George. "Try to look ignorant when you get near the road pickets, same as when I found you and saved you from drink."

"I loves you too, General Jeb. I ain't touched nothing since you saved me. Promise. I gon look ignorant like you say, tills I get to Richmond. Then I might have me a beer."

"Even Christ wouldn't deny you that. Ah, my George, there's a heaven where we'll all prosper together. Even this sissy, Corporal Ainsworth."

GLENNRAY TUTOR. *Black Cat.* 1991. Oil on canvas. 40 x 60 in. Collection of Raymond and Arlene Zimmerman, Nashville, TN. *Glennray Tutor works in a photo-realist style, preferring subjects that are reflective of the everyday South: lawn chairs, back alleys in small towns, abandoned drive-ins, and recently, fireworks with their alien designs but universal promise of excitement.*

They both looked at me benevolently. I felt below the nigger.

George got on the horse and took off South.

At five the next morning we came out of a stand of birches and all of us flew high over the rail-road, shooting down the men. I had two stolen repeaters on my hip in the middle of the rout and let myself off Pardon Me. A poor torn Yank, driven out of the attack, with no arm but a kitchen fork, straggled up to me. We'd burned and killed almost everything else.

Stuart rode by me screaming in his rich bass to mount. The blue cavalry was coming across the fire toward us. The wounded man was stabbing me in the chest with his fork. Jeb took his saber out in the old grand style to cleave the man from me. I drew the pistol on my right hip and put it almost against Jeb's nose when he leaned to me.

"You kill him, I kill you, General," I said.

There was no time for a puzzled look, but he boomed out: "Are you happy, Corporal Ainsworth? Are you satisfied, my good man Deed?"

I nodded.

"Go with your nature and remember our Savior!" he shouted, last in the retreat.

I have seen it many times, but there is no glory like Jeb Stuart putting spurs in his sorrel and escaping the Minié balls.

They captured me and sent me to Albany prison, where I write this.

I am well fed and wretched.

A gleeful little floorwipe came in the other day to say they'd killed Jeb in Virginia. I don't think there's much reservoir of self left to me now.

This earth will never see his kind again.

Alfred Uhry

From *Driving Miss Daisy*

Alfred Uhry won the Pulitzer Prize in drama in 1988 for this play. It is a small play with only three characters, but audiences everywhere have found it to be quietly powerful and appealing. "I wrote what I knew to be the truth and people have recognized it as such," says Uhry.

[*Light goes out on them and in the dark we hear Eartha Kitt singing "Santa Baby." Light up on Boolie. He wears a tweed jacket, red vest, holly in his lapel. He is on the phone.*]

BOOLIE: Mama? Merry Christmas. Listen, do Florine a favor, all right? She's having a fit and the grocery store is closed today. You got a package of coconut in your pantry? Would you bring it when you come? [*He calls offstage*] Hey, honey! Your ambrosia's saved! Mama's got the coconut! [*Back into the phone*] Many thanks. See you anon, Mama. Ho ho ho.

[*Lights out on Boolie and up on Daisy and Hoke in the car. Daisy is not in a festive mood.*]

HOKE: Oooooh at them lit-up decorations!
DAISY: Everybody's giving the Georgia Power Company a Merry Christmas.
HOKE: Miz Florine's got 'em all beat with the lights.
DAISY: She makes an ass out of herself every year.

HOKE [*Loving it*]: Yassum.

DAISY: She always has to go and stick a wreath in every window she's got.

HOKE: Mmm-hmmm.

DAISY: And that silly Santa Claus winking on the front door!

HOKE: I bet she have the biggest tree in Atlanta. Where she get 'em so large?

DAISY: Absurd. If I had a nose like Florine I wouldn't go around saying Merry Christmas to anybody.

HOKE: I enjoy Christmas at they house.

DAISY: I don't wonder. You're the only Christian in the place!

HOKE: 'Cept they got that new cook.

DAISY: Florine never could keep help. Of course it's none of my affair.

HOKE: Nome.

DAISY: Too much running around. The Garden Club this and the Junior League that! As if any one of them would ever give her the time of day! But she'd die before she'd fix a glass of ice tea for the Temple Sisterhood!

HOKE: Yassum. You right.

DAISY: I just hope she doesn't take it in her head to sing this year. [*She imitates*] Glo-o-o-o-o-o-o-o-o-o-o-o-o-o-oriaaaa! She sounds like she has a bone stuck in her throat.

HOKE: You done say a mouthful, Miz Daisy.

DAISY: You didn't have to come. Boolie would've run me out.

HOKE: I know that.

DAISY: Then why did you?

HOKE: That my business, Miz Daisy. [*He turns into a driveway and stops the car*]

CLEMENTINE HUNTER. *Floral Mosaic #5.* 1962. Oil on canvas board. 22 x 28 in. Roger Houston Ogden Collection, New Orleans. *Many of folk artist Clementine Hunter's still lifes are suggestive of quilt patterns, another familiar form of expression for her. Hunter painted scenes of the life she knew at Melrose plantation in Louisiana, where she spent most of her life.*

Well, looka there! Miz Florine done put a Rudolph Reindeer in the dogwood tree.

DAISY: Oh my Lord! If her grandfather, old man Freitag, could see this! What isit you say? I bet he'd jump up out of his grave and snatch her baldheaded!

[*Hoke opens the door for Daisy.*]

Wait a minute. [*She takes a small package wrapped in brown paper from her purse*] This isn't a Christmas present.

HOKE: Nome.

DAISY: You know I don't give Christmas presents.

HOKE: I sho' do.

DAISY: I just happened to run across it this morning. Open it up.

HOKE [*Unwrapping package*]: Ain' nobody ever give me a book. [*Laboriously readsthe cover*] Handwriting Copy Book—Grade Five.

DAISY: I always taught out of these. I saved a few.

HOKE: Yassum.

DAISY: It's faded but it works. If you practice, you'll write nicely.

HOKE [*Trying not to show emotion*]: Yassum.

DAISY: But you have to practice. I taught Mayor Hartsfield out of this same book.

HOKE: Thank you, Miz Daisy.

DAISY: It's not a Christmas present.

HOKE: Nome.

DAISY: Jews don't have any business giving Christmas presents. And you don't need to go yapping about this to Boolie and Florine.

HOKE: This strictly between you and me.

[*We hear a record of "Rudolph the Red-Nosed Reindeer."*]

They seen us. Mist' Werthan done turn up the hi-fi.

DAISY: I hope I don't spit up.

[*Hoke takes her arm and they walk off together as the light fades on them.*]

JOHN MCWILLIAMS. *Escambia County, Alabama.* 1977. Photograph. Collection of the photographer, Atlanta, Georgia. *The elegant, cautionary photographs of John McWilliams often evoke the expansive lyricism of the nineteenth-century landscape painters.*

INDEX

Page numbers in italic denote illustrations. Colorplate numbers are given in parentheses.

Abandoned House Near Montgomery, Alabama
  (Christenberry), *278* (cpl. 103)
Absalom, Absalom! (Faulkner), 10, 207–209
Adams, Henry, 14, 102–103
After the Show (Souchon), *242* (cpl. 84)
Agee, James, 187–188
Ainer Ownesby, Gatlinburg, TN (Ulmann), *181*
Ain't Life Great? In the Big House (Dale), *303*
  (cpl. 113)
Airships (Hannah), 359–362
Alexander, Margaret Walker, 25, 272, 281
All God's Dangers: The Life of Nate Shaw
  (Rosengarten), 182–184
Alligator (von Reck), 42, *43* (cpl. 11)
All the King's Men (Warren), 259–263
"Amazing Grace" (Newton), 13, 63–64
American Notes and Pictures from Italy (Dickens),
  97–99
Anderson, Walter, *176* (cpl. 66)
Andrews, Benny, *328* (cpl. 122)
And the Livin Is Easy (Miller), *12*
Angelou, Maya, 26
Ann Hill Carter Lee (artist unknown), *46* (cpl. 16)
Antrobus, John, 14, 118, *119* (cpl. 41)
Arkansas Traveler, the (Washburn), *149*
Arrival of the Mail/Perspective of Broad Street
  (White), *95* (cpl. 33)
Art of the Old South (Poesch), 11
Arts of the South (Benton), 243, *244–245* (cpl. 86)
Art World (Jennings), *299* (cpl. 108)
Asylum for the Deaf and Dumb, The–Baton Rouge
  (Persac), *94* (cpl. 32)
Audubon, John James, 130–133, *131*
Avery Island Salt Mines (Ninas), *220* (cpl. 78)

Baker, William H., *164* (cpl. 54)
Ball play of the Choctaw–Ball Up (Catlin), *74*
Baptism (Rankin), *281*
Baptism at Triplett Creek (Wolcott), *226*
Barber, Red, 25, 282–285
Bardstown (Gilliam), *301* (cpl. 110)
Bartram, William, 12, 35–37, *36*
Bayou Landscape (Drysdale), *174* (cpl. 64)
Bayou Teche (Straus), *140–141* (cpl. 47)
Bearden, Romare, 25, *248* (cpl. 89), *277* (cpl. 102)
Beauregard, Pierre G. T., *167* (cpl. 57)
Bed (Rauschenberg), *304* (cpl. 114)
Bellocq, E. J., *309*
Benjamin, Judah P., *112*
Benjamin Hawkins and the Creek Indians
  (artist unknown), *67* (cpl. 21)
Benton, Thomas Hart, 25, *231*, 243, *244–245* (cpl. 86)
Berry, Chuck, *341*
Berry, Wendell, 26, 333–334
Betting Money on the Cockfight (Pavy), *298* (cpl. 107)
Betts, Harold Harrington, *200* (cpl. 74)
Billboard. Birmingham, Alabama (W. Evans), *260*
Bird in the Hand, A (McGowin), *273* (cpl. 98)
Birth and Baptismal Certificate for Hanna Elisabeth
  Clodfelder ("Ehre Vater" artist), *65* (cpl. 19)
Black Boy (Wright), 210–214
Black Cat (Tutor), *361*
Black demonstrators, Birmingham, Alabama, 287
Blackwell, Tarleton, *255* (cpl. 96), *319*
Blood, Henry Ames, *189*
Blount, Roy, Jr., 25, 319–320
"Blue Moon of Kentucky" (Monroe), *180*
Bombardment of Fort Sumter, The (Key), *142* (cpl. 48)
Brady, Mathew, 14, *129*
Brammer, Robert, *90* (cpl. 28), *93* (cpl. 31)
Branding slaves on the coast of Africa, previous to
  embarkation (Currier and Ives), *61*
Brown, James, 15
Brown, William Henry, *114* (cpl. 36)
Brumley, Albert E., *178*
Buck, William Henry, *172* (cpl. 62)
Burge, Dolly Lunt, 14, 122–124
Burial of Latané (Washington), 15
Butler, David, 16
Byrd, William, 12–13, 37–39

Cafe Tupinamba (Durieux), *222* (cpl. 80)
Callender, F. Arthur, *173* (cpl. 63)
Calvert Company, *84*
Campbell, Will D., 13, 64, 73–74
Cane (Toomer), 156
"Can the Circle Be Unbroken?" (Carter), 179–180
Capote, Truman, 269–272
Carnival at New Orleans, The, 147
Carter, A. P., 179–180
Carter Family, 179
Cascade (Dodd), *329*
Cash, W. J., 214–215
Catesby, Mark, 12, *24* (cpl. 8), 33–35, *34*
Catfish (White), 42, *43* (cpl. 12)
Catlin, George, *73*, *74*, *98*
Chapman, Conrad Wise, 14, *111*, *135*
Checks (Hollingsworth), *223* (cpl. 81)
Chesnut, Mary Boykin, 14, 104–105
Childhood, A: The Biography of a Place (Crews),
  355–357
Chinchuba to Moss Point (Buck), *172* (cpl. 62)
Chopin, Kate, 152–155
Christenberry, William, *278* (cpl. 103)
"Christmas Memory, A" (Capote), 269–272
Christmas Tree (Hamblett), *269*
Chuck Berry (Grooms), *341*
Churchill Downs, *305*, *306*, 306–308
Civil Rights Quilt (Wells), *302* (cpl. 111)
Civil War: A Narrative (Foote), 111–112, 121–122
Claiborne, Craig, 314–319
Clark, Eliot, *221* (cpl. 79)
Clear Pictures: First Love, First Guides (Price), 320,
  329–330
Clinton, William Jefferson, 26
Cloar, Carroll, 322 (cpl. 116)
Coal Miners, Alabama (Rothstein), *160*
Colonel William Washington at the Battle of Cowpens,
  January 17, 1781 (artist unknown), *47* (cpl. 17)
Confederacy of Dunces, A (Toole), 339–343
Connell, Clyde, *303* (cpl. 112)
"Conquered Banner, The" (Ryan), 128–130
"Contrariness of the Mad Farmer, The" (Berry),
  333–334
Cooke, George, *89* (cpl. 27), *162* (cpl. 52)
Cooper, Don, 25, *326* (cpl. 120)
Cooper, William, *105*
Coram, Thomas, *66* (cpl. 20)
Corn Raising in Carolina (De Bry), *19* (cpl. 3)
Cornwallis, Lord Charles, *57*
Cotton Mill. North Carolina (Hine), *191*
Cox, Ida, 15, 158–159
Creamer, Robert, 282–285
Crews, Harry, 25, 355–357
Crowned Crane (Drayton), *23* (cpl. 7)
Cruise, Boyd, *241* (cpl. 83)
Currier and Ives, *61*, *116* (cpl. 38), *149*

Daingerfield, Elliott, *175* (cpl. 65)
Dale, Ron, 25, *303* (cpl. 113)
"Dance, The," 54–55
Davenport, Rebecca, *276* (cpl. 101)
De Bry, *19* (cpl. 3)
Deceiver of the Whole World, The (Long), *254*
  (cpl. 95)
Degas, Edgar, 15, *161* (cpl. 51)
Delaney, Beauford, 25, *224* (cpl. 82)
Delineations of American Scenery and Character
  (Audubon), 130–133
"Description of Virginia, The" (J. Smith), 29–31
De Soto, Hernando, 27, 28
Diary of a Confederate Soldier (Jackman), 106–107
Diary of Caroline Seabury, The, 108–110
Diary of Dolly Lunt Burge, The, 122–124
Dickens, Charles, 14, 97–99
Dickerson, Vera, *300* (cpl. 109)
Dickey, James, 334–336
"Dixie" (Emmett), *85*
Dodd, Lamar, *329*
Dog Baying at the Moon (Goldthwaite), *334*
Domestic Life of Thomas Jefferson, The, 58–59

Donoho, Gaines Ruger, *215*
Dorsey, Thomas Andrew, 16, *179*
Douglass, Frederick, 13, 80–82, *81*
Drayton, John, *23* (cpl. 7)
Driving Miss Daisy (Uhry), 362–364
Drysdale, Alexander John, *174* (cpl. 64)
Dunlap, William, *251* (cpl. 92), *354*
Durieux, Caroline, *222* (cpl. 80)
Durkin, John, *147*
"Dying Soldier's Letter to His Mother" (Gage), 110

Earl, Ralph Eleazer Whiteside, *68* (cpl. 22)
Earl of Derby with Matt Win, President of Churchill
  Downs, 305
Echoes of Praise (Shuptrine), *225*
Education of Henry Adams (Adams), 102–103
Eggleston, William, *256* (cpl. 97)
Ehren, Susus Frederick von, *315*
Elvis (Parrish), *253* (cpl. 94)
Elvis Playpen with Einstein and Jesus Walking on the
  Water (Mabe), *275* (cpl. 100)
Emmett, Daniel Decatur, 85
"Enoch and the Gorilla" (O'Connor), 263–268
Escambia County, Alabama (McWilliams), *364*
Evans, Minnie, 16, *240*
Evans, Walker, *159*, *180*, 187–188, *206*, *237*, *260*
Everette, Mrs. Thomas, 13, *69* (cpl. 23)
"Everyday Use" (Walker), 343–349
Extreme Southeast Georgia (Cooper), *326* (cpl. 120)

Fairfax Lapsley (Cooke), *162* (cpl. 52)
Farmer, James, 16, 159–160, *177*
Father of the Blues (Handy), 157–158
Faulkner, William, 10, 16, 25, *157*, 207–209, *235*
Feast Made for Laughter, A (Claiborne), 314–319
Federal soldiers destroying the railroad tracks at
  Atlanta during Sherman's march to the sea, 123
Fields Prepared for the Planting (A. Smith), *217*
  (cpl. 75)
Figure/Construction with Blue Border (Traylor), *249*
  (cpl. 90)
Finster, Howard, 16, 25, *250* (cpl. 91)
First Turn at Churchill Downs, the 100th Kentucky
  Derby, 1974, 306
Fishin' at Sunset (Higgins), *170* (cpl. 60)
Flamingo (White), *22* (cpl. 6)
Floral Mosaic #5 (Hunter), *363*
Florida of the Inca, The (Garcilaso), 27–29
Foote, Shelby, 111–112, 121–122
"For My People" (Alexander), 272, 281
Foster, Ephraim Hubbard, and family, 13, *68* (cpl. 22)
Fox Chef (Blackwell), *255* (cpl. 96)
Fox Hunt (artist unknown), *96* (cpl. 34)
Frances Anne Kemble (Sully), *88*
Francis Mill, The (Shuptrine), *321* (cpl. 115)
Fran Tarkenton (Grooms), *295*
Frederick Douglass, 81
Freeman, Roland L., *344*

Gage, Jeremiah, 14, 110
Garcilaso de la Vega, 12, 27–29
Gatewood, Maud, *325* (cpl. 119)
"General's Farewell Address to His Troops" (Lee),
  128
George Washington (Trumbull), 44, *45* (cpl. 14)
"Georgia Dusk" (Toomer), 156
Georgia Landscape (Woodruff), *155*
Georgia Red Clay (Jones), 243 (cpl. 85)
Gerhardt, Karl, 196, *197* (cpl. 71)
Giant Steamboats on the Levee at New Orleans
  (Sebron), *143* (cpl. 49)
Gignoux, Regis, 15, *91* (cpl. 29)
Gilliam, Sam, *301* (cpl. 110)
Girl on Porch. Hinds County (Welty), *331*
Giroux, Charles, *120* (cpl. 43)
"Give Me Liberty or Give Me Death," *52*
"Go Down, Moses," 13, 83–84
Going to Market (Johnson), *183*
Golden Twilight in Louisiana (Giroux), *120* (cpl. 43)
Goldthwaite, Anne, *185*, *334*

Gone with the Wind (film), *127*
Gone with the Wind (Mitchell), 125–127
Grady, Henry Woodfin, 16, 188–190
Graffenried, Baron von, *32*
Grant, Ulysses S., *166* (cpl. 56)
Green, Jonathan, 316
Grooms, Red, 25, *295, 341*
Guillaume, Louis, *166* (cpl. 56)
Gunning, Simon B., *324* (cpl. 118)
Gwathmey, Robert, *209*

H.L. Hunley (submarine torpedo boat), *111*, 111–112, 121–122
Haley, Alex, 13, 60–63
Hamblett, Theora, *269, 323* (cpl. 117)
Hampton, James, 16, *347*
Handy, W. C., 157–158
Hannah, Barry, 25, 359–362
Harris, Joel Chandler, 15, 133–134
Hauling the Whole Week's Picking (Brown), *114* (cpl. 36)
"Have a Good Time While You Can" (Saxon), 146–148
Hawkins, Benjamin, *67* (cpl. 21)
Healy, George P. A., *167* (cpl. 57)
"Heart Is a Lonely Hunter, The" (McCullers), 232–235
He'll Set Your Fields on Fire (Dunlap), *251* (cpl. 92)
Henry, Patrick, 13, 50–52
Henry Darnall III, as a child (Kuhn), *41* (cpl. 9)
Higgins, George F., *170* (cpl. 60)
"Hind Tit, The" (Lytle), 190–192
Hine, Lewis, *191*
Hoening, Julius Robert, *171* (cpl. 61)
Hog Series XVI (Alyce/Piggly Wiggly) (Blackwell), *319*
Holley, Lonnie, *358*
Hollingsworth, William R., Jr., *223* (cpl. 81)
Home Regatta (Baker), *164* (cpl. 54)
Human Figures (Etowah Indian), *17* (cpl. 1)
Hummingbirds in Thistle (Anderson), *176* (cpl. 66)
Hunter, Clementine, *363*
Hunters, The (Andrews), *328* (cpl. 122)
Hurston, Zora Neale, 184–186

"I Blame It All on Mamma" (Mitchell), 216, 225–228
"I Have a Dream" (King), 288–291
"I'll Fly Away" (Brumley), *178*
In Charlotte Street, St. Augustine, Florida (Shapleigh), *198* (cpl. 72)
Indian Village of Secoton (White), *18* (cpl. 2)
Insects (Catesby), *34*
"In the Miro District" (Taylor), 349–351

Jackie Robinson with Branch Rickey, 282
Jackman, John S., 14, 106–107
Jackson, Andrew, *327* (cpl. 121)
"Jambalaya" (Williams), 16, *181*
Jefferson, Thomas, 13, *46* (cpl. 15), *58*, 58–59
Jennings, James Harold, 16, *299* (cpl. 108)
Jesus is My Airplane (Morgan), *178*
Johnson, David, *139* (cpl. 46)
Johnson, Eastman, 14, *109, 165* (cpl. 55)
Johnson, Joshua, *69* (cpl. 23)
Johnson, Junior, 291–296
Johnson, Melvin Gray, *213*
Johnson, William H., 25, *183*
Jones, Nell Choate, *243* (cpl. 85)
Journal of a Residence on a Georgia Plantation (Kemble), 87–88, 97
Journey in the Seaboard Slave States, A (Olmsted), 99–102
Journey to America (Tocqueville), 86–87
Judd, Wynonna, 25
Julio, Everett B. D., 15, *124*

Kandinsky, Wassily, 16
"Keep Your Eyes On The Prize." 286–287
Kemble, Frances Anne (Fanny), 14, 87–88, *88*, 97
Kennedy, J. P., 14, 77–79
"Kentucky Barbecue on the Fourth of July" (Audubon), 130–133
"Kentucky Derby Is Decadent and Depraved, The" (Thompson), 305–308
Key, John Ross, 14, *142* (cpl. 48)
King, B. B., 25

King, Charles Bird, *70* (cpl. 24), *71* (cpl. 25)
King, Florence, 312–314
King, Martin Luther, Jr., 25, 288–291, *289*
Kohlmeyer, Ida, *297* (cpl. 106)
Kuhn, Justus Englehardt, *41* (cpl. 9)

Lafayette, Marquis, *54*
"Landscape of the South, The" (Richards), 75–77
Lanier, Sidney, 150–151
Lanterns on the Levee (Percy), 16, 201–202
"Last American Hero, The" (Wolfe), 291–296
Last Meeting of Lee and Jackson (Julio), 15, *124*
Latrobe, Benjamin Henry, *48* (cpl. 18), *83*
Lawson, John, 12, 31–33, *32*
Lee, Ann Hill Carter, 13, *46* (cpl. 16)
Lee, Harper, 331–333
Lee, Robert E., 128, *129, 166* (cpl. 56)
Lee, Susan, *292*
Leigh, Vivian, *127*
Le Moyne de Morgues, Jacques, *20* (cpl. 4)
Letterbook of Eliza Lucas Pinckney, The, 39–40, 49
Letter on Home, The (Johnson), *109*
Letters of Eliza Wilkinson (Wilkinson), 52–53
Let Us Now Praise Famous Men (Agee and W. Evans), 187–188
"Liberty or Death" speech (Henry), 13, 50–52
Life on the Mississippi (Twain), 134–136, 145–146
Long, McKendree Robbins, *254* (cpl. 95)
Look Homeward, Angel (Wolfe), 203–205
Louisiana Plantation Scene (Pilsbury), *92* (cpl. 30)
Lovie, Henri, *14*
Low Water on the Mississippi (Currier and Ives), *116* (cpl. 38)
Lumpkin, Katharine Du Pre, 15
Luscious Fare (von Ehren), *315*
Lux, Rudolph T., *112*
Lynyrd Skynyrd, 357–358
Lytle, Andrew Nelson, 190–192

Mabe, Joni, *275* (cpl. 100)
Magic Pool (Silva), *218* (cpl. 76)
Magnolia (Catesby), *24* (cpl. 8)
Manchac Cabin (M. Smith), *144* (cpl. 50)
Mann, Sally, *233*
Many Moons Ago (Williams), *229*
Map of Virginia (J. Smith), *30*
Mardi Gras Nap (Sporny), *252* (cpl. 93)
Marion, Francis, 13, *118* (cpl. 49)
Marion's Camp (Washington), *118* (cpl. 40)
Marsalis, Wynton, 25
Mayr, Christian, *72* (cpl. 26)
McCrady, John, 25, *117* (cpl. 39), *201, 262*
McCullers, Carson, 232–235
McGowin, Ed, *273* (cpl. 98)
McWilliams, John, 26, *364*
Mecklenberg County: High Cotton Mother and Child (Bearden), *248* (cpl. 89)
Meeker, Joseph R., *153*
Melon Boats, New Orleans (Millet), *199* (cpl. 73)
Memoirs of the Life of Martha Laurens Ramsay, 59–60
Mencken, H.L., 10, 11, 16
Miller, Tom, *12*
Millet, Clarence, *199* (cpl. 73), *219* (cpl. 77)
Mind of the South, The (Cash), 214–215
Minstrel Poster Detail, Alabama (W. Evans), *159*
Mississippi Family (McCrady), *201*
Mississippi Panorama (Brammer), *90* (cpl. 28)
Mistipee (King), *70* (cpl. 24)
Mitchell, Joseph, 216, 225–228
Mitchell, Margaret, 125–127
Monceaux, Morgan, *327* (cpl. 121)
Monroe, Bill, *180*
Moonlight (Daingerfield), *175* (cpl. 65)
Moonscape (Millet), *219* (cpl. 77)
Moran, Thomas, 118, *119* (cpl. 42)
Morgan, Gertrude, 16, *178*
Morris, Willie, 25, *295*, 336–339
Mosholatubee (Or, He Who Puts Out and Kills), Chief of Choctaw Indian tribe when it was removed to Oklahoma (Catlin), *73*
Mr. and Mrs. Ephraim Hubbard Foster and Their Children (Earl), *68* (cpl. 22)
Mr. Cheevers, potter, and children, Cleveland, and Georgia (Ulmann), *187*
Mrs. Rosa Parks, 285

Mrs. Thomas Everette and Children (Johnson), *69* (cpl. 23)
Mrs. Victoria Bennett, Wilkinson County (Freeman), *344*
Mules and Men (Hurston), 184–186
Music Lives After the Instruments Is Destroyed, The (Holley), *358*
My Parent's Farm (O'Kelley), *278, 279* (cpl. 104)
Mythic Series #31 (Kohlmeyer), *297* (cpl. 106)

Narrative of the Life of Frederick Douglass, An American Slave, 80–82
Natural Bridge, Virginia (Johnson), *139* (cpl. 46)
Natural History of Carolina, Florida, and the Bahama Islands, The (Catesby), 33–35
Negro Soldier (Johnson), *213*
Negro using outside stairway for "colored" to enter movie theatre (Wolcott), *211*
New Orleans from Algiers (Point) (Callender), *173* (cpl. 63)
"New South, The" (Grady), 188–190
Newton, John, 13, 63–64
New Voyage to Carolina, A (Lawson), 31–33
Ninas, Paul, *220* (cpl. 78)
Noble, Thomas Satterwhite, *163* (cpl. 53)
Nolan, Harry, *196* (cpl. 70)
North Toward Home (Morris), 336–339

Oakland House and Race Course, Louisville, Kentucky (Brammer and Von Smith), *93* (cpl. 31)
Object Lesson Series: Lights Out: 1939–1945 (Dunlap), *354*
O'Connor, Flannery, 263–268
Oelschig, Augusta, *247* (cpl. 88)
Office of Daniel Pratt's Cotton Gin Factory (Blood), *189*
Officers of Volunteer Fire Department, 1841 (Mayr), *72* (cpl. 26)
Ohr, George, *338*
O'Kelley, Mattie Lou, *278, 279* (cpl. 104)
Old Log Cabin, The (Powell), 14, *168* (cpl. 58)
Old Plantation, the (artist unknown), *113* (cpl. 35)
Olmsted, Frederick Law, 14, 99–102
"On Correct Behavior in Church" (Woodmason), 49–50
On the Levee at Natchez (Betts), *200* (cpl. 74)
"On the Pulse of Morning" (Angelou), 26
Overseer Doing His Duty, An (Latrobe), *83*

Painting in the South 1564–1980 (Virginia Museum of Fine Arts), 11
Parks, Rosa, 25, 285–286
Parrish, David, *253* (cpl. 94), *274* (cpl. 99)
Pavy, Francis X., *298* (cpl. 107)
Pennington, Estill Curtis, 11, 26
Percy, Walker, 26, 201, 308–312
Percy, William Alexander, 16, 201–202
Persac, Adrien, *94* (cpl. 32), *137* (cpl. 44)
Piano Lesson, The (Bearden), *169* (cpl. 102)
Pictorial Quilt (Powers), *169* (cpl. 59)
Pierre G. T. Beauregard (Healy), *167* (cpl. 57)
Pilsbury, M. L., *92* (cpl. 30)
Pinckney, Eliza Lucas, 13, 39–40, 49
"Pissing in the Snow" (Randolph), 149
Pittman, Hobson, *203*
Plan of a slave ship, 62
Plantation, The, 38
Plantation (Allard), and Oak Tree (Hoening), *171* (cpl. 61)
Plantation Burial, A (Antrobus), 14, 118, *119* (cpl. 41)
Play Ball (Oelschig), *247* (cpl. 88)
Pocahontas (artist unknown), *21* (cpl. 5)
Poesch, Jessie, 11, 26
Poincy, Paul, *195* (cpl. 69)
Poker Night (from A Streetcar Named Desire) (Benton), *231*
Political Rally (McCrady), *262*
Polk, Charles Peale, *46* (cpl. 15)
Polk, James, *327* (cpl. 121)
Pondering Place (Connell), *303* (cpl. 112)
Portrait of a Boy (Delaney), *224* (cpl. 82)
Portrait of Judah P. Benjamin (Lux), *112*
Portrait of Thomas Jefferson (Polk), *46* (cpl. 15)
Portraits in an Office: The Cotton Exchange, New Orleans (Degas), *161* (cpl. 51)

Potter, David, 10
Powell, Lucien Whiting, 14, *168* (cpl. 58)
Powers, Harriet, 13, *169* (cpl. 59)
Powhatan, *30*
Presidential Portraits (Presidents Taylor, Tyler, Polk, Jackson) (Monceaux), *327* (cpl. 121)
Price, Reynolds, 26, *320*, 329–330
Price of Blood, The, A Planter Selling His Son (Noble), *163* (cpl. 53)
Private Mary Chesnut, The, 104–105
Providence (Campbell), 64, 73–74
Pushmataha (King), *71* (cpl. 25)

Ramsay, Martha Laurens, 59–60
Randolph, Vance, 149
Rankin, Thomas, 281
Rauschenberg, Robert, *304* (cpl. 114)
Rebel Cavalry Ball (Cooper), *105*
Red and Blue Club (Faulkner), *157*
Red Palms (Cruise), *241* (cpl. 83)
Reece, Florence, 16, 159–160, 177
Reflections (Gwathmey), *209*
René de Laudonnière and the Indian Chief Athore Visit Ribaut's Column (Le Moyne de Morgues), *20* (cpl. 4)
Revival scene in the rural South, *100*
Rhubarb in the Catbird Seat (Barber and Creamer), 282–285
Richards, T. Addison, 15, 75–77
Richardt, Ferdinand, *138* (cpl. 45)
Rickey, Branch, 282, 282–285
Ride for Liberty, The–The Fugitive Slaves (Johnson), 14, *165* (cpl. 55)
Roadside Stand, Vicinity Birmingham, Alabama (W. Evans), *206*
Robert E. Lee in Richmond (Brady), *129*
Robinson, Jackie, 282, 283, 285
Rodgers, Jimmie, 177
Roosevelt, Franklin Delano, 16
Roots (Haley), 13, 60–63
Rosa Parks: My Story, 285, 285–286
Rosengarten, Theodore, 182–184
Rothstein, Arthur, *160*
Royal Chevy (Parrish), *274* (cpl. 99)
Royal Street Antique Shop (Nolan), *196* (cpl. 70)
Ryan, Father, 15, 128–130

"St. George Tucker's Journal of the Siege of Yorktown, 1781," 56–57
St. John Plantation–St. Martin Parish (Persac), *137* (cpl. 44)
Saturday Night (Shannon), *246* (cpl. 87), 247
Saxon, Lulu, *193* (cpl. 67)
Saxon, Lyle, 146–148
Scartabelli, H. H., *280* (cpl. 105)
Seabury, Caroline, 14, 108–110
Sebron, Hippolyte Victor Valentin, *143* (cpl. 49)
Secret Diary of William Byrd of Westover, 12–13, 37–39
Sevierville, Tennessee (Stevens), *350*
Shannon, Charles, 25, *246* (cpl. 87), 247
Shapleigh, Frank Henry, *198* (cpl. 72)
Shaw, Nate (Ned Cobb), 182–184
"Sheep Child, The" (Dickey), 334–336
Shoeing Mules in Alabama (Goldthwaite), *185*
Shucking Oysters (Green), *316*
Shuptrine, Hubert, 225, *321* (cpl. 115), *336*
Side Show, State Fair, Jackson (Welty), *264*, 266
Signposts in a Strange Land (Percy), 308–312
Silva, William P., *218* (cpl. 76)
624 Orleans Alley, Rear (Gerhardt), *197* (cpl. 71)
Slave Quarters on a Plantation, *78*
Slaves Escaping through the Swamp (Moran), 118, *119* (cpl. 42)
Smith, Alice Ravenel Huger, *217* (cpl. 75)
Smith, John, 12, 29–31, *30*
Smith, Marshall J., *144* (cpl. 50)
Snapping Turtle, a half-breed Choctaw (Catlin), *98*
Solitary Pirogue by the Bayou (Meeker), *153*
Sommers: Kettleburn (Davenport), *276* (cpl. 101)
"Song of the Chattahoochee" (Lanier), 150–151
"Song to Grits" (Blount), 319–320
Sophie's Choice (Styron), 351–355
Souchon, Marion, *242* (cpl. 84)
Southern Ladies and Gentlemen (King), 312–314

"Southern Woman's Blues" (Cox), 16, 158–159
Sporny, Stanley, *252* (cpl. 93)
Steamboat 'Round the Bend (McCrady), *117* (cpl. 39)
Stevens, Will H., *350*
Still Life with Orchids (Scartabelli), *280* (cpl. 105)
Still Life with Radishes (Poincy), *195* (cpl. 69)
Stock car racing (Lee), *292*
"Storm, The" (Chopin), 152–155
Storm Over Loing Valley (Donoho), *215*
Straus, Meyer, 15, *140–141* (cpl. 47)
Strawberry (Bartram), *36*
Streetcar Named Desire, A (Williams), 229–232
Strother, Donald Hunter, *50*
Students staging a fistfight at the University of Mississippi, *87*
Styron, William, 26, 351–355
Submarine Torpedo Boat H.L. Hunley, December 6, 1863 (Chapman), *111*
Sully, Thomas, 88
Summertime (Shuptrine), *336*
Sunday Amusements in New Orleans–The Cockpit (Waud), *145*
Sunday Singing. Frank Tengle's Family. Hale County, Alabama (W. Evans), *180*
Sunny South, 84
Sunset on Dismal Swamp (Gignoux), *91* (cpl. 29)
Surrender of Cornwallis at Yorktown (Chapin), *57*
Surrender of General Lee to General Grant at Appomattox, April 9, 1865 (Guillaume), *166* (cpl. 56)
Swallow Barn, or Sojourn in the Old Dominion (Kennedy), 14, 77–79
"Sweet Home Alabama" (Lynyrd Skynyrd), 357–358
Swinger in Summer Shade (Gatewood), *325* (cpl. 119)

"Take My Hand, Precious Lord" (Dorsey), 16, *179*
Tallulah Falls (Cooke), *89* (cpl. 27)
Tangled in Deep (Gunning), *324* (cpl. 118)
Tarkenton, Fran, 295
Tate, Allen, 16, 205–206
Taylor, Peter, 25, 349–351
Taylor, Zachary, *327* (cpl. 121)
This Is It (Willis), *313*
Thompson, Hunter S., 25, 305
Thompson, Robert Farris, 26
Throne of the Third Heaven of the Nation's Millenium General Assembly (Hampton), 16, *347*
Timrod, Henry, 15
Tisket, A Tasket, A (Hamblett), *323* (cpl. 117)
"To Catch a Runaway Slave," 83
Toccoa Falls, Georgia, *151*
Tocqueville, Alexis de, 14, 86–87
To Kill a Mockingbird (Lee), 331–333
Toole, John Kennedy, 339–343
Toomer, Jean, 156
"Train Whistle Blues" (Rodgers), *177*
Travels of William Bartram (Bartram), 35–37
Traylor, Bill, 16, 25, *249* (cpl. 90)
Trial of the Captive Slaves (Woodruff), *115* (cpl. 37)
"Trout Map, The" (Tate), 205–206
Trumbull, John, 44, *45* (cpl. 14)
Tucker, St. George, 13, 56–57
Tutor, Glennray, *361*
Twain, Mark, 134–136, 145–146
Twilight at Mount Vernon (artist unknown), *44* (cpl. 13)
Tyler, John, *327* (cpl. 121)

Uhry, Alfred, 362–364
Ulmann, Doris, *181, 187*
Umbrella Rock, Lookout Mountain, *76*
Uncle Remus: His Songs and His Sayings (Harris), 15, 133–134
Uncle Tom's Cabin (Stowe), 13
Untitled (M. Evans), *240*
Untitled. From At Twelve: Portraits of Young Women (Mann), *233*
Uptown Street (Saxon), *193* (cpl. 67)
U.S. Post Office Sprott Alabama (W. Evans), *237*

Vanderlyn, John, *54*
Vase (Ohr), *338*
View of Harper's Ferry (Richardt), *138* (cpl. 45)
View of Mulberry Plantation (House and Street) (Coram), *66* (cpl. 20)
View of Norfolk from Town Point (Latrobe), *48* (cpl. 18)

View of River Savannah (Clark), *221* (cpl. 79)
Virginia Capitol, Richmond; front elevation (Jefferson), *58*
Virginia Museum of Fine Arts, 11
Vlach, John Michael, 26
von Reck, Philipp Georg Friedrich, 12, *42* (cpl. 10), *43* (cpl. 11)
Von Smith, Augustus, *93* (cpl. 31)

Walker, Alice, 25, 343–349
War Dance, A (von Reck), *42* (cpl. 10)
Warm Evening (Pittman), *203*
Warren, Robert Penn, 259–263
Washburn, Edward Payson, *149*
Washington, George, 44, *45* (cpl. 14), *54*
Washington, William, *47* (cpl. 17)
Washington, William D., 13, 15, *118* (cpl. 40)
Washington and Lafayette (Vanderlyn), *54*
Water Valley (Eggleston), *256* (cpl. 97)
Waud, A. R., *145*
Weapons of War (Chapman), *135*
Wells, Yvonne, *302* (cpl. 111)
Welty, Eudora, *235*, 235–240, 257–259, *264, 266,* 331
"We Shall Overcome," 287–288
West Tennessee Democrat, 83
West Virginia Madonna (Dickerson), *300* (cpl. 109)
Where the Southern Cross the Yellow Dog (Cloar), *322* (cpl. 116)
"Which Side Are You On?" (Reece and Farmer), 16, 159–160, 177
White, John, *18* (cpl. 2), 22 (cpl. 6), *42, 43* (cpl. 12)
White, John Blake, *95* (cpl. 33)
"Why I Live at the P.O." (Welty), 235–240, 257–259
Wild Iris (Woodward), *194* (cpl. 68)
Wild Turkey (Audubon), *131*
Wilkinson, Eliza, 52–53
William Faulkner and Eudora Welty (unknown artist), *235*
Williams, Hank, 16, 181
Williams, Tennessee, *229,* 229–232
Willis, Luster, *313*
Win, Matt, 305
Wolcott, Marion Post, *211,* 226
Wolfe, Thomas, 16, 25, 203–205
Wolfe, Tom, 291–296
Woman with Striped Stockings (Bellocq), *309*
Women and children in an outdoor rural scene, 50
Wonderful Tar-Baby, *133*
"Wonderful Tar-Baby Story, The" (Harris), 15, 133–134
Woodmason, Charles, 13, 49–50
Woodruff, Hale Aspacio, *115* (cpl. 37), 155
Woodward, Ellsworth, *194* (cpl. 68)
World of the Happy and Free (Finster), *250* (cpl. 91)
Wright, Richard, 16, 25, 210–214

PHOTO CREDITS